The Way of Improvement Leads Home

EARLY AMERICAN STUDIES
Daniel K. Richter and Kathleen M. Brown, Series Editors

Exploring neglected aspects of our colonial, revolutionary, and early
national history and culture, Early American Studies reinterprets
familiar themes and events in fresh ways. Interdisciplinary in character,
and with a special emphasis on the period from about 1600 to 1850,
the series is published in partnership with the McNeil Center for Early
American Studies.

A complete list of books in the series is available from the publisher.

The Way of Improvement Leads Home

Philip Vickers Fithian and the Rural Enlightenment in Early America

JOHN FEA

5·3·11

Best wishes,

[signature]

PENN

University of Pennsylvania Press

Philadelphia

Publication of this volume was aided by a grant
from the New Jersey Historical Commission.

Published by
University of Pennsylvania Press
Philadelphia, Pennsylvania 19104-4112

Printed in the United States of America on acid-free paper

10   8   7   6   5   4   3   2   1

A Cataloging-in-Publication record is available from the Library of Congress
ISBN 978-0-8122-4109-9

For Joy, Allyson, and Caroline

Contents

Introduction

On the morning of Friday, July 16, 1773, Philip Vickers Fithian awoke early and traveled from his Greenwich, New Jersey, house across the Cohansey River to Fairfield. There he spent several days with William Hollingshead, who would soon be installed as minister of the Fairfield Presbyterian church. Together they dined, drank tea, and exchanged the "Usual Civilities" with other friends and relations. The two passed their time together conversing on topics including "the State of Affairs in Philadelphia," Philip's candidacy for Presbyterian ordination, Hollingshead's upcoming sermon "States of Man," and the "useful & well chosen Books" in the minister's personal library. Philip and Hollingshead ate breakfast on Monday with Jonathan Elmer, their representative in the New Jersey Assembly. Later that day this gregarious duo traveled back to Greenwich, where Philip observed a "long Confabulation" between Hollingshead and Andrew Hunter, minister of the Greenwich Presbyterian church, on the subject of "whether there is Scripture Authority for Diocesan Bishops" (which was decided "in the negative"). Here they also encountered Richard Howell, one of Philip's former classmates at the local Presbyterian academy, who shared with them news of his legal studies in New Castle, Delaware. Philip lamented that although Howell was a "young Gentleman of considerable Genius, & has made good Proficiency in his Studies . . . he is remarkably profane in his Principles, & loose in his Behaviour!" After calling on several more friends, Philip returned home late Monday afternoon, "Drank Tea with several Neighbors," and "Went to bed about ten."[1]

By examining Philip's journal over this four-day period, one can learn much about what the young Presbyterian deemed important. His entries reveal the musings of an educated candidate for the Presbyterian ministry. The encounter with Richard Howell demonstrates his concern with personal morality and proper behavior. His breakfast with Elmer suggests an interest in political matters. Reflections on books and philosophy and discussions of current news from Philadelphia invoke a cosmopolitan spirit in the rural confines of "Cohansey"—a series of small townships in southern New Jersey situated approximately forty-five miles southwest of Philadelphia.

Philip's activities illustrate his attempt to rise above the parochialism and rusticity of the Jersey countryside to be a "citizen of the world." By the middle of the eighteenth century the inhabitants of the British North American colonies had become exposed at an ever-increasing rate to the new learning emanating from such cultural and intellectual centers as London, Edinburgh, and Glasgow. Networks of communications and trade allowed such ideas to reach remote corners of the American provinces and connected even the most ordinary farming communities to the world of the British Enlightenment.[2] From the villages of Cohansey, Philip was able to participate indirectly in the eighteenth-century republic of letters—a transatlantic community of scholars sustained through sociability, print, and the pursuit of mutual improvement. Though abstract and boundless, the Enlightenment ideals forged by the republic of letters could indeed shape the "thoughts and deeds" of the republic's members.[3]

Although Philip sought to partake in a fellowship of learning and letters that oriented his mental and social worlds away from the place of his birth, the long mid July weekend of 1773 could just as easily be interpreted through the lens of parochialism. Long-standing personal relationships, local communities of faith, and a sense of social obligation to the men and women who inhabited the soil where he was raised often provided the context for enlightened conversation. Jonathan Elmer was a close family friend. Andrew Hunter was the clergyman who had baptized Philip as an infant, catechized him as a boy, and encouraged him to pursue a career in the ministry. Richard Howell was a former schoolmate. In fact, all the people Philip spent time with that weekend were Presbyterians affiliated with the religious community that gave meaning to life in Cohansey.

Indeed, no one was more aware of the tensions between cosmopolitanism and local attachment than Philip. The need to reconcile the pursuit of Enlightenment ambition with a passion for home or a desire for God was perhaps the greatest moral problem facing the newly educated sons of British American farmers. Philip learned quickly that his pursuit of a life of learning, a vocation in the educated ministry, and a call to serve God and his new country would require a degree of detachment from friends, family, and the very soil of his homeland. Yet, Philip's cosmopolitan turn is incomprehensible apart from these social connections. It was the people, the religious culture, and even the very landscape that continued to hold Philip's affections and that shaped—and transformed—all that he learned beyond its bounds. As a child of the American Enlightenment, Philip could rely on intellectual, religious, and social scaffolding that enabled him to live a life worthy of a man of letters and yet benefit from the virtues of his local attachments. As a patriot, he could continue support for a highly cosmopolitan revolutionary ideology with the intense Presbyterian view of everyday life that permeated Cohansey culture. Ultimately he confronted the task of finding how best to adapt to the social and religious consequences of the modern quest for self-improvement. The result was a cosmopolitan rootedness that, in the context of Philip's agrarian upbringing, I have called his "rural Enlightenment."

The Way of Improvement Leads Home is a cultural and intellectual biography of Philip Vickers Fithian, one of early America's most cited diarists. Historians who study colonial Virginia know Philip well. The journal he kept during the year (October 1773 to October 1774) he spent as a tutor on Robert Carter's plantation in Virginia's Northern Neck not only is a delight to read but also offers one of our most revealing glimpses into the life of the Chesapeake gentry at the time of the American Revolution. If the anecdotal evidence I have collected during the course of this project is any indication, Philip's Virginia diary was a staple of undergraduate and graduate history seminars for two generations of students trained during the cold war.[4] Today, despite the fact that his name no longer appears with great frequency on college syllabi, more people are exposed to Philip's observations than ever before. One would be hard-pressed to find a book on eighteenth-century Virginia that does not mention him. Thousands of families learn about Philip each year at Colonial Williamsburg, where he is a regular part of its public history program. Tour guides echo his words as they lead visitors through the plantations of the Old Dominion. Philip even makes a cameo appearance in *Liberty!*, the popular six-part documentary on the American Revolution that aired on public television in 1997.[5]

Yet, despite Philip's ubiquitous presence in interpretations of colonial Virginia, we still know little about him. With the exception of Vincent McCluskey's 1991 New York University doctoral dissertation, there has never been an attempt to write a biography of the man. His writings are most often used by historians as window dressing for their studies of the plantation Chesapeake. It seems that a quotation from Philip Vickers Fithian is the perfect way to enhance any historical narrative. The lack of detailed attention to Philip's life is somewhat surprising in light of the fair amount of primary source material available to the biographer. Two older collections of Philip's writings are still easily accessible to those interested in learning more about him. In 1900 John R. Williams published many of Philip's personal letters and papers written during his years (1770–72) as a student at the College of New Jersey.

Three decades later Robert Greenhalgh Albion and Leonidas Dodson edited Philip's 1775–76 journals recounting his two short missionary trips to the Pennsylvania and Virginia backcountry and his role as a chaplain with the Continental army in New York.[6] Philip's *unpublished* writings have been virtually untapped by early American historians. This collection, housed in Princeton University's Firestone Library, includes valuable information on his early spiritual, intellectual, and agricultural life.[7] While Philip did not live long enough to produce the kind of paper trail that the era's great statesmen have left us, such neglect of his story is unfortunate. His life sheds light on the history of colonial New Jersey and Virginia, the development of the early Presbyterian Church, eighteenth-century courtship rituals, and especially the impact of the Enlightenment on ordinary people at the time of the American Revolution.

In writing *The Way of Improvement Leads Home*, I have tried to remain as faithful as possible, with a few extended detours here and there, to the genre of biography. What follows is a roughly chronological account of Philip's life. The book begins at the turn of the century in East Hampton, New York, and Fairfield, Connecticut, as Philip's ancestors contemplate a move to the Cohansey River region of southwestern New Jersey. It chronicles the course of his formal and informal education, his experience in plantation Virginia, his love affair with Elizabeth Beatty, his commitment to the American Revolution, and his preaching tour of the Susquehanna and Shenandoah Valleys. Potential readers looking for a good story from the annals of Revolutionary America will, I hope, find one in these pages. At a somewhat more analytical level, this book also attempts to use Philip's story to explain the impact of the Enlightenment in the British American colonies. As a result, I have chosen to leave Philip's story at certain points of the narrative in order to explore more fully the cultural and intellectual milieu in which he lived.

Much of my interest in a book project that uses biography to explain the Enlightenment stems from my experience teaching undergraduates. In an age of the History Channel and best-selling biographies of the country's "Founding Fathers," I have found that a lecture on the Enlightenment in America tends to be a hard sell in the college classroom. Tell eighteen- to twenty-two-year-old college students that they will be spending the next fifty minutes of their lives exploring the intricacies of the Enlightenment and watch their eyes glaze over. Aware of the very real potential that such a topic might elicit boredom, I begin my class devoted to this theme by asking students to recall what they know about the Enlightenment. Someone will usually refer to the Age of Reason, and this will trigger others to start rattling off a short list of the usual suspects—Locke, Rousseau, Voltaire. Others think about the Enlightenment as an elite, secular movement dominated by a small circle of French philosophes who stressed rational thought over a religious worldview. What is missing is a sense that the movement drew strength from and informed everyday lives, dreams, and aspirations in colonial America— and, despite the postmodern turn, continues to do so today. I often ask my students if the idea of self-improvement is important to them and to Americans generally. Although the very act of sitting in a college lecture hall suggests that they are concerned about improving themselves (or at least looking to secure their credentials in the middle class, today's penultimate form of American self-improvement), they often do not know how to respond. Some students take modern notions of improvement and progress for granted and may never have thought critically or historically about such ideas. It is at this point that the story of Philip Vickers Fithian has come to my aid on more than one occasion. I have learned that biography can be used to help students locate the Enlightenment historically and suggest to them that ideas about how to make a better self always rise in a historical context.[8]

With this in mind, Philip's biography illustrates four interrelated themes at the heart of the Enlightenment in eighteenth-century America. While these themes are not new or groundbreaking, they do offer an introduction to what the Enlightenment meant in America and provide the essential framework for understanding the course of Philip's life. First, *the Enlightenment was about self-improvement.* For the first time in history the bettering of one's condition (and by extension the condition of society as a whole) became a real and viable possibility. In this sense, the Enlightenment challenged the prevailing view that people were incapable, largely because of their sin natures, of improving themselves apart from divine intervention. Knowledge about the world and its creatures was now attainable through reason by a variety of people in a variety of places, including ordinary farmers in the rural corners of British America. The Enlightenment was about breaking down social and cultural boundaries through human initiative. Enlightened people could leave the farm to pursue progressive ways of living that challenged the limits imposed on them by traditional forces.

Second, *enlightened people were able to employ reason as a necessary check to the individual passions.* Their lives were characterized by restraint. Sentiment always needed to be contained by the dictates of reason. Passions, whether they be directed toward a particular place, religion, or relationship, were viewed as irrational unless properly controlled. The struggle to subdue desire, to cultivate reason, and—in Philip's case—to distinguish which passions were useful and which ones were dangerous was the mark of a truly enlightened gentleman. Modern people could be tempted by an array of inappropriate and irrational feelings, but local affections for one's homeland and romantic yearnings for members of the opposite sex were perhaps the most damaging to the pursuit of Enlightenment self-improvement. As we will see, Philip had difficulty in these areas his entire life.

Third, *to be rational in the eighteenth century one needed to direct one's passions away from parochial concerns and toward a universal love of the human race.* Enlightened people embraced cosmopolitanism. They championed ideas that belonged to all people and were not confined to a particular locale, region, or nation. The republic of letters was above all else a rational republic with little tolerance for those unable to rid themselves of parochial passions. Its best citizens maintained primary loyalty not to family, friends, faith, or land but to an international commonwealth of humankind. Not all its members could frequent the coffeehouses, clubs, and salons of Paris and London, but they could still think and feel beyond the bounds of their local attachments. They could make choices for their lives that ultimately carried them—geographically or in imagination—away from home. As the historian Gordon Wood has aptly put it, "local feelings were common to peasants and backward peoples, but educated gentlemen were supposed to be at home anywhere in the world." To be too wedded to local attachments was "a symptom of narrow mindedness, and indeed of disease."9

Fourth, *the Enlightenment always existed in compromise with the deeply held Christian faith of the American people.* The American Enlightenment was appropriated most often by the proponents of traditional Christianity. Philip's pursuit of self-improvement was impossible without his Presbyterian faith. His enlightened social world and the rural religious culture in which he was raised were often one and the same. During the eighteenth century some Christians began to believe that they could embrace relatively optimistic views of human nature, particularly in the realm of the human capacity for moral improvement, without abandoning their faith commitments. The Presbyterian Calvinism that Philip inherited provided the theological and moral resources for people to achieve the betterment of self and society. The formal and informal institutions that supported Philip's Enlightenment were all affiliated in one way or another with Cohansey Presbyterian life.10

Philip's "way of improvement" was by no means a smooth one. His passion for "home," which I use broadly in the title of this book to encompass not only his longings for his Cohansey homeland but also his desire for a friendship with his future wife (who lived in Cohansey) and his deep sense of evangelical Calvinist piety (which informed the culture of Cohansey and his Christian calling to the ministry), frequently got in the way of his attempts at Enlightenment self-improvement.

In the messiness of everyday life the Enlightenment ideal was often impractical. It demanded a style of living that only a handful of elite intellectuals could attain. Max Hilbert Boehm, writing in 1932, reminded us that cosmopolitanism has always existed in "compromise with nationalism, race consciousness, professional interests, caste feeling, family pride, and even egotism."[11] However, it is precisely these tensions that make Philip's story so interesting. His attempt at easing them is the focus of this book, the very essence of what I have described as Fithian's "rural Enlightenment." My study of this ordinary farmer argues that an Enlightenment life was complex and complicated. It could be lived locally—even in rural and remote places where the dominant social institutions were churches, where modern and naturalistic explanations of the world often merged with theological convictions held by people of faith, where the lines between ambitious self-improvement and Christian vocation might sometimes be blurred, and where circles of friends improved themselves through conversation amid the regular demands of the agricultural calendar.

On one hand, Philip is an Enlightenment (and American) success story: the oldest son of a grain grower who turns his back on the farm to pursue a college education and a life of learning. On the other hand, his life reminds us that even the most eager of eighteenth-century Enlightenment hopefuls balanced rational quests for improvement with longings that could not be explained by reason alone. Philip's cosmopolitanism was tempered by his multiple bouts with homesickness for his rural upbringing and family farm. His efforts to cultivate human relationships based on sober reason were often undermined by passion, especially when it came to his courtship of Elizabeth Beatty. His personal ambition, self-improvement, and Revolutionary optimism were always understood in the context of his belief in a sovereign God's providential ordering of His creation. Though I cannot say so for sure, it appears that Philip's life is symbolic of the struggles that many young men in the late colonial period faced as they responded to the spirit of the age. In the end, whether or not I convince my readers that Philip Vickers Fithian's story *is* the story of the Enlightenment in America, I still think it is one worth telling.

Chapter 1
A Cohansey Home

Philip Vickers Fithian loved springtime on the Cohansey. As winter bid its farewell to the villages along the river, Philip rejoiced in the morning sounds of birds keeping "a continual round of engaging music." His soul was refreshed by the "feathery choir" of the bluebirds singing their "melody to the God of nature on account of the approaching spring." Even the frogs on the riverbank caught his attention as they filled the evening air "with their shrill and deafening voices." From his bedchamber window Philip could see peach, apple, and cherry trees coming to life on his family's farm. "The Spring now displays its gaiety and exalted grandeur in bloom and pride," he wrote in May 1767; "the Apple and the Cherry trees are in the extremity of their glory, and the Trees of the wood, arraying themselves in green." Delaware Bay's southwesterly breezes felt fresh and warm. Indeed, spring was the time of year when Philip reflected most intently on the virtues of home.[1]

Philip's name for this familiar world was "Cohansie" (Cohansey). Coursing through the center of this place, providing a geographical reference point for all its inhabitants, was the river. The Cohansey River flows south from an unidentified southwestern New Jersey creek past the village of Deerfield and through Bridge-Town, which in Philip's day was a burgeoning local center of political life in the recently formed (1748) county of Cumberland. South of Bridge-Town the Cohansey runs fairly straight beneath a few high bluffs and amid an ever-increasing number of salt hay marshes. The river makes a ninety-degree turn to the east at Fairfield and then begins its winding course toward Delaware Bay. At Greenwich, which sits on a fifteen-foot-high bluff overlooking the river, the Cohansey takes another sharp turn, heading south for its last five miles. At this point the tides become strong, driving a canoe upriver, as Cohansey native and historian Al Zambone has described it, "faster than a man or woman can jog." The river ends in a cove that widens into Delaware Bay, creating a safe harbor for sailors and their crafts. In Philip's day the river united "Cohansie's" two largest towns—Greenwich and Fairfield. (Today, however, it presents an obstacle between the two communities.) For the eighteenth-century merchants and storeowners

GREENWICH, N.J.
AD 1800.

Figure 1. View from the Cohansey River of Fithian's hometown of Greenwich, 1800. Courtesy, Lummis Library, Cumberland County (N.J.) Historical Society.

of the region, and for anyone intent on leaving the world that the earliest settlers developed along the riverbanks, the Cohansey provided access to Philadelphia and points beyond—a gateway, albeit a limited and
underutilized one, to a cosmopolitan Atlantic world.[2]

The writer Wallace Stegner once said that "no place, not even a wild
place, is a place until it has had a poet."[3] Philip Vickers Fithian was
Cohansey's poet. He was a patriot in the classical Greek sense of the
word—a lover of his *terra patria*, his native land. His private writing,
though often romantic and self-indulgent at times, always laid bare the
depth of his connection to the cluster of small townships nestled along
the river's meandering currents. At the time of his birth in 1747 English
men and women had lived in this corner of southwestern New Jersey
for almost seventy-five years. The first seventeenth-century settlers had
established towns on the banks of the river at Greenwich (1684) and
Fairfield (1697), and their descendants had followed its course north-
ward, founding farming communities at Deerfield (1732) and Bridge-
Town (1748). Philip could trace a Fithian genealogy in this place through
three generations.

As he grew in intellect and learning and, as we will see, was exposed to
a kind of life outside of Cohansey that few of his neighbors and none
of his ancestors had ever experienced, the beckoning of home would
become that much greater. As a child of the Enlightenment and one of
the region's first native-born college graduates, Philip could have easily
transcended—culturally, geographically, intellectually—Cohansey's warm
confines. However, he also knew that his pursuit of self-betterment was
held in check by what Karl Marx would later describe as "the circumstances directly encountered, given, and transmitted from the past."[4] In
an eighteenth-century world where young people started to believe that
self-improvement was possible, Philip realized that the limits imposed by
the past anchored him and had just as much impact on who he was and
what he would become as did the optimism of the Enlightenment
stream from which he would drink so deeply.

A sense of place is, like the grain Cohansey farmers grew each season,
cultivated over time. Philip would eventually become part of the first
generation of Cohansey young people to experience a life beyond the
southern New Jersey countryside. Even so, at the age of eighteen, when
he first began writing in his diary, he was more representative of a
generation whose families had lived long enough there to have developed a local attachment to their homeland. Cohansey was the region
where Philip's family, after two generations of migration throughout
New England, was finally able to sink roots and become members of a
founding community of settlers. This meant that they were no longer
strangers—outsiders without a place to call home. If motion defines

the human experience, as it did for many of Philip's immediate ancestors caught up in the whirlwind of migration that characterized the seventeenth-century British world, then place is pause. Philip was born in the midst of the longest pause the Fithian and Vickers families had ever experienced in America. He was thus able to develop affections for his Cohansey home to a degree that his forefathers and foremothers were unable to fathom.[5]

Philip's love of home was also cultivated, quite literally, through his day-to-day life on the farm. He was acquainted intimately with the sights, smells, and sounds of Cohansey. He was familiar with the soil and the agricultural practices that nurtured it. He knew how to bank a stream, make cider, scutch flax, thresh wheat, plow a field, sow corn, and wash sheep. Philip had suffered through the sickness of a late Cohansey summer and prayed his way through the region's spring frosts. The Fithians were yeomen—average farmers familiar with the paradox of an eighteenth-century rural life. They knew the feeling of independence that came with landownership. They had experienced the feeling of helplessness that came with the realization that nature could not be controlled. Philip's identity was shaped by his upbringing in this yeoman culture.

Philip's attachment to Cohansey was inextricably linked to the experiences of those who went before him. His sense of place required an act of historical imagination. Cohansey's physical landscape, the natural environment in which he enjoyed each spring, could not be separated from its local past.[6] Philip was a serious student of Cohansey social history. He recorded, often in meticulous detail, the vital records of his neighbors and friends. He often made a habit of listing all of the marriages and deaths that had occurred during the preceding year in his hometown of Greenwich. He wrote brief tributes to Cohansians who had passed into glory, rejoiced in the marriages of friends and the births of children, and was always aware when newcomers arrived to the region, whether they had come to visit or stay permanently.

Philip took particular care to register his own family genealogy, and he was keenly aware of his place within it. When his grandmother Sarah Vickers died in December 1766, her passing led him to "think seriously" about his own mortality and the meaning of his life in the larger course of human events and family history. He began to construct some of the hereditary bridges that connected him to his past, recording the birth dates of his immediate family and his lineage dating back to Josiah Fithian, his paternal grandfather.[7] Philip's scribal habits are a testament to his knowledge of the people who inhabited the place where he lived. Births and marriages, baptisms and deaths—all were windows into the history of Cohansey and its families. They were sacred events worth noting because they confirmed that God was watching over Cohansey, quietly sustaining the lives of the Presbyterian faithful. The act of recording such data, however private, was a celebration of a particular people, soil, and tradition. Philip saw himself as a laborer in that soil and a recipient of that tradition. History was a discipline that kept him attached to his home.[8]

Philip's custom of transcribing these seemingly mundane lists of names and dates served as a kind of memorial to his ancestors' successful search for roots. His family spent the better part of the seventeenth century looking for a home. In this sense, they were not unusual. Internal migration, or the movement of people *within* the British-American colonies, was the natural extension of overseas migration to America. A move to the Cohansey River in West Jersey at the end of the seventeenth century was the result of a decision, made by one's parents at the beginning of the century, to leave small English agricultural villages for work in more populated areas. A resolution to break with the remnants of the medieval manor could have far-reaching consequences. It might lead to migration across the Atlantic—perhaps, as in the case of Calvinists such as Philip's ancestors, to the Puritan colonies of Massachusetts Bay or Plymouth. For many migrants and their children, the journey did not stop there. Connecticut, Rhode Island, eastern Long Island, or East Jersey might be next on their itinerary before they paused in Cohansey, a third or fourth frontier. Indeed, by the early 1680s a few migrants were making their way to the wilds of West Jersey, buying land there and settling on it. Though it would not be long before the number of travelers to this region would look minuscule compared to the thousands coming to William Penn's "Holy Experiment" in Pennsylvania, the West Jersey colony was still able to tap into a vast array of English men and women in search of a place they could call home, a phenomenon that has been described as the "peopling of the North American continent."[9]

Philip's immediate ancestors were active participants in the peopling process. His parents, Joseph Fithian and Hannah Vickers, descended from two of Cohansey's long-established and best-known families. Hannah's grandfather Philip Vickers had come to New Jersey from Fairfield, Connecticut, sometime around the turn of the eighteenth century. He arrived early enough to obtain choice lands and position himself, by the time of his death in 1703, as one of the region's wealthier yeoman farmers. Joseph's grandfather Samuel Fithian was born in East Hampton, Long Island, and migrated to Cohansey in 1700. Like Philip Vickers, Samuel was part of the region's founding generation. He would die in 1702 as one of Cohansey's few "gentleman" farmers. Joseph and Hannah's marriage in 1740—though no doubt conducted with a degree of Presbyterian frugality—was as close to a royal wedding as would have been possible in Cohansey's grain-growing communities. In a way that few may have realized at the time, their union represented the confluence of two of the more active streams of migration that carried settlers to this region. A half-century earlier over fifty families from Connecticut and Long Island had come to Cohansey to pursue dreams of landed happiness. Hannah and Joseph's wedding was a reminder of how these two streams had cut a New England swath in the landscape of the province of West Jersey.[10]

Philip Vickers came to Cohansey on the tail end of a small migration to the region from Fairfield, Connecticut. In September 1697 twenty-eight Fairfield families joined together to purchase 3,700 acres on the south side of the Cohansey River. Each purchaser received between 100 and 250 acres of land at the rate of nine pounds per 100 acres. Shortly after their arrival they received permission from the West Jersey Assembly to establish the town of Fairfield. The name of the settlement was an obvious choice, although during the first several decades of its history Fairfield would be called "New England Town."[11] Philip Vickers was not part of this original land deal, but he would certainly have been aware of the New Jersey frontier to which several of his Connecticut neighbors had moved. Within a few years of their arrival he would decide to join them.

The English population on the south side of the Cohansey River in 1697 was sparse. A few Baptists and Quakers from East Jersey were living about five miles east of New England Town at a place called Back Neck, but for the most part the Connecticut settlers would be left alone. The river was located in the southernmost sector of the Quaker colony of West Jersey. The first English settlers to Cohansey were members of the Society of Friends who had traveled to America in 1676 with John Fenwick, the English gentleman who made a failed attempt at establishing his own Quaker colony in the region. By the time of the Connecticut migration, Fenwick's colony had come under the jurisdiction of West Jersey, which after 1702 united with East Jersey to form the royal colony of New Jersey. Members of the West Jersey Society, the name for the group of proprietors who owned a considerable portion of the colony's lands, were eager to attract new settlers to their province and thus offered tracts to potential inhabitants at affordable prices.[12] Cohansey was an ideal place for land-hungry Connecticut settlers. New England villages simply could not provide enough acreage to satisfy all of the people who wanted to settle in them. They were overcrowded, and land was virtually impossible to find if one was a newcomer. Those with large holdings in given towns tended to put down roots, develop a sense of place, and participate in the social and political life of their communities. Those who owned small tracts or had no landholdings whatsoever were most likely to leave town when other opportunities presented themselves.[13]

Fairfield, Connecticut, was no exception to this rule. The best lands in Fairfield were allotted to those proprietors or "town fathers" who participated in its founding in 1639. The Fairfield proprietors did everything in their power to limit the amount of land acquired by newcomers. When Connecticut received its royal charter from Charles II in 1662, the town fathers decided that it was in their best interest, in order to protect their property from the Crown, to distribute all remaining undivided lands as soon as possible so that ownership would rest with individuals, who were protected by British liberties. Sixty-nine families received an average of 4 acres each in 1662, and a subsequent division provided an additional 6.1 acres per family.[14] When auxiliary tracts were purchased from the local Indians in 1671, the proprietors decided that only those families who received acreage during the 1662 and 1669 land divisions would be entitled to them. Land was certainly available in Fairfield but only to those with the right family names, and as we will see, "Vickers" was not one of them.[15] By the turn of the eighteenth century, after several additional tracts were added to Fairfield and doled out carefully to the appropriate inhabitants, all of the town's land had been distributed and fenced. As the population of the town increased, the size of its farms shrank and would never grow any larger. Landed inheritances, especially for fathers with more than one son, would slowly diminish in acreage. For at least twenty-eight Fairfield families, the year 1697 was probably as good as any to leave Connecticut for the New Jersey frontier.[16]

Philip Vickers was a blacksmith and a latecomer to Fairfield, Connecticut. He arrived in 1687, a migrant from either New Haven, Connecticut, or Marblehead, Massachusetts. He built a house in town and opened a shop to practice his trade. At some point during the fourteen years Vickers lived in Fairfield, he acquired three acres of land at Sasqua Neck, the site of present-day Southport, Connecticut. Vickers, however, was not part of the original land division and thus had no realistic hope, especially after the town boundaries were clearly defined, of ever expanding his holdings. His dilemma was a common one for those who left for Cohansey in 1697. John Bateman's father, William, for example, was part of a group from Concord, Massachusetts, that came to Fairfield in 1644, but he never appeared on the town's land dividend lists. John Mills, Joshua Curtis, Robert Dallglesh, Joseph Grimes, Michael Hanna, Thomas Kernes, and Edward Lummis were also latecomers who never appeared on these lists. If the names of these men had not been included on the official deed of the 1697 Cohansey land purchase, there would be very little evidence to suggest that any of them, Philip Vickers included, ever lived in Fairfield, Connecticut. They were classic seventeenth-century migrants—men chasing additional acreage for their children and seeking the prestige of town fatherhood that often came with the accumulation of property. Vickers probably lived a rather comfortable life as a Fairfield blacksmith; he possessed a small tract of land, a house in town, and even a slave, named Dorkis. Even so, the level of happiness he achieved in Fairfield was not enough to end his family's American migration, a sojourn that included stops in at least two other New England towns. In 1698 he sold his blacksmith shop, and three years later he did the same with his three acres. Vickers then headed off to Cohansey, with his wife and at least one son, in search of a home.[17]

Samuel Fithian was also searching for a home. Shortly after the Fairfield, Connecticut, settlers arrived in New Jersey they were joined by at least twenty families from the eastern Long Island towns of Southold, Southampton, and especially East Hampton.[18] These migrants were in the midst of their own family sojourns. Many of their parents had come to America as part of the great Puritan migration of the 1630s and had settled in Salem and Lynn, Massachusetts, before crossing Long Island Sound to found the towns on the island's east end. Family historians and other antiquarians debate Samuel Fithian's lineage. Tradition suggests that his father, William, was a Welsh supporter of Oliver Cromwell's army during the English civil war and was present at the execution of Charles I in 1649. According to this scenario, William arrived in Boston sometime in the 1650s and lived in Lynn and New Haven before eventually settling in East Hampton. Others have suggested, perhaps more accurately, that he was of English origin, had little or no direct connection with Cromwell or the English civil war, and followed a path to East Hampton that, though difficult to trace due to lack of evidence, may have taken him through Lynn, New Haven, or Southampton. We will probably never know the route that William Fithian took to Long Island, but we can be sure that he was in East Hampton by 1653 (he received a local land grant) and had made several stops along the way.[19]

When Samuel Fithian met Philip Vickers in New England Town, New Jersey, sometime around the turn of the eighteenth century, they would have had a lot to talk about. Their motivations for moving to New Jersey were similar, and this topic undoubtedly made for much conversation on the walk home from services at the Fairfield church or while sipping beverages together at Edmund and Rachel Shaw's tavern at the town crossroads. East Hampton's seventeenth-century development mirrored that of Fairfield, Connecticut. New England settlers from Salem and Lynn, who, according to Massachusetts governor John Winthrop, were "much straitened by their own nearness to one another, and their cattle being so much increased," came to the eastern end of Long Island in search of more grazing land. Their new home did not offer unlimited opportunities to spread out, but they could expand their holdings through land purchases from the neighboring Montauk Indians. The historian T. H. Breen has taught us that there were clear "winners" and "losers" in early East Hampton. The winners were those who got there first and acquired the best land. As was the case in Fairfield, Connecticut, these earliest settlers maintained strict control over the distribution process. The losers, as might be expected, were those who came late and as a result failed to obtain the best lands or a prominent place in the town's social order. East Hampton developed a sense of "community" defined by those who had enough acreage and prestige to be able to provide large tracts for their children and maintain their political power.[20]

By the end of the seventeenth century the differences between winners and losers in East Hampton were growing. The whaling industry did wonders for the economy of the town. Its success became the envy of royal officials in New York, who did everything in their power to benefit from it. Whaling ushered East Hampton into a thriving British Atlantic economy and brought considerable wealth to those in a position to take advantage of the trade in oil and bone. East Hampton's whaler-founders bought as much acreage as possible from their Montauk neighbors. They fenced their newly improved tracts and cleared outlying areas for their livestock. However, there was one problem that few of the whaler-founders paused long enough to consider or care about: East Hampton was located on the end of an island. By the 1690s short moves of a few miles outside of town to tracts offering additional pastureland were becoming more difficult. There was little room to expand after Montauk lands were purchased, resulting in a small but steady out-migration that continued through the eighteenth century. The New Jersey towns of Newark, Elizabeth-Town, Cape May, and Fairfield—all middle-colony bastions of New England Puritanism—were popular destinations for these migrants.[21]

William Fithian was one of the earliest East Hampton landholders. He received grants in 1653 and 1655 totaling just over six acres. William built a house on the east side of the town's main thoroughfare and lived there with his wife, Margaret, and their five children. William did not participate in the East Hampton whaling trade and seems to have made his living through some combination of woodworking and farming.[22] In 1667 he was named as an overseer of the town and possessed a relatively large taxable inventory valued at £180. At the time of his death eleven years later he owned fifty-three acres, including two home lots in the center of town. William had enough land and personal property to live comfortably in East Hampton, but he did not possess the kind of wealth and political clout afforded to those who had arrived in the town before him. His one-year stint as a town overseer paled in comparison to the positions held by some East Hampton families, such as the Mulfords, Daytons, Talmadges, or Bakers, whose members were elected to serve multiple terms in multiple offices. He also appears never to have pursued Montauk tracts in the aggressive style that characterized some of his neighbors' land pursuits.[23]

On his death in 1678 William left eighteen-year-old Samuel, his second son, one of his main-street house lots and slightly over 21 acres of pastureland. This was a fine and workable inheritance, and Samuel farmed this land for over two decades. In April 1700 he acquired from his older brother Enoch, due to an error in the distribution of his father's estate, 27 additional acres—a small windfall that more than doubled the size of Samuel's holdings. Even so, this new acquisition was apparently not enough to keep him and his wife, Priscilla, and their seven children, ranging in age from nineteen years to several months, from leaving East Hampton. Shortly after he received his new land Samuel packed up and left town for a largely unsettled New Jersey frontier. In December he purchased 304 acres, a massive tract by Fithian standards, on the south side of the Cohansey River and built a homestead for his family at New England Crossroads, the heart of the new settlement established by the Connecticut migrants who had come there three years earlier. He also erected a sawmill, a business venture that he undertook with several of his neighbors, including John Ogden, one of the original 1697 Cohansey land purchasers from Connecticut. Samuel must have taken full advantage of his short Cohansey experience. At the time of his premature death in 1702, at the age of forty-two, he had acquired enough land and social prestige to take the label "gentleman farmer" and was able to pass a substantial inheritance in land and goods to his sons, all of whom would become prominent members of the Cohansey community.[24]

The peopling of Cohansey did not stop once Connecticut and Long Island migrants arrived at New England Town. Not only could internal migration take place over longer distances, such as the roughly two hundred miles separating Fairfield, Connecticut, from Cohansey, but it was also characterized by shorter moves within a region.[25] New England settlers relocated frequently throughout Cohansey, always looking for better land and larger homesteads. When they felt the urge to spread out, many of them went a few miles north, across the river to Greenwich. John Fenwick had envisioned Greenwich, which he also called "Town Neck," as one of his colony's two commercial centers (Salem was the other).[26] Located on the northern shores of the river about six twisting and turning miles west of Delaware Bay, the town was eventually laid out, after Fenwick's death in 1683, with sixteen-acre lots along a one-hundred-foot-wide road that residents would come to call "Ye Greate Street." Greenwich became an official British port in 1687 and was chosen by the West Jersey Assembly as the site of agricultural fairs to be held each May and October beginning in 1695.[27]

Over half of the early settlers of New England Town moved across the river to Greenwich and its rural environs within the first several years of their arrival. Others went farther north along the Cohansey River. Robert Hood and Edward Lummis, both migrants from Fairfield, Connecticut, purchased land at Indian Fields, the once seasonal home of the local Lenape Indians. These holdings would later become the town of Bridgeton. Thomas Harris and Benjamin Davis, also Connecticut migrants, were influential in settling the village of Deerfield in the early 1730s.[28] These local moves throughout Cohansey seasoned the region with the distinct New England Calvinist flavor that we will examine in more detail in the next chapter. Many of those who crossed the river were the children of the first generation of New England Town land purchasers. Philip Vickers stayed on the south side of the Cohansey, but after his death his son made the move to Greenwich sometime before 1735. The sons of Samuel Fithian, including Philip Vickers Fithian's grandfather Josiah, left New England Town for Greenwich shortly after their father's death in 1702.

In addition to the Fithian and Vickers families, the children of Nathaniel Bishop, William Harris, Thomas Maskell, John Miller, William Mulford, and Thomas Parvin, to name only a few, had settled in Greenwich by 1735. These families were joined by Connecticut and eastern Long Island migrants who had not been involved in the original settlement a generation earlier. This group included members of long-standing East Hampton and Southampton families such as the Brewsters, Carlls, Jessups, Pecks, Plattses, and Reeves. Also joining them was a growing number of Scots-Irish, some of whom, such as the Ewing family from Londonderry, came to Cohansey after brief stops in Long Island and other parts of New England. Church subscribers with Scottish surnames such as Campbell, Caruthers, Finley, Keith, and McKnight also arrived during this period.[29] All of these Calvinists came to West Jersey with large families. Samuel Fithian had seven children; Nathaniel Bishop, nine; Nathan Lawrence, six; Edward Lummis, six; William Mulford, ten; Daniel Westcott, eight; John Bateman, twelve; and Edmund Shaw, ten. The biblical exhortation to "be fruitful and multiply" was applied with great vigor by Cohansey's New England settlers and was an important factor in the creation of this Reformed outpost in West Jersey.

Indeed, the social world to which Philip Vickers Fithian was born was beginning to take shape. By the time he reached adulthood, three generations after his great-grandparents' arrival, Philip had developed a historical connection with his ancestors and neighbors that instilled in him a local patriotism he would never relinquish, even when powerful new affections—such as love of humanity and love of nation—threatened to weaken its hold on his life.

Philip's sense of place was the product of his historical and genealogical imagination, but it was also grounded in his family's relationship with the land. New Englanders knew the economic and cultural value of land, and Cohansey offered them tracts considerably larger than those available to them in Fairfield, Connecticut, or East Hampton, New York. Cohansey, as they understood it, was one of the next frontiers of New England settlement—a place where they and their descendants could live free and happy on sizable acreage. Samuel Fithian's Cohansey farm, for example, was five times larger than all his East Hampton landholdings combined.

The first New Englanders to settle in West Jersey realized that Cohansey was no utopia. It was remote, had poorly maintained roads, and, despite the presence of a colonial port at Greenwich, offered limited access to the British mercantile world. However, these problems were minor when measured against the abundance of land at their disposal, the reasonably fertile soil, and the mild winters and longer growing seasons in Cohansey.[30] New Englanders could come to Cohansey and live the yeoman's life to its fullest. Of the 182 heads of household residing in Cohansey between 1670 and 1750 who chose to identify themselves in their wills by occupations or skills, over half (54 percent) opted for the label "yeoman." When alternative agricultural terms of self-identification such as "husbandman," "farmer," or "planter" are factored into the total, the proportion of those who described themselves in relationship to the land rises to just under 64 percent. Similarly, over 65 percent of all land deals conducted in Cohansey between 1676 and 1707 included at least one participant who identified himself as a "planter," a "yeoman," or a "husbandman." When eighteen of the twenty-eight original Connecticut purchasers of Cohansey lands bought additional property in 1697 from the Reverend Thomas Bridge, they chose to identify themselves collectively as "planters." Even Cohansey inhabitants who preferred to describe themselves in probate and land records as craftsmen or artisans—a group that included carpenters, blacksmiths, weavers, millers, coopers, tanners, cordwainers, tailors, saddlers, and hatters—owned land and engaged in some form of agricultural activity.[31]

In seventeenth-century England the term "yeoman" was associated more with social status than with vocation. It was a label applied to a farmer who owned "substantial acreage" worth at the very least forty shillings. Most yeomen, however, owned much more. They not only planned to feed their families with the crops they grew but expected to sell surpluses at market. They were aided in their physical labor by family members and neighbors. English yeomen enjoyed political privileges ("yeoman" and "freeholder" were virtually synonymous categories) and could provide a landed future for their children. In this sense they were a step above a "husbandman," who did not own his land outright or else possessed only a small number of acres. "Husbandman" was a label of both status *and* occupation in early modern England. All those who worked the land, including yeomen, could technically have been considered "husbandmen" by virtue of the kind of work they performed, but husbandmen were usually not able to take the same market risks as yeomen, making them and their families less economically secure.[32]

Much of this English understanding of the yeomanry transferred to the British-American colonies. The label "yeoman" as employed in the colonies applied to small "producers" distinguished by their ability to grow their own food and participate, when possible, in large markets. Yeomanry required a significant tract of land on which to farm. Moreover, the differences between "yeoman" and "husbandman" were less defined in the colonies than in England. In Cohansey these two terms were used interchangeably.[33] Of the 116 Cohansey settlers who identified themselves with an agricultural label between 1670 and 1750, 96 chose the label "yeoman," 14 chose "husbandman," 5 chose "planter," and 1 called himself a "farmer." By the first several decades of the eighteenth-century the latter three labels had been replaced in probate and land records almost exclusively with the term "yeoman."[34]

When a Cohansey farmer sat down to write a will or deed, his decision to call himself a "yeoman" meant more than just the fact that he owned land or understood his place in the social order. Yeomanry was a vital part of his identity as a human being. The label spoke volumes about his character, sense of vocation, and moral sensibilities. Yeomen were people with rights who had at some point in the past triumphed over the moral and economic slavery of wage labor or indentured servanthood. Yeomen carried the weight of civic responsibility on their strong shoulders. As freeholders, they had the right to vote and hold public office. To style oneself a yeoman could also serve as a testament to a farmer's American sojourn. In a century of human mobility driven by the quest for land, to claim yeoman status was a public declaration that one had "made it" in the New World. It symbolized full membership in an early American community and the achievement of a landed American dream. As unimproved land became increasingly more difficult to obtain in places such as Fairfield, Connecticut, and East Hampton, Long Island, and as farms that *were* available were shrinking in size (forcing the diversification of local economies), one could always migrate to a place such as Cohansey and fashion himself as part of the yeoman class.[35]

Yeomen were invested with the independence and the power to voice concern when British liberties were threatened. Because landowners relied only on themselves and their families to obtain their daily bread, they were some of the strongest critics of the royal government when their rights and liberties as citizens of England were threatened. While the image of the colonial yeoman was much employed during the era of the American Revolution, the practice of speaking out against the government from a position of landed independence dates back to the early colonial period. New Englanders, especially those from East Hampton, fought regularly with New York's royal government over issues ranging from taxation to the distribution of land. Revolt and resistance were defining characteristics of the yeoman class.[36]

The idea of landownership was also vested with a religious dimension, especially for Calvinists such as those who came to Cohansey. Calvinism and the theory of British property rights had much in common. Land was part of God's created order. It was meant to be enjoyed and cared for by *individuals*. The tending of a particular plot of earth was a divine calling, and Calvinists took seriously God's command to "replenish the earth and subdue it." Throughout the Scriptures, but especially in the Old Testament, God had given the land to His people to sustain them. There was a Protestant flavor to all of this. Land was acquired and owned by individuals much in the same way that Protestants encountered God as individuals. In other words, property was private and not meant to be shared in a collective fashion—as did the peasants who lived on feudal manors and enjoyed few liberties. The right to own land without outside interference from church or government was rooted in the same philosophical understanding of British liberties that allowed an individual to encounter God without similar intrusions from arbitrary ecclesiastical (most Roman Catholic) or political authorities.[37]

The political and Protestant understandings of landholding came together in 1715 when thirty-six Cohansey residents, including Philip's grandfather Josiah Fithian, fashioned themselves as "yeomen" and refused to pay taxes to New Jersey's royal government because their tax collector, Francis Pagitt, was a Roman Catholic. It is unclear from their petition to Gov. Robert Hunter if these Cohansey yeomen had a gripe with the tax as well as with the tax collector, but it is probably safe to assume that they did not like the former either. The signers of the petition, most of whom can be identified as either Presbyterians or Baptists, could not fathom the notion that the Crown would employ a Catholic constable. Did the royal government not know that the Roman Church was "Utterly Repugnant to the Laws of Great Brittain & Contrary to ye

Rights & Liberties of his Royall Majesties faithfull Subjects"? They remained in doubt over whether Pagitt was "a Lawful Constable" and claimed to have been "Illegally Assessed by an Assesser" who was a "Known & open profest Roman Catholick." To accept the authority of Francis Pagitt was to count themselves "Traytors to his Majesty our King & all True Protestants." By addressing the governor as yeomen, these Cohansey farmers were affirming landownership as a God-given right and expressing a concern that such a right would be placed in jeopardy by a tax collector who served a church known for its suppression of such privileges. We do not know how Governor Hunter responded to the specific demands of this petition, but he did complain to the Lords of Trade in England about the obstinate New Englanders who resided in his colony.[38] Hunter wrote with great disdain that the authors of the petition were "all from New England . . . but whether they be a true sample of the body of the people there, or only a sett of unquiet or restless men, who could be easy nowhere, and so left that Province for this, I cannot determine, but this I confidently affirm, that all the opposition and vexation I have met with in both of these Provinces (New York and New Jersey) has been in a great measure owing to those who have come to us from that."[39]

Some of those who came to Cohansey from Fairfield or East Hampton were yeomen before they arrived in West Jersey. Though Philip Vickers identified himself as a "blacksmith," he did own land in Fairfield, entitling him to vote in local elections. William Fithian even served briefly as an officeholder in East Hampton. However, for many who decided to leave their New England towns for Cohansey, yeoman status and the enjoyment of the privileges that came with it were not enough to satisfy their land hunger. The yeoman classes were constantly engaged in the process of "remaking" themselves on the frontiers of early America. Migration provided a fresh start. The work of clearing land and building dwelling places was worth it in the end if such a refashioning allowed them to become part of a community of landed "winners." At the time of his death in 1703 Vickers could boast a personal inventory valued at over £250, including two "negroes." His son Philip, the maternal grandfather of Philip Vickers Fithian, possessed even greater personal wealth.[40]

For other New England yeomen, a move to Cohansey was a means by which they could climb even higher in the colonial social structure. As we have seen, Samuel Fithian was a "gentleman" at the time of his death. A "gentleman" was a large landholder who had accumulated enough wealth or social capital so that he did not have to perform the daily physical labor that a yeoman life required. While in some cases gentlemen did indeed work with their hands, most of their daily farm tasks were handled by slaves, servants, or sons. Clergymen, for example, were considered gentlemen because of their learnedness. Their farmwork, from reaping at harvest to chopping wood for their fireplaces, was performed by members of their congregations. Gentlemen could be either born or made, but in Cohansey they were almost always made. It was not unusual for a yeoman to work his way up, through the accumulation of lands or some form of social or political leadership in the community, to the status of a gentleman.[41]

A place such as Cohansey offered yeomen and rural gentlemen the economic security they had hoped to obtain by leaving New England. The rapid eighteenth-century growth of Philadelphia as a major British-American port would all but guarantee the long-term success and stability of its multiple hinterlands. Much of Philadelphia's exports were shipped to the lucrative English plantations in the West Indies, where grain was needed to feed the large slave labor force.[42] Though Cohansey was certainly not the most important node in this grain economy, its yeoman farmers might still reap its benefits and fashion their everyday lives with such available markets in mind. This sort of economic opportunity would have proven attractive to anyone considering uprooting and moving to the West Jersey countryside.[43]

It was into this rural world, created by mobile seventeenth-century New Englanders and sustained by a yeoman way of life, that Philip Vickers Fithian was born. By the time he reached adulthood he had an intimate knowledge of Cohansey—its land and its people. Most of Philip's childhood and adolescent years were spent on or close to his father's farm. There is no evidence in his early journal to suggest that he ever left Cohansey. Only months after he was born, the townships on the river were removed from the political jurisdiction of Salem County and placed into the newly created county of Cumberland, whose bounds extended south to West Creek (along the Cape May County border), north to Deerfield, and west to the Tuckahoe River (where it bordered Gloucester County). In 1771 most of Cumberland County's five thousand inhabitants resided in the five Cohansey River townships of Greenwich, Hopewell, Fairfield, Bridgeton, and Deerfield. The daily life of the people of Cohansey had changed little since Samuel Fithian and Philip Vickers arrived at the turn of the century. The inhabitants were still middling farmers who produced grain and raised livestock for Philadelphia markets. Three out of every four taxable residents in the region in 1773 owned between 50 and 150 acres of improved land, prompting Philip to describe his home as a "Spartan-Common-Wealth" where the "midling or lower Class are accounted the strenth & Honour of the Colony." By the time of the American Revolution, one would have been hard-pressed to find an estate larger than 250 acres.[44]

Figure 2. The Greenwich, New Jersey, house in which Philip Vickers Fithian was raised. Courtesy, Lummis Library, Cumberland County (N.J.) Historical Society.

Philip was the oldest of Joseph and Hannah Fithian's seven children. He had five younger brothers—Enoch, Josiah, Jonathan, Amos, and Thomas—and one younger sister, Rebecca. His father owned land a few miles west of Greenwich's Ye Great Street in an area called Town Branch. We do not know the actual size of Joseph's farm, but it contained twenty acres of salt marsh located on either the Cohansey River or one of its tributaries and was probably smaller than the 150-acre tract owned by his brother Samuel, who farmed nearby.[45] Joseph's farm was bounded by two local creeks and was less than a mile from the Cohansey River, allowing young Philip, when working in the fields, to look southward over the rising grain and catch a glimpse of the river's winding course.

Joseph Fithian was not exceptional. Like hundreds of his neighbors in the Delaware Valley, he was a middling farmer who inherited land from his father and worked it hard in order to be successful in the grain-livestock culture of the Philadelphia hinterland. As his father's third son, he watched the best lands and the family house on Ye Great Street go to his older brother Samuel, the executor of Josiah Fithian's estate. Samuel was one of the wealthiest men in Greenwich. At the time of his death in 1777 he had a personal inventory valued at over fifteen hundred pounds. Four years earlier he was assessed for 150 acres of improved land, twenty-eight cattle, and a slave named Anthony, whose erratic behavior Philip occasionally wrote about in his journal. Though Joseph possessed just over one quarter of what his brother Samuel owned in personal goods, he still lived a comfortable life that would have fulfilled his East Hampton–born grandfather's grandest hopes and dreams. While Philip never mentioned specifically his father engaging in physical labor (with the exception of fishing), one does get the sense that much of the work performed on the farm was done by the entire family, Joseph included.[46]

Philip attended grammar school as a boy. He needed to spend at least a year, although probably longer, receiving what he called a "limited necessary Education." This involved learning how to read, write, and develop the math skills needed to maintain an account book and manage a family farm.[47] Somewhere along the way he developed an affinity for writing. From 1766 to 1767 he kept a work journal that chronicled the daily grind on his father's farm and foreshadowed much of his future vocational and intellectual pursuits. However, we must be careful not to jump too far ahead of our story. At the time Philip commenced writing he was eighteen years old and fully engaged in the everyday activities of an agricultural life. His hands were dirty and calloused, and the muscles of his "skinny Ghostly body" were sore from performing nearly every task needed to sustain an eighteenth-century farm.[48] His time was governed by the agricultural seasons, and he had already developed a familiarity with the landscape, the soil, the ecosystem, the plant and animal life, and the tidal waterways of Cohansey. Philip understood the necessity, virtue, and drudgery of physical labor and was fully prepared, like all of Cohansey's yeomen sons, to spend his remaining days performing such work.

The work cycle on Joseph Fithian's farm was rather typical for the Delaware Valley.[49] The calendar year started off slowly, with much of the work conducted indoors. When Philip did go outside into the relatively mild southern New Jersey winter he could be found chopping down trees, splitting wood, loading the logs onto carts or sleds, and delivering them to the family homestead or the houses of friends and neighbors. The bulk of Philip's winter work was focused on the care of the previous autumn's harvest. He spent his winters on the threshing-room floor preparing his father's wheat and rye for market. He was undoubtedly quite skilled at wielding a wooden flail, the device used to separate the grain from its stalks. This was strenuous indoor work, and Philip had no choice but to participate in it. Wheat and rye were the primary commercial crops on the Fithian farm, making this preparatory task essential to the economic livelihood of his family.[50]

Flax production, another one of Philip's jobs that commenced in the fall and continued through the winter, was just as physically demanding as threshing wheat and rye and a lot more tedious. Joseph Fithian probably devoted a patch of his farm to the cultivation of flax so that he might meet his family's most immediate and basic clothing needs and sell the remainder at market. Flax stalks were pulled from the ground during the summer reaping season and were then dried, broken, and threshed in October and November before being stored in a barn to await their "dressing." During these autumn months the stalks were spread over an earthen kiln, and later they were broken into small pieces with a hammerlike device called a flax brake. Once the flax was broken, the entire family began the process of scutching. This was the slow, monotonous, and dusty work of using a knife to remove the tiny particles of wood that still remained in the fiber. When the scutching was completed, the flax was considered "dressed" and the women of the household could begin to cut and prepare the fibers for spinning.[51]

The breaking and dressing of flax continued as the weather grew warmer, but the bulk of Philip's labor was now moved outdoors. He would relish in the rebirth of nature by expanding the family garden and digging ground in the orchard for the planting of new peach and apple trees in the hope that they would soon be "cloth'd with a noble green." He spent several days in March and early April planting string beans, peas, parsley, onions, carrots, cabbage, radishes, and potatoes. He also sowed lettuce and parsnips. The garden, an essential part of every early American farm, provided the Fithians with food for their own consumption. While the Fithians may have shared their vegetables with neighbors, it is doubtful that any of their produce was grown for market. As spring came into full bloom and the Cohansey soil grew softer, Philip left the garden for the fields to begin plowing in preparation for sowing flax, corn, and pumpkins. He was not fond of this aspect of springtime labor, complaining after one particularly difficult day behind the plow that he was "extremely weary" and "much fatigued." In addition to plowing, Philip carted and spread wagonloads of dung in the hope of restoring (through fertilization) depleted soil and minimizing the months his father would need to let his lands lie fallow. The little time Philip had left on the spring work calendar was spent repairing fences, washing sheep, seine fishing in the Cohansey (for terrapins and rockfish), and "bottoming some chairs."[52]

Philip was fully attuned to the changing seasons in his homeland. If God had blessed the people of Cohansey, then summer was a time of bountiful harvest. The Fithian farm abounded with "fruits of various kinds" that were "precious to behold" in their "milky sweetness." The garden yielded summer melons and cucumbers distinguished by their usual "native excellency."[53] The thought of fresh fruit was a pleasant distraction amid the farmwork required of him during June, July, and August. Rural life now turned to the harvest—the highpoint of the agricultural year. The significance of the harvest season may have prompted Philip to start writing. It is not surprising that he chose June 28, the first day of the 1766 reaping season, to begin recording his daily activities in the pages of his work journal.

From the end of June through late July, Philip reaped wheat and rye, mowed and raked hay, and pulled flax stalks from the ground. This was a time when community values coexisted with the individual and self-interested economic concerns that made the Delaware Valley "the best poor man's country in the world."[54] Cohansey grain growers hired single men to aid them with their harvests each summer, but most relied on their families and the generosity of friends and neighbors to help gather their crops. In the summer of 1766, after eleven days of reaping on his father's farm, Philip lent his services to his uncle Samuel and four other farmers in Greenwich. The following year he worked for six additional area farmers. The community nature of the harvest made the difficult and repetitive practice of wielding a sickle or scythe in the hot Cohansey sun more bearable. Each summer one could look forward to working together with friends, neighbors, and relatives. West Indian rum flowed freely during breaks from work.[55]

In the summer, in addition to reaping, the Fithians made repairs to the system of banks and sluices that they constructed to control the drainage of their salt marshes. These banks, which could run up to seven feet in height, were built to reclaim marshland along the Cohansey River with the ultimate goal of creating meadows suitable for the grazing of livestock. In the center of each bank was a sluice box—an open-ended wooden case with a flapper (or gate) that allowed a controlled amount of river or creek water to enter and exit the meadow. First employed by the Dutch in the eleventh century, banking was used throughout the Cohansey River region and much of the larger Delaware Valley to allow plant life in the marshes to feed off the rich nutrients of the river bottom. The process produced some of the most fertile land available in the region, and the salt hay that these meadows yielded offered a better-tasting diet to cattle tired of eating fresh hay and grass.[56]

During the eighteenth century, before companies took up the responsibility of building and maintaining banks and sluices, the work of diking belonged to all the farmers who owned the land beside a given river or creek. The labor required to construct these banks was back-breaking. Stones, mud, and sod (and on occasion timber and masonry) were carted to the site of the bank. Drains were dug and sluice boxes built and fitted. Much of this work demanded a thorough knowledge of the tidal patterns of the Cohansey River and its tributaries since repairs had to be made quickly in order to avoid the high tidal waters that could damage unfinished banks or flood unprotected meadows. Philip was well acquainted with bank construction and repair. He spent many July and August days pushing wheelbarrows and carrying canoes full of mud to the banks. His familiarity with carpentry was useful for framing sluice boxes, and he helped his father reap the benefits of the banks by mowing the family's twenty acres of salt marsh.[57]

The nature of this work made summers on the Cohansey the unhealthiest season of the year. Agricultural labor was plagued by the ubiquitous presence of mosquitoes. These pesky insects were everywhere and became more concentrated and oppressive as one approached the river. The well-traveled eighteenth-century Swedish botanist Peter Kalm noted the prevalence of mosquitoes and other insects on the Cohansey to a degree he had never seen before. He described gnats that "suck up so much blood that they can hardly fly away." They were "so numerous in some places that the air seemed full of them, especially near swamps and stagnant waters." He added, "when they [mosquitoes] stung me here at night, my face was so disfigured by little red spots and blisters that I was almost ashamed to show myself."[58] Mosquitoes were more than just a nuisance. They were also carriers of a local sickness—a disease that Philip, the natives of Cohansey, and other early American inhabitants of marshy environments called the "fever and ague"—that raged throughout the region, usually in late August and early September. This was most likely the same strain of malaria that plagued many in the colonial Chesapeake and from which settlers in Cohansey had suffered since the 1670s.

Philip's Cohansey, in other words, was not the healthiest place to live. Peter Kalm remarked that "strangers who arrive here are commonly attacked by sickness the first or second year after their arrival, and it acts more violently upon them than upon the natives, so that they sometimes die of it." The illness Kalm remembered included symptoms such as headaches, severe chills (which Kalm described as being "so great that both the patient, the bed upon which he lies, and everything else, shakes violently"), high fevers, and chest pains. He tentatively suggested that the disease was related to the "peculiar qualities of the air," the "putrid water," and the abundance of "morasses and swamps . . . where stagnant, stinking water is to be found."[59] Philip's immune system did not adapt well to these conditions. He was a sickly young man (he complained about his "poor scurvy frame") and occasionally missed a day or two of farm chores because he had contracted the ague. It was more common, however, for Philip to carry out his daily work, some of which was performed in the mosquito-infested marshes of the Cohansey tidewater, while suffering through these "fits." After being sick for two weeks in September 1766 Philip wrote, "It is at present a remarkable sickly and unhealthy time, it is said there is hardly one family in the place; but what some of them are sick, and some families not able to help one another."[60]

Though Philip managed to get through his fever and ague fits, many inhabitants of Cohansey did not. When this illness was accompanied by an extreme form of diarrhea often referred to as the "bloody flux," the results could be deadly. This combination was responsible for a handful of deaths every summer. In some years the concern was more serious than in others. Philip recorded six deaths from this illness between April and December of 1766. Ephraim Harris of Fairfield described a time during Philip's childhood when "the Lord sent the destroying angel to pass through this place," adding, "Not a house escaped" and "not a family was spared from the fatal calamity. . . . So dreadful was it that it made every ear tingle and every heart to bleed."[61] Philip occasionally obsessed about the impact of the disease on his own life and showed great empathy for his fellow Cohansians suffering from it. In 1775 he wrote:

That many disorders, chiefly the Flux, are now raging in the lower Counties, Chester, Newcastle & c. I pray God Delaware may be a Bar & stop that painful disorder, Enough has it ravaged our poor Cohansians. Enough are we . . . enfeebled & wasted with the Ague & Fever. Our Children all grow pale, puny, & lifeless—Foreigners are affrighted & flitt off. The manly Natives lose their Colour and Agility. Our girls, which are now, in the neighbouring Provinces, Standards of Beauty, droop-dead-Eyed from Room to Room, & shrink back from every Glass, vexed into a Belief, when the living Lustre of their Eyes is gone & the Warmth & Vivacity of their Heart, that so rude a Winter can never be repaired by the Influence of Spring.[62]

The fever and ague season usually passed in mid-October, a victim of the first autumn frost. As Philip regained health, he turned to the variety of tasks required for the farm's transition from harvest to winter. The threshing of wheat and rye, the beating of flax, and the cutting down of corn stalks took up much of his time during the fall. At the end of September he was back in the fields for about a week plowing orchards, spreading dung, and sowing grain for the coming season. Vegetables were pulled from the family garden. Livestock was slaughtered and, in the case of the hogs, "put up to fat." Other responsibilities included more fishing and more carting of wood. Philip also spent thirteen workdays during the fall of 1766 making apple cider. Since most colonists in early America did not trust water and milk was in short supply, cider was the drink of choice. In Cohansey it could also serve as a useful tonic for those engaged in bouts with the dreaded fever and ague. Philip participated in every aspect of the cider-making process. He spent his morning picking apples from the trees (and gathering them from the ground) of the family orchard, "squeezing" and "grounding" them into liquid form, and storing the finished product in barrels where it would either be left in the barn to ferment or used in the making of apple butter. Philip's family made twenty-eight barrels of cider (about seven hundred gallons by the estimation of one local historian) in the fall of 1766. He never mentioned what his father did with the cider when it was finished, but he probably sold or traded some locally and used most of it for family consumption. It was not unusual for a farm household to maintain an open tap of hard cider for the adults and diluted cider (or "water Cyder") for the children.[63]

As Philip moved through the agricultural seasons his thoughts were often preoccupied with the weather. This was yet another sign of his intimate knowledge of the Cohansey landscape he called home. It is common for people to begin their farm diaries with references to current weather conditions. It is even more common for historians who study diaries to ignore these references, skimming over such apparently unimportant jottings on their way to the "real lives" of their subjects. This is unfortunate for it misses a vital dimension of what actually defined "real life" in places such as eighteenth-century Cohansey. Philip obsessed about the weather. He did not start his journal entries with notes on the weather because such remarks represented proper form or provided an adequate preamble to the day's more important events. Philip wrote about the weather because his family and neighbors were at its mercy: "We know not what a Day may bring forth."[64] The weather, more than anything else, provides our best insight into the limits of an eighteenth-century agricultural life. No degree of human initiative could tame it. Few technological improvements could ease the anxiety that it brought to farmers.

When winter refused to yield to spring, the cold weather could lay waste to the Fithians' orchard. Philip described consecutive days of frost in late April 1766 and thought they would certainly "kill all our peaches." The summer's tempests "of rain, wind and thunder," arriving to Cohansey from the southwest, wreaked havoc on the Fithians' fields, "blowing down the Flax, Wheat & Corn very much." At other times the rain inundated the fields to such an extent that Philip was able to "track an Ox or a Cow" across them.[65] Cohansey farmers never watched the weather more closely than during the harvest season. Philip often devoted an entire journal entry to an hour-by-hour chronicling of a particular day's weather patterns: "cloudy this morning"; "about nine or ten o'clock it broke away so that the sun shone"; "about noon it rained again in showers"; "at 3 o'clock there came a thunder gust from the

west, and rained excessively hard"; "a while in the evening it cleared
very pleasant." The unpredictable weather during the 1766 harvest season brought great anxiety to Cohansey farmers. When the rains came as
consistently as they did during this particular summer, the Fithians were
given only a small window of time to harvest their crops. Philip had
never seen Cohansey farmers so apprehensive. "From this time to next
Wednesday," he wrote, "will be the most hurrying and engaging time for
harvest Men that perhaps ever was known; on account of the later
rains."[66]

While these concerns were certainly real, they were made less frighten-
ing by the power of the Presbyterian God. During times like the summer
of 1766, Philip placed his hope for a successful harvest in the hands of a
God who knew what was best for the farmers of Cohansey and worked all
things together for the good of those who loved Him. During times of
uncertainty Philip did not turn to superstitions or the wisdom of man-
made almanacs but instead did his best to rest in God's care for his family. In 1766 the God who controlled the weather looked favorably on the
people of Cohansey. "When the descending rains seemed to threaten us
with entire desolation," Philip reflected, "God is pleased to withhold the
Showers." Though God could have chosen not to save the Cohansey harvest, this time around He elected to answer the prayers of His people.
The only response was thankfulness, a virtue that was not lost on any of
God's creation in Cohansey. Even the "beasts & birds," Philip proclaimed
with appreciation, "express a sense of their joy and gratitude, for the
plentiful provision, by their chearfulness and merryment."[67]

At other times, however, unfavorable weather patterns could be interpreted as signs of God's judgment. In the summer of 1769 Cohansey suffered through a particularly difficult drought. "This part of our World
where we dwell," Philip wrote, "is at present, a melancholy Witness for the
Truth of the doleful Appearance of a pinching Drought." He described
drooping vegetable plants and farm animals, irritated by hunger and
flies, running "disordered" through "dusty fields." Yet, Philip believed
that these "parching Droughts of Summer" did not come by chance.
They were part of God's will for the people of Cohansey. In fact, using the
language of the well-known Puritan jeremiad, Philip believed they were a
punishment for the sins of the people in his neighborhood: "It is the
Work of the Almighty to punish sinful Man, & thus he may in Justice
continue to afflict us, till we forsake our sins."[68] The limits the weather
placed on the everyday life of Cohansey farmers reminded them of the
inability of human beings to alter the plans of a sovereign God. Their
Calvinism was lived and confirmed within the context of their agricultural lives. Their spiritual and economic lives flourished and languished

under the watchful eye of the One they believed to be the creator and sustainer of all things.

By the time he reached his twenty-first birthday, Philip's attachment to his Cohansey home was deep. This was the place where his ancestors had finally found a resting place amid a culture of seventeenth-century mobility. This was the natural world—soil, livestock, tides, and crops— that Philip, as the son of a yeoman, knew well. Cohansey was also special because of its people, and its people were Presbyterians. In 1729 Philip's grandfather Josiah, along with Thomas Maskell and Noah Miller, bought six acres from Nicholas and Leonard Gibbon on behalf of the "Descenting Presbyterian inhabitants of the North Side of Cohansey" (Greenwich). The land would be used as a parsonage for the Reverend Ebenezer Gould, who had recently arrived in Greenwich to minister to the township's Calvinist population. Josiah Fithian was remembered as a man of great piety, and his grandson Philip would follow in his stead.[69] Whether it was God's sovereign control over the weather or a local history that reflected His faithfulness through the generations, Presbyterianism was an indispensable part of Philip's connection to home. At the same time it also offered him the tools he would need to leave home for greener intellectual pastures.

Chapter 2
A Presbyterian Conversion

March 31, 1766, was the most important day in Philip Vickers Fithian's life. It was a Monday, and Philip was still reflecting on the sermons that Rev. Simon Williams had preached the day before. On Sunday morning the Deerfield minister expounded on the Twenty-fourth Psalm—"lift up your heads O ye gates! . . . lift them up, ye everlasting doors; and the King of glory shall come in." His afternoon text came from the seventeenth chapter of the Gospel of John—"I in them, and thou in me; that they may be made perfect in one; and the world may know that thou hast sent me and hast loved them, as thou hast also loved me." Philip was moved by these sermons. He noted that they "were delivered with a great deal of life, and earnestness and the assembly which was exceeding large, was very solemn and attentive."[1]

The Greenwich meetinghouse may have been crowded on this particular Sunday, but Philip undoubtedly felt that Williams's texts were chosen specifically for him. Since January he had been pondering daily the salvation of his soul. These sermons reminded him, at a crucial moment in his religious journey, that Jesus Christ came into the world so that sinners might know him and be made "perfect." If the door of Philip's heart would only be "lifted up," the "King of glory" would enter. The following day, as he sat in his room and penned his daily journal entry, three months of intense spiritual seeking came to a climax. Philip had finally experienced an evangelical breakthrough: "But I, upon the loving request of God, and Christ, made to me, by the mouth of his ministers, have embraced the offers of perpetual reconciliation through Christ; and do purpose by God's grace, a reconciled person, to strive against sin, and to serve God with all my power constantly, therefore I may be assure to have righteousness, and eternal life given to me for the obedience of Christ imputed to me as it is sure that Christ was condemned and put to death for the sins of the redeemed imputed to Him."[2]

Philip's conversion experience secured his identity as a member of a place drenched in early American Presbyterianism. When he talked about "Cohansey" as the native soil in which he worked and lived, he always understood these dimensions of home in the context of his faith.

Philip grew up in one of the most concentrated pockets of Presbyterianism in British America. While the Society of Friends, Baptists, Seventh-Day Baptists, and Anglicans could each claim one small congregation in the Cohansey region, Presbyterian life was sustained by four churches, all located within ten miles of one another. Congregations at Fairfield, Greenwich, Deerfield, and nearby Pittsgrove in Salem County sacralized the landscape with strong doses of Calvinism and were, without competitor, the most important nodes in Philip's social world.

Philip and Cohansey Presbyterianism grew up together. The course of his life—his friendships and his future bride, his Princeton education, his vocation as a clergyman, his intellectual passions, his service in the American Revolutionary War, and, of course, his relationship to God—was influenced by his participation in a Presbyterian culture that reached maturity in the Jersey countryside at the same time that he was reaching his own level of Christian and intellectual maturity. Both Philip's sense of "home" and, eventually, his "way of improvement" are unexplainable outside the historical narrative of Presbyterianism in this region. In the years between his birth in 1747 and his conversion eighteen years later, the churches of Cohansey had transformed themselves from struggling religious outposts, divided by the effects of religious revivalism, into vibrant congregations, fully integrated into a growing colonial Presbyterian denomination. In the process the region became a religious environment where the evangelicalism of Philip's conversion experience merged with the Enlightenment to influence the lives of its young people. At the same time that Presbyterianism informed the local world of Cohansey it was also at work in providing Philip and his friends with the resources necessary to move intellectually beyond its bounds.

As we have seen, Philip descended from the English settlers who made their way to America during the great Puritan migration of the 1620s and 1630s. His ancestors traced their beliefs to the Reformed wing of the Protestant Reformation, particularly the teachings of the Swiss theologian John Calvin and his followers. As an heir to a Calvinist heritage, Philip grew up believing that God was sovereign over all of his creation, that human beings by nature were depraved, and that God, as an act of grace, chose to redeem some of his sinful creation through the sacrificial death of Jesus Christ.[3] Philip's descendants from Fairfield, Connecticut, and East Hampton, Long Island, arrived in Cohansey as Congregationalists or "Independents." This meant that they defended the right to govern their congregations without interference from a supervising ecclesiastical body. "Visible saints," defined as churchgoers who could testify publicly to a conversion experience, presided over such churches.

Independent congregations exercised their own church discipline, chose their own ministers, and erected their own meetinghouses.[4]

However, by the mid-seventeenth century some New England Puritans had begun adopting the more "Presbyterian" form of government that had long been the norm among Scottish Calvinists. At the local level Presbyterians relied on "sessions" made up of settled ministers and elders—not a vote by the saints—to make decisions pertaining to congregational life. Sessions were required to submit to the religious authority of presbyteries, governing bodies comprised of the clergy and appointed lay representatives from a given geographical region. A presbytery was responsible for examining and then appointing ministers to vacant pulpits, solving disputes in local congregations, and enforcing church doctrine. Presbyteries, in turn, were governed by the Philadelphia Synod, the highest authority in early colonial Presbyterianism. For Presbyterians, the visible "church" included all individuals who had entered into a covenant with God and his people through baptism. On this point Presbyterians would have parted ways with most Independents, who believed that a conversion experience was required for full church membership.[5]

When Philip's ancestors arrived in Cohansey, they helped to establish a church at New England Crossroads, an area of Fairfield Township not far from the place where Samuel Fithian, following his arrival to the area in 1700, built his homestead and sawmill. The Fairfield church functioned as an autonomous congregation in the Independent style for the first decade or two of its existence.[6] Identified as "Cohanzy," the church is mentioned in the early minutes of the Philadelphia Presbytery (founded in 1706), but it is not clear whether its members embraced Presbyterianism at this time or merely began to consult with the presbytery for ecclesiastical guidance as needed.[7] Eventually, after churches were founded at Greenwich (1707) and Deerfield (1735), all Cohansey Calvinists, including those at Fairfield, united with the Philadelphia Presbytery. In fact, Cohansey became as close to a homogeneous Presbyterian place as would have been possible in the religiously diverse middle colonies. Over half of the inhabitants of Fairfield, Greenwich, and Deerfield were affiliated with a Presbyterian congregation.[8]

Yet, a relatively large number of Presbyterians in a relatively small place did not always translate into a stable religious community. Cohansey Presbyterians struggled during the first half of the eighteenth century to secure the services of permanent clergy. Ministers were both an essential and a rare commodity in middle-colony Protestantism.[9] While the Protestant Reformation secured the rights of all laypersons to read the Bible without a priestly interpreter, most Presbyterians believed that clergymen versed in Calvinist theology and the original Greek and

Hebrew texts explained the Bible best. Indeed, one late eighteenth-century historian of the Presbyterian Church at Pittsgrove noted that before the arrival of visiting ministers, "the people of this Quarter were very uncivilized & knew little or nothing about religion."[10] This colonialwide problem was only exacerbated in Cohansey, a remote place by the standards of eighteenth-century travel. Requests for ministers from Cohansey congregations were often subordinated to the needs of larger churches in or near port cities.[11] By settling in such a remote locale, educated ministers removed themselves from the intellectual vibrancy of early American urban life. A one-way trip to Philadelphia from Greenwich, for example, would take roughly half a day (twelve hours). Clergy would have to work harder at obtaining religious books and travel longer distances to attend presbytery meetings.[12] Cohansey might be a nice place to start a ministerial career, but few could imagine finishing one there. The laity suffered the most from this shortage of ministers. Congregations were unsure from where their next spiritual meal might come. In 1717 the Presbyterians at Greenwich expressed "the difficulties with which they in many instances have had to struggle" through "dark and gloomy seasons" when they had been "left to coldness—to deadness and dullness on the things of God" due to the fact that "for a great part of our time we have been destitute of the stated preaching of the word."[13] Cohansey congregations, desperate for any available ministerial aid, often forged relationships with clergymen who were morally or doctrinally suspect. On several occasions the Philadelphia Synod had to intervene in the affairs of sessions intent on calling a pastor who was ill-equipped.[14]

The difficulties that these congregations faced in the early decades of settlement, however, were but a small tremor compared to the damage brought to Cohansey Presbyterianism in the early 1740s by the fault lines of religious revivalism. The First Great Awakening unleashed on the British Atlantic world a new style of Protestant religion that took to new heights time-honored Christian concerns with the spread of the gospel. Proponents of this form of Protestantism, which I will call "revival evangelicalism," preached the necessity of the New Birth, or the belief that one could be regenerated by the spirit of God immediately, apart from the communal nurturing of a local congregation. Revival evangelicalism divided the Presbyterian Church. Factions developed among the clergy over how to respond to this new emphasis on individual and immediate conversion.[15] On the one hand, ministers who came to be called "Old Side" refused to allow the evangelical-conversion experience to trump conformity to the Westminster Confession of Faith (the most important creedal statement of Presbyterian faith) as the distinguishing mark of the Presbyterian Church. They emphasized the importance of a visible church made up of all who were baptized into the community and willing to conform to the teaching of the Westminster Confession and submit to the authority of the synod, presbyteries, and local church sessions. The church, they argued, would always include the converted and the unconverted. Clergymen labeled "New Side," on the other hand, claimed to be members of an invisible church of the converted. New Siders believed that subscription to the Westminster Confession was important but that the intellectual assent to a body of correct theology, without the New Birth, could not save one's soul. Old Side clergy did not think that New Side preachers behaved in an orderly way. They complained that the New Side displayed little concern with the proper state of the church in this world because they were too busy winning converts to the spiritual fellowship of the next world.

The differences between these two factions were played out in fierce battles over the practice of itinerant preaching and ministerial education. The Old Side affirmed that placing educated ministers in local congregations, working in conjunction with presbyteries and synods, was the best way to keep an orderly Presbyterian Church. Itinerancy often undermined the authority of these local guardians of Presbyterian communities.[16] Much of the Old Side disgust with this practice was directed toward Gilbert Tennent, the minister of the New Brunswick (New Jersey) Presbyterian Church. In his sermon *The Dangers of an Unconverted Ministry,* Tennent exhorted New Side itinerants to identify, in public orations, local ministers who could not testify to an evangelical conversion experience. He then encouraged the parishioners of these unconverted pastors to leave their churches and seek out a congregation with a minister who was preaching a message in sympathy with New Side concerns.[17] Old Side clergymen were often willing to admit that some of their number could not testify to a conversion experience. Some even saw this as a serious problem. However, they disapproved of the way that New Side ministers exposed this problem by outing unregenerate pastors in public sermons rather than from behind the closed doors of the synod or presbytery.[18] The New Side countered by arguing that itinerancy was necessary because Presbyterian laypersons were spiritually perishing under the care of "graceless and unfaithful Ministers." The salvation of souls, they believed, was a higher priority than the preservation of order.[19] The Philadelphia Synod, which was controlled by Old Side clergy, did not see it this way. In May 1737 the synod declared that probationary clergymen (or those licensed but not ordained or installed in a specific church) would no longer be permitted to preach in vacant pulpits without the permission of the presbytery that had authority over the congregation with the vacancy. The following year the synod directed its ruling specifically to those clergymen who traveled within the bounds of presbyteries other than their own and had a "Tendency to procure Divisions and Disorders."[20]

The debate over itinerancy was related to a similar battle fought over how to define the historic Presbyterian commitment to an educated clergy. Much of the controversy in this regard centered on Log College, a Presbyterian academy in Neshaminy, Pennsylvania. Directed by the Reverend William Tennent (Gilbert's father), Log College established a reputation for graduating ministerial candidates who championed revival evangelicalism. According to the Old Side, much of what was wrong with the Presbyterian Church could be blamed on Log College alumni traveling throughout the region preaching divisive sermons in vacant pulpits outside the bounds of their presbyteries. Some of them had performed poorly on licensing examinations, prompting the Philadelphia Synod to question the school's ability to properly train Presbyterian ministers for ordination.[21] In 1738 the synod pushed forward a proposal requiring a ministerial candidate to possess a degree from a European or New England (Harvard or Yale) college. Resistance to this decree came from the newly formed New Brunswick Presbytery, a haven for Log College graduates. Since the synod's education proposal meant that alumni of the Neshaminy school would not be permitted to serve the church as clergymen, the New Brunswick ministers refused to abide by it. In defiance of the order, they continued to ordain Log College men.[22] The synod responded, after much debate and several attempts to reach a compromise, by expelling the rebel presbytery in 1741. Following its expulsion the New Brunswick Presbytery and its supporters in other presbyteries, the most significant being the Presbytery of New York, united in 1745 to form the Synod of New York.[23] The Presbyterian Church in British colonial America would remain formally divided between Old Side (Philadelphia Synod) and New Side (New York Synod) factions until they were reunited in 1758.

The Great Awakening in Cohansey was a rural microcosm of the problems facing the denomination during the revival. Aware of the vacant pulpits at Greenwich and Deerfield, the New Side targeted the region as an ideal place to fan the flames of revival evangelicalism.[24] In 1739 Gilbert Tennent spent about a week in Cohansey, where his preaching was accompanied by "Surprising effects in comforting and establishing old pious professors and awakening the thoughtlessness of almost every age and character." Those who remembered his Greenwich visit added that "the church, on the Sabbath days, was filled with people, who came and joined in worship."[25] The Deerfield ministry of the Reverend Samuel Blair, a New Side colleague of Tennent, was "attended with a divine power" that prompted "careless sinners . . . to enquire what they should do to be saved."[26] The "Grand Itinerant" himself, George Whitefield, made two trips to Cohansey in 1740 and preached "to some thousands, both morning and afternoon." He recorded that the "Word struck the hearers till the whole congregation was greatly moved, and two cried out in bitterness of their souls, after a crucified Saviour."[27] The evangelical fervor initiated by these revival preachers consumed the laity of the ministerless Greenwich and Deerfield Presbyterian churches. New Brunswick itinerants, including Samuel Finley, John Campbell, William Dean, and Daniel Lawrence, began to converge on this Presbyterian outpost.[28]

Because the church records from the period have been lost, we cannot know as much as we would like about the kind of impact the Awakening had on the Cohansey congregations affected by it. We do, however, get a sense of the revival's influence through the controversies that occurred in the region's churches. In Greenwich, for example, the local minister became a victim of Awakening politics. When Rev. Ebenezer Goold was suspected of flirting with Anglicanism, he was driven out of the church by the pro–New Side session. A rumor had circulated in the congregation that Goold had an "Inclination of Conformity to the Church of England" and had considered "going to England for orders." The Philadelphia Presbytery dismissed the charges and did its best to restore peace among Greenwich Presbyterians, but the damage had been done. After serving the church for eight years and presiding over the construction of a new meetinghouse, Goold sensed rightly that his congregation had now lost confidence in him. In 1739 he left Greenwich for a church on Long Island. Goold had accomplished much during his tenure in Cohansey (he was the longest-tenured minister in the congregation to date), making it surprising that a remote congregation would end a relationship with a settled minister who, for what little we know, seemed willing to stay longer. He most likely left because the congregation was swept up by the preaching of visiting revival ministers. Anglicanism, as we will see in Chapter 5, was a form of Protestantism with a different understanding of conversion than that of New Side Presbyterians. Goold and the Greenwich congregations thus appeared, at least from the perspective of the church's leadership, to be moving in different theological directions. As a result, the Greenwich Presbyterians, for the next six years, would exchange the daily presence of a settled minister for the evangelical messages of visiting New Brunswick preachers.[29]

Awakening politics also affected the congregations in northern Cohansey. Deerfield and Pittsgrove were neighboring townships with large Presbyterian populations. When the Philadelphia Presbytery proposed the creation of a single congregation with one minister and one meetinghouse to serve Presbyterians in both communities, the Deerfield and Pittsgrove churches balked at the idea. They preferred instead to construct their own buildings and hire their own clergy. In May 1739 the presbytery gave into the demands of these congregations and allowed the Pittsgrove church to build a meetinghouse of its own, on the condition that it be located nine miles from the meetinghouse in Deerfield, which had been constructed two years earlier. One month later members of the Deerfield session complained that the congregation at Pittsgrove was moving ahead with the erection of a meetinghouse "not above six miles from theirs, contrary . . . to the order of the Presbytery, and tending to their Damage." What the presbytery minutes do not mention is that the Pittsgrove congregation had also hired Rev. David Evans, a noted Old Side sympathizer, as its clergyman. The Deerfield church, which had still not filled its vacant pulpit at the time of Evans's arrival and had made a definitive embrace of the New Side, was clearly disturbed by Pittsgrove's choice of minister. Deerfield broke off all relations with Pittsgrove and its Old Side pastor, sought out a closer fellowship with the Greenwich congregation, and like the Presbyterians at Greenwich, began to be supplied by New Brunswick ministers. The geographical boundaries of the Deerfield Presbyterian community became increasingly more important to those residents in 1739 after their neighbors in Pittsgrove, through the hiring of Evans, aligned with the Old Side.[30]

Meanwhile, on the south side of the Cohansey River, the Awakening met with little support from Fairfield's Old Side minister Daniel Elmer. Elmer was opposed to revival itinerants invading his ecclesiastical domain, but there was nothing he could do about it. The Philadelphia Synod no longer had any authority over the Deerfield and Greenwich churches once they aligned themselves with the expelled presbytery of New Brunswick. In many places in the middle colonies it would have been difficult, due to the distance between congregations, for laypersons dissatisfied with the Old Side tendencies of their pastor to follow Gilbert Tennent's advice in *The Dangers of an Unconverted Ministry* and find another Presbyterian congregation that was more in line with their religious preferences. However, in Cohansey all one needed to do was cross the river. This is what many Fairfield parishioners did, including Elmer's own son, Daniel Elmer Jr. Elmer Jr. was affected by the preaching of George Whitefield and became a leading organizer of New Side activity in the region. He inherited from his father-in-law an old and vacant Baptist meetinghouse in nearby Back Neck and utilized it as a preaching station for Presbyterian itinerants.[31] One Sunday morning the elder Elmer, with his son present in the congregation, chose "the subject of schism" as the theme of his morning sermon. During the course of the message Elmer Jr. left the church in protest. He would never return until after his father's death, choosing instead to worship at the Greenwich Presbyterian church, where the New Side supply ministers were preaching a message more in tune with his evangelical sympathies.[32] The evangelicalism of Whitefield and the New Side Presbyterians proved attractive to many of Elmer's congregation, a situation that "Occasioned much uneasiness in the church."[33] While the majority of Fairfield parishioners remained loyal to Elmer Sr., others opted to leave the church and attend services at Greenwich. As late as 1754 the Synod of Philadelphia was sending delegates to "Mr. Elmore's Congregation" to try to "remove the difficulties he compleans of."[34]

In summary, the Fairfield church was split into two factions; the Greenwich church had ousted its settled clergyman in order to open the pulpit to New Side itinerants; the Pittsgrove and Deerfield congregations went their own separate ways based on the New Side/Old Side differences; and the relationship between the Fairfield church and the Greenwich church (and by association the Deerfield church) had been strained. Josiah Fithian, as a pillar of the Greenwich Presbyterian church, was probably sympathetic with New Side evangelicalism, but like the rest of the congregation and the larger denomination, he would have certainly been saddened by the divided state of Cohansey Presbyterianism and sought ways to bring about much-needed community healing.

In 1743 Robert Jenney, the Society for the Propagation of the Gospel (SPG) missionary-priest assigned to the city of Philadelphia, informed his Anglican superiors in London that "The Presbyterians are almost broken to pieces."[35] He was right. Presbyterians were left reeling in the aftermath of the Great Awakening. At the local level, among the congregations and communities where religion was lived, the Presbyterian landscape of the middle colonies was an ecclesiastical war zone. Congregations were rent by the controversial way in which the New Birth was spread. The witness of the Presbyterian Church in the British American colonies had been tarnished by this religious culture war. The passions associated with revivalism, the otherworldly focus of religious enthusiasm, and the divisive nature of New Side preachers and their followers had contributed to the "shattered" state of the church in a way that the supporters of revivalism could not ignore.

Presbyterians would be successful in healing their wounds and rebuilding their congregations after the revival storms by making accommodations to the spirit of the age. The church, in other words, made its peace with the Enlightenment. Between 1745 and the American Revolution, the New Side Presbyterianism of the First Great Awakening was transformed. Enlightenment concerns with social order, the rational control of the passions, and the celebration of the things that united rather than divided human beings and their institutions meshed well with the concerns of both the Old Side *and* the New Side. Presbyterianism converged with the Enlightenment in this era to provide the scaffolding necessary to rebuild the church and enable it to engage the surrounding culture. These developments in Reformed Christianity had profound implications for the way the Enlightenment was lived in eighteenth-century America. In fact, the changes to the post–Great Awakening Presbyterian Church provided one of the primary windows through which many colonials, particularly in the mid-Atlantic, experienced the Enlightenment. Two decades after the Great Awakening, evangelical Presbyterianism and the Enlightenment were hand-in-glove in a way that would have been inconceivable in the early 1740s, a time when the beliefs and behavior of Presbyterian evangelicalism stressed an anti-intellectual piety less concerned with rational or confessional explanations of the faith and more concerned with saving as many souls as possible from eternal damnation. How did this happen? What did such a convergence between the Enlightenment and evangelical Presbyterianism look like in Cohansey? Most important, how did all this impact the young life of Philip Vickers Fithian?

Presbyterian attempts to heal the wounds inflicted by the Great Awakening were part of a general cultural trend pervading the British American colonies in the period between the First Great Awakening and the American Revolution. The values of love, brotherhood, and unity gained popularity in provincial life as means of sustaining social cohesiveness and moral order in an era of political instability, imperial warfare with France and its corresponding threat to British civilization, demographic changes and ethnic strife stemming from new patterns of immigration, and of course, an acrimonious religious revival. As the historian Steven Bullock has noted, those influenced by the social theory of the Enlightenment—a vision of everyday life defined by reason, balance, and order—believed that selflessness and benevolence could serve as a potent antidote to the "particular divisiveness of American society." Such a vision was appealing because it required persons to unite around the things that were common to all human beings and look beyond the particularities that made them different. For Christians, this kind of universalism was not unlike Jesus' prayer in the Gospels (John 17:21) that his church "all may be one"; but it was also an ideal at the heart of the Enlightenment in America. When cultivated in a rational way, love, and its sister virtues of peace and harmony, offered hope to those attempting to navigate the turbulence of mid-eighteenth-century British American life.[36]

This new cultural spirit had profound effects on American religion during this period. By the mid-1740s denominations rent by the Great

Awakening were seeking ways of putting aside their theological differences and uniting around the religious beliefs that they held in common. Other denominations, some of which had reputations for disorder and religious enthusiasm during the Awakening, began to work toward better and more efficient means of organization. For example, attempts were made in 1745 to bring German and Swedish Lutherans together under a unified synod. While both of these groups could trace their history to the Lutheran wing of the Protestant Reformation, they were divided in America by language and the degree to which they were willing to embrace continental pietism. Similarly, in 1747 German Reformed ministers established the Coetus of Pennsylvania, the first official body of German-speaking Calvinists in America. One year later the Moravian Church brought much-needed order to its fold by establishing a synod for ministers. Even the Society of Friends, a group on the fringe of colonial Protestantism (but still quite mainstream in the Delaware Valley), began to emphasize spiritual unity around obedience to Quaker moral codes.[37]

The successful reunion of Presbyterians in 1758 was another example of this religious and cultural season. In May, Presbyterians representing the Philadelphia Synod and the New York Synod met in Philadelphia to confirm a proposed plan that would put their broken denomination back together again. As part of the settlement, both sides agreed to affirm the Westminster Confession of Faith *and* the importance of conversion to the Christian life. The Old Side conceded that the Great Awakening was a "gracious work of God," and the New Side concurred that conversion was a rational process void of enthusiastic behavior. The licensing of ministerial candidates was turned over to the presbyteries, though the Plan of Union warned against clergymen publicly accusing fellow ministers of "Heterodoxy, Insufficiency, or Immorality." The union did not end all of the bitter feelings or theological differences between the Old Side and the New Side, but some degree of peace had been restored among British American Presbyterians. After seventeen years of division the church could now move forward into the uncertainties of a revolutionary age with a renewed sense of unity and purpose.[38]

Philip Vickers Fithian was ten years old at the time of the reunion. He spent most of his days working on his family's farm, attending grammar school, and familiarizing himself with the ebb and flow of the Cohansey River. He had no idea how the kind of Presbyterianism that emerged from this reunion would shape his future and provide a framework for his understanding of the relationship between his spiritual life and his moral life. The culture of post–Great Awakening Presbyterianism laid the groundwork for Philip's pursuit of a formal education and a vocational path to the Presbyterian ministry. It furnished him with a sense of service to the public good that he would come to embrace with all his being.

The Presbyterian move toward reconciliation in the aftermath of the great revival began before the awakening fires had a chance to cool. While many New Side clergymen were still roaming the region on their feverish quest for souls, Presbyterians who feared that the Great Awakening had the potential of moving too strongly in a radical direction preached sermons and published tracts in favor of moderation. Jonathan Dickinson, the settled clergyman at Elizabeth-Town, New Jersey, forged a well-respected career from attempts to broker some sort of compromise that might bring the Old Side and the New Side back together.[39] Dickinson never abandoned his belief in the importance of conversion and experimental religion, and he defended the revival as a work of God on more than one occasion. However, he was convinced that evangelicalism must be practiced rationally, without the passion-driven behavior that led to the rift in the colonial Presbyterian Church. Moderates, many of whom were members of the New York Presbytery, condemned New Side clergymen's practice of invading the pulpits of fellow ministers and pronouncing them as unconverted. They preferred that ministerial candidates be educated in respectable, well-established schools. Thus, they worked diligently in the 1746 formation of a college—the College of New Jersey at Princeton—that could offer students the best of Enlightenment learning and Presbyterian evangelicalism. Such attempts to balance piety with a rational approach to Presbyterian faith reflected one of several ways that the Enlightenment influenced the church in the decades following the Great Awakening. As Henry May has argued, the attempts to balance reason with religious passion provided the intellectual and cultural venue in which the Enlightenment had its greatest impact in the British American colonies.[40]

By 1742 Jonathan Dickinson's moderate evangelical camp was growing. In February, Gilbert Tennent wrote a letter of apology to Dickinson for some of his misguided behavior during the height of the Great Awakening. He repented over the "excessive heart of temper which has sometime appeared in my conduct" and claimed to have since developed a "clear view of the danger of every thing which tends to enthusiasm and divisiveness in the visible church." Tennent expressed regret over nearly every issue that had led to the Old Side/New Side divisions of the previous years, including the role he played in dividing churches, his "pernicious" practice of declaring fellow ministers unconverted, and his "perverse" defense of an uneducated ministry.[41] He eventually accepted a call to pastor Philadelphia's Second Presbyterian Church and started publishing essays and sermons, such as *The Danger of Spiritual*

Pride Represented (1744); *Irenicium Ecclesiasticum, or a Humble Impartial Essay upon the Peace of Jerusalem* (1749); *Brotherly Love Recommended* (1748); and *Blessedness of Peace-Makers Represented* (1765). He also began to dress in a more refined fashion and became more "literary" in his sermons.[42]

As the number of moderate Presbyterians grew steadily in the years following the Great Awakening, these clergymen began to practice an evangelical Calvinism that was concerned not only with the other-worldly aspects of faith but also with the ways in which evangelicalism might serve the moral good of *this* world. While evangelicals focused first and foremost on a proper "vertical" relationship with God attained through conversion, they also began to take seriously their responsibility to promote Godly "horizontal" relationships within society through obedience to the ethical commands of Scripture grounded in God's moral law. Presbyterians in this period advocated a moral theology rooted in the social requirements of Christianity.[43] Early American Calvinists believed that the Old Testament law was ultimately a means of exposing sin and pointing people to the regenerative power of New Testament grace, but it could also serve, secondarily, as a moral rule for the larger society. Furthermore, New Testament exhortations such as the Golden Rule or the Fruits of the Spirit were loaded with social requirements that when obeyed contributed to a society that was ethical and upright. Evangelical Calvinists upheld God's moral law as a standard to measure public virtue.[44] Thus, even with its millennial vision, otherworldly focus, and commitment to original sin, evangelical Calvinism could still contribute to an orderly and benevolent world.

This Presbyterian social vision was evident in Samuel Davies's last valedictory address to the senior class at the College of New Jersey. Davies had gained a reputation for promoting religious revival among the growing number of Presbyterians in Virginia and quickly became one of the church's most prominent clergymen, leading to his appointment as president of the Presbyterian college at Princeton in 1757. In a 1760 address that was later published as *Religion and Public Spirit*, Davies challenged each student to serve his generation as a "proper Member of human Society." God's purposes in this world, he exhorted, are carried out through the cultivation of "*social* Connections" and a "love" of one's fellow human beings. Davies wanted his graduates to serve the church, but he also urged them to use their liberal education to "Extend the Arms of your Benevolence to embrace your Friends, your Neighbours, your Country, your Nation, the whole race of Mankind, even your Enemies." The goal was to "leave the World wiser and better, than you found it at your Entrance." The Princeton class of 1760 had a mandate from their president to work for the public good and serve the various communities in which they found themselves without being seduced by "private Interests."[45]

Davies's address illustrates the complicated interplay between Presbyterianism and the Enlightenment in early American religious discourse. His emphasis on *this* world and his exhortation to improve society placed *Religion and Public Spirit* at the center of the eighteenth-century British Enlightenment. Enlightened people hoped that the "present age" could be "more enlightened than the past." Armed with this progressive ideal, they strove to leave the world better than it was when they entered it. Societal improvement and the moral advancement of public life were important to this generation of Presbyterians, even those who, like Davies and his New Side colleagues, had built a reputation for being more concerned with their followers' preparation for the next world than their meaningful contribution to this one. Davies's call to treat one's fellowman with a spirit of brotherly love reflected the Enlightenment's universalistic approach to the world and the general spirit of social virtue at work in the culture of America's educated classes in the decades following the First Great Awakening. Piety was important, but so was moral improvement.

A rational faith that tempered enthusiasm and a Calvinism that took seriously the church's social obligations had always been important to the ministers of the Old Side. It was now, however, becoming a vital component of New Side thought as well. In this sense the New Side's moderate turn led its supporters to become more amenable to long-standing Presbyterian commitments to the authority of synods and the importance of settled and educated clergymen. *All* Presbyterians were now extolling the God of order, and they were ready with Scripture to defend him. Some of the passages of the Bible that they employed were 1 Corinthians 14:40 ("Let all things be done decently and in order"); 1 Corinthians 14:33 ("For God is not the author of confusion, but of peace, as in all churches of the saints"); and 2 Thessalonians 3:6–7 ("Now we command you, brethren, in the name of our Lord Jesus Christ, that ye withdraw yourselves from every brother that walketh disorderly, and not after the tradition which he received of us. For yourselves know how ye ought to follow us: for we behaved not ourselves disorderly among you").[46] These verses were summed up best by a post-Awakening Gilbert Tennent when he wrote that "God is not the Author of Confusion, but of Peace, and therefore of Order, which is the Contrary of Confusion, and the cause and antecedent of Peace."[47] Presbyterians were convinced that their church was built on this biblical understanding of order as encapsulated in the Westminster Confession. Anyone who challenged such order through divisive behavior was acting in a manner that was ungodly and sinful.

As Presbyterians looked to the Bible to help construct an orderly church, they also turned to faculty psychology. This discipline, a subfield of moral philosophy, taught them that a society maintained order when its members learned to regulate their passions—the appetites, desires, and emotional longings present in all human beings. Passions were not wrong or disorderly in and of themselves, but they could become dangerous when not guarded by reason. The human faculties were ordered in a hierarchical manner. Reason, the chief faculty, must be cultivated with diligence so that it was strong enough to control the unruly, and naturally more powerful, passions. When passions were allowed to rage out of control, the faculties would become unbalanced, resulting in immoral and unenlightened behavior.[48] Thus, when Enoch Green, the minister who replaced Simon Williams at the Deerfield Presbyterian church, warned his congregation about the dangers of slothfulness, a practice that led to an uncultivated mind where the "lusts and passions grow rampant," he was reflecting both a Christian understanding of order *and* what Henry May has called the "moderate Enlightenment." Those who did not control their passions were not only prone to sin but also, as Green wrote, a "disgrace to civil society" through their "neglect of every social duty."[49] Faculty psychology was at the core of the unified Presbyterian Church's understanding of revivalism. Unless the passions were carefully restrained, the work of God would become relegated to bedlam, as evidenced in many of the enthusiastic New Side stirs of the Great Awakening. The moral dimensions of the Enlightenment, particularly its emphasis on reason over passion, offered a language that Presbyterians could use to restore order to their broken church.

By 1749 Gilbert Tennent was convinced that his passions had led him astray during the height of the Great Awakening. As he continued to express his change of heart, he regularly employed the language of faculty psychology. Tennent blamed his earlier condemnations of fellow (Old Side) ministers on his inability to control his passions. "Passion is a Blind Guide," he wrote, and it could lead, in his case, to a "Ferment of sinful Anger" that boiled in opposition to the "Righteousness of God." On the matter of those newly converted laypersons who ignited division in local congregations, Tennent noted regretfully the "Ignorance and wild fire" that "sometimes attend the Zeal of young Converts, who are Ignorant and of a passionate Temper." Tennent wrote in *Irenicum Ecclesiasticum*, "When People are divided and prejudiced against each other, they are apt, thro' the force of their Passions, to misapprehend one another's meaning," resulting in "Persons under strong Temptations in order to make themselves appear Consistent, or support what they call their Credit, to speak of Things that should be buried in silence, in an undue Manner."[50] Tennent's emphasis on the passions and the spiritual asceticism required to control them merged nicely with the concerns of the Enlightenment and helped to define its American character.[51]

As the leadership of both the Philadelphia and New York Synods began reclamation work on their broken denomination, part of the efforts would need to be directed toward the Jersey countryside. With the curbing of evangelical passions, Cohansey Presbyterians stood poised to enter a new era of religious life through the mending of congregational rifts and the establishment of a renewed religious order. The churches at Greenwich and Deerfield both found permanent ministers. Andrew Hunter was installed at Greenwich in 1746. A New Side supporter and classical scholar who had been ordained by the New Brunswick Presbytery, Hunter presided over both the Greenwich and Deerfield churches until the Presbyterians of Deerfield petitioned for their own minister in 1760. His New Side credentials were strong. He had close connections to some of the leading prorevival clergymen of Log College fame, and none other than Gilbert Tennent preached his ordination sermon.[52] Two decades later and a few miles up the Cohansey River, the Deerfield church installed Enoch Green in 1767. Green was a recent graduate of the College of New Jersey and had just returned from a missionary tour of Presbyterian churches in Virginia. Shortly after his arrival he opened a small Presbyterian academy to prepare young men for matriculation at his alma mater. Both Hunter, who would stay in Greenwich for close to thirty years, and Green, who remained at Deerfield for nine years before his untimely death in 1776, would guide these churches through some of their most fruitful periods of eighteenth-century growth.

After the death of Daniel Elmer in 1755, the Fairfield church turned to its New England roots to find his replacement. Thomas Ogden, an elder in the congregation and the son of an original Fairfield, Connecticut, settler to Cohansey, wrote to Ezra Stiles, the president of Yale College, to inform him that the church was "divided in this time, but have now agreed, by advice of our Presbytery, to invite a minister from Connecticut." If they could be "happily supplied" with such a settled clergyman, Ogden wrote, he was certain that members of his congregation would "bury all their contention" and "unite under his ministry."[53] The Fairfield session eventually issued a call to William Ramsey, a 1754 graduate of the College of New Jersey. Only twenty-five years old at the time of his installation, Ramsey was an ideal candidate for the divided Fairfield church. Though he was born and raised in Lancaster County, Pennsylvania, he had received his ministerial license in Fairfield County, Connecticut, and could not be linked, as could most mid-Atlantic clergymen, to either the Old Side Philadelphia Synod or the New Side New York Synod.[54] Ramsey was thus poised to do the difficult work of restoring unity to this divided congregation.

The young pastor went right to work in Fairfield's spiritual precincts. He traveled throughout the township paying extensive pastoral visits to his disgruntled parishioners. Ramsey was the primary catalyst in healing many of the church's wounds and restoring the strained relationships with the Greenwich and Deerfield churches across the river. Even Daniel Elmer Jr. returned to the Fairfield congregation and was appointed an elder in 1760.[55] Ramsey was said to have preached "in Season and out of Season . . . Visiting and Exhorting from house to house with considerable success."[56] The new clergyman took a genuine interest in the spiritual condition of his charges by meeting with them in their homes to catechize, counsel, and restore a sense of spiritual community. While such practices would be required of any Presbyterian minister in the British Atlantic world, they took on added weight among such a divided congregation. Ramsey invested himself deeply in the people of Fairfield. He married Sarah Seeley, the granddaughter of one of the region's first settlers from Connecticut, and was granted 150 acres of land in the area, where he built a parsonage for himself and his family.[57] It appeared that he would be in Cohansey for a long time.

Ramsey's labors among the Fairfield Presbyterians resulted in the congregation's first religious revival in 1765. His work of communal restoration and his regular preaching on themes of "the grace and salvation . . . freely offered to sinners . . . upon condition of their repentance" triggered a "Remarkable and Amazing out Pouring of his (God's) Holy Spirit; on most all the whole Congregation." There "was Scarcely a house in which there was not one or more under deep Concern about the salvation of their Souls."[58] The church session records for March 6, 1765, read, "large group of people brought into full communion with the church," and they note that the congregation was experiencing a "Blessed shower of Divine Influences for some months past."[59] Ramsey described the revival as a "harvest time in this church Blessed by God." Thomas Harris, whose father, Ephraim, was a member of the church during the revival, remembered that "there was a very great and remarkable outpouring of the spirit and reviving of Religion in the congregation so that in the fall about 100 was added to the church."[60] Harris's estimate of new admissions was a bit high but not by much. Seventy-six people joined the Fairfield church in 1765 and 1766, representing an astronomical growth in new members.[61] Moreover, the local awakening was contagious. It spread across the river to the congregations at Greenwich and Pittsgrove and brought a sense of spiritual harmony among the Presbyterians of the region.[62]

As they presided over this local awakening, the Cohansey ministers were concerned not as much with the quantity of those revived as with the quality of their new members—making sure to ground them firmly in the Reformed faith and in the assurance of salvation. William Ramsey was "very careful and accurate in describing the nature of true religion, and in distinguishing the reality from the base appearance." In other words, there was a theological and rational depth to his converts. Enoch Green described Ramsey as a "master of a rational, consistent, sound system of divinity" who "firmly adhered to our received standards" and "in sentiment was strictly Calvinistic."[63] He exemplified an evangelical New Side passion for souls tempered by a conservative Old Side concern with order, seasoned by the values of the British Enlightenment.

The 1765 Cohansey awakening was a community revival in the sense that most, if not all, of the communicants shared common surnames stemming from the original settling of the region in the late seventeenth and early eighteenth centuries. In Fairfield converts with names such as Bateman, Dare, Diament, Harris, Ogden, Sayre, Westcott, and Whitaker, to name a few, all had historic ties to the history of the town's Presbyterian church. None of the new communicants in Fairfield were baptized at the time of their admission to the communion table, confirming that those revived were already members of the local covenant community via their baptism as infants. They were no doubt intimately acquainted with Cohansey Presbyterian life and culture and were thus quite familiar with the recent history of division within the congregation. Many of them had probably attended services at the church from the time they were born, and some were old enough to have experienced the First Great Awakening. As the historian Michael Crawford has noted, "Conversion of a large number of unassociated individuals did not constitute a revival of religion. Revival meant the transformation by grace of a community, a group of people bound together as a single moral entity, be it a social unit, church, or nation, by a covenant, implied or explicit."[64] The arrival of Ramsey and the renewed sense of congregational unity he fostered through his ministry prompted these Fairfield Presbyterians to commit or recommit their lives to God through a deeper relationship with the local church and the sacraments.

This revival did not breed divisiveness, as was the case with the intruding New Side itinerants of the First Great Awakening. Even to contemplate any sort of resistance to this Cohansey awakening was to undermine the very nature of it. Indeed, Ramsey "justly deserved to be called a Peacemaker, and was very successful in his endeavors to maintain peace in his own flock, for whenever the flames of contention began to kindle, his prudence and good sense found means to extinguish them."[65] By the 1760s sensational, divisive, and enthusiastic outpourings of God's spirit foisted on local communities by outsiders were becoming things of the past. The Cohansey awakening was conducted in an orderly fashion. It was the sort of revival that Old Side sympathizers could defend.[66] Gilbert Tennent described best what was happening in Cohansey in these years. In *Irenicum Ecclesiasticum*, his extended apology for his First

Great Awakening behavior, he wrote that there was "nothing more amiable, than to see Brethren, who have been broken from one another by Division, and prejudiced against one another by angry Debate, seeking the Lord in UNION and Harmony." Such a spirit was at the heart of the local community revival that affected Cohansey. "There is nothing more efficacious, to excite Mankind to embrace the Gospel," Tennent believed, "than the mutual Love and Unity of the Professors of it." Religious harmony and the love of all fellow Presbyterians—an ideal steeped in both Christianity and the universalism of the Enlightenment creed (and not the divisive, passion-driven efforts of revival itinerants)—would be the true and most effective catalyst for the propagation of the gospel to the unconverted.

Enoch Green, Andrew Hunter, and William Ramsey were products of the New Side First Great Awakening. Their connections to Log College and the College of New Jersey equipped them for careers of evangelical service. However, these clergymen were not enthusiasts or schismatics. Their concerns with otherworldly Christianity coexisted with the necessity of promoting a moral and ordered society in *this* world. They served their communities in the hopes that they might redeem society or at the very least bring it into moral conformity with the teachings of the Bible. In the process they helped to build a strong Presbyterian enclave out of the disorder that resulted from a half-century without regularly settled clergy and a divisive Awakening. Enoch Green put it best when he described his colleague William Ramsey as a minister who "had much at heart the welfare and eternal felicity of the flock more immediately committed to his charge" and "spared no pains in cultivating principles of virtue among them in his private interviews." Ramsey "made it his business to enlighten the understanding, to inform the judgment, to *regulate the passions*, to rectify the will, to advance the divine-life, and restore the moral image of God, defaced by man's apostacy."[67]

Cohansey young people were particularly influenced by the 1765 revival. Thirteen-year-old Ebenezer Elmer, the son of Daniel Elmer Jr., was impressed by the new spiritual concern in the Fairfield church. He wrote in his diary that "the young, in general, became very much engaged, and we had a meeting at least twice a week during all the summer and fall" and that "About sixty new members were added to the church."[68] As we have seen, Philip Vickers Fithian was also deeply affected by this revival. Prompted by a serious concern over the state of his soul, Philip began a journal in January 1766. Like Ebenezer Elmer, he was completely caught up in the spiritual excitement that pervaded Cohansey life in these months. The pages of his diary became a place to encounter God privately and come to grips with God's plan of redemption for humankind. Philip was the perfect candidate for conversion. As the child of one of the first families of Cohansey Presbyterianism, he had breathed the heavy Reformed air of the region from his birth. He was baptized in the Greenwich congregation and catechized by Andrew Hunter. Philip thus knew what it meant to be a Presbyterian. He had been drilled in the rudiments of Calvinist faith and could probably recite from memory portions of the Westminster Shorter Catechism. However, by the age of eighteen he had arrived at a stage in his religious life where he had become "much troubled in my Mind about the state of my soul." He now sought something more than a mere intellectual adherence to a body of doctrine. "My former evidences of faith and Love to God seem clouded," Philip wrote, and "Sin seems to rage and prevail more furious against Me." So, on a rainy Monday evening in the winter of 1766, Philip started a hopeful "endeavour to fix my trust in him as the only object of happiness."[69]

For the next several months Philip's mental world would remain singularly focused on the salvation of his soul. Like all Protestant conversion experiences, his spiritual seeking was intensely personal in nature. His deepest religious thoughts were known only to God and the pages of his journal. Yet, even as Philip sought God through private reflections and meditations, he did not go through this season of conversion alone. To put it differently, Philip was not converted as one of hundreds of people standing in a large crowd listening to an itinerant preacher rail against sin and offer God's plan of salvation to anyone within earshot. While such itinerants were often effective in convicting their hearers of sin and the need for a savior, they rarely hung around long enough to lead potential converts to Christ and nurture them in their newfound faith.

Philip's spiritual search and ultimate conversion were different. They were conducted within a fellowship of Cohansey Presbyterians bound together by the ordinances of the local church. Most of the questions he was asking of himself and his spiritual condition arose from the biblical exhortations he heard week after week from settled and permanent ministers in Cohansey pulpits. These clergymen understood that God's favor was bestowed on those connected to a local body of believers whose membership pursued God privately through their devotional practices and corporately through a regularly ordered church. Andrew Hunter reminded his congregants during the height of the revival that grace came to sinners through the preached word, prayer, meditation, reading, and participation in the sacraments—all appropriate means "for sinners to fly to the Lord Jesus Christ." Philip benefited greatly from this renewed sense of order in the Cohansey Presbyterian congregations and wore out a path of travel between Greenwich, Fairfield, and

Deerfield to attend services. He heard at least three sermons each week, reflected on their content in the pages of his diary, and prayed about how he might most effectively apply their messages to his life. Philip owed the revival of his soul to the work of the spirit of God. However he also, whether he realized it or not, was indebted to a transformation in the colonial Presbyterian Church that brought unity in the wake of division and provided the southern New Jersey countryside with ministers willing to work at creating the kind of loving, harmonious, and ordered religious environment where a true revival might flourish.

The content of the sermons that Philip heard in the first three months of 1766 reveals that Cohansey's clergymen were obviously aware that they were presiding over a religious awakening. Since none of their sermon notes has survived, we are unable to know all that they uttered from their pulpits. Even so, because Philip chose to record the biblical passages from which they preached and the general themes they extracted from those passages, we have a better sense of the nature of evangelical preaching during a revival and its impact on an average hearer under religious conviction. The act of recording the passage and topic of every sermon he attended was an important spiritual discipline for Philip that also sheds considerable light on the process of his conversion.

Like all Presbyterian evangelicals, Cohansey clergymen hammered away from their pulpits on the sinful condition of humanity. Hunter worked his way through the Psalms to what appears to have been, at least in Philip's case, great effect. During a sermon on the Forty-fourth Psalm, Hunter "laid down our plain character as Man, proving him to be the most sinful, rebellious, and detestable creature while in his natural sinful state." A similar sermon on the 144th Psalm "considered Adam in his state of innocency" and the "dreadful expectations" of "divine vengeance" that he and his descendants faced "when he fell from, that happy condition."[70] Such preaching took its toll on Philip. In good Calvinist fashion he readily lamented over the sinful character of his natural state and his inability to do anything to merit God's favor. His diary entries were not unlike those recorded in the diaries of dozens of seventeenth-century Puritan converts: "God hath been pleased to let me see more of the hardness and depravity of my heart Still I am in an indifferent uneasy condition"; "I feel this morning in a very sober and melancholy condition on reading the state of our first parents in their state of innocency, and their desperate fall from that happy condition"; and "O wretched creature that I am, daily sinning against the dearest love."[71] Recognizing one's depravity and the impossibility of saving oneself was the first step in any Protestant conversion, but for Calvinists, this recognition of the utter crippling and disabling power of sin over the human will was indispensable.

The preaching of what Presbyterians called the "terrors of the law"—the sense of fear that came with realization that human beings were incapable of ever keeping the commandments of God to the degree of perfection that God required—was always followed in Cohansey by sermons on the hope of redemption. As Philip was reminded after hearing Hunter preach a sermon from the fifth chapter of the Gospel of Matthew, Jesus Christ came not to destroy the "law of the prophets" but to fulfill it. The death, burial, and resurrection of Jesus Christ offered solace to Philip as he came to understand the depths of his depravity. He was comforted in the knowledge that Christ had made "full satisfaction . . . in the behalf of sinners to divine justice." If these clergymen believed that God was indeed pouring out his spirit in a special way upon the people of Cohansey, then the spiritual diet they were prepared to offer in each sermon was straight gospel. It was not unusual for Andrew Hunter to preach Sunday morning on the terrors of the law and the "natural sinful state" of all humanity and then, after allowing his hearers to go to their homes for dinner, return in the late afternoon with a sermon on the "method of our recovery from that sinful and dangerous condition."[72]

Philip listened to sermons on law and grace for the first three months of 1766. Like any good Protestant under the conviction of sin, he suffered through periods when he was "low" and "melancholy." He grappled relentlessly with himself over his true standing before God. Philip would rejoice one day in "the infinite love, and condescention" of a God who saw fit to provide a means of salvation, while the next day he would cry out: "O! that I had a heart given up in entire love to Christ, and perfectly conformed to his holy commandments." Hunter and Ramsey reminded him to prepare for death by pursuing a "saving interest in the Lord Jesus Christ." Such an exhortation was particularly relevant amid the disease-stricken climate of Cohansey. This need to consider the eternal destination of his soul was no doubt heightened when Philip received the "distressing news of the Death of one of my friends, Viz. Hope Mills." Hope was taken suddenly by a bout with smallpox, forcing Philip again to come to grips with a sovereign God who could at any time bring an end to earthly life.[73]

As January turned to February, Philip was no longer writing explicitly about his own depravity. He was now choosing to record passages from Cohansey sermons on the promise of eternal life, the "beautiful sight when sinners flock to Christ as a cloud" and the "promise of a more glorious day of grace to come." Hunter challenged Philip with Christ's offer to "Come unto me all that labour and are heavy laden, and I will give you rest." Cohansey ministers were no doubt still preaching sermons on the "terrors of the law," but Philip had now seemed to reach a point in his spiritual sojourn where he was ready to learn—and write—more about grace.[74]

By the first week of March, Philip was thinking about repentance. This was the moment, common in the Calvinist understanding of conversion, when Philip was prompted to leave his old way of life and turn toward God as the only means of salvation. Again it was Andrew Hunter, from the pulpit of the Greenwich Presbyterian church, who made this abundantly clear to him. "To day I heard a sermon from the 25th Chapter of Luke, at the 47th verse," Fithian recorded, "in which sermon, he discovered wherein true evangelical repentance consists."[75] Repentance led naturally to conversion. Once Philip turned away from his sin there was no place else to go but into the loving arms of the Savior. Unlike modern evangelicals, Fithian never specifically identified the exact moment of his conversion, but on March 31, 1766, he had his spiritual breakthrough.

Philip was saved, but his spiritual quest had only begun. For most eighteenth-century Presbyterians, a conversion was only as good as the spiritual fruit that it produced. Assurance of salvation was confirmed over a life of faithfulness to God in everyday living. Shortly after he "embraced the offers of perpetual reconciliation through Christ," Philip started to write less about God's plan of redemption and more about the necessary disciplines that were essential to living a Christian life. The virtue of self-denial seems to have especially caught Philip's attention when he heard it presented in sermons. In mid-April, Hunter spent two weeks preaching on this theme from the ninth chapter of the Gospel of Luke. Philip knew that denial of one's own passions and desires was an important mark of a true believer. He needed to reorient his goals to fit God's will, a process that required him, in the words of Jesus, to "take up his cross daily and follow me." Philip's experience during these months was undoubtedly influential in his decision to pursue a ministerial vocation. He took God's call on his life seriously and prayed that he could live a life of service to others.[76]

Philip also knew that self-denial required him to bring every dimension of his life under the authority of God's Word. In a lengthy spiritual reflection written shortly after his conversion, he prayed that God would grant him the power to "regulate" his life "by the Word of God." His affections needed to be centered on "things above" rather than on "things on the Earth." His "Joy" needed to spring from his love of God. His "desire," "thoughts," "fear," and "trust" were to be directed toward his newfound Savior, and his "hatred" needed to be focused on "evil" alone. Philip's "speech" needed to be both "edifying" and "always with grace," and his daily activities should be directed toward good work. Such a spiritual and moral transformation was unimaginable, however, without an open and humble admission of his inability to pursue such holy living through his own efforts. Philip's spiritual striving would be worthless without God's grace guiding him along the way. Good works flowed logically from a conversion experience.[77]

The long months of spiritual struggle and joy that Philip experienced in the winter and spring of 1766 reached a glorious culmination for him in May when he and his fellow Greenwich Presbyterians received the Lord's Supper. Cohansey Presbyterian churches normally celebrated communion twice a year. It was a time when Presbyterians identified most fully with Christ by remembering his atoning death on behalf of their sins. The communion season was a time of both solemn reflection and great rejoicing. The distribution of the Sacrament was normally preceded by a day of fasting and prayer. Philip attended morning and afternoon sermons on this day of preparation, listening to a sermon by Hunter on the Passion of Christ. The following day—Sunday morning—the Lord's Supper was administered at Greenwich. The church was always crowded on the Sunday of the communion festival, and Philip wrote, "There was a great many people" and the "assembly was very solemn and attentive." Hunter's text came from the fifth chapter of the Book of Romans: "But God commandeth his love toward us, in that, while we were yet sinners, Christ died for us." Philip was stirred by the message. Reflecting on his own recent conversion, he recorded his newfound rapture in the "infinite love" and "free grace" that Christ showed to all sinners. "Infinite love indeed!," he wrote emphatically— "That he should die for us, while we were yet sinners."[78] When compared to other Cohansey communion seasons, the May 1766 celebration was probably much the same, but for Philip, it was surely the most meaningful participation in the Lord's Supper of his entire life. Over the course of the proceeding months he had passed from death to life. He had received a new identity as a child of God and could now claim an eternal home in heaven.

At the time of Philip's conversion, the Presbyterian Church in America was stronger than it had ever been. In 1765, approximately two decades after SPG minister Robert Jenney had all but written off the Presbyterians, the German Lutheran minister Henry Melchior Muhlenberg made an observation about the state of religion in the British American colonies that reads like that of a twenty-first-century sociologist trying to explain why some churches grow and others do not: "The English Presbyterian Church is growing so rapidly among the English in America that in a few years it will spread and surpass the Episcopal and all the rest. The *progress* is due to the fact that they have established ministers, keep strict discipline, and tolerate no ministers except those who had good moral character and the ability to speak, and who are content with small salaries and able to endure hard work. Those denominations here which do not have these characteristics, just the opposite, are consequently decreasing and making room for the Presbyterians."[79] Ten years later, during a missionary trip to Pennsylvania, Philip encountered a fellow traveler who remarked that he had spent some time in Fairfield and found the inhabitants of the region to be "sober, uniform in their Manner, & every Way so religious."[80]

This was the world in which Philip was born and raised. Presbyterianism informed the moral culture that made this geographical space a home. By the middle of the century Cohansey had become fully integrated into colonial Presbyterian life.[81] The region's churches had healed their revival wounds, attracted educated clergymen steeped in Enlightenment learning, and embraced a moderate brand of Presbyterianism that stressed a rational evangelicalism lived and practiced in ordered religious communities. Cohansey was Presbyterian country, and Philip Vickers Fithian would soon become its favorite son, but only after he encountered a cosmopolitan and intellectual world that would force him, like all liberally educated people throughout Western history, to come to grips with his roots and his childhood faith. He would soon embark on his way of improvement.

Chapter 3
Ambition

As Philip worked and prayed, he thought a great deal about his future. He would turn twenty years old at the end of 1767, and his identity as Joseph Fithian's eldest son weighed heavily on his deliberations. He knew his place in Fithian family history. His great-grandfather Samuel had never met any of his great-grandchildren, but he certainly must have had their future prosperity in mind when he decided to leave East Hampton for New Jersey in 1700. Over half a century later Philip was a beneficiary of Samuel's decision to migrate. The course of his life, it appeared, had already been set. He would inherit his father's farm, work it faithfully in the way that Joseph had taught him, and live a sober but relatively happy life in this "Spartan common-wealth." To imagine anything different was to break with the yeoman experience that had rewarded his family over the course of three generations.

Philip *did* imagine something different, however. He grew up in an era when the thought of breaking with the past did not seem as scandalous as it had before. His restlessness with the traditions of his rural upbringing reflected the spirit of a revolutionary age. All the pieces for a life of self-improvement seemed to be in place. Philip would have access to educated Presbyterian minds to a degree that was unprecedented in the Cohansey countryside. Cohansey's Presbyterian ministers—Andrew Hunter, William Ramsey, and Enoch Green—were evangelicals concerned with bringing spiritual, moral, and intellectual development to society, and they believed that such change began with young people. These clergymen exposed Philip to new worlds of learning, and he took every opportunity to sit under their teaching. After Philip's conversion in 1766, he began to think seriously about pursuing a formal education in preparation for the Presbyterian ministry. Philip's vocational dilemma—the decision to work behind a plow or a pulpit—was a moral one. Should he respect the legacy of his family's time-honored way of living and settle for a life on the land, or should he break with the past in pursuit of an education that would probably take him away from the family farm? Was a compromise possible? Could he reconcile his love for "Cohansie," the place to which he was so deeply attached, with a life of professional mobility? These questions are essential to understanding the meaning of the Enlightenment for the children of yeoman farmers in the early American hinterland. Indeed, they would haunt Philip for the rest of his life.

Philip grappled with these vocational issues on the pages of his diary. Between 1766 and 1767 he kept a work journal in which he recorded short, terse entries describing the daily labor he performed on the family farm. As we saw in Chapter 1, his writing in this journal revealed his attachment to the agrarian life of his Cohansey home. However, Philip also kept another diary, a record quite different from his work journal. It was begun as a day-by-day chronicle of his spiritual condition and evolved into a place where he could react to local gossip, copy poetry and newspaper articles that caught his attention, comment on the content of Cohansey ministers' sermons, and reflect on his reading in spiritual and contemporary literature. These pages provide a glimpse into an oasis of learning and reading amid the daily rigors of Cohansey farm life. "For I can now with truth declare," Philip wrote, "that the most happy hours I find in life or could even wish to enjoy are those when I am quite alone & have free, undisturbed Liberty to ponder over the Sentiments of some famous Writer." Philip was dwelling in Greenwich, but he inhabited two distinctly different cultural worlds. He cut "hoop-poles" in the morning and returned to his room in the evening to read Sir Richard Blackmore's poetry. He ended a day of carting firewood by perusing the third volume of the *Universal History*. He spent one day planting corn and reading Homer's *Iliad* and another reaping rye and copying the obituary of College of New Jersey president Samuel Finley.[1]

Philip was developing interests that prompted him to envision a future quite different from that awaiting most of Cohansey's young men. The Reverend Enoch Green had just opened a small classical school designed to prepare students for careers in law, medicine, politics, and the church. Philip wanted desperately to attend. Joseph Fithian, as a middling grain grower of reasonable wealth, could certainly afford to send his son to school, but he would need some convincing. Few native-born Cohansians had ever attended college, and Philip's interest in formal education apparently met with little enthusiasm from some of Joseph's neighbors. Early American yeomen valued schooling as long as it was limited to the necessary training needed to operate a family farm. Advanced education undermined family values. It pulled farm children away from their agricultural obligations to their fathers. Philip was Joseph's oldest son and most reliable laborer. Joseph's seventeen-year-old son Enoch was crippled by a leg infection, his son Josiah was only fifteen years old, and his youngest boys, at the ages of nine and seven, were not yet ready to take up serious farmwork. (Also in the household were an infant, Thomas, and a sister, Rebecca.)

Cohansey yeomen, like all early American farmers, believed that agriculture represented a superior way of living. It provided independence and comfort. In the Delaware Valley, where the grain market thrived during much of the eighteenth century, farming was the most economically successful way of life for ordinary people. The physical work required to sustain a family farm in Cohansey was difficult, but for Presbyterians sensitive to the consequences of Adam and Eve's Fall, such toil was a necessary part of their daily lives. Agricultural labor was the closest one might come to a flourishing human existence in a sinful and imperfect world. Life on the land offered Calvinists a lesson in the limits imposed by a sovereign Creator on his fallen creation. Men of leisure and luxury, or those who did not work by the sweat of their brows, were concerned more with selfish pursuits and personal improvement than with the necessary toil performed by those whom Thomas Jefferson would later call "the chosen people of God."[2]

Philip was probably sympathetic to some of his neighbors' thoughts about higher education, but this did not stop him from writing a letter to his father "begging him to put me to School." In this letter and a similar one written over two years later, he answered his Cohansey critics and defended the importance of education for society in general. Philip was living in a unique moment in Cohansey Presbyterian life. He recognized that the founding of Green's academy provided a small window of opportunity to obtain the type of education he had long desired. Philip's conversion and call to the ministry came late in life, and he thus had little time left to pursue a vocation outside of the grain field. A school such as Green's was new to Cohansey, and as Philip put it, there was only a "remote expectation" that it would continue after its headmaster left the region. Since few clergymen stayed long in Cohansey, Philip saw immediate enrollment in the school as "the only opportunity I shall ever have, of acquiring that, which through my whole Life I have most desired."[3]

In his letters to his father, Philip offered an alternative vision of human work to the one common among the grain growers of Cohansey. Farmers, for example, criticized men of learning because they did not exercise regularly and were thus more prone to illness than those who worked with their hands. Philip noted that many in Cohansey talked regularly about the "inactive lives of the learned, or those who are seeking knowledge." While Philip readily admitted that his critics were correct—scholars *were* more susceptible to poor health—the cultivation of the mind was a form of work that he deemed to be just as important as farming to the improvement of society. "For the Health, & good natural

Constitution of Men," he wrote, "have been freely forfeited in their painful Search after Knowledge, & given up as Witnesses for the Truth of the arduous & difficult Ascent to the Pinnacle of Science."[4] If leading an educated life meant that Philip might more readily suffer from physical illness, he was willing to take the risk. In a sickly and mosquito-infested place such as Cohansey, where immune systems were constantly under attack, such a risk was not to be taken lightly.

Philip's apology for education also challenged the economic values of Cohansey society. Cohansey's middling farmers believed that they were living happy lives because they owned farms and had accumulated a modicum of wealth through their participation in the ever-stable Philadelphia grain market. They lived, after all, in the "best poor man's country in the world." If Philip were to turn his back on the relative prosperity associated with this way of life, he would need to redefine the pursuit of happiness in a noneconomic way. In a statement that would be the envy of any twenty-first-century college professor who has tried to explain to a student why a major in a humanities discipline was a good idea, Philip favored the love of liberal learning over the quest for personal wealth or comfort: "I hold a free Education in so great Esteem, that I should choose for my Lot, to live in the World in low Condition, if Providence thought it necessary, as to Wealth and all outward Greatness, under the Frown of Fortune, & be blest with Learning, rather than possess the most ample Estate, & be blind with Ignorance." He requested that his "whole Patrimony . . . be applied to help in finishing my Education, even if it should be expended."[5] By asking Joseph for his inheritance to pursue a vocation that diverged drastically from the yeoman culture in which he was raised, Philip was breaking with the traditional world of the early modern farm, a culture sustained by family labor and a generational attachment to the land. What were the chances of such a prodigal ever returning to this way of life? One thing is clear from Philip's letters to his father: the pursuit of education as a form of self-improvement meant that part of him would no longer be held back by the farm and the limits it placed on his life. He noted that "there are many Principles which we drink in in early youth, as close, & almost as dear as our very Natures, & which many cannot throw off but carry with them all their Days, these must be laid aside, & if possible forgotten in obtaining true Knowledge."[6]

Philip's letters to his father also delved deeply into Enlightenment language about the civilizing function of education. According to many proponents of the Enlightenment, education was one means by which societies evolved into a higher order of civilization. Perhaps with his Cohansey objectors in mind, Philip noted that human beings were "prone to mischief" because of their "vicious tempers" that caused them to "debauch the best Principles of Education." Men without "Instruction and Refinement" were "advanced but a little above their fellow Creature the Brutes" and were completely "ignorant" of the principles necessary to live with any degree of "Decency & Comfort in common life." Philip justified his education to his father by arguing that "Men of Letters" had the capacity "to refine & often to reform Mankind to correct their Principles & check their Vices."[7] For the enlightened man of letters, opportunities to obtain knowledge were always available. Philip wrote, "When we accomplish one Difficulty, that presents us to the Embrace of another, this being finished we see the third; to use an old, but very just Simile, it is like a person endeavouring to surmount a Cluster of Hills, he ascends the first & a second appears, when he is at the top of that he beholds another, & when he can see some he ascended first no longer, he sees so many before him that he seems only beginning to ascend; thus illimitable are the Attainments of Learning. Yet we are not to suppose these Difficulties as Barriers hindering our Attempts to attain it, but as Incitements to Activity & Greater Diligence."[8]

Philip's lifelong love of reading and ideas had found a potential outlet in Green's academy. He could, for the first time, envision his way of improvement. He would now be confronted with ambition—the engine that would carry him along this road. Ambition was one of the Enlightenment's most powerful passions. Eighteenth-century moral philosophers linked it to the political sphere. The word comes from the Latin *ambitio*, which in its original context referred to the way in which a politician garnered votes in an election campaign. An ambitious person was motivated by a desire for power, fame, or social rank. He or she set out to escape the limits of a traditional way of life or the confinement associated with an attachment to a particular piece of earth. As the historian Jason Opal has noted, ambition rested on the premise that one should "not be hemmed in by parental precedents and local needs." The very nature of ambition ran counter to the values that defined the world of the farmer. Philip was thus indulging a passion in which few Cohansians had ever indulged.[9] For civic humanists, or those who sought to place the general good over personal gain, ambition was a dangerous passion with immoral or unethical connotations. If virtue was the foundation of a republic, then ambition worked to undermine the moral frameworks of political and social life. For Presbyterians, ambition could lead to the worst forms of selfishness and worldliness. John Witherspoon, the Presbyterian president of the College of New Jersey and a future mentor of Philip, listed ambition as an "evil" passion.[10] God called people into vocations according to the gifts he gave them, but the sin nature, which sometimes operated under the guise of ambition, was ever enticing them to follow career paths inspired by the unhealthy quest for fame and wealth. After graduating from the College of New Jersey at Princeton, Philip's friend and classmate Andrew Hunter Jr. wrote to him to relay the unfortunate news that many of their friends and classmates were "getting into business as fast as possible, whether they are called or not."[11] Worldly ambition could cause a person to miss the true call of God on his or her life.

Ambition, however, did not always have to be associated with republican condemnations of luxury or Calvinist jeremiads about the evils of selfishness. Most of the early settlers of the British American colonies, including Philip's own descendants, were ambitious migrants in search of modest wealth through the acquisition of land. They set out zealously to satisfy their own economic and social interests. Some of the first settlers of the Delaware Valley, particularly the members of the Society of Friends, were able to reconcile their pursuit of wealth, power, and social prestige with their Quaker faith, feeling equally at home in both the "MeetingHouse" and the "CountingHouse." The New England migrants who settled Cohansey at the turn of the eighteenth century upheld a similar understanding of ambition. These were Calvinists who viewed success on earth as a sign that they were numbered among God's elect.[12] Ambition could be directed toward a variety of noble ends. Philip, for example, was working toward a career as a Presbyterian minister.

Philip was aware of the dangers inherent in ambition, but he refused to reject its usefulness as a means of motivating him in everyday life. Ambition was good as long as it was controlled. While in college at Princeton he composed an essay defending this passion, arguing that every human has a "Secret Desire of being greater than any of his fellow Mortals." Such desire was "agreeable and useful in life" as long as it was held under "due Regulations."[13] Later he would describe the form of self-improvement that was not directed toward honorable purposes as "vulgar Ambition." In a similar composition, Philip directly related ambition to education. "Education rightly conducted very much assists laudable Ambition," he argued. Education and ambition were the marks of any civilized, liberal, and modern human being. To illustrate this idea, he imagined a picture of an "uninstructed barbarous Creature void of Education & Ambition" displayed alongside a picture "of that Person who by the Influence of a well conducted Education is excited to the Study & Practice of great & Noble things." The differences in the portraits, of course, would be obvious to any observer.[14] We cannot tell conclusively to what extent Philip actually believed these ideas about ambition since he wrote about the subject for the College of New Jersey's Whig Society, a debating club that was more concerned with the effective presentation of an argument than with the debater's personal convictions on a given topic. However, by the time he had started studying with

Enoch Green, he certainly saw himself more as a practitioner of "great and noble things" than as an "uninstructed barbarous Creature."

Philip had presented his case. His future now rested in his father's hands. To help him make this important decision Joseph turned to Rev. Andrew Hunter. As Hunter was one of the only educated men in the region and a trusted family friend, Joseph would have put much value on his advice. Fortunately for Philip, the clergyman had been the primary catalyst in encouraging his young charge to attend Green's academy. Later, Philip would remember the role that Hunter played in his religious education and would thank him, at least on the pages of his journal, for "his generous Proposal, & frequent vigorous Solicitations of my Father, who was not easy to be persuaded of how much Importance Learning is." Joseph had two meetings with Hunter concerning his son's schooling, and Philip, ever aware of his father's doubts about higher education, experienced great anxiety over their outcome. In the end, whatever Hunter told Joseph must have been convincing. On August 11, only five days after Philip first mentioned the possibility of studying at the academy in his journal, he recorded, with more than a hint of jubilation, "This morning I had the gracious and agreeable news from my Father that next week I am to go to school to Mr. Green." Philip's dream would become a reality, but not before he completed his summer farmwork. He spent the next four days mowing and carting hay, his mind probably filled with eager anticipation for the start of his new life. On August 17 he moved up the Cohansey River to Deerfield, and the following day he was immersed fully in the study of Latin verbs and adverbs. While his transition from an agricultural life to an academic life may have been abrupt, Philip was more than ready. He had been waiting a long time for this moment.[15]

Philip was a member of the first class of students to pursue their educational ambitions at Enoch Green's academy, one of several such schools founded by Presbyterians in the decades following the First Great Awakening. Green's academy was part of a Presbyterian educational renaissance that included the establishment of the College of New Jersey at Princeton in 1746 and over sixty-five academies, mostly in Pennsylvania and New Jersey, founded between 1727 and 1802.[16] "Green Hall," as Philip called it, was modeled after the dissenting academies in England and Ireland. The English dissenting academies, the most notable of which was Philip Doddridge's Northampton Academy, offered broad training in the liberal arts to students who, due to their nonconforming religious beliefs, were not permitted to attend Oxford or Cambridge. Similarly, Irish academies, founded by Scots-Irish clergymen in the late seventeenth century, provided an education to Church

Figure 3. The Deerfield, New Jersey, Presbyterian church (built in 1771 but shown here as it stood in 1858). Courtesy, Lummis Library, Cumberland County (N.J.) Historical Society.

of Scotland ministerial hopefuls in preparation for study at a Scottish university such as Glasgow or Aberdeen.[17] After the First Great Awakening, American academies, under the direction of local ministers, began to crop up in towns such as Faggs Manor, Pennsylvania (Samuel Blair); West Nottingham, Maryland (Samuel Finley); Carlisle, Pennsylvania (John Steel); New London, Pennsylvania (Francis Alison); and Lancaster, Pennsylvania (William Pequea). Unlike Log College, which trained solely ministers, the later Presbyterian academies were preparatory schools, founded to educate students for matriculation at the College of New Jersey and other colonial colleges or prepare them for professional apprenticeships in law or medicine.

Although not all of Green's students opted to continue their education in a colonial college, those who did were well prepared. Green Hall students who attended the College of New Jersey were placed in the junior class, having been adequately schooled in Latin, Greek, mathematics, rhetoric, and logic—all required subjects for freshmen and sophomores at Nassau Hall.[18] Most of these Presbyterian academies were located in rural areas such as Deerfield, where the cost of schooling was less expensive. The popularity of these institutions became clear in 1768 when the trustees of the College of New Jersey scrapped a proposal requiring students to take all four years of their studies in residence at Princeton. The successful opposition to the proposal came from those who believed that the rural academies offered a more convenient and affordable way of meeting the first two years of Princeton's curriculum requirements.[19]

Green had assembled an impressive group of students in his first academy class. Richard Howell pursued a course in law at New Castle, Delaware, following his graduation from the academy. He served as an officer during the American War of Independence, opened law offices in Greenwich and Trenton, and was eventually elected governor of New Jersey, a post he held from 1793 to 1801. Another of Philip's classmates, Joseph Bloomfield, came to Deerfield from Woodbridge, New Jersey, and would also distinguish himself as an officer during the Revolutionary War before practicing law at nearby Bridge-Town. Bloomfield became a rising star in New Jersey Republican politics and succeeded Howell as the state's governor, serving from 1801 to 1802 and 1803 to 1812. Thomas Ewing, a Greenwich native and one of Philip's closest friends, studied medicine after leaving Deerfield and eventually opened practices in Greenwich and Cape May. He served as an officer during the Revolutionary War and was elected, in 1781, as a member of the state legislature. Andrew Hunter Jr., the nephew of the Greenwich minister by the same name, graduated from the College of New Jersey with Philip in 1772; presided over several small New Jersey academies; taught mathematics, astronomy, and natural philosophy at his alma mater from 1804 to 1808; and ended his career as chaplain of the United States Navy. During the roughly nine years (1767–75) in which the academy was open, Enoch Green sent six of his graduates to the College of New Jersey, including a winner of the Latin Salutory Prize (Samuel Leake, A.B., 1774), the highest honor awarded to a student at the college.[20]

Philip's education at Green Hall did not stop once he completed his daily course work. The academy's students maintained regular contact with each other outside of the classroom. They visited one another's homes, nurtured friendships, and conversed via personal letters. In the eighteenth century friendship was an important means of fostering moral improvement. Personal affection and sympathy between friends created a bond that contributed to the development of individual and social virtue.[21] With such moral weight invested in this kind of relationship, it was important that rifts among friends be settled quickly. Thomas Ewing, for example, wrote to Philip to make amends for a breach in their friendship: "I do beg your pardon for accusing you falsely, and I hope [you] will forgive me; so that we may know our friendship tied with such an inveterable knot . . . [will] never be destroy'd till our bodies and souls are separated from this world by Death." Enlightened friendship also required mutual encouragement on the road to self-improvement. In 1771 Ewing wrote to Philip at Princeton, "My dear friend, your advancement is so nearly connected with my happiness that one is absolutely consequent to the other; every step you take toward the *Ne plus ultra* of literature, animates me to think that my friend is capable of making progress in the path which has immortalis'd so many of the British genius."[22]

Shortly before he left Deerfield, Philip sent his cousin Amy Fithian, the daughter of his Uncle Samuel, "An Epistle . . . on the Excellencies of Friendship." In it he affirmed that "there is something useful & very mystical in the private mutual Transactions of two Persons directed by Principles of Virtue & Honour to take a Vow of Friendship & to maintain individual unconditional Harmony." Friendship served a civilizing function. Philip remarked that the attainment of true friendship required humans to "bridle over our Inclinations" and "guard our Actions" in order to avoid the passionate side of human relations that was governed by a "thousand jealousies." In this sense, friendship helped to balance the human faculties. Philip went on in his epistle to note that friendship, which should be "cultivated with unremitted diligence," distinguished the refined individual from the social interactions of the "Brutal Creation." It was "the most refined, satisfyingly earthly Joy that a human creature can endure" and "worthy of Pursuit of every wise and intelligent Person."[23]

Cohansey Presbyterians also made friends as a form of Christian fellowship, a kinship among believers ordained by God for the promotion of spiritual growth. Such friendship found its source in the grace of God and could be enjoyed only by those of like-minded religious faith. This was the kind of friendship that Saint Augustine, one of the most important ancient influences on Calvinist theology, described when he said that there can be "no true friendship unless those who cling to each other are welded together . . . in that love which is spread throughout our hearts by the holy spirit which is given to us."[24] This type of relationship, according to Philip, was "sacred" and the highest form of friendship in which one could engage. It represented, but only in part, the eternal friendship that the believer would share with God in eternity. It was also conducive to societal improvement. Invoking the languages of both Christianity and enlightened civilization, Philip reminded his cousin that "to make friendship[s] happy, these should all be guided by a Principle of Piety and Religion without which human Nature is rude barbarous & unpleasant."[25]

Philip referred to the social engagements between friends and other acquaintances as "conversation." Such human interaction could contribute to moral improvement as long as it was "good" or "useful."[26] The

Presbyterian attempt to foster this kind of useful conversation sheds light on an informal circle of young people, with Philip at the center, striving to model themselves on the "republic of letters," another name for the fellowship of learning cultivated by some of Europe's leading intellectuals in the late seventeenth and eighteenth centuries. The republic of letters was sustained by personal correspondence between men of ideas and had the potential of incorporating an even larger citizenry through the dissemination of printed materials such as magazines, newspapers, and books. It became an imagined community of the learned in which the educated men of the American colonies could enjoy full participation. Such a manifestation of the republic of letters could even be found in remote corners of the British world among the young academy students of Cohansey. Provincials such as Philip might gain membership into the republic of letters by completing a course of learning at a colonial college; staying abreast of current trends in the fields of science, moral philosophy, and religion; or generally seeking to live lives of intellectual and moral self-improvement.[27]

Philip's classmates gave each other classical names, occasionally penned their letters in Latin, and patterned their conversations after the enlightened culture of the London coffeehouse. As fitting with the citizens of the republic of letters, they corresponded with one another. Letters were composed, discussed, and critiqued for both content and form. For example, Philip recorded a visit from his friend "Amasio" in which the two students "disputed the nature of a variety of letters." Members of this circle of friends exchanged correspondence on such topics as the proper objects of the passions, the eternal fate of sinners and atheists, and the virtue of women. The contents of the letters would often be shared with others and discussed at length among the group, creating a scribal community of readers. Philip asked his friend Sally Dare to comment on the theme of Amasio's recent letter, which Dare had apparently also read. He requested that Dare recollect "our pleasing interviews and the Discourses that attended them particularly by Amasio's principles" and urged her to "present me a letter, containing the full contents of your heart respecting it, and I will likewise offer you my sentiments upon them."[28]

Other letters delved into more political and philosophical topics. Philip wrote a letter to his friend Rowena comparing the hostile relationship between England and her colonies with the politics of Rome under Julius Caesar. He encouraged her to develop the type of civic virtue needed by all colonists to defend their liberty against the Crown. The participation of Sally Dare and Rowena in these conversations suggests that this rural circle of enlightened friends was not confined to men. As we will see below, they served as both a form of enlightenment improvement and a sort of Presbyterian courtship circle.

Some of Philip's local letters could be quite philosophical in nature. James Ewing shared some thoughts on moral philosophy with Philip: "Moral philosophy or Ethics is an art which treats of virtue & vice and prescribes rules for attaining one, and avoiding the other; according to this definition we shall leave religion (that is revealed religion) as belonging to theology and Divinity." He asserted that "virtue" was the "only way to Happiness" and stressed that knowledge of self was absolutely essential to the promotion of such virtue. Yet, he also held that both virtue *and* religion were needed to foster such happiness. He made sure that he "would not be understood to mean that virtue, or moral good, without Religion was the way to Happiness." This was a heady exchange for two sons of Cohansey farmers who had not yet reached the age of twenty.[29]

While the contents of these letters certainly reveal the writers' concern with morality, sociability, and politics, the style in which the letters were composed was also important. Letter writing was a sign of refinement, especially for rural folk striving for some degree of gentility.[30] Philip and his Deerfield classmates critiqued each other's writing. James Ewing ended his letter on moral philosophy by asking Philip to overlook any errors in style: "I know your friendly heart will overlook my failing, so beging you would excuse any litteral mistake." James's brother Thomas told Philip that the "polite" way to conduct a "friendly literary correspondence" was to avoid filling letters with "useless declarations" of "dying love." After leaving Deerfield, Andrew Hunter Jr. read some of the letters Philip had sent to his father from Princeton and corrected him because his epistolary style was not "free, open kind and respectful." Most of Philip's letter-writing circle lived within a ten-mile radius of him, and he could thus have easily communicated with them in a face-to-face manner. Letter writing, however, was not designed merely to pass along information. Form was the mark of a gentleman—an essential skill required of any rural academy student on the road of self-improvement.

After two years of study with Green at Deerfield, Philip enrolled in the junior class at the College of New Jersey. There he entered a training ground for enlightened gentlemen ready to make their mark on a revolutionary society. President John Witherspoon, who had arrived at Princeton in 1768, had transformed a largely New Side seminary with the primary mission of training Presbyterian clergymen into a college with a curriculum grounded in the Scottish Enlightenment and a commitment to the cause of American liberty. Central to Witherspoon's vision was the creation of a community of inquiry where young men could become citizens, through reading and study, of the transatlantic republic of letters. The new president believed that "great and eminent men have generally, in every nation, appeared in clusters," and he challenged his students to maintain friendships and relationships for the purpose of mutual improvement.[31] Despite its rural setting, Princeton was a place where the parochialism that students brought with them to college was eroded through exposure to a cosmopolitan world of ideas.[32] This notion was at the heart of an eighteenth-century liberal arts education. Witherspoon's students would be public servants who entered British American life through a variety of professions and vocations, including law, politics, medicine, and the ministry. Princeton was the ideal place for Philip to reconcile his ambition with a life of service to God and society.

Witherspoon's most influential reform at Princeton was in the area of moral philosophy, the intellectual centerpiece of any early American college curriculum. The president's lectures on the subject emphasized the learning of moral lessons as one of the fundamental aims of religion. He borrowed freely from the "New Moral Philosophy," or the "British moralist" school. Led by the Glasgow moral philosopher Francis Hutcheson, the New Moral Philosophy taught that a virtuous life could be attained through the development of what Hutcheson called the "moral sense," an ethical compass placed by God in every human being. The moral sense, when trained through reading, education, or sociability, enabled persons to arrive intuitively at ethically correct assumptions. In this sense, the New Moral Philosophy was as much a "science" as natural philosophy; it was practiced through an experimental and rational analysis of the human condition.[33] In adhering to the idea that personal virtue could be attained through rational and natural means, Witherspoon's ethical thought was rooted firmly within a British Enlightenment that made the science of morals a focus of attention.

Princeton's president believed that moral behavior would not, and could not, contradict the teachings of the Bible—God was the author of both the Scriptures *and* moral principles. However, he also maintained that morality could be constructed through *inductive* experimentation. Witherspoon's embrace of the British moralists meant that Princeton was departing from an approach to ethics in which morality was *deduced* by systematizing the revealed commands of divinely inspired Scripture. Jonathan Edwards, the third president of Princeton, taught that "true virtue" was impossible without a personal relationship with God, the ultimate source of all good works and public morality. By suggesting that the human will was strong enough to overcome the sin nature, thus allowing even unbelievers to lead morally upright lives, Witherspoon was taking early American Calvinist ethics in a more enlightened direction.

Despite his devout evangelicalism, a primary reason he was called to the presidency of Princeton, Witherspoon often placed more emphasis on virtuous acts and the teaching of morals than on traditional evangelical concerns such as conversion or revivalism.[34]

Witherspoon's moral philosophy fit well with the cosmopolitan goals he sought to instill in his students at Princeton. In the course of his lectures he taught them that human beings possess two kinds of affections. The first, which he called a "particular kind of affection," included the natural loyalties one had to family, friends, and country. These attachments could promote societal happiness, but they were by nature "narrow" and "less extensive" than the second kind of affection, which Witherspoon described as a "Calm and deliberate good will to all."[35] His commitment to the moral superiority of universal affections even extended to his understanding of patriotism, a position that might surprise those familiar with his active role in the American Revolution (which we will explore in Chapter 6). Witherspoon taught that while "the love of our country, to be sure, is a noble and enlarged affection . . . yet the love of mankind is still greatly superior. Sometimes attachment to country appears in a littleness of mind, thinking all other nations inferior, and foolishly believing that knowledge, virtue and valor are all confined to themselves."[36] This understanding of the affections was inherently Christian in nature. Human beings were created by God, and Christians should thus display benevolent affections to all people regardless of local or national attachments. Christian universalism was compatible with enlightened cosmopolitanism. Local attachments, while important, were backward and morally inferior to the love of humankind. Philip would learn rather quickly at Princeton that it was far better to be a citizen of the world than a citizen of Cohansey.

Philip moved to Princeton in the fall of 1770 and prepared for the college's rigorous entrance exams. He would take the same exam, conducted by President Witherspoon and his tutors, given to sophomores at Princeton who sought entrance into the junior class. It required students to "render Virgil and Tully's orations into English and to turn English into true and grammatical Latin." Philip was expected to translate a New Testament passage from Greek or Latin (to English), "be acquainted with vulgar arithmetic," read English "with propriety," and write "without grammatical errors."[37] Enoch Green had prepared him well. Shortly after passing his exam, he wrote to his father to inform him of his admission to this "flourishing *Seminary* of Learning" where he was adequately prepared to take "another grand Step towards the Summit of my Wishes."[38] Philip would spend the next two years living in Nassau Hall, a three-story stone building equipped with boarding rooms for 147 students (Philip counted 81 students in 1770), an assembly hall, a

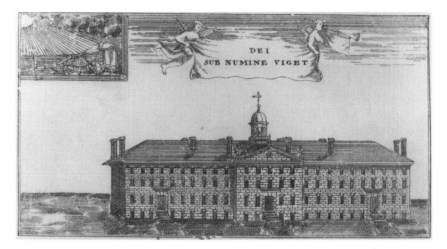

Figure 4. "Nassau Hall," 1760. Courtesy, Department of Rare Books and Special Collections, Princeton University Libraries, Princeton, N.J.

library of over two thousand volumes, and a dining room large enough to accommodate the student body. At the time of his matriculation, Nassau Hall was the largest building in the British American colonies. Its sheer size, the fellowship of students and scholars who resided and taught within it, and the extensive library it housed must have been both overwhelming and exciting to this twenty-two-year-old son of a Cohansey farmer on the road of self-improvement.[39]

Philip's transition to Princeton, however, was not without its difficulties. For reasons that are unclear, he enrolled late. Rather than taking his exam with the rest of the incoming junior class in September, he and Andrew Hunter Jr. were not examined until November. He also arrived without a gown—an essential part of an eighteenth-century college student's daily wardrobe—and would not acquire one until he had been at Princeton for three months (students who appeared in public without wearing one were fined five shillings; we do not know if Philip was required to pay this fine). These, of course, were minor setbacks, but they caused a great deal of apprehension for Philip, who had never been away from Cohansey for any extended period of time and now found himself trying to fit into an intimidating and foreign academic culture. He found comfort in the letters of his mother, Hannah, who did her best to sympathize with her son. "I suppose you are uneasy about your Gown," she wrote in her first letter to Philip after he arrived at Princeton. She assured him that Reverend Hunter had ordered cloth for the garment but that it had not yet arrived. Hannah then called her anxious son's attention to the teachings of Jesus in the Sermon on the Mount: "this is perhaps a small Cross & you must my dear Son take your Cross Daily & follow Christ if you will be his disciple."[40]

If Philip had a hard time adjusting to some of the cultural differences between life in Cohansey and that in Nassau Hall, his long days in the fields of Greenwich would have certainly prepared him physically for the schedule he would face each day at Princeton. A typical day at the College of New Jersey began at 5:30 A.M. with morning prayers, a required part of life at Nassau Hall. Those students who chose to sleep late or skip prayers altogether could expect to be reported to Witherspoon or one of the college tutors, and appropriate disciplinary action would be taken. Following prayers, students generally studied for an hour before breakfast was served at 8:00. After breakfast, Philip had another hour to "play, or exercise" before the morning recitations got under way. Most of the intellectual work that took place in the Nassau Hall residences was conducted in preparation for these daily recitations with college tutors. Students were expected to demonstrate knowledge of the topic assigned for the day and be prepared to recite passages from assigned texts, listen to the tutor's thoughts on a particular subject, or answer any questions that the tutor might pose.[41] After recitation, Philip ate dinner with the rest of the student body, had "Liberty to go out at Pleasure," and participated in mandatory study hours. Evening prayers began at 6:00 P.M., and supper was served at 7:00. Students were required to be back in their rooms by 9:00 P.M.

Sunday was the only day in which students broke from this daily routine. All Princeton students were required to attend two sermons, one at 11:00 A.M. in the Princeton Presbyterian Church and the other at 3:00 P.M. in the "College Hall." Philip looked forward to hearing John Witherspoon preach each week and told his father that he was "indeed much pleased" with his sermons, describing them as "almost inimitable." On Sunday evenings a service was held in Nassau Hall for "any who belong to the College & choose to attend." This service included singing, prayer, and the reading of a sermon by one of the college tutors. Members of each class then gathered together in their rooms for an informal time of Psalm singing and prayer. Since Philip was a new member of the junior class in 1770 (he had not matriculated with most of these students during their first two years at Princeton), he merely observed this Sunday night student ritual until he felt more comfortable participating.[42]

The daily schedule that Princeton students endured was rigid, and as John Murrin has quipped, "it takes an act of historical imagination to discover how any intellectual excitement got smuggled into the students' daily routine."[43] Unlike in contemporary colleges and universities, which solicit potential students with innovative classroom strategies and an array of bells and whistles initiated by departments of student development, students in eighteenth-century colleges were slaves to routine. "Habit" was an essential virtue at the College of New Jersey, and Philip spent some time contemplating this topic in an essay he wrote for the college Whig Society. It was only through the day-to-day engagement with ideas and the rote practice of skills learned that students acquired "great Readiness & Facility in the Performance of many Things" that would otherwise be "wholly impracticable" or at the very least "difficult and perplexing." One became an accomplished orator by speaking regularly in public. One could be "well skilled in the Theory of Navigation," but unless he had been "placed upon the broad Ocean many Leagues from the Shore in a Ship accommodated with every Instrument for his Purpose" he would be as "ignorant of the Methods necessary to direct a Ship to her Port as an Indian is of Geometry." Philip's reference to uneducated Native Americans is telling, for it was the ability to learn through habitual practice that distinguished the civilized gentleman from the uncivilized savage. "Education of Habit is truly admirable," he wrote, and "those who enjoy them in their Purity are certainly exalted much above the common Herd of Men."[44]

While he was at Princeton, Philip studied Greek and Latin, logic, rhetoric, and classical writers from Homer to Horace. He was also exposed to the New Moral Philosophy, current works in mathematics and science, belles lettres, and modern poetry. During his junior year he focused on algebra, geometry, trigonometry, natural philosophy, English grammar, and composition. Attendance at Witherspoon's lectures, which consisted of the president dictating his notes to the class and the students copying them verbatim into their notebooks, was required of all seniors. The final year of study included logic and an additional course in natural philosophy as well. Seniors were also required, every five or six weeks, to present orations "of their own composition" before a public audience made up of students, faculty, and the larger community. A Princeton education was only as good as the college library. Philip had access to a large collection of theological works and a significant number of volumes in literature and history, mostly classical. Students who wanted more contemporary fare, such as the growing pamphlet literature produced in response to the imperial crisis with England or a recently published popular novel, might find it in the student-run libraries of the college literary societies.[45]

The year Philip arrived at Princeton, Witherspoon bought the orrery (an instrument for demonstrating the movement of the planets) created by the Philadelphia scientist David Rittenhouse. It was a purchase that enhanced greatly the scientific apparatus of the college, prompting Witherspoon to tout Princeton's program in the sciences as "equal, if not superior, to any on the continent."[46] Philip was intrigued by natural philosophy because more than any other course of study it challenged some of the assumptions about the world that many of his Cohansey friends and acquaintances had long accepted. For example, he learned that "by the Help of Philosophy we find that the Earth wheels annually round the Sun as Centre; & us whirled about daily on its own Axis, which is contrary to all Appearance, & the Scriptures too." He was aware that many, on being exposed to such information—especially the notion that science might contradict the teachings of the Bible—would be "ready to call down the Vengeance of Jove in wrathful Lightning upon the impious Rebels who dare utter such blasphemous language." However, Philip was an educated gentleman who now knew better. He was a man of science and learning who could articulate the finer points of Copernican astronomy. He did not need to waste his time with the superstitions of home.[47]

While Philip may have attended Enoch Green's academy with young men who would become some of New Jersey's prominent postRevolutionary public servants, ambition would carry his Princeton classmates to fame on a national stage. They included future politicians and early republican literary figures such as Hugh Henry Brackenridge, Aaron Burr, Philip Freneau, and James Madison. What is striking, and even a bit odd, is that during his two years at the College of New Jersey, Philip never mentioned any of these men in his private writings, nor did they mention him in their papers. Philip would have certainly seen these men on a daily basis—the Princeton class of 1771 (which included Brackenridge, Freneau, and Madison) had only thirteen students, while Philip's class of 1772 (which included Burr) had twenty-four. Moreover, as a member, and eventually the "Assistant to the Moderator," of the college's Whig literary society, Philip would have worked closely with them. He presented essays and orations before the Whig Society and participated in the Whigs' 1771–72 satirical "paper war" with the rival Cliosophic Society.

We can only speculate as to why Philip does not mention any of these future American leaders or why he is absent from their writings. Perhaps students at Nassau Hall tended to segregate themselves based on social distinction or vocational pursuit. Philip tended to befriend other ministerial hopefuls from less privileged or agricultural backgrounds, such as Israel Evans, Andrew Hunter Jr., Oliver Reese, and James Templeton, while Madison, Brackenridge, and Freneau, who were a year ahead of him in their studies, formed their own social clique.[48] Whatever the case, Philip would have benefited, even if it was indirectly, from rubbing shoulders with these young men of great potential who came to Princeton to study with Witherspoon.

Philip found plenty of time amid his academic schedule for amusements and diversions from study. He took afternoon trips with his "sweet mates" into the Princeton countryside "for exercise & pleasure."[49] He would later recall his participation in a host of college pranks, including "giving each other *names* & *characters*; Meeting & Shoving in the dark entries; knocking at Doors & going off without entering; Strowing the entries in the night with greasy Feathers; freezing the Bell; [and] Ringing it at late Hours of the Night." He also enjoyed the informal time he spent with the members of the Whig Society. In addition to writing essays and disputing them with the Cliosophic Club, the Whigs engaged in a variety of extracurricular activities, including stealing hens and turkeys from neighborhood farms, "ogling Women with the Telescope," and hazing new students by concocting "frightful compositions with Gun-Powder, & lighting them in the Rooms of timorous boys."[50] As at modern-day college campuses, at Princeton the pursuit of learning came with a great deal of time for play.

Philip's quest for self-improvement intensified during his two years at Princeton. "I have here . . . an Opportunity of acquainting myself with the Writings of great & famous Men, & to improve by their Instruction," he wrote to his mother. "And all these Advantages . . . that I have now been mentioning to advance ourselves in Science, are exceedingly helpful in acquiring the one other most important Branch of Science, I mean Acquaintance with Myself."[51] The College of New Jersey was a very diverse place by eighteenth-century standards. While most colonial colleges attracted students from one or two colonies, Witherspoon recruited his classes from throughout the British-Atlantic world, creating a cosmopolitan culture unlike that at any other American institution of higher education. Philip looked forward to observing "the Conduct & Temper of the Students in this Seminary; Which is filled with Young-Men not only from almost every Province, in this Continent" but "also many from the West Indies, & some few from Europe." Philip was aware that an enlightened education such as the one he was receiving at Princeton would allow him to study the differences in his classmates' education and manners, an exercise that he found both "agreeable and profitable."[52]

He was slowly transforming himself, at least in an imagined sense, into a citizen of the world. His affections were becoming increasingly more oriented to the "generality" of humankind. His experience in college was facilitating his move from an agricultural life to that of an educated gentleman. Roughly one-third of the students who studied under Witherspoon at Princeton between 1769 and 1775 were the sons of yeoman farmers. John Vardill, a professor at Kings College (Columbia) in New York, told prospective students that if they came to Kings they would "mingle with virtuous blue bloods," but if they chose Princeton they would "suffer exposure to the lower standards of farmers' sons." Princeton graduates left their homes as plowmen and returned as professionals, although many of them, in contrast to the average graduate of other colonial colleges, did not return. More than any other place in America, Witherspoon's college embodied the spirit of self-improvement that defined the Enlightenment in America. Philip would later conclude that his stay at the college was "the most pleasant as well as the most important Period in my past life." He would triumphantly announce in a paper presented before the Whig Society, "Hail fair Nassau! Here within thy Walls Men of Genius & Learning met with due Encouragement, here the Ignorant by Care & Diligence may arrive to the summit of Knowledge, here Vice & Idleness are discountenanced; & are banished hence; here Learning & Piety & Justice & Freedom are united & rule as one." He told his father that he "had much Cause to be delighted with my Lot, I would not change my Condition, nor give up the Prospect I have before me, on any Terms almost whatever."[53]

However, as Philip basked in his newfound participation in the republic of letters, he still could not detach himself from passionate longings for his Cohansey home. The fostering of cosmopolitan affection was harder than he thought it would be. As he neared the end of his study at Princeton, Philip reflected with uncertainty about his life after college, wondering wistfully if the way of improvement he was traveling would ever lead him home. He began to feel "stronger than ever" about his "Obligations" to his family, no doubt a reference to the work required on his father's farm. He longed to "see my near Connections" in Cohansey. During this period of homesickness Philip, as he would do time and again along his way of improvement, took solace in his faith. He tried to convince himself, as Witherspoon was teaching him, that true happiness came not from a particular place, "nor is it the Presence nor Absence of Relations, & Friends, tho' most near, & tender to us, that can give us, for any length of Time, either substantial joy, or Grief." Philip instead found comfort in "the favoring Presence of our Common Father, who is the Almighty God." God alone, Philip believed, could serve his deepest human needs, especially if he had to remain removed from his beloved homeland for an extended period of time.[54] He was beginning to learn that a life of improvement often came with a measure of loss—a condition cured only by placing his trust in an omnipresent God who transcended any particular locale.

Philip's "obligations" would call him home sooner than he expected. Halfway through his senior year at Princeton, he received a troubling letter from Rev. Andrew Hunter. "I am very sorry that I have the melancholy occasion to inform you of something that will try all the religion and fortitude you have," Hunter wrote. "I need not keep you in longer suspense," he continued, "your Parents are both dead." It is unclear just what kind of illness killed Philip's parents, but they died six days apart—Hannah on February 2, 1772, and Joseph on February 8, 1772. Whatever caused their deaths, it must have been sudden, for Joseph had yet to record a will, making Philip, as the eldest son, the only person with the right to administer the estate. Hunter urged him to travel to Cohansey as soon as possible, "for all must lie as it is till you come." The letter included thirty shillings to pay for Philip's stage ride from Princeton to Greenwich.[55] Following the settlement of the estate, Hannah and Joseph's personal property was sold and the family homestead was leased, temporarily, to tenant farmers. Philip's siblings were scattered. Enoch, who was twenty-two years old and disabled, needed special care. He along with Philip's youngest brothers—Jonathan (age fourteen), Amos (age twelve), and Thomas (age four)—went to live with their Uncle Samuel. Josiah (age nineteen) was eventually apprenticed to a trade, and Rebecca (age sixteen), who appears to have taken the loss of her parents harder than the rest, spent some time living with the Bullocks, a Presbyterian family in Philadelphia. For the next year or so the Fithian children would need to put their trust in a "Providence who takes care of the Fatherless."[56] It is surprising, especially in light of his propensity to record his deepest thoughts, that Philip wrote little beyond the occasional passing reference about the death of his parents. Since he had given up journal writing during his years at Princeton, we have no idea how he reacted to this awful news.

While Philip certainly mourned both of his parents, the death of his mother, Hannah, would have been particularly difficult for him. Hannah had great affection for her oldest son and was more pleased than anyone about his decision to pursue a ministerial vocation. "I hope that the Lord hath Work for you to do in the World," she prayed, "O that he would furnish you with every necessary Grace & Qualification for his Service." With Philip away at school, she did her best to nurture affectionate relationships between the members of her family, providing Philip with news from home and urging him to write letters to his brothers and sister. Hannah also maintained a constant concern for Philip's soul—exhorting him to remain pious amid the worldly distractions of college life. "Youth is a dangerous Time," she wrote, and "it is not possible for you to know it until Experience teaches you . . . flee youthful Lusts." Hannah also feared that Philip's exposure to book learning might puff him up and jeopardize his spiritual relationship with his Savior. She urged him to recall the moment of his conversion and God's providential care for his life. "It is easy to profess Religion," she wrote to Philip at Princeton, "but it is hard to be a Christian. Without holiness no

Man Shall see the Lord. . . . Remember what the Lord hath done for you & let it humble you." Two years after her death Philip remembered Hannah while he was working as a tutor in plantation Virginia: "I . . . had a fond indulgent Mother, when I was sick, or otherwise distress'd, she was always patient til my Health & Ease returned." Hannah was ever ready with the physical and spiritual sustenance that she believed Philip needed on his road to improvement. She knew her son well, and he would miss her dearly. His final letter to her, written a month before her death, expressed sentiments that foreshadowed what was to come. Philip prayed in the letter that God would "give us all Repentance unto Life, that [as] Parents, & Children, we may be all translated to Christ's heavenly Kingdom."[57]

The loss of his parents meant that Philip was now one more step removed from the agrarian world of his childhood. Someone would need to care for his younger siblings, a reality that no doubt made Philip wonder if a sovereign God was using his parent's death to lead him back to Cohansey. Perhaps his vocational choice had already been made for him. Philip did, however, find a way to get back to Princeton. He finished the academic year and graduated in September 1772. After graduation he had the option of staying in Princeton to continue ministerial studies with Witherspoon at no cost, but his obligations were calling him home. As we will see in the following chapter, Philip spent the next year in Cohansey, caring for his family and living with Enoch Green in Deerfield, where he would begin preparation for the Presbyterian ministerial licensing exam. During these dark days Philip learned that death and ambition have little in common. He realized that mourning always awakens one to the fact that life has its limits. We will never know how the course of his career may have changed if his parents had lived longer, but it is safe to say that things would have been different along Philip's way of improvement.

Philip spent much of his final year at Princeton developing a friendship with Elizabeth "Betsy" Beatty. He had met her in the spring of 1770 when she came to Deerfield to attend her sister Mary's wedding to Enoch Green. As a student at Green's academy and a young man who was not shy around the ladies, Philip managed to spend some time with Betsy during her one-month stay. She was the daughter of Charles Beatty, the minister of the Presbyterian church of Neshaminy, Pennsylvania, and one of the colonies' most respected clergymen. Charles was quite familiar with the Presbyterians of Cohansey. He knew personally several of the region's ministers (he would preach William Ramsey's ordination sermon at Fairfield in 1757) and had sent two of his sons, Charles and Reading, to study at Green's academy. Betsy was a member of one of the first families of early American Presbyterianism. Philip's pursuit of her reveals both how far he had come on his path of self-improvement and how confident he was in that reality.

Like most young men, Philip had a definite interest in courtship and marriage. He did not miss the opportunity to comment in his journal or in letters to friends on the company he kept with the Presbyterian women of Cohansey. Many of the women were regular participants in the group of young writers and moralists who surrounded Green's academy. Philip frequently shared his thoughts on friendship with his female acquaintances and initiated correspondence with girls he hoped to court. On one occasion, while he was a student at Deerfield, he was pursued by two women at the same time.[58] The opposite sex was a popular topic in Philip's correspondence with male friends. When George Green noted that he saw "pretty young Ladies at Deerfield" during a visit, Philip reminded him that "there were several more in Greenwich." (Green looked forward with great anticipation to his next trip to Cohansey.) As he studied law in New Castle, Delaware, Samuel Leake envisioned walking home with Philip after a day of study discussing "amours and ladies." Oliver Reese, his Princeton classmate, informed Philip of his regimen of postgraduate study for the ministry: "I study divinity one hour and think of the ladies the next." Philip described the women of Deerfield as "skilled in all the Niceties of domestic life" and active members in the exchange of news and gossip. The coterie of young females who surrounded Green Hall were the "Oracles of New Jersey." He praised them for their ability to "fully understand" and "easily explain" the "dark, knotty inexplicable Doctrines of Divinity." They possessed "extensive knowledge in the Affairs of the Neighbors" and carried on correspondence with "Connections" up to "ten or Fifteen Miles in every way."[59] In other words, they were clearly members of this rural manifestation of the republic of letters. Until he met Betsy, this was the community of women in which Philip envisioned himself finding a wife.

Betsy was a new face in Deerfield. She would eventually become a transient member of this circle of female friends, but the fact that she was an outsider made her especially enchanting to the single men of Cohansey. Philip had spent enough time with Betsy while she was in Deerfield to begin a friendly correspondence with her. In his first letter, written shortly after she returned to Neshaminy following her sister's wedding, Philip wrote, "You can scarcely conceive . . . how melancholy, Spiritless, & forsaken you left Several when you left Deerfield! A sullen of Disagreeable Silence Succeeded the Conversation and Songs which your Presence excited. Every Countenance discovered a flattering, doubtful, bewildered Mind." Philip hoped for a prominent place "in this gloomy Row of the disappointed." He told Betsy, in a flurry of

metaphorical language that would characterize all of his correspondence with her, that since she had departed Deerfield he could not
"walk nor read, nor talk, nor ride, nor sleep, nor live, with any Stom-
ach!" The "transient golden Minutes" that they had spent together, he
added, "only fully persuaded me how much real Happiness may be had
in your Society." Philip was smitten.[60]

Betsy did not reply to this letter, and much of Philip's initial passion
for her society waned temporarily as he headed off to college. However,
while at Princeton he had more than one opportunity to see her again.
He joined fellow classmates on weekend excursions into the country to
visit Charles Beatty's church at Neshaminy (about thirty miles from
Princeton), and it was during these visits that he made his first serious
attempts to court Betsy. Though Philip and Betsy would spend much
time together over the course of the next several years, the establishment of a correspondence was equally important to the development of
their relationship. Betsy had given Philip permission to write to her, a
clear sign that she approved of his desire to move the friendship forward. As the foremost historian of courtship in America has written, "letters are more than the artifacts of a relationship; in many cases, they
were, for a time, the relationship itself."[61] Philip often wrote to Betsy following a face-to-face meeting in order to express the sentiments that he
had experienced during the course of their conversations. By February
1772 he was signing his letters with the name "Philander" ("loving
Friend"), an obvious indicator of his affection for his new correspondent. A significant portion of Philip and Betsy's courtship was conducted through letters, but the exchange of sentiments usually flowed
in only one direction. Betsy almost never responded to Philip's letters.
Her failure to do so is difficult to explain. Perhaps Betsy did not like to
write. Perhaps she preferred more intimate encounters or feared the
lack of privacy inherent in letter writing. Or perhaps she was unsure of
her suitor's intentions and did not want to encourage him with a reply.
Her failure to correspond is not unusual by eighteenth-century standards. Philip may have fretted when he did not receive a return letter
from Betsy, but women generally did not write as much as men, especially when it came to love and courtship letters.[62]

By summer 1772 Philip's visits to Neshaminy to see Betsy became
more frequent and his letters to her became more sentimental. He now
began to address Betsy as "Laura" (a probable reference to Petrarch's
devotion to Laura), a name of affection that he would use for the rest of
his life. He was bothered by the fact that Betsy never returned any of his
letters (he thought about not writing to her until she responded), and
yet, at least in Philip's mind, their relationship was growing. He now felt
comfortable sharing the daydreams that distracted him from his studies

at Princeton: "I lead you by the Hand in a cool bright Evening, & once more, in that lovely garden oh! in that pleasant, pleasant Garden, hold Conversation in Rapture with you!"[63]

One of the many turning points in their relationship occurred follow-ing the death of Betsy's father in September 1772. Charles Beatty had died prematurely during a fund-raising visit to Barbados on behalf of the College of New Jersey. Philip expressed benevolence and love to Betsy during her time of grief. His sympathy for her was genuine. Philip had lost his parents seven months earlier, and now Betsy's mourning "excited in my Heart a fresh & feeling sense of the same Pain, which had not yet Subsided, when on a sudden it was renewed & increased by Sympathy with you." Using Calvinist language that would have been con-soling to the daughter of a Presbyterian minister, Philip tried to comfort Betsy: "It hath pleasured Heaven, whose work we ought to view & rever-ence, to make you & I & our Families orphans! The ways of Providence are indeed mysterious & the Design is to us unknown." He connected on a deep level with Betsy during this season of sorrow. Her mother had died in 1768 when she was a teenager, and now she, like Philip, was with-out parents. This shared experience, understood in the context of a Calvinist God who controls life and death, brought the couple closer to-gether.[64] Ten days later, while she visited Philip at his Princeton gradua-tion, Betsy gave him, in his words, "an expressive & visible Token, or Pledge, of . . . real Friendship."[65] Though the nature of this pledge is unclear, Philip was pleased by it.

A great deal changed in Philip's life between 1767 and 1772. He broke with the yeoman tradition of his family. He graduated from col-lege. He lost his parents, the most important anchors of his agrarian childhood. He fell in love. As the British colonies began to contemplate independence from England, Philip was experiencing personal changes that, to him, were just as revolutionary. He lived in an era when patriots were willing to risk everything, including their very lives, to do just what he appears to have done—transcend the parochialism of colonial life and replace it with a progressive vision of the good life tied to self-improvement. His way of improvement would one day be described as the pursuit of the American dream, but for now it reflected best the modern impulse of the Enlightenment in British America. Viewed from the twenty-first century, Philip's life path looks quite normal. However, from the perspective of those who lived through this transformation, the choices were hard, if not excruciating, to make. As Philip would soon realize, American ambition had its price.

Chapter 4

Rural Enlightenment

On September 30, 1772, Philip Vickers Fithian became a member of Princeton's twenty-fifth graduating class. He could now count himself among a privileged group of men who had received degrees from colonial colleges. Commencement was indeed a gala event at Nassau Hall, attended by "Persons of Rank and Fortune, from almost all provinces of the Continent." John Witherspoon began the festivities with prayer at 10:00 A.M., and the program, which included a break for dinner, was not completed until the late afternoon. Philip was one of thirteen orators (chosen from a class of twenty-four) at a ceremony dominated by student speeches related to the imperial crisis with England. He participated in a disputation (with Isaac Alexander, a fellow student from North Carolina) that required him to support the thesis "Political Jealousy is a Laudable Passion."[1] It must have been a day of mixed emotions. Philip had acquired that which he most desired in his life—a formal education. However, Joseph and Hannah, the parents who had supported him financially and spiritually during his two years away from home, were not alive to celebrate with him.

After graduation Philip went home. He planned to study for a postgraduate degree and prepare for his ministerial licensing exam. He would live with the Peck family in Deerfield and pursue his studies under the direction of Enoch Green. It must have been strange to return to his homeland without the demands of farmwork beckoning him on a daily basis or the pious exhortations of his mother reminding him of what mattered most. Though Uncle Samuel and Rev. Andrew Hunter were there, Philip was now responsible for the future of his younger siblings. His world had changed dramatically since he had left for college, but so had he. A liberal education had transformed him into someone different from most of his neighbors. He had entered a social rank inhabited only by the region's ministers and a small handful of professionals, mostly doctors and lawyers. Philip needed time to reconnect with his homeland and redefine his place within it. He needed to ponder his vocation and consider, among friends, family, and the quiet of the countryside, where the next steps on his way of improvement might lead. He wanted to reconcile the cosmopolitanism of the republic of letters that he had imbibed at Princeton with the local attachments of his Cohansey home. Philip spent the succeeding year living the Enlightenment in the context of everyday rural life in the British colonial countryside.

Philip's decision to return to Cohansey raised some eyebrows among his more urban-dwelling college friends and other refined acquaintances. College of New Jersey graduates seldom went home, and when they did, they did not stay long. Several of his classmates chose to stay at Princeton after graduation to study divinity with John Witherspoon. Philip opted to continue his studies with Green in Deerfield. In the months following graduation he also turned down teaching offers at grammar schools in Philadelphia and Maryland. Why would he go back to remote Cohansey when the world of the educated gentleman awaited him? Cohansey did not have the cosmopolitan sophistication of Philadelphia or the academic vibrancy of Princeton. On one level, his choice was an obvious one. Following the death of his parents he needed to care for his younger siblings. Philip, at least at this stage of his life, was not willing to pursue the life of a world citizen when there were such pressing responsibilities at home. However, before we assume that his return home was a step backward on his way of improvement, it is worth noting that Cohansey possessed the kind of environment that Philip believed was conducive to self-development. His training in classical literature reminded him that a pastoral existence provided the best opportunities for reflection.[2] The countryside, Philip believed, was inherently good, a locale where true happiness could be found. Enlightenment historians always connected the fall of Rome to the decrepit moral conditions of urban life. The farmer was the source of Roman virtue, and the countryside was the best place to avoid the temptations of the world. Deerfield certainly fit the bill in this regard. Philip could study without the distractions of the city. Charles Clinton Beatty, a student at Green's academy in 1773, described Deerfield as "void of news or strange things as a Tree is in Winter time of leaves."[3] Philip believed that potential citizens of the world would, ironically, benefit from starting their intellectual journeys in a rural place removed from the centers of cosmopolitan life. He began occasionally to write poems on the advantages of the countryside and recorded thoughts on his reading of Horace, Ovid, and Virgil, Latin authors known for the celebration of their rural surroundings.

Philip's familiarity with the pastoral tradition was evident in a letter he received from his friend Samuel Leake, who had left the confines of Green Hall to continue his studies in New Castle, Delaware. Leake informed Philip that the people of New Castle were "generally affable and polite," but "the generality have not so good, sound, true, doctrine and knowledge of religion and morality as the people in the country." Leake, who would also graduate from Princeton, described his new life as filled with "much noise, bustle, and many diverting objects, all which greatly prevent close application to studies." He preferred "Latin schools" set in the country, where "Houses are private retirements, the orchards, and coppices abound for meditation, and the fields suitable for exercise and healthy walks while every surrounding object will not tend to draw off the mind, but a fruitful subject for thought; and all this without any allurement to profanity, or extravagance, wheretofore school and country together unite to render the scholar sober, frugal, pious, learned, and wholly absorbed in thought." Leake concluded his letter with a qualification: "Do not think that I dislike the town, for I do not. I am pleased with the town, and the company of the people; but I only offer my sentiments respecting which of the places are most suitable for the education of youth."[4]

As Philip tried to live in a manner informed by this pastoral ideal, he would on more than one occasion face cosmopolitan temptations. He often felt a bit isolated in Cohansey. In a letter to Benjamin Armitage, a friend from Philadelphia, Philip expressed just a touch of envy: "you are favour'd with furnishing out a letter with new, agreeable, & strange things, when I am here in the rude, the delightsome country & prisoned up the greater part of my time in a little silent, warm chamber."[5] He was conflicted—the country was both "delightsome" and a place to be "prisoned up." Yet, he continued to defend country life to correspondents who seemed playfully to disparage his decision to return to Cohansey. The language of rural virtue would serve him well toward these ends. For example, he asked his urban friends to visit him so that they might enjoy the "course pleasures of the country." He filled his letters with descriptions of Cohansey. Philip told Laura Armitage, Benjamin's sister, that he was indeed "happy" in this corner of southwestern New Jersey despite the region's distance "from the splendid town." A few weeks later he made his location clear to Laura and Polly Bullock, friends from Philadelphia: "I write from the country Ladies; where the evening dews & sunny days & autumnal flowers and falling leaves, & busy farmers, & sprightly girls & lovesick Swains, where Plenty & Pleasure & Health making a consistent variety, keep over Bodies & minds in a successive enjoyment of something new & pleasing." He added that "the country wears a new robe & more lovely dress since commencement, to me it surely breathes a purer Air, everything looks cozy, unconcerned & cheerful." Philip sent off a quick retort to his friend Amanda after she complained with dread about a trip from the "delightful city" to the "howling wilderness." Didn't Amanda realize,

Philip queried, that her rural upbringing made her far "superior" to her urban neighbors?[6]

Philip had always loved Cohansey and had been attuned to its "charms" from the time he was a child, but his education now led him to perceive his home differently. He no longer wrote about the rigorous farmwork of his youth. Cohansey was now a place of rural simplicity. He painted a rosy picture of the countryside in these letters, a portrait befitting the Roman pastoralist who romanticized a rural life without ever experiencing it. Philip was now an aspiring gentleman with little time or inclination to engage in the daily work of the farmer. (This transition, of course, was made much easier by the fact that after his parents' death he did not have a family farm on which to work.) He reinvented the country to conform to the new social rank that his education had secured for him. It ceased, in his mind, to be a place of production and became, as Donna Landry has described it, a place of "consumption and pleasure, recreation and retreat."[7] When Philip did mention the region's "busy farmers," they were lumped together with other romantic images of rural life, including "lovesick Swains" and "sprightly girls."[8] Philip knew better than to romanticize the country in this way. He was fully aware that the life of a Cohansey grain grower required tedious labor. He did not write about the country as a leisured outside observer who had never poured his sweat into its cultivation. Yet, he does seem to have created in his own mind, with the help of his training in the pastoral literature of the ancients, a new Cohansey that could serve as a place of learning and improvement—a local manifestation of the republic of letters. In the end, his reinvention of the countryside did little to change his affection for his homeland. He still loved Cohansey and its people. The pastoral images he now called on aided him in his attempt to reconcile his attachment to this place with his cosmopolitan education and the aspiration that stemmed from it.

This transformation was clearly evident during the 1773 harvest season, Philip's first since his return to Cohansey. What role would he play in this important agricultural season, a time when most able-bodied males were called on to reap? Clergy rarely performed physical labor. As gentlemen, they could afford to hire reapers to take in their harvests for them. Agricultural work took time away from preparing sermons and meeting the spiritual needs of the community. Philip, however, was not a minister yet. His identity was still unclear. He was listed as a "yeoman" on his father's 1772 probate inventory, and as a son of Cohansey, he undoubtedly felt uncomfortable being indoors studying while the rest of the community was in the field. Yet, as an educated young man pursuing a path of self-improvement, he had his own intellectual work to do. As a result, he would never participate in this rural ritual to the degree that he once did. When Philip planned to spend a harvest morning in study, he was called away from his books: "Began this Morning to study; but at the strong Request of my Landlord, & the Family, I was prevailed with to stay & provide Water, Rum, etc. . . . for the Reapers. Reapt also a little myself." On another day during the harvest Philip wrote, "My landlord is reaping. After Breakfast I went out with the Reapers. Bound up some Sheaves, provided them with Drink & reaped a little . . . I rode among the people to secure Reapers for him (Mr. Peck) on Monday next & was so successful as to provide five good reapers for him & two for Mr. Green." Though Philip did spend some time reaping during the summer of 1773, his assignment had changed. His harvest labor was no longer as difficult as it had been during his adolescence on his father's farm in Greenwich. His primary job was now that of serving drinks and recruiting reapers.[9]

Without responsibilities in the grain field, Philip could indeed live the kind of contemplative life afforded to those who resided in the country. He spent a great deal of his time in Deerfield undertaking a voracious schedule of reading. If he learned anything while he was a student at Princeton, it was that liberally educated gentlemen were not bound by a college curriculum. Following graduation his way of improvement would be conducted outside of a formal educational setting. In this regard, books were one of the most effective means of maintaining his membership in the republic of letters from his location in southwestern New Jersey.

In the months after the death of his mother and father, there were many hours when Philip "looked over, sorted, and adjusted" his personal library. Like most early American Presbyterians, Philip read to enhance personal piety. Each morning he studied a chapter from the Greek New Testament (his focus during much of this year was on the Acts of the Apostles), and he meditated on its principles throughout the day. Such a practice was at the heart of evangelical spirituality. It also enabled him to sharpen his knowledge of Greek in preparation for his ministerial licensing exam. Philip supplemented his devotional reading with biblical commentaries. One of his personal favorites was Philip Doddridge's *The Family Expositor or a Paraphrase and Version of the New Testament.* Doddridge was extremely popular among British American evangelicals. His *Rise and Progress of Religion in the Soul,* published in 1744 (and reprinted in America in 1745), was one of the best-selling books in the colonies. Doddridge strove to foster an evangelical faith rooted in a careful balance of religious affection and academic credibility. Such an approach to Christianity would have been appealing to Philip as he sought to nourish a Presbyterian faith, befitting of his academic training with Green and Witherspoon, that was both intellectually sound and warmly pious. "Dr. Doddridge's Paraphrase," as Philip called it, was the eighteenth-century equivalent of a modern study Bible. It included an English translation of the New Testament supplemented by the editor's "critical notes" on the text. Doddridge's goal was to provide a Bible that could be used for family devotions and personal study. His *Paraphrase* was lighter, but no less essential, spiritual fare for Philip.[10]

Since Doddridge catered to the heart rather than the head, the *Paraphrase* served as a nice balance to Philip's theological reading in Benedict Pictet's *Christian Theology* and Thomas Ridgeley's *Body of Divinity*. Pictet was a seventeenth-century Genevan theologian. He wrote *Christian Theology* in order to present Calvinist doctrine in a plain and familiar style that would be accessible to students and laypersons. The book became a standard text of Reformed orthodoxy among British American Presbyterians. Though published in Latin, *Christian Theology* was void of lengthy commentaries on the theological controversies of the day. It instead presented Reformed thinking on doctrinal topics such as God, man, salvation, Christ, calling, justification and sanctification, the church, and the sacraments in a straightforward and readable manner. Philip purchased his copy of *Christian Theology* from Rev. Andrew Hunter and read it consistently throughout the summer of 1773 in preparation for his licensing exam.[11] *Body of Divinity*, the eighteenth-century work of the English Calvinist Thomas Ridgeley, was a much weightier and intellectually sophisticated tome. It was a one-thousand-page extended commentary on the Westminster Larger Catechism, the Presbyterian confession of faith. Philip used Ridgeley's text as a "system" to organize his theological convictions.[12]

As we have seen, large portions of Philip's reading fell within the field he labeled the "ancients." Horace, Longinus, Virgil, and Ovid supplemented Homer's *Iliad* and Lucian's *Selected Dialogues* on his reading list. For the circle of students and alumni of the College of New Jersey, knowledge of the ancients became an important part of the curriculum of self-improvement. In addition to discussions of pastoral themes, Greek and Roman literature provided models of public spirit and disinterestedness, attributes that John Witherspoon believed were essential to the political development of a new nation. The ancient writers were the earliest formulators of free government and thus worthy of example and imitation. Study of these authors, especially in their original languages, would force students throughout the colonies to grasp the ancient understanding of such concepts as virtue, civil society, republicanism, and duty. Though Witherspoon taught his students to read the classics with caution due to their pagan character, they were still sources of useful knowledge for Christian scholars. An ability to quote from ancient literature was a sign of a truly educated gentleman. Knowledge of the classics was a distinguishing characteristic of all who held membership in the republic of letters.[13]

Philip also continued to keep abreast of modern, contemporary, and popular literature. He occasionally quoted from Benjamin Franklin's *Poor Richard's Almanac* and was familiar with a host of popular novels. He owned eight volumes of Joseph Addison and Richard Steele's *Spectator* and read them almost as regularly as he read his Greek New Testament. His habit was to study a chapter in the New Testament in the morning and the *Spectator*, "in my Course," in the evening.[14] Philip read the *Spectator* in precisely the way in which Addison and Steele intended it to be read. It was meant "to be punctually served up" as an essential part of the "Tea Equipage" of "well-regulated" and educated families. Set in the British coffeehouse culture of the eighteenth century, part of the Anglo-American world's burgeoning public sphere, the *Spectator* provided an ongoing conversation on politeness, refinement, good sense, improvement, and civility. It championed moderation as the key to a decent society, condemning both the enthusiasm that stemmed from uncontrolled passions and the stoicism that resulted from too great a reliance on reason. It was a devotional in manners that one read as a means of moral improvement, and it promoted a lifestyle appropriate to an enlightened society.[15]

Philip's Cohansey reading list also had a certain cosmopolitan emphasis. He read extensively, for example, in the *Universal History*, a multiauthored chronicle of Western civilization. As Ned Landsman has argued, eighteenth-century histories such as the *Universal History* exposed readers to "far-distant places, especially those to which they were connected by empire and trade."[16] Such works were equivalent, in many respects, to travel literature. They allowed readers to expand their imaginations and transcend mentally their parochial surroundings. The *Spectator* offered similar models of the cosmopolitan life. Addison, in *Spectator* number 69, described his experience visiting England's Royal Exchange, where he witnessed the representatives of several nations all engaged together in trade. He rejoiced that he could observe such human diversity in isolation without being recognized by the strangers. "As I am a great Lover of Mankind," Addison wrote, "my Heart naturally overflows with Pleasure at the sight of a prosperous and happy Multitude . . . the Natives of several Parts of the Globe might have a kind of Dependence upon one another, and be united together by their common Interest." In the marketplace all had abandoned their particular national or ethnic identities, and Addison could thus "fancy" himself, like the "philosophers of old," as a "Citizen of the World."[17] Though Philip had never encountered the kind of London cosmopolitanism described by

Addison, he could still, as he read, engage the republic of letters with a sense of unlimited ambition. "Perhaps my Mind, contracted & fluttering, as it appears to be," he wrote in 1775, "will expand & show out a Capacity ample, & important, as Locke's, or Newton's, or Witherspoon's."[18]

As Philip studied, he continued to pursue his relationship with Elizabeth Beatty. Things seemed to be going well between them. Betsy was beginning to warm to Philip's advances, and their friendship appears to have reached new heights. She continued to make regular trips to Deerfield to visit her sister, and Philip embarked on the occasional visit to Princeton to see friends. They would thus have a good chance of spending the time together that was necessary to sustain a courtship. However, somewhere along the way things went terribly wrong. Philip misread Betsy's September 1772 pledge of friendship following the death of her father as something much deeper than it was apparently intended. In the months after his college graduation, he began to come on strong—a bit too strong for Betsy. His letters were now full of romantic gestures and flowery disclosures of his sentiments. In December, while visiting Princeton, Philip proposed marriage (Betsy was in Deerfield at the time) in a passion-filled letter that he would later describe as a "wild and incoherent epistle":

I know not how, in the present State of my Mind, to address myself to you in such a manner as will be decent & proper for one, & at the same time, acceptable to you: But there remains no Medium: I cannot refrain, & I may not disguise the Feeling of my Heart; You are the Person_____. The amiable Objects, on which, after a perfect Acquaintance, I have so far placed my Esteem, that I cannot easily avoid making Proposals to you, for a nearer Alliance. . . . Can you hear me tell you this? . . . Can you be comfortable & Satisfied in his Society who is always uneasy in your Absence? . . . Can you listen to my ardent Wish, & when it Seems to be in your Power, allow me the Expectation of arriving at my Standard of Contentment & Felicity here below? Can you consent as you are entering, young & unexperienced, upon the thorny dangerous Paths of Life, to accept of One for Company in the Way, who is your truest Friend?

Philip told Betsy that he would be back in Deerfield the following day and that it was his intention to "wait on you with these sentiments, tomorrow afternoon at three o'clock." In the meantime he encouraged her to "consult with your own Heart" so that they could "debate the matter together" over what Philip planned to be a three-hour conversation. By six o'clock that evening, after their conference together, he would ask her for "a full and conclusive Answer" to his proposal.[19]

Philip was making demands, but he knew that he was vulnerable. The power in this relationship belonged to Betsy, as it had throughout much of their courtship.[20] We do not know the details of what happened on

December 3, 1772, between three and six o'clock, but the Deerfield meeting did not go well for Philip. Betsy rejected his proposal. Twelve days later Philip sounded like a man who had been scorned. He sent Betsy a long poem entitled "To Laura: An Epistle," in which he asked, "Why does my Heart these raging Tortures feel / Whose Force I cannot from the World conceal?" Betsy's refusal of his proposal was clear from another stanza: "for Laura quite unfeeling hears / My tenderest Vows & disapproves my Fears / At least, I fear, She's careless & at Rest / While Love of Friendship glows within my Breast." Philip was left to ponder the status of their relationship, if indeed any relationship still existed. He ended his poetic epistle by expressing his continued love for Betsy: "In one great Wish, that Laura may be mine / And I dear Laura, may be only Thine / Then would these Tumults in my Bosom cease / Calm'd by your fullest Friendship into Peace."[21]

Philip's letters during December 1772 shed a flicker of light on why Betsy decided not to accept his offer of marriage. She confided to a friend her reasons for turning down the proposal, but she did not realize that this unidentified person to whom she confided was also one of Philip's close companions. By the end of the month the gossip mill was churning in the small world of Cohansey, and Philip thought he now understood the reason for Betsy's decision. When he was sure of this intelligence, he penned a letter expressing his sorrow that she had "cruelly communicated that to another which I should have hoped from your Friendship you would have first of all made known to me." According to what Philip had heard, Betsy did not take his proposal seriously because she was wary of his reputation for gallantry, an eighteenth-century social practice that could be employed by young men as a form of seduction. The gallant used all his persuasive charms to win the affections of the "weaker" sex. Then, once his conquest was complete, he left her in order to ply his craft on another unsuspecting victim. In this case Betsy had heard a rumor that she was not the first or only woman to whom Philip had proposed marriage. We cannot be sure if this accusation was true, but in Philip's defense, there is no evidence of a marriage proposal to another woman in any of his extant writings. He seems to have been justified when he wrote to defend himself and his reputation. On the other hand, Philip was no stranger to the company of young Presbyterian ladies. He had been accused of gallantry before and would be accused of it again. Yet, he insisted that his proposal to Betsy "was the first & only one, of the like Nature, that I ever made." Somewhere along the way Betsy had received some false information. However, Philip's propensity to write her passion-filled letters that at times were unfitting for a Presbyterian gentleman did not help his cause.[22]

Philip was embarrassed by all that transpired during December 1772. He wrote one more letter to Betsy before she "debar[red] him from the liberty of corresponding" with her. Philip wanted Betsy to know she was "dismissing from . . . [her] Intimacy as faithful a Friend as you have below the Skies!" Though Betsy's refusal had put Philip "in a momentary and transient Flutter," he would not grieve, for "When Laura is gratified; I am wholly at Ease." He realized, however, that the time was right to formally end their relationship. He closed the letter by announcing his intention to "renounce, abjure & annul every Tie, Band, Engagement, or Penalty" between them.[23] Though friends from Princeton wrote to raise his "drooping spirits" during this sorrowful time, it was generally not a good Christmas for Philip Vickers Fithian.[24] He had learned a valuable lesson from his courtship with Betsy. He had been too sentimental and had not behaved like a Presbyterian gentleman. His particular affections were too strong and highly irrational. He would later see the error of his ways and would apologize profusely to Betsy for his "romantic and foolish flights." He asked her to "destroy" some of his letters written in 1772 by sending them "to Oblivion in Flames." He claimed to "blush and condemn myself" after examining what he had written.[25] If Philip were to continue on his way of improvement, he would need to work harder at holding his passions in check and expressing his sentiments in a more rational manner. He now knew firsthand the dangers that untempered emotional attachment posed for the educated gentleman. Philip would get another chance to prove himself with Betsy, but for now their relationship had stalled, with little hope, at least from his perspective, of ever restarting again.

Philip did his best to forget about Betsy by investing himself in the lives of his friends. While Joseph Addison of *Spectator* fame relished in the state of his cosmopolitan loneliness as he observed the international gathering of traders at London's Royal Exchange, Philip took comfort in the fact that everyone in Cohansey knew his name and friends were everywhere. He spent so much time visiting during the summer of 1773 that it is easy to imagine his local jaunts through the neighborhood as the primary generator of the social gravity needed to hold the Cohansey Presbyterian community in place. Philip's habit of visiting was one means by which he tried to bring Cohansey and the republic of letters together in creative ways. He was aware that his rational cosmopolitanism and passion for local attachments were often at odds. How might he live the life of an educated gentleman and still maintain his affections for home? As his postgraduate year in Cohansey reveals, Philip believed that such reconciliation was possible. The life of self-improvement did not need to be lived separately from the life of rural community. Philip's

Cohansey was not only a quiet place that afforded him time in isolation with his books; it was also a site of sociability. When Philip visited with his friends and acquaintances he was in essence participating in his own moral improvement and the larger betterment of society.

Philip's visiting patterns and personal relationships reflected the most recent trends in British ethics. As we have seen, the New Moral Philosophy made the connections between sociability and virtue an important theme of inquiry. By the late eighteenth century Presbyterians, especially the circle affiliated with the College of New Jersey, had espoused a system of religion and morals that mingled evangelical faith with Enlightenment beliefs about progress and an orderly society. Drawing from the best British moral philosophy available to them, Presbyterians taught that there was a direct correlation between the way people treated one another in their personal lives and the general improvement of the world around them. Virtue was possible, they believed, *without* a personal encounter with God through conversion; and if one could indeed perform virtuous acts without the special help of God, it followed logically that all human beings—the converted and the unconverted—were responsible for the betterment of society. It was the universality of the moral sense and its status as a natural source of virtue independent of divine grace that entwined this ethical approach with the values of the Enlightenment.

Francis Hutcheson, the Glasgow professor who most deeply influenced the moral thought of John Witherspoon at Princeton, believed that the conscience was cultivated through conversation, friendship, and family life—the stuff of community. For Hutcheson, writes Susan Purviance, sociability could lead to moral improvement "whether the matters at hand are weighty or frivolous, or whether the subject is current events, the arts or local gossip." Hutcheson went so far as to argue that the moral sense was not "objective" in its nature but that correct ethical decisions were validated within communities of like-minded friends. Though Witherspoon often used the term "conscience" to describe the moral sense and placed more emphasis on the rational than the affective dimensions of that faculty, he too stressed the need for sociability to train and nurture the conscience.[26]

The ethical system of moral philosophers such as Hutcheson or Witherspoon was thus useless unless applied in a particular community. Witherspoon's suggestion that local passions—such as the love of friends, family, and place—were always inferior to a universal love of humankind sounded great in theory, but any general affection for humanity required an intimacy that came only from face-to-face encounters with actual people inhabiting real places. Christians were to love all human beings because they were God's highest order of creation

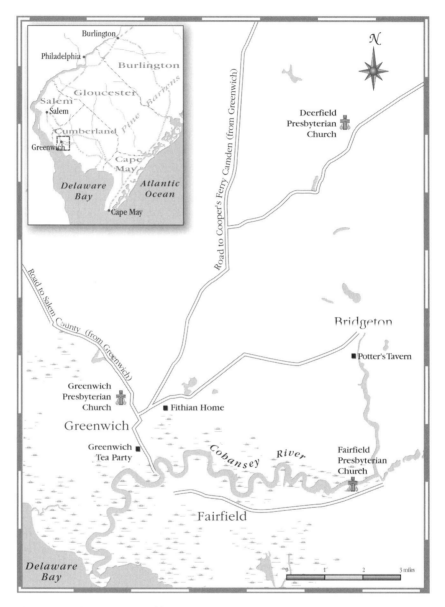

Figure 5. Cohansey, circa 1776.

and shared his image, but the fulfillment of the Golden Rule required the presence of particular neighbors to love. Just as one could not satisfy the ethical demands of Christianity without serving others, one could not practice the social values of the British Enlightenment without a connection to a place or community concerned with the pursuit of mutual and moral improvement. Through his visiting patterns Philip satisfied, simultaneously, the requirements of both moral systems. The eighteenth-century world would improve one neighborhood at a time. Moreover, the universal nature of this moral Enlightenment meant that it could be practiced anywhere. It was not solely the domain of the elite circles of gentlemen who frequented the coffeehouses of London, the salons of Paris, or the juntos of Philadelphia. Philip could return home to his beloved Cohansey and not miss a step on his way of improvement.

Philip's feet wore a well-beaten path through Cohansey during the spring and summer of 1773. He made the ten-mile walk from Deerfield to Greenwich in order to spend time with his family and friends. He occasionally stayed with his siblings at his Uncle Samuel's house in Greenwich. He also bedded with the Ewings, whose patriarch, Maskell Ewing, entertained Philip with readings of "the much talked of Comedy call'd 'the Mistakes of a Night.'" When he was not spending the night in Greenwich, Philip often returned to Deerfield well after dark. He made a habit on his arrival of drinking tea with the Pecks before retiring in preparation for another day of study. Occasions for sociability abounded during the rest of the summer and into the autumn. There were expeditions into the woods to gather huckleberries; rural curiosities to observe, such as the slaughter of a one-thousand-pound ox on a neighboring farm; and evening chats with friends.

While dining with the Pecks at Deerfield one afternoon, the "Oracles of New Jersey" (Philip's name for the women of Deerfield) shared what they had heard about Philip's behavior during his most recent journey to Princeton. Philip, they said, had "figured the Beau—Affected the Behavior of a Rake" and "Gallanted the Ladies." (Perhaps Elizabeth Beatty's perception of his behavior was correct after all.) In September, Philip joined several friends in a midnight serenade of select houses in Greenwich. Since this was something "entirely new" for the village, Philip felt it was necessary to spend the day after the serenade soliciting local reviews of the performance: "I walked over into Town, after our serenade, as Poets, & other Authors do in London [when they] visit Coffee Houses, to know if our Performance is damn'd or applauded by the Inhabitants."[27] Greenwich was a long way from London, but Philip did his best to transport the metropolis's culture of criticism and conversation to his humble Cohansey surroundings.

As the date of the first part of his licensing exam drew near, Philip paid regular visits to Rev. Andrew Hunter in Greenwich for last-minute advice and counsel. Hunter believed that Philip was prepared for the exam and urged him to present himself before the presbytery when they met in Cohansey at the end of July to install the Reverend William Hollingshead, a recent graduate of the College of Philadelphia, at the Fairfield church. (William Ramsey died suddenly in 1772.) Philip and Hollingshead spent long hours together walking the mosquito-infested fields and woods of the Fairfield parsonage discussing life in Philadelphia and the requirements for Presbyterian licensing. After much consideration, Philip took Hunter's advice and declared himself a candidate for the Presbyterian ministry. Since there were only four ministers present at the July 28 gathering of the presbytery—a low attendance record not uncommon for such meetings when held in the Jersey countryside—his initial examination was postponed until November. In preparation for that meeting he was asked to compose a sermon on the "Nature of Regeneration" and an exegetical study "that shall prove by plain & full Arguments that the Torments of the Damned will be Eternal."[28]

Some of Philip's visits with Cohansey friends were more purposefully designed as exercises in self-improvement. Though news and ideas traveled slowly into the southwestern New Jersey countryside, some of the most recent popular literature found its way into Philip's hands. Presbyterians read novels with a certain degree of caution, but when consumed carefully, within a larger community of familiar readers, such literature could be used to cultivate virtue. During the summer of 1773 Francis Brooke's epistolary novel, *The History of Lady Julia Mandeville*, was a topic for useful conversation among a group of Philip's Cohansey friends. *Lady Julia*, published first in London in 1763 and republished in Philadelphia three years later, was a collection of fictional letters exchanged among innocent young Julia; her lover, Henry Mandeville; and Lady Anne Wilmot, a coquettish and witty acquaintance of the two lovers. The novel was sentimental in nature and offered insight into matters of sensibility and refinement in the eighteenth-century Anglo-American world. Like many sentimental writers of the era, Brooke used the novel as a form of social commentary. For example, Julia read the popular courtesy books of her era that stressed modesty, chastity, concern for one's reputation, and other virtues. The novel ended with a duel between Henry and Lord Melvin, an aristocratic friend of Julia's family who was to marry the heroine. Henry was fatally wounded in the duel, providing Brooke with the perfect outlet to condemn this "savage" practice. In light of his recent experience with Elizabeth Beatty, Philip may have also been attracted to the novel's representation of Julia and Henry's courtship.[29]

On an evening near the end of the Cohansey harvest season, while some young people were gathered together "talking carelessly, as usual upon various Subjects," one participant in the conversation, who was sitting nearby reading *Lady Julia*, asked the group (who apparently had also read the work) whether they felt the novel was "well-written & entertaining." A member of the group replied that the book was "in his Opinion ... Well Written, highly entertaining, & best calculated for the refreshing & improving our Behaviour, of any Novel now extant." A female participant in the conversation, whom Philip described as a "proposed wit," offered a different perspective. She told "the young Fellow that there were only two or three Select Letters in the Whole Book that could deserve his, or anyones attention." Further disagreement ensued about the character of Lady Anne Wilmot, Julia's lively and outspoken alter ego. One member of the group viewed Wilmot, as many eighteenth-century critics of the novel had done, as representative of the "finished character of a Coquet," comparing her to "four or five [real-life] Ladies, whose Behavior ... exactly coincided with her in the novel." The woman responded by defending the character of Lady Anne against the accusation and expressing shock that the same man, in a previous discussion of the novel, had described Wilmot as a "Prude." The apparent contradiction between the two interpretations of the character of Lady Anne Wilmot, according to this female "wit," revealed the young man's ignorance since a woman could not be both a "Coquet" and a "Prude." At this point Philip interjected, seeking some moderation of what was becoming an impassioned debate. He "observed" that both parties were "mistaken in their opinion about the Characters, & each [was] too warm in their own Cause." The character of Lady Anne Wilmot, Philip argued, was not "What the *Spectator*, calles a 'fine Woman,'" but the "Gentleman's" argument that the character was a "Coquet" was not totally accurate either. Ever the diplomat, Philip "turned" the conversation quickly to a new topic—a discussion "upon Mr. Locke's Opinion 'That the Souls of all mankind when first infused into our Bodies have equal abilities.'"[30]

The debate over the merits of *Lady Julia* was not based solely on the novel as a piece of entertainment (although that too was mentioned) but was also centered on its "refining" and "improving" qualities. The original reader of the novel engaged himself with a fellowship of other readers, forming an interpretive community that haggled over the moral value of this literary work. *Lady Julia* was "useful" to the degree that it served as a model of virtuous living for Philip and his Cohansey friends.[31] This case also reveals that good conversation was also orderly conversation. The woman in the discussion did not participate in a useful mode of conversation because she was "ready to believe any remarks which are made upon the Characters in general in Conversation, to be pointed and severe." The overheated passions of this "proposed wit" were not conducive to the right kind of human interaction. Disruptive and inordinate outbursts undermined the rational order of conversation and did little to promote the improvement of the group's members. It is worth noting that this reading circle occurred as part of the daily agricultural rhythms of Cohansey life. The harvest season, with its community-based labor patterns, provided the impetus for this friendly gathering. This ritual of the agrarian calendar afforded an opportunity for a cosmopolitan conversation worthy of a local manifestation of the republic of letters.

Around the same time as the harvest discussion of *Lady Julia Mandeville*, several of Philip's young Presbyterian friends began meeting in more organized communities of benevolent criticism. They formed the Bridge-Town Admonishing Society, an informal club that met in the Cohansey town of Bridge-Town, founded "by the voluntary agreement of several Persons . . . for the regulation of each others conduct & to fulfill them with punctuality & Sincerity; as also to improve ourselves in several parts of useful and ornamental knowledge." Members wrote letters admonishing each other and providing their thoughts on a variety of subjects. Philip's March 1773 address to the group reveals that the members of this "little well-formed club" had ambitious and cosmopolitan goals. He believed that the society would "gain a reputation abroad" and be "great and memorable" as long as the members fostered a sense of "harmony & Union amongst themselves."[32] The Bridge-Town Admonishing Society was no doubt modeled on the culture of the London coffeehouse as presented in Addison and Steele's *Spectator* and the clubs for mutual improvement, such as Benjamin Franklin's Philadelphia "Junto," that were cropping up all over British America at this time.[33] Its emphasis on oral presentation and the discussion of a particular problem or question important to the larger culture also evoked the spirit of the Whig and Cliosophic literary societies at the College of New Jersey. All of these clubs and societies were imbibed with the same cosmopolitan spirit that Philip had hoped to achieve with his own circle of friends in Bridge-Town. What made the Bridge-Town Admonishing Society unique was its attempt to blend the enlightened goals of the coffeehouse, the junto, and the Whigs and Clios with the spiritual friendship common among evangelical Presbyterians. The society's location in such a remote corner of the British Atlantic world is once again worth noting. These kinds of Enlightenment communities could be formed anywhere, even in Cohansey.

Philip exhorted the club members to "remember that our personal entertainment & improvement as individuals depends on the diligences of the Members in general." Discord and division in the club, as in the larger society, were prompted by a "disease of the mind" that Philip defined as the "passions turned out of their original course and fixt upon wrong objects." When passions were allowed to spiral out of control, as in the novel-reading circle described above, the harmonious relationship between the human faculties would become unbalanced and result in a "disease" that could contribute to social discord. Passions could be guarded in two ways. As Calvinists, Philip and his fellow Cohansey Presbyterians believed that the "disease" was rooted in man's moral depravity as a child of Adam. It could thus be remedied by a dose of "special grace," available only through regeneration. The negative *effects* of the passions, or what Philip called "the violence of the disease," could be moderated (in the absence of a conversion experience) through "strict and constant attention to the dictates of reason." While divine grace was essential to *sanctify* dangerous appetites, all humans possessed the moral power to *regulate* the passions. Jealousy, envy, revenge, or pride could destroy the mutual trust of the society and prohibit the openness that would permit members to correct one another morally. The disease was thus "communicable"—its unchecked spread would slowly destroy the group. In his address to the society, Philip said, "How dangerous then, would it be if not quite destructive to our comfort & Happiness, in this Society, if any hurtful passion should grow to be predominant amongst us? . . . Let us therefore banish the first appearance of the passions so destructive to Society; & mutually thrive by Friendship & diligence to promote our common good which will also tend to our personal improvement, that our society may rise & flourish."[34]

In the midst of his intense regimen of study and visiting, Philip received news from his friend Andrew Hunter Jr. that John Witherspoon was seeking worthy candidates for a position as tutor on the plantation of Robert Carter III in Westmoreland County, Virginia. The offer was attractive. The job paid very well (sixty-five pounds annually) and provided a room for study, an "eligant" library of books, and a personal servant.[35] It would allow Philip to travel outside of Cohansey again and expose him to the relatively foreign culture of the Virginia gentry. As an educated gentleman on the rise, how could he forgo such an opportunity?

Robert Carter was the grandson of Robert "King" Carter, one of colonial Virginia's largest landholders and one of the most powerful men in southern society.[36] He inherited a plantation in the Northern Neck and eventually settled down at Nomini Hall, the manor house his father, Robert Carter II, had built along the Potomac River. Like many Virginia gentry, Carter pursued a life of learning and cultural refinement. Education was central to that lifestyle, and Carter made sure that his ten children received the schooling necessary to those ends. In his search for a tutor Carter preferred those trained "on the continent" because they had a better command of spoken English than those educated overseas. He favored graduates of northern colleges because he thought that they were schooled in a higher moral climate than the graduates of the College of William and Mary.[37] Carter had probably heard John Witherspoon preach in Williamsburg shortly after the Scotsman was appointed president of the College of New Jersey in 1768 and concluded that Princeton was an obvious place to secure a teacher for his children.

Philip's decision to leave Cohansey for Virginia was not an easy one. It meant he would have to postpone his ministerial career. While he had a "strong inclination to go," his advisers, probably Andrew Hunter and Enoch Green, opposed the idea, encouraging Philip to "enter with as great speed as convenient into that plan of Life" for which he had been educated. Philip was twenty-six years old when Carter's offer arrived. His closest friends and extended family members felt it was time that he started "settling to some constant Employment." He could not help but agree with them—a year in Virginia would certainly slow his professional progress.[38] If he accepted the position, his examination before the Philadelphia Presbytery, originally scheduled for November, would have to be put off until the spring of 1774.

Philip's age was not the only reason he was discouraged from accepting this tutorial post. His Presbyterian advisers did not have a high regard for the moral ethos of Virginia society. They warned their charge that life in plantation Virginia would lead him "into the midst of many dangerous Temptations" such as "Gay Company" and "frequent entertainments." Enoch Green spoke from experience. Before coming to Deerfield he had spent six months traveling through Virginia as an itinerant Presbyterian missionary, and his trip undoubtedly contributed to his negative perception of the colony. Philip was warned that the people of the Old Dominion were "profane and exceeding wicked" and that such an environment would pose a serious threat to his spiritual growth. It was a land with "little practical devotion" and "no remote pretention of Heart religion." There he would find "no Calvinist Books nor hear any Presbyterian sermons."[39]

What is most surprising about Philip's willingness to consider accepting Carter's offer is the toll it might take on his parentless brothers and sister. If Philip believed he had a responsibility to continue in Cohansey and care for his siblings, he said little about it on the pages of his diary. Perhaps Enlightenment ambition got the best of him and he opted to pursue his own career opportunities over the needs of his family; or perhaps Philip did tend to the needs of his siblings but simply did not write about these matters at length in his journal, a piece of private writing that always had a self-absorbing quality. It is also easy to underestimate the extended care that his Uncle Samuel's family provided for him. Samuel's wealth and large home could have easily accommodated the younger children of his deceased parents. In the end, the decision to have Enoch, Josiah, Jonathan, Amos, and Thomas live with Samuel would not have been unusual by eighteenth-century standards. Granted, Enoch would need special care due to his disabled leg, but Josiah and Jonathan would serve as additional farmhands for Samuel. Amos would eventually, with Philip's help, be apprenticed to a local shoemaker, and Rebecca would be temporarily sent to live with the Bullocks in Philadelphia. That left six-year-old Thomas as the only sibling not yet old enough to pursue regular work. Moreover, Philip could use his earnings from his Virginia tutoring job to help support his siblings.

Philip had a lot to think about at the end of the summer in 1773. He agonized over his decision. Local wisdom, in the form of "those who have the Direction of my Studies" and who "have all along, with the warmest friendship interested themselves to procure my welfare," was telling him to stay. However, John Witherspoon, who embodied the spirit of the cosmopolitan republic of letters, to which Philip longed for membership, urged him to go. "Dr Witherspoon desires & advises me to go," he confided in a letter to Elizabeth Beatty, but "My Directors here seem backward, & rather unwilling." In August, Philip made a trip to Princeton to consult with Witherspoon, a meeting that finally convinced him to accept Carter's offer. Before he knew it, Witherspoon had him observing the Presbyterian grammar school at Princeton in order to acquaint himself "with the plan of Teaching & Examining; & with the Authors that are generally taught." Witherspoon was a commanding presence in Philip's life, and it is unlikely that the student could have ever said "no" to the teacher's face. Even so, the people of Cohansey knew Philip better than any college president could, and he did not want to disappoint them even if they were "backward."[40] After returning to Cohansey and informing his "nearest relations" about the decision, the anxiety he felt was palpable. He wrote to Witherspoon to ask him if there were other Princeton students who might be willing to take his place in Virginia. Witherspoon did not reply, but a letter from Andrew Hunter Jr. let him know in no uncertain terms that "the Dr. insists on my Going to Virginia." For more than a month after agreeing to take the tutoring position, Philip was haunted by the doubts that arise when local attachments and cosmopolitan aspirations come into conflict.[41]

In Philip's case, cosmopolitan desire trumped local attachment. He did not go back on his promise to Witherspoon and Carter. He listed three reasons why he decided to go to Virginia, all of which to one degree or another contributed to the enlightened goals he had set for himself. First, Carter's offer of a private room and the use of his impressive library afforded Philip "a longer opportunity for Study than my friends would willingly allow me if I should remain at home." Second, Philip sought "a more general acquaintance with the manners of Mankind; and a better Knowledge of the Soil, & Commerce of these neighbouring Provinces." Third, he desired "a more perfect acquaintance with the Doctrines, & method of Worship in the established Church in these Colonies."[42]

On October 20, 1773, Philip left Cohansey and headed for Nomini Hall. In the days leading up to his departure he was measured for a coat, had his boots mended and his horse "shod," and battled his way through a bad fit of the "fever and ague." He also embarked on another round of visits, which can only be described as a long good-bye. Philip's activity was unspectacular during this week and thus is easy to overlook, but the seemingly endless socializing in which he engaged reveals his deep psychological and moral connection to his Cohansey community. On October 12 he was in Deerfield making his "final Adieu" to the Pecks. The friendships and close ties with the people who lived there weighed heavy on Philip's emotions. He confided to his journal: "The Thought of Leaving home haunts me at Times." The next evening Philip was in Greenwich for some additional farewells. He supped with the Brewsters, a prominent Greenwich Presbyterian family. After the meal he passed the evening with his friends Daniel Mashells and John Gibbon.[43] On October 15 he ate dinner with two Princeton classmates, Andrew Hunter Jr. and William Smith. Three days later, after recovering from his bout with the fever, he met with his cousin Joel to execute a will in order to secure portions of his father's estate for his brothers and sister. He stopped and said good-bye to the Ewings and the Wallings, two more Greenwich Presbyterian families, and on the evening before his departure he paid a visit to Rev. Andrew Hunter and all of his "Relations." "How hard it is at last," he wrote, "My Heart misgives, is reluctant, in spite of me; But I must away!" At six the next morning he was on a horse heading for Virginia. John Peck and William Hoshel, two friends from Deerfield, rode with him for the first eight miles of the journey.[44]

As Philip traveled to Virginia, thoughts of Elizabeth Beatty still raced through his head. In the months since his disastrous marriage proposal in December 1772, Betsy had made extended trips to Deerfield to visit her sister Mary Green and brother-in-law Enoch. Philip, who was living and studying at Deerfield, could not help but see her often, noting that they had "frequent Opportunities of conversing" while she was in town. However, Philip sensed that things between them were not the same. Betsy was acting in a "cold" and "indifferent" manner toward him, behavior that was making him "uneasy" in her presence. Since Philip's affection for Betsy remained strong and he could no longer bear the awkwardness of their meetings, he decided, after a three-month layoff following the rejection of his marriage proposal, to express his feelings to her in writing once again.[45]

In his letter Philip confessed that his marriage proposal of the previous December had been poorly timed and was the result of "over-anxious Desire," but he admitted that Betsy's current indifference toward him was stirring his passions into a "strange Commotion." Philip remained persistent, refusing to take Laura's coldness as a sign of her "formal and absolute Refusal" of his company. A feeling of desperation seems to have overcome him. He pleaded with Betsy to take him back and in the process abandoned all sense of Presbyterian decorum he had picked up during the course of his education. He told her that he was "in the fullest sense" her "Slave."[46] March 1773 was, without a doubt, a low point for the aspiring Presbyterian gentleman. John Witherspoon and the rest of his mentors would have been sorely disappointed in him.

Philip continued with the letters and poetry to Betsy during her spring 1773 stay in Deerfield, but they did not achieve their desired ends. He pulled out all the stops to get his "dear Laura" back, writing, "Why does my silly Bosom rise / And vent its grief with fruitless sighs? / Shall I sit whining over my pain / And die for one I can't obtain? / Have I been kept so long at School / To die of Love, as dies the Fool / . . . For once control'd in my Desire / My raging Bosom's all on Fire."[47] This kind of romantic poetry exposes the tensions Philip was feeling. His schooling had taught him that above all else one cultivated a modern identity through self-control, but the sentiments he had for Betsy were overwhelming him.

We get a rare a glimpse of how Betsy might have responded to Philip's correspondence from a letter she wrote sometime during the course of her courtship with him. Since it is undated and addressed only to "Sir," it is impossible to know for sure if Philip was the intended recipient. However, the contents of the letter seem to suggest that it was indeed written to him, perhaps shortly after Betsy received his series of romantic letters and poems.

Sir,

To comply with indiscreet requests is equally heinous in the performer as the Desirer—a correspondence between Young people of different Sexes, however, Innocent, is generally looked upon as containing Matters of Love & Gallentry— But you will say the abuse of blessings is no reason to set a Just Value upon them—true—But we must first correct the Errors of Mankind in this particular, before we can dare to enter upon such an Enterprize & come under the Lash of a Censorious World—I shall not say your demand is unreasonable, but I am persuaded a compliance now would be unreasonable—Letters of Business, for those of Friendship are such as I highly approve of, but what the Vulgar call Love Letters are equally useless & Insipid—they betray the Ignorance of the author & are at best but a Compliment or rather an affront upon the Ladies good Sense—& now give me leave to tell you, that however agreeable a continuance of your epistles may be, they can never force me to a Compliance of an untimely request. This upon Mature deliberation will appear equally Just to yourself as Sir

Your hb'le Servant

E. Beatty[48]

Her letter reveals the moral dilemma that Philip encountered in all of his correspondence with Betsy: he found it difficult to write in an epistolary style defined by self-control. It was Betsy, the daughter of a prominent clergyman, who best exemplified the masculine virtues of rationality that Presbyterians valued so highly. Philip, on the other hand, could not stop himself from writing "useless" and "Insipid" love letters teeming with sentimentality, a pattern of behavior reflective of the eighteenth-century feminine virtues of sensibility and passion. As long as Betsy maintained power in their relationship, Philip would need to stick to writing letters of friendship and avoid dabbling in "vulgar" attempts at "Love & Gallentry."

By late spring 1773 Philip appears to have, at least for the moment, gotten the message. Betsy had returned to Pennsylvania, and Philip had immersed himself, perhaps to ease the pain, in his studies and rounds of visiting. He did not write to her again until August. The occasion for renewing his correspondence at that time was the trip he made to Princeton to consult with John Witherspoon about his new job offer in Virginia. During his stay he took a familiar ride into the country to see the Beatty brothers in Neshaminy. Betsy was also there, and Philip had the occasion to drink tea with her and engage in "some fine Conversation." Their meeting was carried over to the following day as Philip attended Betsy on the short wagon jaunt to her brother John's house in Newington, Pennsylvania.[49] As was his custom, Philip sent a letter to Betsy the evening of the day he had left Newington and returned to Princeton. Compared to his letters from the previous March, this piece of correspondence was quite tame. He used this letter to inform Betsy about the momentous decision he had before him regarding his tutoring opportunity in Virginia.[50] Though Philip would remain with the Carters only for one year, at this stage of his deliberations the length of his stay was undetermined. His Virginia sojourn could have been more permanent, and if it was, Philip wanted to know where he stood with Betsy. How would she respond to his decision to go to Virginia—a place far removed from the Deerfield-Neshaminy-Princeton Presbyterian orbit in which she regularly traveled?

Betsy, as might be expected, did not reply in writing to Philip's letter, but sometime during his visit with her in Neshaminy and Newington something had changed in their relationship. Her feelings for Philip were apparently renewed. In the meantime Philip seems to have managed to temporarily get his passions under control. A letter he wrote to Betsy on August 31 expressed his concern over the "Danger of the Impropriety I may possibly be guilty of in this continuing my Intimacy with you." In another letter he warned Betsy that his future correspondence would no longer be "embellished with Splendid, Pompous, or Fashionable Phrases ... made up of obtrusive & equivocal Sentiments." He promised that from this point forward he would write "intelligibly," conveying only his most "simple Thoughts." He even reacted in a rather even-tempered manner to a rumor that Betsy had found another suitor and was going to be married. Though the rumor was false—probably a cruel hoax played on him by one of his friends—Philip let Betsy know that he "turn[ed] it all off with a Smile" and that if indeed she were getting married, he wished her well and hoped she would be happy. Was this the same Philip?[51]

By October, Philip was making preparations to leave for Virginia. He was pleased that Betsy seemed to be showing more interest in him, but he was sorrowful that his Virginia trip, which he now described as an "unexpected Accident," would divide him from her company. He told Betsy that he had turned down several other opportunities (the teaching positions in Presbyterian grammar schools mentioned above) that would have kept him close to her. Since she showed little interest in moving their relationship along rapidly, and since he was too "timid" to discuss their future together in the wake of his ill-timed marriage proposal, he believed he had no other alternative but to accept Robert Carter's offer. After arriving in Virginia, he told Betsy that he would not have left Cohansey if she had been "less uncertain" of her "future Purpose."[52]

The year between Philip's graduation from Princeton and his trip to Virginia allowed him to reacquaint himself with his beloved homeland. His activities during this period suggest that the life of an educated gentleman could be lived within the confines of home. The year spent reading in preparation for ordination, cultivating the affective bonds with friends that were essential to a civil society, and learning hard lessons from his relationship with Elizabeth Beatty simultaneously enhanced his local attachment to Cohansey and sharpened his skills as a learned gentleman. His way of improvement, rooted in Presbyterian notions of moral and societal progress, was lived daily in the context of this remote landscape. Indeed, for Philip, "rural Enlightenment" was not an oxymoron.[53]

Chapter 5
A Virginia Sojourn

The time Philip spent in Virginia was the closest this cosmopolitan dreamer would ever come to a cross-cultural experience. At first glance the Northern Neck of Virginia might appear to be just as remote as the southwest New Jersey countryside; but the Carters, and planters like them, had developed a culture there that would have been quite foreign to the son of a "Spartan-Commonwealth." If Philip could not frequent the genteel worlds of London, he could at least immerse himself in the life of colonials who sought to imitate that world. He would become a classic participant-observer in plantation Virginia. Like a cultural anthropologist studying an unfamiliar culture, Philip took extensive field notes on the practices and behaviors of his subjects. However, as a newly minted gentleman, he did not hesitate at times to shed his scholarly objectivity and immerse himself fully in plantation life. The entire experience would offer some valuable lessons for him on his way of improvement.

After nine days of travel between Cohansey and Virginia, Philip arrived safely at Nomini Hall. Robert Carter's eldest son, Ben, welcomed him and showed him to the room that they would be sharing over the course of the next year. Philip and Carter's sons, Ben and Bob, and Carter's nephew, Harry, lived in a school building on the Carter plantation. Philip and Ben occupied a room on the second floor. Two days after his arrival the tutor was in attendance at Anglican worship, and the following Monday he began teaching. His school consisted of eight pupils—Carter's sons, nephew, and five daughters. After his first day in the classroom, he penned a short letter to Enoch Green, informing him that the Northern Neck was "a most delightful Country" and that he was pleased to discover that Nomini Hall was in a "civil, polite neighbourhood." He found the Carter family to be "remarkable for regularity, and oeconomy" and "of the highest quality and greatest worth of any in Virginia." When he finally did meet Robert Carter sixteen days later (Carter had been in Williamsburg on business), Philip was immediately impressed, describing him as "agreeable, discreet, and sensible." Though Philip had been there only a short time, Virginia seemed to offer him everything he had hoped for when he agreed to take the job.

If his "most important connections" had not remained at home in Cohansey, he would be "strongly solicited to stay [in Virginia for] many
years."[1]

Philip spent most of the year between October 1773 and October
1774 in Virginia's Northern Neck. The journal he kept during his stay
has become a staple for historians of eighteenth-century southern plantation culture. It is an incredibly rich and unusually descriptive primary
source chronicling everyday life, from the spectacular to the mundane,
at Carter's manor house Nomini Hall. Philip's stay in Virginia would be
yet another step on his way of improvement, but it also taught him that
his enlightened pursuits could sometimes be hampered by irrational
yearnings for home and sentimental longings for his "fair Laura."

Philip's greatest incentive for taking the tutorial job at Nomini Hall
had been the freedom he would have for study, reading, and thoughtful
reflection. He arrived during what historians have called the "intellectual golden age" of the colonial Chesapeake Bay region—a time when
planter families, such as the Lees, Fitzhughs, Randolphs, Byrds, and
Carters, built large personal libraries to stay linked to the life of the republic of letters.[2] Books were important to the culture of the Virginia
gentry because the exploration of ideas was precisely what separated
them and their way of life from the uneducated masses. Rhys Isaac has
written that "those fitted for book learning were assumed to be of a superior nature to those who did the material work that sustained the civilization; the elite and their valued knowledge should be as completely
disassociated as possible from the servile preoccupations of those who
worked with their hands." The gentry class was so removed from physical labor that many of them, as Kathleen Brown has noted, were forced
"to take exercise in order to remain in good health."[3] During his Virginia sojourn Philip would glean a better understanding of why his Cohansey neighbors found the luxury of the plantation gentry to be so
reprehensible.

Carter's library was an impressive one, even by the high standards of
Virginia planters. It was the largest private collection of books Philip
had ever seen. The tutor felt quite comfortable amid the 641 titles and
more than 1,000 volumes, which included books on subjects ranging
from law to "Latin and Greek Classicks" and Anglican divinity to such
"late famous writers as Locke, Addison, Young, Pope, Swift, Dryden, & c."
Philip's descriptions of his experiences in Carter's library sound as if
he were entering an imaginary world where his intellectual heroes
reigned supreme: "I spent much of this Day in Mr. Carters Library
among the works of mighty-Men." He even took the time to take inventory, recording the title of every book in the Nomini Hall library. Philip

Figure 6. Robert Carter III of Nomini Hall, 1753. Courtesy, Virginia Historical Society.

was intrigued by the host of English gentleman's magazines Carter received, often perusing them the moment they arrived in order to acquaint himself with the most current trends in refined living. It was Carter's large collection of "late famous writers" that distinguished his library from the one at the College of New Jersey, which contained mostly old theological texts and ancient literature. Newspapers were also a means of staying connected at a time when revolutionary sentiments were rising in colonial port cities. Philip was pleased that Carter subscribed to the *Pennsylvania Gazette* so he could remain informed of newsworthy happenings in New Jersey and Philadelphia.[4]

Since Philip had also envisioned his stay in Virginia as a time when he could continue preparation for his Presbyterian licensing exam, he spent many hours in his room poring diligently through Pictet's *Christian Theology* (which he described as "plain and useful") and preparing the sermon he would soon deliver before the Philadelphia Presbytery. His teaching responsibilities would require him to refresh his knowledge of English grammar and history, mathematics, and classical literature (mostly Homer, Horace, Virgil, and Salust), but he also found time for more entertaining reading. He continued to work his way through the *Spectator* and supplemented it with Laurence Sterne's *Tristram Shandy* and the poetry of the black writer Phillis Wheatley, which he read in the *Universal Magazine*.

Philip learned much from his time at Nomini Hall about the refined habits of an educated gentleman. Colonial Virginia's white plantation culture was sustained by unwritten codes of genteel life. Philip told his eventual successor John Peck that "a young Gentleman traveling through the Colony . . . is presum'd to be acquainted with Dancing, Boxing, playing the Fiddle, & Small sword, & Cards." He continued, "If you stay here any time, your Barrenness in these must be detected." It was evident from the outset that the manners essential to function properly in Virginia society were quite different from those needed in the grain-growing villages of Cohansey. Philip often commented on the importance that "posts of honour & mental acquirements" played in Virginia gentry life. Education was the most valuable of the "mental acquirements," and educated visitors found themselves welcomed and accepted. Fithian wrote to Peck, "if you should travel through this Colony, with a well-confirmed testimonial of your having finished with Credit a Course of studies at Nassau-Hall; you would be rated, without any more questions asked, either about your family, your Estate, your business, or your intention, at 10,000£; and you might come, & go, & converse, & keep company according to this value." It was becoming ever clearer to Philip just what his education was worth—in both wealth and social standing.[5]

Philip often used his Cohansey home as a point of comparison with Virginia. He observed correctly that New Jersey lacked the geographical and social landscape that separated the Old Dominion's gentlemen of wealth from the colony's middling and lower sorts. In Cohansey the "laborious part of man, who are commonly ranked in the middling or lower class, are accounted the strenth & Honor of the Colony." They received regular "encouragements" from "Gentlemen in the highest stations."[6] Such social mingling was next to impossible in Virginia. The plantation system contributed to a carefully bound social structure that separated the wealthy tobacco growers from the rest of the colony's inhabitants. The planters, according to Philip, were "exalted much above other Men in worth & precedency." The vast acreage of their plantations, the political power they wielded at Williamsburg and in their Anglican parishes, and the shoring-up of their status through an abundance of slave labor led to infrequent encounters with the poor folk below them and contributed to the deferential mood of the colony. If Virginia planters were feeling "anxious" about their patriarchal status or were being threatened by the rebellious and revolutionary spirit of the age, it certainly did not seem that way to Philip. Even Robert Carter, who experienced doubts about the morality of owning slaves (he would eventually free them), the theological certainty of his Anglican faith (he would later become a Baptist and eventually a member of the Swedenborgian Church), and the economic stability of tobacco farming (he was, like most planters, deeply in debt to English merchants), seemed through Philip's eyes to be the master of his domain.[7]

Virginia planters believed that their emphasis on education and learning was manifested in refined human relationships. Sociability and conversation, they affirmed, were important building blocks in the construction of a genteel identity. Ensconced in rural locales away from major cultural centers, planters were "determined they should not return to barbarism in the wilderness."[8] Polite behavior was just one way the planter class exemplified the social graces of true gentlemen, and Philip was more than prepared to learn that way of life. He informed Peck, "One considerable advantage which you promise yourself by coming to this Colony is to extend the Limits of your acquaintance; this is laudable, & if you have enough prudence & firmness, it will be of a singular advantage. . . . You come here, it is true, with an intention to teach, but you ought likewise to have an inclination to learn."[9] Enoch Green and John Witherspoon had taught their pupil that conversation was vital to a civilized life, and Philip found the dinner table at Nomini Hall, with Robert Carter and his frequent guests, a worthwhile place to experience such sociability. Hospitality and conversation over elaborate meals was one way in which the Virginia gentry displayed their cultural superiority and power.[10] Philip recorded the topics of conversations at meals, which included marriage and widowhood, nursing children, dancing, books, manners, and science. Carter was well read in philosophy and astronomy and would often trigger discussion by bringing books on those topics to the table. He was often in the habit of skipping meals in order to pursue his music or scientific interests, leaving Philip

to preside at the dinner table. The tutor reveled in these evening collo-
quies since they enabled him to receive news, cultivate a sense of cosmopolitanism in the woods of the Northern Neck, and consequently
improve and refine himself.[11]

On other occasions Philip participated reluctantly in the social life of
planter society. As an eligible bachelor, he received many invitations to
dinners, balls, and dances held among the wealthy families of the Northern Neck. Such events allowed the gentry to display their social power
through fashion and conspicuous displays of wealth and consumption.[12]
It was during these occasions, when the Virginia gentry were at their
finest, that Philip most decried his austere upbringing. He was notably
self-conscious about his inability to dance since the practice was an important part of assimilation into Virginia culture. He was often asked to
grace the dance floor, but he always declined respectfully. Yet, unlike Virginia evangelicals (such as the Separatist Baptists) who despised this practice for the air of worldliness it represented, the reason Philip did not
participate in this ritual was a simple one: he did not know how to dance.
He wrote in his journal that although "I was strongly solicited by the
young Gentleman to go in and dance I declined it, however, and went to
my Room not without Wishes that it had been a part of my Education to
learn what I think is an innocent and an ornamental, and most certainly,
in this province is a necessary qualification for a person to appear even
decent in Company."[13] He regretted his lack of skill in this area because it
hindered him from participating fully in genteel society. Dance was a
symbol of the politeness and enlightened refinement that Philip found so
worthwhile about Virginia culture. The synchronized and graceful movements of those engaged in a well-orchestrated minuet reflected a proper
form of entertainment for a truly civil and ordered society. Philip observed that the teenagers "danced with great ease and propriety . . . and it
was indeed beautiful to admiration to see such a number of young persons set off by dress to the best Advantage, moving easily, to the sound of
well performed Music, and with perfect regularity."[14] Dancing was an aes-
thetically beautiful practice that separated Virginia planters from more
uncivilized people and groups in revolutionary America.

Philip also went to Virginia to acquire a "more perfect acquaintance
with the . . . established Church." Robert Carter was a devout Anglican
who served as a vestryman and warden of the Northern Neck's Cople
Parish. He and his family had a choice of two Anglican churches in the
parish at which to worship, and their new tutor had ample opportunity
to tag along. As a ministerial student, Philip was a wide-eyed observer of
the established religion, and some of his observations were quite critical.

He commented most on Anglican sermons. Unlike Presbyterians and those of other dissenting religious traditions for whom the exposition of a biblical passage was the focal point of Sunday worship, Anglican services were centered on the liturgy of the Book of Common Prayer. Needless to say, Philip was a bit surprised when Thomas Smith, the rector of the Ucomico church, preached a sermon that lasted only fifteen minutes. From this point forward Philip made a habit of timing Smith's sermons, informing John Peck that his messages were "seldom under & never over twenty minutes." Anglican priests delivered what he called "cool, spiritless harangue[s] from the Pulpit."[15]

As Protestants, both Anglicans and Presbyterians affirmed the sacrificial death of Jesus Christ as the only means by which sins were forgiven and eternal life was secured. Anglicans, however, taught that Christ died for all of humanity, not just a select few. They upheld a belief in what most eighteenth-century Calvinists disparaged as Arminianism, the view that humans played a part in their salvation by responding to the gospel with a spirit of repentance that, if genuine, would result in a moral life. Presbyterians and Anglicans could agree that God's grace was bestowed on Christians through the reading of the Bible, prayer, devotional meditation, and the Sacrament. However, for Presbyterians, these practices were designed to lead one of God's chosen to the point of conversion, while for Anglicans, they were meant to motivate all men and women, regardless of conversion experience or status as "elect," to live holy lives informed by Christian virtues.[16]

Philip was also sure to make note of the striking differences between Presbyterian and Anglican patterns of Sabbath observance. Sunday in Anglican Virginia was not only a day of worship but also a time for tobacco growers to discuss business. "The Gentlemen go to Church to be sure, but they make that itself a matter of convenience & account the Church a useful weekly resort to do Business." They discussed "the price of Tobacco, Grain & c. & settling either the lineage, Age or qualities of favourite Horses." Philip was troubled that such activity often prevented Anglican gentlemen from arriving at services on time—"It is not the Custom for Gentlemen to go into Church til Service is beginning, when they enter in a Body, in the same manner as they come out; I have known the Clerk to come out and call them into prayers." He was appalled one Sunday morning when he found an advertisement for the latest price of pork posted to the church door.[17] Such customs, when approached through the grid of Philip's northern evangelical faith, were in direct violation of the biblical warrants to honor the Sabbath. After witnessing several Anglicans assembling to chop and gather wood on a Sunday afternoon, Philip summarized his thoughts succinctly: "We do not spend Sundays thus in Jersey."[18]

Philip also commented on Anglicanism's failure to provide Virginians with the theological resources necessary to condemn the cruel treatment of slaves. He thought that Robert Carter managed his slaves humanely, but he was shocked by the paltry weekly diet (a "peck of Corn, & a pound of Meat a Head") that he provided for them. "Good God!," he wondered, "Are these Christians?" Most of Philip's condemnation of slavery fell on Carter's neighbors and was directed less toward their participation in the institution (Philip's Uncle Samuel also owned at least one slave) and more toward the methods of punishment they employed. After hearing one gruesome tale of an overseer's habit of salting the open wounds of his slaves, Philip neglected to offer any detailed moral judgment in his journal, leaving his sense of outrage to "a righteous God, who will take vengeance on such Inventions." On a similar occasion, after listening to Carter describe his friend George Turburville's practice of chaining his slave to a coach, Philip wondered whether Turburville would be "admitted into the peaceful Kingdom of Heaven where meekness, Holiness, & Brotherly-Love, are distinguishing Characteristicks."[19]

Though Philip's thoughts about Anglicanism remained largely confined to his private journal, public criticism of Virginia's established church was by no means novel in the 1770s. Baptists and Methodists made similar comments about Anglican sermons, Sabbath observance, and slavery. Indeed, these groups posed a legitimate threat to the mother church and the social order that it sustained in the Old Dominion.[20] Before we too hastily lump Philip with these controversial Virginia dissenters, it is important to remember that his personal religious and moral beliefs also had some things in common with those of the Anglicans. Philip's assessment of Anglican practice, for example, was not always negative. Though he remained concerned with the brevity of Anglican sermons, he praised them for their "sound morality" and "deep studied Metaphysicks." He described a homily by Isaac Gibberne, the priest at the Nomini church, as a "warm discourse." While attending worship on Good Friday, Philip heard Thomas Smith deliver "the usual Prayers . . . and a long Sermon very suitable and well-chosen."[21]

Philip shared the Anglican commitment to a rational Christian faith. Virginia Anglicans hoped that their pulpit oratory might arouse the affections of their hearers and motivate them to live pious lives, but they were careful to use the liturgy and the Book of Common Prayer as means of tempering and controlling religious passions. Their sermons were thus, as John K. Nelson has described them, "balanced, ordered, dispassionate, and polished" and preached in a "plain style" that was not unlike the sermons of seventeenth-century Puritans.[22] Though their commitment to this form of rational piety may not have always found its way to local parishes (as Philip was quick to point out), the Anglican concerns over enthusiasm and religious passion were similar to the concerns of the Presbyterian Church in the aftermath of the First Great Awakening.

Though Anglicans often looked askance at Reformed evangelical practice that emphasized immediate conversion, they shared with post–Great Awakening Presbyterians a similar Enlightenment-based moral philosophy. Virginia Anglicans were influenced by latitudinarianism, an approach to religion that downplayed doctrinal differences between Christians and emphasized ecumenical unity in the body of Christ. The latitudinarian emphasis on human love and societal harmony was in tune with the general flavor of British American culture in the middle decades of the eighteenth century. Anglicans were thus prone to stress religion's contribution to the improvement of society over the eternal rewards it provided to the believer. As we saw in Chapter 2, Presbyterians were also influenced by this Enlightenment culture of brotherly love, particularly in their attempts to forge a reunified church in the decades following the divisive Awakening. Presbyterians knew all too well that theological particularities were often promoted by preachers who were slaves to religious passions and disorderly in their conduct. They favored a faith that would provide a rational undergirding to the social order just as much as they championed traditional evangelical commitments to conversion and otherworldly piety.[23]

These similarities between Anglicanism and Presbyterianism were evident in the ways both groups engaged the religious culture of colonial Virginia. At the time of Philip's arrival, the staid world of the colony's Anglican parishes was under attack from an ever-growing movement of Separatist Baptists. A visitor to the Carter plantation informed Philip that the Baptists in nearby Louden County were "growing very numerous; & seem to be increasing in affluence." Their practices were "destroying pleasure in the Country; for they encourage ardent Pray'r; strong & constant faith, & intire Banishment of Gaming, Dancing, & Sabbath-Day Diversions." Parson Isaac Gibberne preached "several sermons in opposition to them, in which he has labor'd to convince his People that what they say are only whimsical Fancies or at most Religion grown to Wildness & Enthusiasm!"[24] Anglicans believed that Separatist Baptists, with their primitive faith and a religious genealogy descending to the most enthusiastic Great Awakening Baptists in New England, lacked a concern for the way Christianity contributed to the good of society. Their otherworldly perspective and their emphasis on the democratic implications of evangelical conversion posed a serious threat to the social and moral order of Anglican Virginia. As a fellow evangelical, Philip shared many of the same concerns of the Baptists. He could relate to their tirades against gambling, card playing, and the failure of Virginians to keep the Sabbath. However, Philip also shared the concerns of Anglicans related to the disruptive conduct of these dissenters. His agreement with the established church on these matters reflected similar informal alliances forged between Presbyterians and Anglicans against Baptists in other regions of the Old Dominion.[25]

As his stay progressed, Philip became more and more comfortable with Anglican religious life. Robert Carter asked him on occasion to conduct Anglican prayers at Nomini Hall, and Philip "heartily agreed" to fulfill his requests. Although it usually troubled his conscience, Philip also took advantage of, and came to appreciate, the Virginia law that required attendance at church only twice a month. He often used Sundays to catch up on his studies. One summer Sunday morning a Carter slave, known only as "Daddy *Gumby*," asked Philip if he would be attending services later that morning. When Philip told him that it was too hot to go to church, Daddy Gumby issued a rebuke to the tutor: "Too hot, Good God, too hot! I shall affront you, Master—Too hot to serve the Lord!" After the encounter Philip confessed that he "felt a little non plus'd," but apparently not enough to prevent him from skipping church.[26]

While Baptist ministers were considered whimsical and enthusiastic by Anglican divines, Philip discovered that Presbyterian clergymen were well respected in Virginia. The Carter family had high praise for the Reverend James Waddell, pastor of a small Presbyterian congregation in the Northern Neck. In describing Waddell, Philip noted that "People of Fashion in general countenance, & commend him," and he praised him for his "irreproachable Character."[27] Philip's Presbyterianism was never a problem in the Carter household. Frances Carter, whom Philip acclaimed for her "great propriety" and "very extensive Knowledge," believed that the established church was "without Exception the best of any invented or practised in the world"; but she added that she felt the "Difference[s] between the Church & Presbyterianism to be only exceeding small." In a remark fitting of her latitudinarian faith, she wished that the two churches could be "intirely united."[28]

During his experiences in Virginia, Philip struggled with the ramifications of his decision to pursue the life of an educated gentleman. Men of the Enlightenment were, above all else, rational beings. Philip had learned from his Presbyterian upbringing and college training in faculty psychology that if a society were to be virtuous, enlightened, and refined, the "passions" had to be regulated. The gentleman's life must therefore be one of restraint.[29] For Philip, as his relationship with Elizabeth Beatty made abundantly clear, holding the passions in check was never easy. While in Virginia he composed a sermon on the regulation of the "inordinate affections." The passions had long been a source of great perplexity to him, and yielding to them brought only temporary fulfillment and satisfaction. As a student at Green's academy he wrote, "Today my mind seems much engaged (as it too often is) upon natural and low objects, reaching after them with vain solicitude; endeavoring to grasp them into the arms of my passions; and when I obtain the most of my desires, they sink from me like fleeting vanities." Philip exerted much mental labor in training his rational faculty, finding that such rigorous exercise was a "painful process." "It is an arduous task to bring the Mind to close application;" he complained, "& still greater to lay up and retain useful knowledge." Such knowledge could be acquired only through "Industry, Applications, & Pains."[30]

For a gentleman pursuing world citizenship, homesickness was an especially debilitating passion. Love of home and attachment to a given place were irrational because they elevated a commitment to a specific land and specific people over a universal devotion to the human race. How could a person move freely within the boundless republic of letters when he remained wedded to his homeland? To the Enlightenment mind, emotional attachment to a particular people in a particular locale was nothing more than irrational sentimentality. It was rooted in unpro gressive ideals such as prejudice, romantic love, religious faith, and tradition. It was, to use John Witherspoon's formula, an "inferior affection."[31] Philip's life journey from Greenwich to Nomini Hall and from Cohansey farmer to educated gentleman provides a vivid example of how one individual crafted a new modern identity. Yet, the longing for home that he expressed at every point of that journey reveals a young man tormented by the sacrifices necessary to assume an enlightened self.

Whether he was in the hallowed corridors of Princeton's Nassau Hall or in the library of Robert Carter, Philip was always aware of Cohansey. "Strong & sweet are the bands which tye us to our place of nativity," he wrote from his Virginia bedroom. "If it is but a beggarly Cottage, we seem not satisfied with the most elegant entertainment if we are totally separated from it." Though the genteel life of plantation Virginia was certainly attractive to the young tutor, and at one point early in his visit he had considered staying for a long time, Philip decided rather quickly that he had no interest in making his permanent home there.[32] On arriving at Nomini Hall and throughout his entire stay in the Old Dominion, Philip suffered acute bouts of homesickness. He felt "uneasy," "bewildered," and "haunt[ed]" about his decision to leave Cohansey. He made a habit of gazing out the window of his room and then turning to his diary to write about home. "I went to the window before I was drest . . . I could not help casting my Eyes with eagerness over the blue Potowmack and look homewards." Time spent in Virginia did not seem to help. The longer he stayed, the more intense his homesickness became. One cold Sunday morning in January 1774 Philip skipped church services and wrote, "I feel very desirous of seeing Home: of hearing good Mr Hunter Preach; of seeing my dear Brothers & Sister; Indeed the very soil itself would be precious to me!—I am shut up in my chamber; I read a while, then walk to the North window, & look over the Potowmack through Maryland towards Home." These were hardly the private thoughts of a citizen of the world.[33]

Philip was well aware of the irrationality of his longing for home. He labored to harmonize the gentlemanly accoutrements he enjoyed at Nomini Hall with his passion-laden feeling for Cohansey. Though he delighted in the quiet contemplation and scholarly isolation of Carter's plantation, he also realized that such intellectual opportunities had little meaning to him outside of Cohansey and the people who inhabited that place. "This may seem strange," he wrote in June 1774,

but it is true—I have but very few acquaintances [in Virginia], & they easily dispense with my Absence—I have an elegant inviting apartment for Study—I have plenty of valuable & entertaining Books—and I hav business of my own that requires my attention—At home my Relations call me proud and morose if I do not visit them—My own private business often calls me off & unsettles my mind. . . . All these put together, when they operate at once, are a strong incitement to divert me from Study. Yet I love Cohansie! And in spite of my resolution, when I am convinced that my situation is more advantageous here, yet I wish to be there— How exceedingly capricious is fancy! When I am Home I then seem willing to remove, for other places seem to be full as desirable—It is then Society which makes places seem agreeable or the Contrary—It can be nothing else.[34]

By August 1774 Philip had come to the point where he was "low Spirited" and could not "eat nor drink" because he was thinking "constantly of Home." He even felt, using the theological language of his Presbyterian upbringing, that "Sometimes [I] repent my having come into this Colony."[35]

Philip may have learned from John Witherspoon and the *Spectator* that local affections were narrow and inferior when compared to a universal affection for the entire human race, but he found this lesson difficult to apply when his passions for home were so strong. In the eighteenth century homesickness or "nostalgia" was considered a mental disorder. It was first diagnosed among seventeenth-century Swiss mercenaries who suffered from an intense zeal to return to their cantons whenever they gathered around campfires to sing native songs. At its worst, those who suffered from nostalgia confused the past with the present or, in a few rare cases, saw specters of loved ones back home. More mild cases were accompanied by nausea, loss of appetite, or fever. One eighteenth-century medical encyclopedia defined nostalgia as "a vehement desire in those absent from their country, of revisiting" and placed its entry on the pages between "Nymphomania" and "Anorexia." It was a disease that revealed what Svetlana Boym has called the "contradictions of modernity." Nostalgia was incompatible with Enlightenment notions of self-improvement, and yet it was also a consequence of the Enlightenment. In many cases of nostalgia—and this was certainly true of Philip—it was the social and geographical mobility required of a world citizen that led to the disorder.[36]

Philip was certainly suffering from a mild case of nostalgia during his Virginia sojourn. Homesickness of this variety was most intense during times of uncertainty or displacement, similar to what Philip had experienced when he left home for the Northern Neck. Modern historians have attacked nostalgia because it is often associated with yearnings for a return to lost worlds no longer obtainable. It undermines the values of the historical discipline in its celebration of an idealized past that rarely existed in the way that the nostalgic perceive of it in the present. The myth of the eighteenth-century, self-sufficient yeoman farmer, or the popular perception of post–World War II America as a place populated exclusively by happy, white, middle-class suburbs comes to mind.[37] Yet, in the eighteenth century the longing to return to a geographical homeland was not necessarily equivalent to the yearning for a utopianlike past that had long vanished. The desire for home could still be satisfied in a real and genuine way. In fact, this is what most medical professionals of the era believed was the disease's only reliable cure. Philip's Cohansey was not a lost world—at least not yet. It was still there and had actually changed little. It was a place of real and meaningful friends and relationships. The moral attachment that Philip, even as a twenty-six-year-old college graduate, felt to his childhood home had not subsided. The possibility of going home again was a real and enticing one for Philip. His longing to be present in Cohansey once more was only enhanced by his taste of life outside of its bounds. This was a place where he still considered spending the rest of his life. Philip, of course, had changed a great deal since he left home. He had most likely grown ambivalent about going back to agricultural work and probably imagined he would return to Cohansey in some sort of educational or ministerial capacity. Yet, as we will see later, he did not surrender the idea of moving back to his father's farm. God might have other purposes for his life, but when Philip prayed he no doubt asked that his way of improvement might lead him home.

Philip was also homesick because he had somehow managed, before he left for the Old Dominion, to rekindle his friendship with Elizabeth Beatty. Philip wrote letters to many of his friends during his stay in

Virginia, but no one received more letters from him than Betsy did. His epistles from Virginia continued in their moderate fashion. In the early months of his stay he was preoccupied with teaching, and as a result his correspondences with Betsy, like all the letters he wrote shortly after his arrival, were filled with mostly news and observations. Privately, however, he continued to find it difficult to exercise restraint. During a brief return to Cohansey in order to take his ministerial licensing exam before the Philadelphia Presbytery he was overcome with passions for Betsy and home. "A thousand things perplex me," he wrote in his diary. "I am unwilling to leave Home. I have already overstaid my Time—I am vexed at having to continue here [in Virginia]—I have left the girl I love. . . . O ten thousand Difficulties embarrass me!"[38] When Philip wrote to Betsy, he was overcome by a flood of passion and sentiment that he found nearly impossible to contain. "In Spite of all my strongest opposing efforts," he wrote, "my thoughts dwell on that Vixen *Laura.* I strive to refuse them admission, or harbour them in my heart, yet like hidden fire they introduce themselves, & seize, & overcome me when perhaps I am pursuing some amuseing or useful Study." It had now been one year since his marriage proposal, and he was still dealing with the rejection. Though he was enjoying his time with the Carter family and learning a great deal about Virginia culture, he could not help "reflecting on my situation last winter, which was near the lovely Laura for whom I cannot but have the truest, and warmest esteem possible! If Heaven shall preserve my life, in some future time, I may again enjoy her good society."[39]

During his stay with the Carters, Philip had multiple opportunities to meet and court the daughters of some of Virginia's most prominent planters. Matchmaking was a popular social practice in plantation Virginia, and the Carters were constantly trying to find him a suitable marriage partner in the hopes that he would stay in the Northern Neck beyond his one-year commitment. Philip delighted in his chance to meet these young ladies and often commented in his journal on their physical appearance, sense of fashion, and courtly manners. He spent considerable time socializing with Jennie Corbin, the sister-in-law of John Turburville, the owner of the manor house located about one mile away from Nomini Hall. However, Philip also made it clear in both his public declarations and private writings that his heart belonged to Betsy. He remained so devoted to her that the Carter boys, who were notorious for their infatuation with the girls in their neighborhood, questioned whether or not he ever thought about the opposite sex. "Yes, Harry, & Bob," Philip responded in his diary, "*Fithian* is vulnerable by Cupid's Arrows—I assure you, Boys, he is, Not by the Girls of Westmoreland— O my dear Laura, I would not injure your friendly Spirit; So long as I breathe Heavens vital air I am unconditionally & wholly Yours."[40]

As Philip became more assured that Betsy was interested in hearing from him (he even received a letter from her!), his correspondence from Virginia began once again to take on a more sentimental flavor. This return to sentimentality coincided with his reading of some of the latest popular fiction, particularly the writings of the eighteenth-century novelist Laurence Sterne. Philip had started reading Robert Carter's copy of Sterne's most famous work, *The Life and Opinions of Tristram Shandy* (1760–68), but he never managed to complete the first volume, claiming that Sterne's title character was too "droll" for his taste. He did, however, read Sterne's *Letters from Yorick to Eliza* (1773), a series of love letters written by Yorick, an Anglican minister (a pseudonym for Sterne), and Eliza Draper, a young married woman with whom Sterne had carried on a three-month sentimental affair before she had to leave England to return to her husband, a royal official stationed in India. The letters were so dripping with passion for the writer's "dear Eliza" that some scholars have suggested that Sterne wrote them as satires on the sentimental nature of late eighteenth-century fiction.[41]

In August 1773 Philip wrote to Betsy that he had "just been reading Yorrick's celebrated Letters to Eliza." The text had been recently published in Philadelphia, so Philip's copy must have been hot off the press. From this point forward his letters to Betsy were modeled on the form and style of Sterne's *Letters*. He could indeed relate to Yorick's plight. Not only were they both infatuated with a woman named Eliza[beth], but also he, like Yorick, was a minister (or at least training to become one) living away from the one he loved with no certainty that he would ever see her again. Though Philip would have considered Yorick's practice of writing romantic letters to a married woman extremely inappropriate, he knew all too well the sense of longing that the author felt for Eliza and the way in which the practice of letter writing eased the emotional agony of a long-distance relationship. He thus connected at several levels with Sterne's *Letters*, describing them as "familiar," "plain," and "beautiful." Philip told Betsy that he had grown to "love Eliza, from the admirable Description he (Sterne) has given of her." Betsy, however, was a far superior woman: "There is in America an Eliza I would venture, from Yorrick's own Picture, to set against it & let Yorrick himself be Judge—should I venture never so largely, I am sure I should succeed."[42]

The literary marks of Sterne's *Letters* were everywhere in Philip's correspondence with Betsy. He often concluded his own letters with Sterne's familiar "Adieu, Adieu." He regularly addressed her as "Eliza."[43] Sterne advised his Eliza, before her departure for India, to "Reverence Thyself," while Philip, on leaving Cohansey for Virginia, advised Betsy (among other things) to "Honor Yourself."[44] Sterne toasted Eliza at his elaborate dinner parties, and Philip toasted Betsy before similar events on the Carter plantation. Sterne encouraged Eliza to begin the practice of rereading his letters to her in India and then, when time permitted, to put them in chronological order as a means of remembering him during their period of separation. Philip did not ask Betsy to do the same with his letters (he wondered if she even saved them), nor could Philip sort the correspondence he received from Betsy since he had only, at the most, two letters. What he could do, however, was organize the copies of the letters that he had sent to Betsy over the years. In May 1774 he wrote her what he called a "chronological" letter cataloging the theme of every piece of correspondence he had sent to her since they first became acquainted four years earlier. He advised her to burn or destroy most of his more passionate epistles, but the very process of ordering his letters in this way was a means of emotionally connecting with his "Eliza."[45] Philip could also be more overt in his borrowing from Sterne. In another May 1774 letter to Betsy he copied an entire section from letter six of Sterne's *Letters from Yorick to Eliza*, replacing the name "Eliza" with that of "Laura": "You are not handsome, **Laura**, nor is yours a face that will please the tenth Parts of your Beholders____But you are Something more, for I scruple not to tell you, I never saw so intelligent, so animated, so good a Countenance, nor ever was there, nor will there be, that Man of Sense, Tenderness, & Feeling in your company three Hours, that was not, or will not be your Admirer & Friend in Consequence of it, if you assume or assumed no Character Foreign to your own, but appeared the artless Being Nature designed of you for____A Something in your Voice & Eyes you profess in a degree more persuasive than any Woman I ever **yet behold**."[46]

By modeling his correspondence on Sterne's letters to Eliza, Philip was fashioning himself as a man of feeling. He had, at least in his relationship with Betsy, dabbled in what G. J. Barker-Benfield and others have called "the culture of sensibility." By the second half of the eighteenth century, Enlightenment rationalism was under attack from a culture that celebrated a new form of gentleman. This new man was no longer asked to govern himself by the stoic dictates of reason alone but was invited to express his emotions in public and private, even to his female friends and correspondents. The kinds of love letters that Betsy had condemned were now being embraced by genteel culture as an important part of a masculine identity. Such feeling, which was often described in terms of "sympathy" or "sentiment," came with a certain moral quality. Like the latitudinarian religion Philip encountered in Virginia, love and benevolence, when applied in everyday life, would produce a better society. A real gentleman was able to communicate his affections for the opposite sex in much the same way that Sterne had done with Eliza and, to some extent, the way Philip was doing in his letters to Betsy.[47] The culture of sensibility offered Philip a language that, unlike the Presbyterian rationalism in which he was raised and educated, did not condemn his passionate side as sinful. He now confronted the moral quandary over whether or not such a language was compatible with his religious convictions.

The culture of sensibility found its moral roots in the writings of British philosophers such as Anthony Ashley Cooper, third earl of Shaftesbury; Adam Smith; and Francis Hutcheson. All of these writers, to varying degrees, taught that the innate moral sense was an affective human faculty that was cultivated best through personal relationships. While few ordinary people in the eighteenth century read the weighty tomes of these moral philosophers, they did read novels, and as a result the culture of sensibility was popularized in the British world through the rising genre of sentimental fiction. Writers such as Sterne, Samuel Richardson (author of *Pamela* and *Clarissa*), Henry MacKenzie (author of *The Man of Feeling*), and even Addison and Steele in the *Tatler* and the *Spectator* provided powerful examples of the kind of sensibility that the new gentleman needed to display.[48] This kind of fiction, according to John Mullan, could empower readers to take action in their everyday lives and relationships. Sentimental novels did not merely "reflect" the social world of the eighteenth-century gentleman but actually carried the power to shape or "produce" the society inhabited by the reader. When Philip read *Letters from Yorick to Eliza* he participated in a "special relationship" with Sterne's words and the feeling behind them. The work connected him, at an emotional level, to what he was feeling for Betsy.[49]

However, reading in this way, as Philip knew all too well, could be dangerous. The culture of sensibility, with its emphasis on feeling and emotion, could invoke the kinds of passions that might easily undermine the rational order of society. In one respect, the sympathy portrayed by some sentimental writers—Sterne included—was simply impractical, "eccentric," and over the top. While it is understandable that Philip would have found a kindred spirit in Yorick, he needed to be careful that he did not go too far in his appropriation of this kind of fiction. The moral philosophers who advocated sentimental behavior as a means of sustaining a virtuous society made sure to stress that such affections needed always to be held in check by reason. Even the most popular sentimental writers knew that sympathy and emotion could be carried too far. The man of feeling was not an enthusiast or a slave to his emotion but instead pursued a "softened Stoicism" or a "moderated sensibility." As one historian has put it, sensibility "demanded tears, not sobs; tenderness rather than emotional storms."[50] For Philip, this was easier said than done.

Sentimental fiction and the passions it could invoke in readers such as Philip were also dangerous from the perspective of his religion. Laurence Sterne was not the kind of author Presbyterian ministers normally turned to when they wanted to teach their parishioners about courtship and marriage. This does not mean that Presbyterians avoided this literature. Francis Alison, a staunch Old Side Presbyterian, a moral philosopher, and vice provost of the College of Philadelphia, for example, was a subscriber to the Philadelphia edition of Sterne's *Collected Works*.[51] Some of the most prominent Presbyterians in America dabbled in this material and could actually use it—as we saw in the context of Philip and his friends' discussion of *The History of Lady Julia Mandeville*—as a means of moral improvement. Presbyterians prided themselves in their active engagement with current trends in intellectual life and popular culture, but there was the need to filter this sort of reading through the grid of a Reformed worldview before putting it into action in everyday life.

There was clearly a place, as Philip knew from sitting through John Witherspoon's moral philosophy lectures, for sentiment and feeling in Presbyterian ethics. Witherspoon was heavily indebted to Shaftesbury and Hutcheson, who both thought that benevolence and sympathy were essential moral virtues. In a survey of the moral thinking of his age, Witherspoon wrote, "Dr. [Samuel] Clark[e], and some others make understanding or reason the immediate principle of virtue. Shaftesbury, Hutchinson [Hutcheson] and others, make affection the principle of it. Perhaps neither the one nor the other is wholly right. *Probably both are necessary* [italics mine]."[52] However, if indeed reason and affection went hand in hand, Witherspoon was more cautious than most about giving too much credence to the affective dimensions of the moral sense, especially when it came to his views on courtship and marriage. Philip never corresponded with Witherspoon concerning his relationship with Elizabeth Beatty, but if he had, his Princeton mentor would have had some strong words of admonishment for him.

Witherspoon advised young people to avoid relying too heavily on their parents in choosing a mate, but his concessions to modern courtship practices stopped there. Marriage and family, Witherspoon believed, were sacred institutions that should not be held captive by popular culture. As an astute observer of the cultural trends of his day, he knew that the cult of sensibility was posing a formative challenge to an Enlightenment model of morality in which ethical choices were based largely on the rational exercise of the human conscience. He saw great danger in the way that such a culture, with its powerful appeals to the affections and its democratic dissemination through popular literature, might influence how people understood marriage and courtship. He summed his position up best in the last of his lectures on moral philosophy: "Therefore the propensity of the sexes to one another, is not only reined in by modesty, but is so ordered as to require that reason and friendship, and some of the noblest affections, should have place. And it is certain that they have, if not a more violent, at least a more lasting and uniform influence in the married state than sensual desire."[53]

In a series of letters written to the *Pennsylvania Magazine* in 1775 and 1776, Witherspoon condemned sentimental literature (including, at least on the issue of marriage, Addison and Steele in the *Spectator*) as offering "a certain refined idea of felicity, which hardly exists anywhere but in the writers imagination." Popular novels made up a "class of writings to which the world is very little indebted." Sexual desire and romantic intimacy were natural and "noble" instincts instilled by God in all of his human creation ("I hope no body will think me so clownish as to exclude sentiment altogether"), but they were best satisfied in the context of marriage. He thought that young people exposed to sentimental fiction were apt to "indulge themselves with romantic expectations of delight, both ecstatic and permanent." Such flights of fancy only exposed marriage "to the scoffs of libertines," who knew, but did not tell their readers, that their "raptures must soon come to an end."[54]

The sentiments of courtship and marriage, according to Witherspoon, should be handled like "certain medicines that are powerful in their operation, but at the same time require the utmost caution and prudence as to the time and manner of their being applied." Love, when under the "restraint of reason, and government of prudence, may be greatly subservient to the future happiness of life." Writers such as Sterne, who dabbled in "an extravagance of sentiment and language on this subject that is at once ridiculous in itself," were only setting their readers up for disappointment. The "high sentimentalists" promoted expectations that were "impossible to gratify," and the "gallantry of courtship" they portrayed in their novels promised things that "the downright reality of matrimony cannot afford." Instead, Witherspoon believed that marriage should be governed by common sense. True happiness in a marital relationship could come only through mutual esteem and respect for one another and the love and connection between partners that arise from the raising of children.[55]

There was probably little about Witherspoon's views of marriage and courtship with which Philip disagreed. Yet, the culture of sensibility, with its powerful celebration of the passions and romantic love, was tugging him in an opposite direction. Since he was living in the home of a Virginia gentleman where he felt pressure to conform to the refined manners of a genteel life, was exposed almost daily to the daughters of plantation owners, and had regular access to sentimental literature, it was inevitable that the thoughts of Laurence Sterne and

John Witherspoon would wage a constant war for control of his iden-tity. As a result, his letters to Betsy continued to read as if Philip were riding an emotional roller coaster.

Philip left Nomini Hall in October 1774 and would never again re-turn to Robert Carter's plantation. John Peck, his Deerfield friend, would succeed him. Throughout Philip's stay he often reflected, in a general fashion, on life in the Old Dominion. As an evangelical Presby-terian, he concurred with friends and mentors who warned him that spending any length of time in Virginia would jeopardize his faith. He noted the "great advantage of the Precaution I received from my friends" and believed that their sound advice influenced him to set "out on a safe, and prudent Plan" while there. Following this course led to his reputation in Virginia as one who was "dull, unsociable, & splenetic," but such repute was the price he had to pay in order to avoid any un-necessary challenges to his evangelical convictions. He hoped that Carter and the other Virginia gentlemen he met would understand his behavior and be pleased with his modeling of the "strict & rigid virtue in those who have the management of . . . children."[56] During his Virginia sojourn Philip became aware that a college education qualified him for at least limited participation in this world of books, conversation, and self-improvement. The genteel culture of the region had seeped into his private thoughts, diary, and letters. Life in the plantation Chesapeake would have been quite foreign to his deceased parents and most of his Cohansey friends, but Philip belonged. The trip was the culmination of what, at first glance, appeared to be a journey away from his beloved Co-hansey and toward the world citizenship valued by all true members of the republic of letters.

At the same time, Philip's Virginia sojourn reminded him that he had a long way to go in his quest to become a rational citizen of the world. His stay with the Carters helped him to realize that unruly passions could be major stumbling blocks on his way of improvement. His education was changing him for the better, but it also made him see the virtues of home more clearly. His passions for the Cohansey of his youth—and the poten-tial of marital bliss with Betsy—caused him to wonder if he, or anyone for that matter, could ever truly embrace the cosmopolitan spirit of the re-public of letters. He realized that he was living in a perpetual state of limbo—his dreams were boundless, but his roots remained strong.[57] As he entered upon the life of an ordained Presbyterian clergyman and came face-to-face with the cause of revolutionary liberty, he would con-tinue to search for some sense of reconciliation between these worlds.

Chapter 6
Revolution

As Providence would have it, Philip became a Presbyterian minister in his own backyard. His licensing exam commenced in Neshaminy, Pennsylvania, the site of the November 1774 meeting of the Philadelphia Presbytery. However, midway through his trials, when it was time for the three-day meeting to adjourn, a committee was appointed to convene the following month in Pittsgrove to conclude his interview. The faces of his examiners on December 6 were familiar. In fact, the entire gathering might have easily passed for a celebration of Cohansey Presbyterianism.[1] William Hollingshead, Philip's friend and the minister of the Fairfield church, opened the day with a sermon. He then joined four other southern New Jersey Presbyterian clergymen, including Enoch Green of Deerfield and Nehemiah Greenman of Pittsgrove, in querying the candidate in natural and moral philosophy, geography, and, of course divinity (he had preached a sermon, delivered an academic lecture, and interpreted a Latin passage the previous month in Neshaminy). Despite the fact that several of the clergymen involved in the exam had a vested interest in seeing Philip succeed, the committee did not treat him with kid gloves. They interrogated him for the better part of the day. Finally, at nine o'clock that evening, he was presented with a license to preach the gospel. Overwhelmed by the realization that he had passed the exam and entered the ranks of the clergy, he turned to his diary: "I feel myself not able; I feel myself unqualified; I feel myself unworthy & every way vastly unequal to this great undertaking—Give me Strength, O Shepherd of Israel; furnish me with every necessary qualification; with wisdom, Fidelity, Zeal, Prudence & Perseverance." Such Calvinist humility, expressed in a literary style that would make his journals popular among historians over two hundred years later, was not uncommon for Philip. This time, however, his reflections did not stop there. He went on to pray for a "sense of my duty in these times of distraction & Misery," pleading with God to "Furnish me with an uniform & unbiass'd love for my Country; & give me courage to engage in every method that has a tendency to save her from Ruin, even if my life should be in Danger in the Competition."[2]

It may seem odd that Philip, on the day he became a Presbyterian minister, would pray that God would fill him with an ample dose of patriotic zeal, but these were revolutionary times. The First Continental Congress had met in Philadelphia earlier in the year, and the skirmishes at Lexington and Concord were only five months away. Philip, like nearly all colonial Presbyterians, had already made up his mind about where he stood in relation to the imperial crisis with England. He had followed events closely. In 1765, as an eighteen-year-old farm boy, he would record on the largely blank pages of his journal "the very agreeable news of the repeal of the Stamp Act."[3] While in Virginia he kept abreast of revolutionary affairs through Robert Carter's newspapers and the intelligence he garnered from the planter's well-connected neighbors. He described the toasts, songs, and "great Professions of liberty" among the Virginia gentry after receiving news of the Boston Tea Party. The Virginians "are warm and active in supporting the liberties of America," he informed his Uncle Samuel, and he added that the House of Burgesses had called for a colonialwide fast "to invoke almighty God to assist our falling country, and save us from oppression and Tyranny." Following the passage of the Intolerable Acts in March 1774, the "conversation . . . on American affairs" often went late into the evening.[4] By December militia had begun drilling in some of the colonies and Philip, now back home, had been licensed to preach by a colonial church that had wed its moral agenda to the cause of American liberty.

Philip knew the importance of pursuing a life of service to his country. Such civic responsibility, he had been taught, could be exercised only by the virtuous. True public servants were unselfish and not easily taken in by the temptations of corruption or commerce. They exemplified self-control by keeping their passions in check. The success of the American Revolution depended on the personal morality of the colonial people, but for Presbyterians, this was not a revolution for Christians alone. Rev. John Witherspoon and his disciples believed that all members of provincial society, even nonreligious or marginally religious persons, could act virtuously because, as human beings created in the image of God, they had a moral sense, or conscience.

The moral beliefs of eighteenth-century Presbyterians had much in common with ancient notions of public life that historians have described as "civic humanism" or "republicanism." Greeks and Romans who followed this line of thinking believed that republics were successful only if citizens sacrificed their own interests for the good of their country.[5] There was nothing, of course, particularly Christian about such an idea. Granted, Christians were required to obey governmental authority, but a true believer's ultimate sacrifice and allegiance were to be directed toward God, not the state.[6] Nevertheless, the sacrificial spirit that republican civic duty required did overlap a great deal with both the biblical virtue of selflessness and the ethical beliefs of the New Moral Philosophy. Christians were to serve other people. Moral beings, Christian or otherwise, were to act benevolently toward one another. Presbyterians believed that these self-sacrificing virtues could be easily directed toward political independence if the cause were just. They thought that Christian and moral-sense traditions could infuse the largely pagan civic humanist ideal with an ethical quality that made it worthy of their embrace in a time of revolution. All good patriots could drink from the moral reservoir created by the blending of God's law and the human conscience. The nourishment in virtue that this well provided would give them the strength to resist tyranny and establish a republican form of government.[7]

Several historians have noted the convergence of the New Moral Philosophy, Presbyterian ethics, and republican political thought in revolutionary-era public discourse. Yet, little work has been done to determine how such ideas were applied by ordinary people living within local communities.[8] Philip's response to the American Revolution provides us with a glimpse of the ideas as they were practiced. Because the vocabularies of the three systems of moral thought overlapped, Philip moved freely among them in his musings on revolutionary virtue, making it nearly impossible to decipher which moral language he was employing at any given time. These ideals became part of his thinking while he was a student at Witherspoon's Princeton, but they were nurtured at home, in the context of a rural Presbyterian enclave along the Cohansey River whose inhabitants were some of the most ardent and overlooked patriots of the time. Thus, when Philip prayed for courage to save his country from ruin, "even if my life should be in Danger in the Competition," his words not only had a prophetic quality but also, for a Presbyterian, were wholly appropriate. God would answer Philip's prayer on more than one occasion.

Before Philip could perform his patriotic duties, he needed to learn how to preach. His first six months as a Presbyterian minister were spent supplying pulpits in Cohansey and the surrounding southern New Jersey region. The Presbytery apparently believed that Cohansey would be the best place for the young preacher to hone his skills. The everyday rhythms of home and the nurturing presence of Andrew Hunter and Enoch Green provided a safe environment for Philip to gain experience behind the pulpit. He preached his first sermon in the intimate confines of the Deerfield church. As he climbed the pulpit on that particular December Sunday to deliver an exposition from the Book of Job, he was "much frighted." During the opening prayer his nerves got the best of him and he asked God, in a supplication that must have provided the congregation with some comic relief, that the "King may become a nursing mother & the Queen a nursing Father to the Church." Philip was horrified by this "material blunder," but he managed to recover and get through the sermon without the use of his notes and "with little difficulty." The next Sunday, Christmas Day, he preached at Fairfield from the Gospel of Matthew. He used his notes a bit more this time, and his anxiety had apparently subsided. He claimed that he "was none affraid."[9]

The real test of Philip's pulpit skills would come later in the month when he preached several sermons at the Greenwich Presbyterian church. The prospect of delivering a sermon at Greenwich was daunting for several reasons. Greenwich was the largest Presbyterian congregation in southern New Jersey. It was the church in which he had been baptized and catechized and where his spiritual mentor, Andrew Hunter, had served the Presbyterian faithful for thirty years. It was also the place where evangelical heroes such as Whitefield, Tennent, and Finley had preached during the First Great Awakening, a fact that most likely did not escape Philip's historically sensitive mind. As he looked over the pews from his perch in the Greenwich pulpit he could see that the "House was very full" with people eager to hear Cohansey's favorite son expound on the Scriptures. Philip made it through his first sermon at Greenwich with little problem, but the following week the congregation was sprinkled with "several Strangers of Note," a scene that made the young preacher "dashed & terrified." Later in the month, with Hunter seated in the front of the congregation, Philip developed a case of the jitters so great that it temporarily paralyzed him in the pulpit. During the course of his message before a packed Greenwich meetinghouse he went into a panic. His thoughts escaped him, his speech failed him, and he came "within an Inch," he claimed, of losing his sight. "How unwelcome, how distressful, how unpopular is this involuntary flutter!" he wrote.[10]

It had now been over six years since Philip started on his way of improvement, and despite the minor difficulties that one might expect, his decision to pursue the life of an educated Presbyterian clergyman was being confirmed with every sermon he preached. Indeed, Philip was fulfilling what he had long believed to be his God-given vocation. He was now ready to move slightly beyond the bounds of his homeland and test his pastoral skills on people who were less familiar. After a month in Cohansey's churches, Philip was sent to the scattered Presbyterians who lived along the New Jersey coast in the settlement of Egg Harbor. With no established congregations in the region, Egg Harbor was a popular training ground for young Presbyterian preachers—a ministerial boot camp where the likes of Charles Beatty, Andrew Hunter, and Enoch Green had at one time or another preached and distributed the Lord's Supper.[11]

Philip was not thrilled with the assignment. The journey to Egg Harbor required an eight-hour horseback ride through the largely unsettled, pine barren region of New Jersey, a place that Cohansey Presbyterians called "the desert." Despite the fact that many esteemed clergymen had visited the region before him, Philip imagined the people there to be uncivilized and thus largely uninterested in hearing from a refined Presbyterian minister. Even those in a relatively remote and distant place such as Cohansey thought of these coastal settlers with disdain. The region contained some of the worst soil in New Jersey, making farming difficult and forcing its inhabitants to earn their livings by coal, iron, and lumber production. The Delaware Indian population, though never large in southern New Jersey, was denser in these parts, and Philip probably heard rumors of racial mixing between the natives and the white settlers of the area.[12] Roughly ten years earlier the Swedish Lutheran clergyman Carl Wrangel had passed through the vicinity and noted that the people lived "like savage heathen, without the slightest knowledge of God" and had "no other homes than hovels in the woods."[13] Yet, Philip had his orders. The gospel needed to go forward. He would perform his duties in the pines and get back to Cohansey as soon as possible.

The new minister spent six weeks in the Egg Harbor region. He addressed crowds of forty or fifty people at a time in log meetinghouses and spoke to smaller groups in individual homes. He visited the sick and preached to the workers at Batsto Furnace, one of the mid-Atlantic's most important ironworks. He delivered sermons to the Lenape at Brotherton, the Indian mission run by Rev. John Brainerd. In addition, he got his first glimpse of the Atlantic Ocean by peering through the cedar trees on the beach in what would become Atlantic City; it was a sight that filled him with "admiration." Despite all that he had heard about the people of Egg Harbor, Philip was pleasantly surprised that they utilized his services "with great civility." When he arrived, he expected that the region's Presbyterians, because they lived in a "wild and unpeopled" country, would be warm to any "clamorous Lubber who has assurance enough to make a rumpus & bluster in the pulpit." He described the inhabitants of the region, even before he met them, as "straggling, impertinent, vociferous Swamp-Men." Instead, Philip found a community of discriminating Presbyterians who required their visiting ministers to be "Good-Speaking" and have "good-sense, Sound Divinity, and Neatness and Cleanliness" in "Person and Dress." While there, he even ran across some "English . . . Gentlemen of Fortune and Breeding."[14]

At precisely the time he was gaining valuable experience in southern New Jersey pulpits, Philip was facing a crisis in his personal life that was to him every bit as tumultuous as the political one confronting the American colonies. He found himself in the midst of a rivalry for the affection of a young woman—a precarious predicament for any young minister, but one especially dangerous in a rural community such as Cohansey, where rumors and gossip could quickly become the order of the day. In October 1774, two days before he left Virginia, Philip, clearly distressed, wrote in his diary, "But this sad thing which I hear of that turn-Coat *Laura*, that She loves & courts one Mr *Rodman.*" He was crushed. His natural inclination was to lash out. Philip had "made a Solemn vow" to remain faithful to Betsy, but his promise was not "inviolable," especially if she had "listened to another." His unruly passions flared as he swore to "retreat from every former Promise" he had made to the girl he had once hoped to marry. He would "treat her with contempt; & Sincerely pity, instead of resent, her ineffectual Caprice." Philip, of course, was caught up in the pain of the moment. He could never write off Betsy that easily; his affections for her ran too deep. Instead, once he cooled down a bit, he would do everything in his power to dissuade her from continuing in her courtship with Rodman and hopefully reestablish his place as her sole suitor. His work was cut out for him.[15]

Philip's attempts to win Betsy back in the months between October 1774 and March 1775 contain all the drama of a modern-day soap opera. Consequently, one is hard-pressed to find much of the refined and enlightened approach to courtship that might characterize the life of a Presbyterian gentleman. Philip tried to keep the entire affair private, but this was virtually impossible in Cohansey. Not only was the Presbyterian community aware of the details of this courtship triangle, but they also intervened in the matter on more than one occasion. The entire episode—which Philip described to Betsy as "the present popular Clamour, in which you & I have so considerable a Share"—seems to have rivaled British tyranny as a popular subject of conversation in Cohansey.[16] What exactly happened over the course of these months, and especially during the final few weeks, is difficult to piece together since we are forced to view the entire affair through Philip's letters. Thus, Betsy's thoughts, when available to us, can be accessed only through the grid of Philip's interpretation of them.

On his arrival in Cohansey following his Virginia sojourn, Philip continued to visit with Betsy as if nothing had changed. After spending a late November day with her and several of her female friends at the home of Rev. Nehemiah Greenman in Pittsgrove, Philip wrote Betsy a series of letters—which he called a "Collection of Sentiments"—to comfort her after her companions had returned home, presumably to Philadelphia or Newington. Philip did not directly mention Rodman in these letters, nor did he ever reference specifically Betsy's relationship with him, but he did fill his epistles with "sentiments" devoted entirely to his views on love, courtship, and female sensibility. While these letters were designed to amuse and inform Betsy, their content suggests that Philip was also using them as a way of winning back her sole affection. He copied to Betsy long passages from the diary he had kept at Nomini Hall, deliberately choosing excerpts in which he pledged his loyalty to her amid the temptations posed by the fashionable and refined young plantation ladies of Virginia. He sent her a copy of his journal entry from the previous March in which he responded to Robert Carter's suggestion that he marry a Virginia girl who could offer a dowry worth fifty thousand pounds sterling. He wanted Betsy to see that his response to such an offer was the same now as it had been then: "I declare with as great Pleasure as Truth that the Esteem and Fidelity which I possess for my ever-dear Eliza would make me, without Reflection, evade & refuse the Offer."[17]

These months were, as might be expected, a painful time in Philip's life. The joy and satisfaction he experienced from passing his Presbyterian licensing trials were tempered by the sorrow he felt from thinking about the possibility of Betsy marrying another man. In his letters Philip did not hesitate to express his pain to Betsy. By early December rumors were swirling about the couple. Some Deerfield friends claimed to have heard that Betsy had turned to Rodman because Philip was so "remarkably & impertinently intimate" in his behavior with her. In another second- or thirdhand story Betsy made "an ill-natured Remark" concerning Philip's decision to go to Virginia. Whether these rumors were "Trash or Substance," they put Philip in a "lowly Posture." To describe his sadness he turned to Joseph Addison in the *Spectator*, who compared the agony of ending a courtship or marriage to the nagging throb of a swelling finger. Philip asked Betsy to sympathize with this sort of steady and constant pain by reading the author's thoughts on marriage in *Spectator* number 183.[18] His emotional aching, however, did not hinder him from hoping for a future with Betsy. During December 1774 and January 1775 he wrote and visited more frequently than he ever had before, prompting one neighbor to wonder how Philip "Could find Time to visit Ladies, if he attended properly to his necessary Studies."[19]

By mid-January, Betsy was committed to her new suitor but still unwilling to end her friendship with Philip. This gave him hope and left the door open for him to write. On January 16 he reaffirmed to Betsy that he was "much at ease" in her friendship but wanted more, claiming that he could not be "compleatly happy" until he was "with Reason & Evidence fully convinced that you have countenanced & approved my Proposals and agreed to a nearer Alliance with me." It is unclear whether or not Philip had made Betsy another offer of marriage, but whatever the nature of his latest "proposal," she had not entirely rejected it. Moreover, the relationship Betsy shared with Rodman must have been serious, for Philip's letter has a forbidden quality to it. It appears that both Philip *and* Betsy were pushing the bounds of proper etiquette by continuing to exchange intimate letters—Philip writing them and Betsy receiving them—while she was pursuing a committed relationship with another man. Philip thought that there was something unethical about their correspondence, especially amid the current revolutionary climate. He described their "conduct" as inappropriate at a time when the people of Cohansey were mustering the virtue necessary to protest politically against "a Tax on our Liberty which shall never be taken off."[20]

Betsy was clearly considering marriage with Rodman, and Philip urged her to make her choice carefully: "There is so large a Measure of Earthly Contentment at Stake when we are fixing upon a Companion for Life, that every prudent Precaution should previously be considered." This, of course, was good advice no matter what the circumstances, but coming from Philip it wreaked of meddling. He advised Betsy "to be as certain as you can, indeed you should be fully convinced, that the Man you are willing to marry expects to live more agreeably with you than he could with any other Woman of his Acquaintance." Philip warned Betsy about marrying someone who practiced "gallantry." He lectured her on the dangers of "Infidelity with Regard to marriage" and reminded Betsy that when either party in a courtship could not be trusted to remain entirely faithful, the best thing to do was to end the relationship: "it is better to break off even with the Misery of one, than by carrying it on to make both wretched."[21] We know nothing about Rodman, but Philip seems to have been attacking his character here, alerting Betsy to the fact that he knew things that she did not about her suitor's relations with members of the opposite sex. If Rodman had not committed some form of infidelity, Philip certainly believed that he had the potential for such behavior. He thought that this was information, or gossip, that Betsy needed to know.

Philip now began to sound a great deal like John Witherspoon's letters on marriage and courtship. Marriage needed to be rescued from the cult of sentimentality that held the entire culture of the refined classes hostage. He warned Betsy not to be taken in by the cunning and flattery that had long been the mark of a sentimental gallant. The fact that Philip had engaged in similar romantic fantasies in earlier correspondence with Betsy did not seem to matter now. Women, he wrote, are often too "fond of being admired and flattered" by men and will thus "humour a Man so far as to agree to spend their Lives in his Company." A relationship based on this type of superficial affection was doomed to failure. Marriage partners should be chosen based on "ordinary Conversation" rather than on a man's ability to "praise & adore" a woman's "Charms." When such flattery came to an end, so would the marriage, resulting in "Solitude, Melancholy, and Grief" for the couple involved. Philip ended with a strong exhortation: "Upon the whole, my dearest Girl, you will allow me however deeply interested, to recommend it to you, that you never give away your Name nor Person but to the Man you sincerely love."[22] The letter was nothing short of an attempt to convince Betsy to break off her courtship with Rodman. Philip wrote out of concern for the future welfare of the woman he loved, but his caring admonishments were obviously driven by motives that were blatantly selfish.

Philip had clearly crossed a line of propriety here. His Cohansey mentors and friends were not only aware of it but also felt an obligation to do something about it. Two weeks after he penned the aforementioned letter, and roughly around the same time he was preparing to go to Egg Harbor, Philip wrote Betsy again to inform her that he had "a most violent and dangerous Encounter chiefly on your Account, with two of the governing Masters of human Conduct." While he never mentioned who these "masters" were or what they wanted to confront Philip about, the nature of their encounter becomes clearer in his journal entry written four days later, after Philip met with Andrew Hunter to obtain instructions for his journey to the coast. Hunter not only advised Philip concerning his ministerial duties in Egg Harbor but "gave me correction too about my Intimacy with Laura, & such as was not so agreeable as I should wish."[23] Since Philip was without parents to turn to for advice, Hunter represented a figure of moral authority and guidance on matters such as this. Philip was now experiencing the disciplinary and reproving dimensions of an eighteenth-century Presbyterian community. The friends and relations who made his homeland so beloved were intervening in his life to offer correction, and Philip did not like it.

Hunter's involvement suggests that Betsy and Rodman must have been moving toward marriage, making Philip's letters subversive and unbefitting of an educated gentleman and Presbyterian minister. Yet, despite these rebukes, Philip continued to believe that he had a better read on Betsy's sentiments than anyone else. He thus chose to ignore, perhaps for the first time in his life, Hunter's reprimands. Philip wrote to Betsy to tell her that he had been "severely lashed by Hunter," adding that he would defy any adviser who suggested that he curtail his pursuit of her. "And til I am told by your own Lips that you disavow & renounce every former Engagement," he wrote, "I shall still continue, *let the World say what it will*, to harbour & nourish in my Breast this soft & increasing Friendship for you which was produced at the happy Moment when I first beheld you, & which hath now grown into pleasing Raptures—I will indeed so long as it pleased a kind & merciful Providence to feed & continue the glimmering Taper, this Lamp of Life [italics mine]."[24]

The corrections, however, kept coming. When Philip returned from Egg Harbor on March 5, three letters were awaiting him. He copied them, noting that they were written in a disguised hand and sent secretly "to dissuade me from continuing any Intimacy with Laura, who despised my Friendship." Philip's reference to Laura despising his friendship suggests that a major shift must have occurred in their relationship. Sometime during February, Betsy seems to have closed Philip's small window of hope and decided to move forward with Rodman. Philip now had three letters from friends who were trying to save him from any further embarrassment. The first letter came from a friend who claimed that he was not "so unobserving as to be ignorant of any of your Advances to Miss [Beatty]." His rebuke was stern: "I am sorry you intrude yourself so often, & with so little Reserve, where the World all around, but especially your most valuable Friend, cannot but observe you are much unwelcome." The writer suggested that Philip had been "blinded with an overstrong Esteem for that young Lady," and he hoped that he would "play the fool no longer." His use of the words "intrude" and "much unwelcome" suggests that Philip was interfering in a relationship between Betsy and Rodman that everyone in the community realized had a degree of formality about it.[25]

The second letter began with a question: "Are you crazy & bebedlam'd that you go on so madly?" It continued, "I cannot think but you have common Sense; & it is commonly allow'd that you have a good understanding—But you seem to be trying to make us believe that you have in fact neither the one nor the other." This correspondent claimed to have heard that Rodman had "lately absolutely obtained . . . a firm & unchangeable promise from Miss [Beatty] to be his & [n]one others Companion." He made it clear that Philip was out of the picture and advised him to stop being such a "whining Dunce." He told Philip that instead he should take the noble route and "make it more convenient" for Rodman and Beatty "to carry on their Design with Success." The closing paragraph of this letter was especially revealing. Philip was undoubtedly to blame for much of this scandal, but the author was also "as much amazed at the Infatuation of Miss [Beatty]." He hoped that she would "open her Eyes & take a considerate View, before she rashly steps . . . into Wretchedness."[26] Apparently Betsy was not an innocent victim in this affair and may have never entirely closed the door, until perhaps recently, on the possibility of a deeper relationship with Philip. Maybe she did love Philip but could not muster the courage to rise above social pressure and break things off with Rodman. We will never know.

The final letter, addressed simply to "Rash Youth," came from "a true & intimate Friend & Companion of him who is now your able and successful Rival in Miss [Beatty]s Kindness & Countenance." This writer, apparently a friend of Rodman, admonished Philip for not behaving in a gentlemanly manner. "One would expect Sir," he wrote, "from the Manner & Place of your Education & from your Acquaintance in a polite Part of America that you should be possest of a far greater Share of Civility when you are contending with a Gentleman for the Heart of a Lady, than you either discover or pretend to." It continued with a warning for Philip to turn his "fondness into another Channel & be no longer an impertinent & unmeaning Interruption to the declared & manifestly welcome Visits' of my Friend."[27]

Philip's only answer to these epistles came in a letter to Laura written three days after he received the third of these letters of reproof. He wrote: "I must not omit to tell you that I received since I saw you several Letters of Advice from Anonymous Persons who, call themselves Well-wishers, concerning this most disagreeable & slanderous Report, to which you are not a Stranger. I have resolved, however, *from what you kindly told me the other Day*, that I will listen neither to Relations nor Friend, but as often as it is convenient I will run, I will fly, with Pleasure with Desire to your Company which I prefer to either [italics mine]." His response shows his rejection of the wisdom of his friends. In doing so, he was also turning his back on an essential part of Presbyterian moral thought—the importance of friendship and sociability in the making of ethical decisions. Moreover, the importance of self-control, at least when it came to the opposite sex, was a lesson Philip never seemed to learn. His sense of rational decorum disappeared whenever his relationship with Betsy was in jeopardy. Philip was willing to discard all the polite behavior and refined manners of a Presbyterian gentleman in order to pursue his deepest yearnings and passions for Betsy, even if she was in a relationship with another man at the time.[28]

This response also tells us that Philip's own assessment of his relationship with Betsy was correct. The fact that he had read the signals accurately was confirmed by a definitive statement from Betsy ("from what you kindly told me the other Day") that her affections for him were superior to those she felt for Rodman. We do not know what happened between Betsy and Rodman, but sometime in the days prior to this letter she must have had a change of heart that led her to end her relationship with him and embrace Philip's "proposals" exclusively. If it were not for his stubborn rejection of his friends' advice and his willingness to follow his passionate love for Betsy, Philip would have probably lost her to Rodman. Instead, he scheduled a time to dine with her and, at her request, entertain her with the German flute. Another unmistakable sign that his relationship with Betsy was restored came in a long letter apologizing to her for his improper manner of correspondence of late and expressing hope that she would not judge his character based on the content of his epistles. Philip the enlightened Presbyterian gentleman, conveniently enough, was back.[29]

As Philip learned how to challenge authority in the social realm, he was also learning to do the same in the political realm. In general, American Presbyterians positioned themselves among the strongest supporters of independence. The official Presbyterian pronouncements on the Revolution were informed by Whig ideas about the protection of liberties, particularly religious liberties, from an English government that was placing those freedoms at risk. Great Britain's taxation schemes and intolerable acts served as evidence that its government was corrupt, if not sinful, and Presbyterians had a religious and moral obligation to resist it. Philip was certainly no stranger to the kind of virtue that Presbyterians believed was needed to sustain a revolution and a republic. He had cultivated moral friendships while he was a student at Green Hall and the College of New Jersey. He used novels, letters, and the social practice of visiting to foster virtue in the fields and villages of Cohansey. As an active member of the Bridge-Town Admonishing Society he met regularly with young men concerned with moral improvement. As the hostilities between England and its colonies reached a fever pitch, such local communities of virtue—both formal and informal—would be essential to the preservation of liberty.

Much of what Philip knew about politics came straight from the social contract philosophers of the era. John Witherspoon's lectures on moral philosophy taught Philip that when government is "found to be pernicious and destructive" people have the right to "recall their obligation [to that government], and resettle the whole upon a better footing." If governmental power is "exercised in a manifestly tyrannical manner," he added, "the subjects may certainly if in their power, resist and overthrow it." Such Lockean principles were at the heart of his ideas about civil society, politics, and specifically the American Revolution.[30] In this sense, Witherspoon's case for independence was no different than the arguments put forth by most educated revolutionaries in the colonies. His writings sounded a familiar refrain: British taxation was unjust; Great Britain was enslaving its American colonies; the distance separating the mother country from its colonies made it impossible for England to claim moral and political authority over America. Witherspoon believed that the revolution should be supported by all ethical people. He affirmed that the "cause in which America is now in arms, is the cause of justice, of liberty, and of human nature."[31]

As a Whig, Witherspoon thought that the American Revolution was just. As a Presbyterian, he thought that it was ordained by God. War and

Figure 7. John Witherspoon by Charles Willson Peale, after Charles Willson Peale, 1783–84. Courtesy, Independence National Historical Park, Philadelphia, Pa.

revolution reflected the sinfulness of humankind. As a Calvinist, Witherspoon was not surprised by the behavior of the English government. Human beings, by their very nature, were conditioned to act in corrupt and immoral ways. However, it was also his Calvinist beliefs, specifically his trust in divine providence, that allowed the Princeton divine to argue that God could use the horrendous conditions of war to further God's larger causes in the world. In his famous 1776 sermon *The Dominion of Providence over the Passions of Men,* Witherspoon employed providential history to remind his listeners that the founding and development of the American colonies resulted from God's use of human sin to promote his own good purposes. For example, Protestantism, and the overwhelmingly Protestant character of the colonies, would have been impossible if Martin Luther's followers had not been forced by the Roman Catholic Church to flee to "every part of the world." God used the British destruction of the Spanish Armada to humble the leaders of a nation who were "determined to crush the interest of the [Protestant] reformation." Similarly, if Charles I had not persecuted English Puritans, those dissenters could not have carried "the knowledge of Christ to the dark places of the earth," particularly New England. By appealing to the providential nature of the Calvinist God, Witherspoon was leading his hearers to consider the American Revolution as an important epoch in spiritual history. Despite the death, destruction, and sin that war might bring, it was ultimately part of God's plan, and the end result, which Witherspoon believed would be an American victory, would bring God glory.[32]

Witherspoon, like many patriot clergymen of his day, claimed to be able to decipher God's sovereign will on the question of American independence. *The Dominion of Providence over the Passions of Men* does not make a sophisticated theological argument for independence but simply assumes, based on secular Whig principles, that Providence was on the side of the colonies: "If your case is just, if your principles are pure, and if your conduct is prudent, you need not fear the multitude of opposing hosts. If your case is just—you may look with confidence to the Lord and intreat him to plead it as his own." If this statement was not enough to convince his readers, Witherspoon provided some specific reasons why God would naturally support the American cause. America, for example, was morally superior to England. Apparently sinful human nature did not have the same effect on the people of the American colonies as it did on the imperial administration in London. "I cannot help observing," he wrote, "that though it would be a miracle if there were not many selfish persons among us, and discoveries now and then made of mean and interested transactions, yet they have been comparatively inconsiderable both in number and effect." The colonies offered relatively few examples of "dishonesty and disaffection" because their people exercised greater public spirit than the people of England. And, perhaps most importantly, God was on the side of the Revolution because Americans, as we saw in Chapter 2, had fully embraced the universal and harmonious qualities of the Enlightenment that had permeated their culture in the decades since the end of the First Great Awakening. The colonists did not get caught up in the passions of division, particularly religious strife. They enjoyed a great degree of "order and public peace" and transcended "local provincial pride and jealousy." Americans understood the "absolute necessity of union" to the success of their cause.[33] The Revolution was thus the climax of the Enlightenment in America, and this meant, for Presbyterians of Witherspoon's age, that it was also pleasing to God. American provincials had sacrificed their selfish passions for the greater good, embraced the God of order, and staked their claim for independence on the natural, moral, and political laws, instilled by the Creator, that governed all human beings.

If God was indeed on the side of independence, then it was the job of Presbyterians to make sure he stayed there. Witherspoon encouraged his church to revolutionary action. He called for nothing short of a religious revival, but not the kind of spiritual awakening that we associate with the great revival of the 1740s or even the passion-driven stirrings that occurred at the College of New Jersey in 1770 and 1772, student revivals that Witherspoon frowned on because of their enthusiastic nature. The Princeton president instead called for increased attention to the "public interest of religion, or in other words, zeal for the glory of God and the good of others." He wrote, "What I have here in view is to point out to you the concern which every good man ought to take in the national character and manners, and the means which he ought to use for promoting public virtue, and bearing down impiety and vice." The "best friend to American liberty," Witherspoon argued, was the person "who is most sincere and active in promoting true and undefiled religion." If the Revolution were to be a successful one, people needed to counter English vice with American virtue. This was not the religion of the "peculiar distinctions" that were prone to divisiveness and normally associated with specific denominations or sects, but rather a universal Protestantism that was capable of securing God's favor and providing the colonies with a moral edge over their British adversaries. Witherspoon, fitting with his enlightened ethical views, encouraged his readers to find such virtue either in "God's moral government" *or* "the operation and influences of natural causes."[34] Only evangelical religion could save one's soul, but when it came to promoting the public good there was little difference between the virtue that flowed from the lives of believers and the virtue that all people could cultivate through conscience.

Related to this revival of public religion, American revolutionaries needed to be industrious. The results of industry would bring economic benefit to the colonies at a time when it was desperately needed, and hard work was conducive to virtue. In this portion of his sermon Witherspoon drew on classical republican attacks on luxury.[35] "Idleness," he wrote, "is the mother or nurse of almost every vice" and leads men "on to the most abandoned and destructive courses." Industry, on the other hand, was "the sure way of obtaining the blessing of God." Witherspoon placed the burden for such industry on the backs of ordinary American farmers: "He who is inured to the labor of the field, is prepared for the fatigues of a campaign," he wrote. His message would have had much appeal in the agricultural and Presbyterian precincts of Cohansey. Those who resided in Philip's homeland were the children and grandchildren of the yeoman farmers who, in 1715, resisted colonial taxation and challenged what they believed to be the tyranny of a Roman Catholic tax collector. These were the same people who questioned Philip's decision to pursue the life of an educated gentleman because it would force him to sacrifice the health and physical rigor associated with an agricultural life. They were also the friends and relations who advised him against going to Virginia because the life of the plantation gentry posed a threat to his moral sensibilities. Indeed, these rural Presbyterians, in all their masculine revolutionary spirit, knew exactly what kind of religion, virtue, and industry Witherspoon was calling them to take up. They would no doubt have smiled when they read the words of their most celebrated colonial religious leader: "The active farmer who rises with the dawn and follows his team or plow, must in the end be an overmatch for those effeminate and delicate soldiers, who are nursed in the lap of self-indulgence, and whose greatest exertion is in the important preparation for, and tedious attendance on, a masquerade, or midnight ball."[36]

The formal Presbyterian statements on the American Revolution were not as overt or as thorough as Witherspoon's *The Dominion of Providence over the Passions of Men*, but they were driven by the same understanding of religious, moral, and public duty. Witherspoon, in fact, was one of their primary authors. The combined Synod of New York and Philadelphia announced that "there is no example in history, in which civil liberty was destroyed, and the rights of conscience preserved entire." Liberties and "inestimable privileges" that the colonies had "hitherto enjoyed without interruption since the first settlement of this country" were now in jeopardy, and Presbyterians, perhaps more than the members of any other Protestant denomination, would rise up in their defense. The synod instructed laypersons to support the Continental Congress with prayer and defend their rights as "FREEMEN and BRITONS."[37] Presbyterians understood the Revolution in distinctly moral terms, for a nation without virtue had no platform from which to direct its supplications to God. Ministers urged their congregants not only to confess personal sins but also to repent of "those prevalent national offenses which may be justly considered as the procuring of causes of public judgments." Only if Americans confessed public transgressions of "profaneness and contempt of God and his Name" or "pride, luxury, uncleanness" or "neglect of family, religion and government" would God "hear our supplications, and interpose for our protection or deliverance." The synod added, "It is undeniable that if universal profligacy makes a nation ripe for divine judgments, and is the natural means of bringing them to ruin, reformation of manners is of the utmost necessity in our present distress." The inclination to engage in immoral activities worked counter to freedom. It was a sign of dependence, representing the enslavement of an undisciplined will to the passions. Moral citizens, living ordered lives, as John Witherspoon had exhorted them in *The Dominion of Providence over the Passions of Men*, were the foundation of the colonial character needed to resist British tyranny.[38]

Similar sentiments could be found in Cohansey pulpits. Enoch Green at Deerfield announced in March 1776, "This Contest is glorious, this cause is just" and "Victory seems to incline to America. There is cause to hope ye Lord of History is on our Side and will favor our righteous Cause." Americans had "Truth and Law and Reason and Justice" in their corner, so it was also logical that God was there too. Like Witherspoon and the Synod of New York and Philadelphia, Green warned his hearers that the real enemy was not the British army but American sin. "I have it observed, by a good Man, that the Sins of ye Lord are more to be feared then Lord North, ye King, Ministry and all ye Fleets and Armies of Great Britain." Morality and liberty were closely related—God would support liberty only among a virtuous people.[39]

Philip reached maturity in this patriotic culture. He was taught at Princeton that it *was* appropriate to exercise the passions in the defense of liberty. In his 1772 commencement disputation he echoed the words of the eighteenth-century political tract of John Trenchard and Thomas Gordon, *Cato's Letters*, by defending the notion that "political jealousy is a laudable passion." His speech distinguished between "domestic and ecclesiastical jealousies," which were harmful, and "political jealousy," which was "rational & uniform & necessary." As Philip had learned all too well through his courtship with Elizabeth Beatty, "jealousy" was normally a dangerous "disease" that could blight friendships and lead to "suspicions" among acquaintances. However, when channeled in the right direction, it was also a useful passion. The truly "jealous" citizen kept a careful and virtuous watch on his government leaders to guard against vice and corruption. Political jealousy served as a unifying force—a common political ideology of resistance grounded in a common morality—that held a community together in times of strife and preserved societal order. Philip said that it had a "natural tendency" to "unite people" around interests that were closely associated with the preservation of the nation.[40]

It is only through this understanding of political jealousy that we can begin to fathom why a supposedly civil and enlightened Presbyterian such as Philip might have engaged in an act of local political rebellion that could be described as uncivil and unenlightened. The members of the Bridge-Town Admonishing Society, along with other public-spirited young Cohansey Presbyterians, initiated what has become the most celebrated event in Cumberland County's public memory—the Greenwich tea burning. Sometime in mid-December 1774, approximately one year after the famed tea party at Boston Harbor, the British brig *Greyhound*, carrying tea to Philadelphia from Rotterdam, docked on the Cohansey River at Greenwich and unloaded its cargo for safekeeping during the night. On December 18, the day of his first sermon as a licensed Presbyterian clergyman, Philip wrote: "Early last week a Quantity of Tea said to be shipped at Rotterdam was brought & privately stored at Dan Bowens in Greenwich."[41] Since Greenwich was a port within the Salem-Cohansey customs district, such a stop was not out of the ordinary. The fact that the *Greyhound* was transporting tea, however, made its arrival a serious community concern.

By the turn of the eighteenth century tea had become an integral part of everyday life in colonial America. Perhaps more than any other consumer product, it represented the British character of the American provinces. Colonists could not get enough of it, purchasing roughly three hundred thousand pounds of tea between 1770 and 1773 alone, a period, interestingly enough, when it was taxed as part of the dreaded Townshend duties.[42] Tea was served at nearly every stop along Philip's way of improvement. The culture that surrounded this beverage provided the venue for many of his visits throughout Cohansey—visits that, as we have seen, were essential to the fostering of his own moral and intellectual development. If Philip had followed the advice of Addison and Steele, he would have read his daily passage of the *Spectator* with a hot cup of tea nearby. Charles Clinton Beatty, Philip's future brother-in-law, wrote to his sister Betsy at Deerfield, "if you have tea [in your future household] you will have visitors enough, you will see every old wife in the neighbourhood each week, you will hear all the news that is stirring and many other useful things." As T. H. Breen has noted, "It was hard to imagine maintaining the normal fabric of social relations without tea."[43]

However, after Boston patriots dressed as Mohawks dumped tea into Boston Harbor in December 1773, the status of this popular drink changed dramatically across the colonies. Lord North, the British prime minister, punished the people of Massachusetts by issuing a series of measures in spring 1774 known in the colonies as the Intolerable Acts. These acts closed the harbor until the tea was paid for (Boston Port Act), restricted the number and character of Massachusetts town meetings (Massachusetts Government Act), moved trials to locations where defendants would be able to obtain sympathetic juries (Administration of Justice Act), and quartered British soldiers in unoccupied buildings in the colony (Quartering Act). In response to the Intolerable Acts and other British injustices, the First Continental Congress convened in Philadelphia in September and quickly issued a statement, known as the "Continental Association," calling for both the nonimportation *and* nonconsumption of British goods. The enforcement of this legislation would rest with local committees at the town and county levels.[44]

In the wake of the Boston Tea Party and the formation of the Continental Congress, the drinking of tea became a great "political sin." Its consumption became a moral issue in local communities, a test of one's commitment to the American Revolution.[45] Philip's letters and diary entries, which repeatedly made reference to his tea-time visits with friends, now mentioned coffee as the beverage of choice. For example, after writing an especially sentimental letter to Betsy, an epistle that he would later deem to be entirely inappropriate for a Presbyterian gentleman, Philip asked her if she would use his lines "to boil your tomorrow-Morning's Coffee."[46] Reading Beatty asked his teacher and brother-in-law Enoch Green whether or not his sister Mary, Green's wife, still kept tea in their household: "Does Mrs. Green drink Tea yet? I hope not, if she does, and you allow her, you will perhaps fall under the denomination of a Tory."[47] Presbyterians, however, thought that drinking tea was more than a political transgression. In addition to his call for a revival of public religion and a renewed emphasis on personal industry, John Witherspoon exhorted all Presbyterians and lovers of liberty to be frugal in their habits of consumption. He echoed the Continental Congress with his suggestion that people of true public spirit exercise "Temperance in meals, moderation and decency in dress, furniture, and equipage," but he also reminded his hearers that self-denial was first and foremost a religious virtue. Nonconsumption was an example of how Christianity should be applied to all dimensions of life. "Consider, therefore," Witherspoon exhorted, "that the Christian character, particularly the self-denial of the gospel, should extend to your whole deportment." He compared the kind of frugality required of Presbyterian patriots to an ancient Christian baptism where adult converts were asked to "renounce the world, its shews, its pomp, and its vanities." He added, "The same thing, as it is suitable to your Christian profession, is also necessary to make you truly independent in yourselves, and to feed the source of liberality and charity to others, or to the public."[48]

Witherspoon's reference to the need for patriots to be "truly independent in yourselves" also revealed, once again, his commitment to the moral character of the Enlightenment. Independent people evidenced self-control and moderation in their lives: "the frugal and moderate person, who guides his affairs with discretion, is able to assist in public counsels by a free and unbiased judgment." In other words, because independent people were not enslaved to their passions, they were capable of acting fairly in matters pertaining to public affairs. Those unable to exercise the rational faculties conducive to a life of self-control were also deemed incapable of curbing their desires for British consumer goods. The undisciplined colonist was a "rioutous and wasteful liver, whose craving appetites make him constantly needy," and he was thus unfit to sacrifice for the public good during a time of revolution. The theological and moral commitments of early American Presbyterianism, Witherspoon believed, provided a powerful ideological resource for sustaining the virtue necessary to resist the consumption of tea or any other British product.[49]

Witherspoon's ideas, which had been inculcated in all his Princeton students, Philip included, provide the proper context for understanding the Greenwich tea burning. Following the arrival of the *Greyhound,* Philip wrote, "A pro Tempore Committee was Chosen to secure it till the County Committee be duly elected." The formation of this tempore committee of five prominent Greenwich residents occurred on the same day as the election in Bridge-Town of a county committee as ordered by the Continental Association. On December 22, shortly after the *Greyhound's* tea was secured in Daniel Bowen's basement, thirty-five men were chosen to form this political body, which became known as the Cumberland County Committee. Their job description included the enforcement of the Continental Congress's nonimportation and nonconsumption decrees and the identification and discipline of local Tories who defied such orders. The members of the Cumberland County Committee included Cohansey Quakers, Baptists, and Anglicans, but as might be expected, it was dominated by Presbyterians. It is difficult to determine exactly how many of the members of the committee were affiliated with one of the Cohansey Presbyterian churches, but it was at least half. Philip's cousin Joel Fithian was elected to the committee, and so was Philip's childhood friend and Bridge-Town Admonishing Society member Thomas Ewing. Samuel Leake, a former student at Enoch Green's academy, a correspondent of Philip's, and a recent graduate of the College of New Jersey, was also chosen. Leake had gained some notoriety in Presbyterian circles when the college trustees stripped him of the honor of serving as Princeton's Latin salutory orator due to his participation in the 1774 burning of the college's supply of tea (along with an effigy of Massachusetts governor Thomas Hutchinson) on the lawn of Nassau Hall.[50]

The Greenwich tempore committee turned the problem of the *Greyhound* and its tea over to the members of the newly formed Cumberland County Committee. A meeting of the committee was scheduled for the next day, December 23, to discuss what to do about the matter, but when the members awoke the following morning they soon realized that their problem had grown exponentially. The agenda for their meeting would no longer be focused on how to respond to a small shipment of tea stored in a local basement, for during the night Cohansey patriots disguised as Indians had removed the stash from Bowen's house, taken it to the town's market square located near the end of Ye Greate Street, and burned it. Philip described the event tersely: "Last night the Tea was, by a number of persons in disguise, taken out of the House & consumed with fire."[51]

The Greenwich tea burning was a radical act. It created quite a stir in the usually sober world of Presbyterian Cohansey. The participants could face criminal charges ranging from forcible entry and trespassing to the destruction of property and rioting. The tea burners were motivated by similar events in Boston and Princeton, the nonconsumption decrees of the First Continental Congress, and the fact that Daniel Bowen was known in the community for his Tory sentiments. Almost all of the burners, twenty-three according to local lore, were young Presbyterians who were most likely driven by their duty to exercise the "laudable passion" of political jealousy. The group included a future governor of New Jersey (Richard Howell); a future member of the United States House of Representatives (Ebenezer Elmer); a future mayor of Trenton, New Jersey (James Ewing); and a future chaplain of the United States Navy and College of New Jersey trustee (Andrew Hunter Jr.). At least sixteen of those involved would serve in some military capacity during the American War for Independence.[52]

While the tea burning may have been an outlet for the zeal of young Presbyterian patriots, it did not meet with approval from the residents of Cohansey or the Cumberland County Committee. Philip took a quick survey of the people of Greenwich. "Violent, & different are the words about this uncommon Manoeuvre, among the Inhabitants," he wrote. "Some rave, some curse & condemn, some try to reason; many are glad the Tea is destroyed, but almost all disapprove the Manner of the destruction."[53] The committee (which may have included two tea-burning participants—Joel Fithian and Thomas Ewing) issued a condemnation of the event. Members claimed that the tea party was "entirely contrary to our resolves" and declared that the committee would not protect any of the perpetrators from justice.[54]

The owners of the tea, of course, were not thrilled with the events of December 22 either. John Duffield and Stacey Hepburn, Philadelphia merchants, sued seven of the participants in an effort to recover their losses. The tea burners indicted in the case—Richard Howell, Joel Miller, Alexander Moore Jr., Ephraim Seeley, Silas Newcomb, Henry Seeley, and Abraham Sheppard—were defended by Bridge-Town lawyer

Figure 8. Monument to the "Greenwich tea burning," circa 1908. Courtesy, Lummis Library, Cumberland County (N.J.) Historical Society.

Joseph Bloomfield, a graduate of Green's Deerfield academy and a future governor of New Jersey. (In one of the more interesting twists in New Jersey political history, a future New Jersey governor, Richard Howell, was defended by another future New Jersey governor, Bloomfield. The two men would end up on different sides of the political spectrum in the 1790s and 1800s.) Bloomfield was assisted by Elias Boudinot of Elizabeth-Town and George Read of New Castle, both Presbyterians. The tea burners also faced criminal charges, but New Jersey governor William Franklin's attempts to prosecute them were frustrated by the local sheriff, Jonathan Elmer, the brother of two of the tea burners and a prominent Cohansey physician. Elmer not only stacked the local jury with members sympathetic to the tea burners but also appointed his own brother, Daniel, as jury foreman. After several failed attempts by Franklin's chief justice William Smyth to convict the Greenwich patriots, the case, along with the aforementioned civil suit, was postponed indefinitely due to the arrival of war.[55]

Philip's role in the tea party remains somewhat of a mystery. He recorded the event in his diary but did not specifically mention his own involvement. If he did participate, he probably hesitated to record many details out of a concern that such incendiary activities were unbecoming of a newly licensed minister. He may have also feared the legal and civil repercussions he would face if the royal government learned of his role in the incident. Such explanations make sense in light of the fact that he delivered his first sermon at Deerfield only four days before the tea party. Tradition and oral history, which were largely consulted in the assembling of the list of tea burners that appears on a monument to the event erected at Greenwich circa 1908, support the idea that Philip was present at the bonfire. This "official" list of participants comes from the early nineteenth-century local historian Robert Gibbon Johnson. In conducting research for his 1839 history of Salem County, Johnson interviewed eighty-seven-year-old Ebenezer Elmer, one of New Jersey's leading early national politicians and a participant in the tea party. While Elmer's memory may have been fading at the time, he did list Philip as one of the tea burners. Cohansey antiquarians have even suggested, with little evidence apart from local tradition to support their claim, that those involved in the tea party organized themselves at Philip's home on the outskirts of town. (The road where his childhood house stands has been renamed Tea Burner's Road.) In addition to the motivation provided by the tea parties at Boston and Princeton, the Greenwich affair may have also drawn inspiration from a similar event in Annapolis, Maryland. On his return trip from Virginia, Philip witnessed the patriots of Maryland's capital and their Baltimore neighbors, "full of patriotic fire," burn a London brig carrying seventeen chests of tea. Philip mentioned the Annapolis tea party only once in his journal but most certainly would have retold the story to Cohansey friends, and his account may have provided some incentive for action when the *Greyhound* made its way up the river two months later.[56]

Whatever Philip's role, he was fully aware of the circumstances surrounding the event, was probably involved in some capacity, and was likely pleased with the result. The tea party confirmed for him that political jealousy was indeed a "unifying" force. The virtuous act of burning tea connected the Cohansey patriots to the revolutionaries of Boston,

Princeton, and Annapolis. It served as one means by which the solidarity and unity essential to the success of the American Revolution were achieved. Cohansey Presbyterians engaged imaginatively with a universal and cosmopolitan set of religious, political, and moral ideals, but in the end the action that stemmed from those ideals was local. Such acts of resistance made them revolutionaries.[57]

If would be difficult, following the Greenwich tea burning, to find a region more in tune with the Revolutionary call of Witherspoon, the Continental Congress, and the Philadelphia and New York Synod than Cohansey. Ephraim Bateman, a member of the Fairfield church who was born during the American Revolution, may not have been exaggerating or engaging too heavily in Jefferson-era mythmaking when he wrote in 1801, "it is worthy of remark that during the revolutionary war not a single disaffected person or tory was to be found here."[58] The Cumberland County Committee fueled the resistance in the region and claimed that Cohansey patriots were the first in the southern part of New Jersey to take up arms for the cause of liberty. Ever aware of their vulnerability to British warships, the committee asked the Continental Congress for gunpowder to protect themselves and their property from "ministerial robbers, should they think proper to enter our Bay."[59] The region's Presbyterians contributed military leadership—officers, soldiers, chaplains, and surgeons—to the patriot cause. For example, of the sixty-two men listed on the Pittsgrove muster roll of "Minute Men in 1775," at least forty-two (69 percent) were affiliated with the local Presbyterian church.[60]

The Cumberland County Committee, which met weekly at the county courthouse in Bridge-Town during most of 1775 and into 1776, took their job seriously. They continued to monitor the consumption of tea in Cohansey, even when it was being consumed by one of their own. In March 1775 Silas Newcomb, a county judge who sat on the committee, confessed to his fellow members that he "had drank East-India Tea in his family ever since the first day of March instant." To makes matters worse, Newcomb made it abundantly clear that he was "determined to persist in the same practice." Others in the committee spent considerable time and effort trying to convince their wayward member of his error, but when Newcomb would not repent of his actions they had no choice but to "break off all dealings with him, and in this manner publish the truth of the case, that he may be distinguished from the friends of American liberty." In the rural confines of Cohansey, a region teeming with revolutionary spirit, Newcomb's punishment was the equivalent of wearing a scarlet letter. We do not know how the committee or the people of the region chose to ostracize him, but their disciplinary action must have worked. Two months later Newcomb was before the committee again to "make formal acknowledgement" of his "former misconduct" and promising in the future to "regulate my conduct agreeable to the aforesaid Association, and a majority of said Committee." He would later go on to distinguish himself as a colonel and brigadier general in the Continental army.[61]

Members of the committee also made it their mission to identify and punish those Cohansey inhabitants who displayed behavior that was in opposition to the work of the Continental Congress. They did not hesitate to use military force to achieve their ends. In July 1775 the committee sent a band of local militia, lined up in formation with drums banging, to the home of Robert Cayford, a Bridge-Town innkeeper who was guilty of repeatedly opposing "the general measures pursued by the united American colonies." Cayford was accused of publicly mocking militia volunteers, calling them "rebels, rascals, & c.," and instilling "into others his own pernicious principles." The committee declared him "an enemy to the rights of America" and, like their response to Newcomb's tea drinking, demanded that the inhabitants of Cohansey "break off all dealings with him." When the militia arrived at his house, Cayford was not there, but two other loyalists, Robert Wheaton and Richard Shay, were quickly snatched up nearby. When the armed party, which had now grown to nine men, continued their hunt for Tories at the home of J. Wheaton, they nearly encountered their first gunfire of the Revolution. Wheaton "flashed a gun" at the patriots before he was captured and taken to the courthouse with the others. The agitators were jailed overnight and scheduled to appear before the committee the following morning. The next day, July 22, the men confessed their political crimes before the members of the committee and were released on "good behavior."[62]

The following week this small cadre of local Tories was again up to its old tricks. Robert Wheaton was overheard uttering threatening words about the tyrannical behavior of some members of the committee. Other local inhabitants had expressed reservations about the committee's rough treatment of loyalists. Buoyed by this support, which eventually came to include a few members of the committee, local Tories continued their public condemnation of these guardians of the Cohansey revolution by swearing revenge against several prominent patriots, including Richard Howell, Joseph Bloomfield, and Matthew Potter. Ebenezer Elmer, who witnessed most of these events as a member of the local militia, summarized the state of Cohansey life during these days: "What distressing times do we See! Confusion, war, bloodshed, abroad and at home. Will the Lord who is the Supreme Generals of the Armies of the whole earth, appear to us & deliver us from our troubles, or we shall come to ruin!"[63]

With the committee presiding over the region's revolutionary activities, Cohansey became an armed camp. Philip described his homeland existing in a "melancholy state" filled with "Battalions of Militia & Minute-Men embodying—Drums & Fifes rattling—Military Language in every Mouth." He added, "Numbers who a few Days ago were plain Countrymen have now clothed themselves in martial forms—Powdered Hair, Sharp pinched Beavers—Uniform in Dress with their Battalion—Swords on their Thighs—& stern in the Art of War—Resolved, in steady manly Firmness, to support & establish American Liberty, or die in Battle!"[64] Militia companies were mustering and training in Greenwich, Bowen's Cross Roads, Bridge-Town, Fairfield, Deerfield, and Dividing Creek. The Fairfield militia marched through the streets of New England Crossroads, the place where Samuel Fithian had settled almost eighty years earlier, firing their guns before the onlooking crowds. Ebenezer Elmer noted that there was "such noise and confusion in the Country little can be done." People were now referenced with military titles: "Capt. Preston" and "Adjutant Bloomfield" and "Lieut. Holmes." The military activity continued to be entwined with the Presbyterian culture of the region. Captain Howell's soldiers marched to and from services at the Greenwich church "in form." Other companies paraded "up to Deerfield to hear the chaplain," presumably Enoch Green, preach on Continental fast days. In the midst of it all, and somewhat ironically, the session of the Fairfield church, perhaps forgetting the egalitarian and democratic ideals they were fighting for, conducted their annual sale of pews, an event that reflected the township's social hierarchy through the seating of the meetinghouse.[65]

While old customs such as pew renting still remained, and would persist well into the nineteenth century, the region's ministers—Enoch Green, William Hollingshead, and, as we will see, Philip Vickers Fithian and Andrew Hunter Jr.—volunteered as chaplains in the Continental army and the New Jersey militia. They also offered sermons in favor of independence and colonial resistance to British tyranny. Enoch Green's use of his Deerfield pulpit to propagate Whig ideas is especially telling in this regard. In a 1776 sermon on the occasion of his appointment as a chaplain to the New Jersey militia, he grounded his understanding of colonial rebellion in the history of British liberties, arguing that the "King derives his power from the people." He continued with a history lesson on the English civil war and the Puritan resistance to Charles I: "Little better than a century ago," he preached, the people "resisted and opposed a Tyrant, King Charles . . . and they took . . . their rights and vanquished the Tyrant." George III's newfound "Tory" sentiments prompted Green to encourage his listeners to begin making gunpowder in preparation for war. The language that Green employed in this sermon was similar to a message on tyranny and liberty he had preached at Deerfield six years earlier. In this sermon Green noted, "Because we were enslaved" and had become "Slaves to Sin—to ye Tyrant Satan . . . we are all fond of Liberty." He added, "as long as we are out of Christ, we are enslaved to ye worst kind of Bondage, enthralled by ye Tyrant of Hell." By the time of the American Revolution, Green's theological and biblical understanding of tyranny and liberty had taken on a new political meaning. The enslaver and tyrant was no longer Satan but George III and his army. Liberty was no longer the freedom from sin and the right to enjoy God's presence forever in heaven but the individual rights secured to all people by the Enlightenment. The champion of liberty was not Christ but the New Jersey militia, for which Green would serve as chaplain.[66]

It was also during the tumultuous year 1775 that a group of educated inhabitants of the region, many of whom were part of Philip's social circles (especially the Bridge-Town Admonishing Society), founded the *Plain Dealer*, a weekly manuscript newsletter designed to share and exchange "useful knowledge" in the Cohansey countryside. The *Plain Dealer* was the embodiment of a revolutionary public sphere. Placed every Tuesday morning at Matthew Potter's tavern in Bridge-Town, the newsletter was a collection of essays that focused on the political and moral matters facing the region in these troubling times. All who were interested in reading or discussing the essays presented to "Mr. Plain Dealer" were invited to the tavern to peruse the latest issue. The "Secretaries" of the paper, which included Cohansey patriots such as Joseph Bloomfield, Thomas Harris, Richard Howell, and Ebenezer Elmer, invited "both male and female who have ability or inclination to serve the public in this way, to give . . . a lift in carrying on this work."[67] The *Plain Dealer* was set in a place where the general public could discuss the ideas articulated in the essays and even respond to them in writing. The authors of the essays remained anonymous so that they might "communicate their sentiments to the public without the inconvenience of being known or personally criticised."[68] Philip probably did not write for the *Plain Dealer*. As we will see in Chapter 7, he was on a missionary tour in Pennsylvania and Virginia during the period (December 25, 1775, to February 12, 1776) when the paper was published. We do know, however, that as the patriotic temperature of the region began to rise, Philip made repeated trips to Bridge-Town to meet with his Admonishing Society and participate in revolutionary events. He also kept up a correspondence with Joseph Bloomfield, one of the paper's editors.[69] As part of this circle of local patriots, Philip would certainly have been familiar with the paper's contents.

The *Plain Dealer* was an attempt to apply the political ideals of the age to the local circumstances of Cohansey life. It was written to provide commentary on "every subject that may occasionally fall in the way; at least upon all such as have any reference to the present situation of public affairs or the particular circumstances of our place." The paper was designed as a forum where the educated could express their ideas and "diffuse useful knowledge, among the generality of mankind."[70] Those with the "leisure for study & opportunity of improving the mind" were called upon to employ themselves "in forming just Ideas of things and arranging them to others with clearness and precision" in order to "enlarge our own sphere of knowledge" and "contract a habit of thinking and reasoning more justly than those who neglect to exercise their intellectual faculties in this way." The writer of the first essay, who went by the revolutionary pseudonym "Cato," defended the importance of an informed citizenry to the cause of enlightened civilization. Cato wrote that "the only effectual method ... to rectify the errors and remove the superstitious prejudices, which at this time more especially occasions many of the evils that threaten our ruin, is to convince the Judgment and inform the understanding."[71] An invitation to participate in this rural public sphere was also extended to those who did not have the same level of education as some of the region's educated farmer-scholars, as long as the topics on which they chose to write were suitable to the social life of Cohansey. Cato wrote to "Mr. Plain Dealer": "By thus adopting them [these essays] to the spirit of the times, and the Ideas manners and capacities of your readers, even though they should fall infinitely short of all former attempts of the kind of eligance of language, sentiment, & propriety of diction, yet they will nevertheless have their merit & perhaps prove more serviceable in the place than better performances by abler hands."[72]

The essays in the *Plain Dealer* focused on both the conflicts with England and the social problems of Cohansey society. The author of *Plain Dealer* number 2 chided those in the region—most likely Quakers—who for religious reasons refused to take a stand against the "unjust and tyrannical impositions for conscience sake." These "rank Tories" were more concerned with private religious belief and otherworldly concerns than with the exercise of public virtue. They differed from the "True Whigs," who stood courageously against the corruption and vice of arbitrary power and exercised the virtue essential to the revolutionary cause.[73] Similarly, appended to *Plain Dealer* number 8 was a transcript of a speech delivered to Joseph Bloomfield's militia company the evening before it headed off to war. The speechwriter addressed the moral temptations that the soldiers would face on the battlefield, warning them to "live sober, temperate, & regular, & carefully guard against all those vices & irregularities, that are too common in Camps & Armies, particularly profane Swearing and the excessive use of spirituous liquor—These will injure your health, blast your reputation, & unfit you for service of your country."[74] The author of *Plain Dealer* number 7 used the death of Gen. Richard Montgomery as a model of the kind of bravery, heroism, and civic virtue needed to sustain the fight for liberty: "Does not the generous breast of every virtuous *American* boil with indignation, at those remorseless monsters in human shape, *a British Ministry & Parliament*, to whose cruelty and oppression, *a Warren, a Montgomery*, and many others of our brave Countrymen have fallen victoms? . . . let us draw our swords, and never return them into their scabboards, till we have rescued our Country from the Iron hand of Tyranny, And secured the pure enjoyment of Liberty, to generations yet unborn!"[75]

Another topic that drew heated debate in the newsletter and most likely triggered similar conversation in Potter's tavern was the courting practice of "Bundling," the custom of young people of the opposite sex sleeping together in the same bed while remaining fully clothed. Little is known about this young person's ritual, but theories and interpretations about its meaning to young men and women abound. All, however, agree that the practice was common among "the more humble and less cultivated classes" and was more of a rural phenomenon than an urban one.[76] For those who wrote about the topic in the *Plain Dealer*, it was also a moral problem. *Plain Dealer* number 4, written by "Juvenis," described a specific incident, which he apparently witnessed, of a young man and woman together in bed, in the dark, "Solacing themselves with Loves." When the man in bed realized that he and his young lady friend had company, he leaped up and tried to explain to Juvenis that the practice of "bundling" was the "custom of the place" and was the only way he knew how to "gain the esteem of the girls." Using this story as his guide, Juvenis went on to criticize the practice as an improper and indecent means of courtship and an affront to female modesty.[77]

Juvenis's account of this case of bundling drew a great deal of ire from the other readers of the *Plain Dealer*, and his essay sparked replies. These responses, all of which questioned the validity of the story and the reliability of its teller, admitted that bundling was practiced in Cohansey but challenged the notion that it was a widespread custom in the region. Many saw Juvenis's essay as an unfair assault on the moral character of their rural community and an exaggerated account of a courtship ritual that occurred only in a few isolated incidences. "A Country Bachelor" responded by noting that Juvenis was probably a "young Gentleman not well acquainted in this place; who happening in some of his first excursions in the Country to meet with an instance or two of this indelicate method of Courting, & being told perhaps in mere waggery that it was customary in this place, ungenerously asserts that the Custom is universal." He defended the virtue of Cohansey's young people and hoped to "remove some of Those base aspersions which he (Juvenis) Cast upon the fair Sex.[78]

It is clear that all of the respondents believed bundling was morally wrong. However, the manner in which the readers of the *Plain Dealer* rose up to challenge the assertion that it was a prevailing practice in the region reveals the way in which the newsletter was used as a forum to uphold public morality. Residents of Cohansey were quick to defend the virtue of their rural society against a stereotypical attack from an outsider. When taken in the context of the political essays included in the *Plain Dealer* and the virtuous agenda of the Presbyterians responsible for it, morally corruptible activities were a hindrance to the virtue needed to resist English tyranny and create a moral republic. Social and cultural practices such as bundling and the language of political resistance appeared to be closely connected in the minds of the rural Cohansey Presbyterians who debated and conversed about such topics in Potter's tavern.[79]

As the revolution continued its march through Cohansey, Philip was striving to fulfill two related callings, one to the ministry and the other to his country. His way of improvement was preparing him, every step of the way, for a time such as this—a moment when he would get the opportunity to come to the defense of both God and nation. Philip would not waver in his fulfillment of these commitments, but he also expressed a great deal of doubt and confusion about the direction his life would, and should, take. Where was God leading him to serve the Presbyterian Church? In what capacity was his new country calling him to use his education for revolutionary purposes? How would the answers to these questions impact his affection for his Cohansey home and his love, now seemingly secured, for Betsy? As the whirlwind of revolution swept over the British American colonies, Philip would be caught up in his own storm of uncertainty. By this point he knew that his way of improvement was never as straightforward as he had once imagined it, but he still had no idea exactly where it was leading him. He would find out soon, however, that it was leading him home.

Chapter 7

The Call of God

On May 9, 1775, Philip began a fresh page in his journal with the words "I left home." The sentence exudes a sense of finality. He had never written about leaving Cohansey with such certainty. Separated from the rest of that day's diary entry for emphasis, these three words speak volumes about Philip's mindset as he prepared to embark on an itinerant tour of the Pennsylvania and Virginia backcountry. He had spent the last five months at home gaining valuable preaching experience, but he knew his chances of settling into a ministerial career in one of the region's Presbyterian churches was slim. God was summoning him, perhaps once and for all, away from his beloved Cohansey. The time had come to answer the call.

Yet, Philip remained doubtful. The rest of his journal entry for that day suggests that he was still uncomfortable with the prospect of a permanent departure from home. As any eighteenth-century gentleman might have done, he turned to the Latin pastoral writers—in this case Ovid—to help him make sense of his decision. He copied a short passage from *Metamorphoses* exalting the cosmopolitan life: "Ignotis errare Locis, ignota videre / Flumina gaudebam; Studio minuente Laborem" (He loved to roam through unimagined places, by the banks of undiscovered rivers; and the joy of finding wonders made his labors light). "How soft is Ovid's Language!" Philip commented, "But can I apply it to myself?—Is my Inclination for rambling into other Provinces, & seeing new & strange Faces, & Manners, stronger than to fix down at once on some little Farm, in this Cohansie, my native dear Sod?" The emotional attachment to his "native dear Sod" remained strong. It was still the place of his childhood labors in his father's fields, the location where his family members and friends resided, and the new home of Elizabeth Beatty. This time, however, reason prevailed. Philip concluded that "my Duty, from the Course of my Education, calls me abroad." Service to the Presbyterian Church meant resigning himself to a life of geographical mobility.[1]

Philip's education and the cosmopolitan opportunities for "ramblings into other Provinces" that came with it were not the only things calling him away from home. His decision to pursue such an education in the first place was rooted in a belief, initiated amid the 1765 Cohansey revival and confirmed by the region's ministers, that he had received a call from God. An eighteenth-century Presbyterian minister's life was not his own. God called people to serve him in a variety of places and circumstances. Working through the wise council of synods and presbyteries, God opened and closed doors of ministerial service. When such a door was opened, clergymen were required to walk obediently through it. When God closed a door of opportunity, clergymen needed to pray that he would lead them to one that was open. There were many biblical precedents for this kind of Christian discipleship, and Philip knew them well. God called Abraham to leave his home in Ur for what would become the "promised land." Jonah was sent to preach to the people of Ninevah. Jesus told his disciples to leave father and mother and follow him. Saul (Paul) was knocked off his donkey on the road to Damascus and commissioned to evangelize the Gentile world. While all of these biblical heroes thought twice about leaving home, in the end they all remained obedient to the call.[2]

Philip understood that his passion for home was not only unbecoming of an enlightened gentleman but also could be a hindrance to the work God wanted him to do in the world. Writing in the context of his future life with Betsy, he committed himself to the possibility of living anywhere, even if it was "among the Mountains of Pennsylvania or Virginia—Or in distant, fertile Transylvania—in the most interior Wilds of rising America—or . . . in some foreign Quarter of the Globe." This was a cosmopolitanism rooted more in a sense of Christian calling than in the universal principles of the Enlightenment. Ministers were citizens of a world that was ordered and sustained by God and his purposes. A clergyman was not truly "home" in this world unless he was doing the will of the Lord. As he prepared to leave Cohansey, Philip prayed: "Great God—I am going on thy Business, & I trust by thy Appointment: grant me, then, in mercy, thy Direction, thy Blessing & a large Portion of they Grace & Spirit—Make me a faithful, an able, & useful Shepherd, that I may have thy Plaudit for my Recompense at last—!"[3]

On a less spiritual and more practical level, Philip left home because there were no ministerial openings for him within the bounds of the Philadelphia Presbytery. He was, in this sense, a victim of his denomination's success. The presbytery no longer had to suffer through the clerical shortages of its infancy. By 1775 the number of ministers licensed by the presbytery had grown to exceed the number of vacant pulpits. The "frontier" of early American Presbyterianism had moved from places such as Cohansey to the new Scots-Irish settlements in Virginia's Shenandoah Valley and Pennsylvania's Susquehanna Valley. Young clergymen began to leave Philadelphia and its hinterlands for remote regions where churches were desperate to obtain the services of educated ministers. Many of these backcountry congregations were tiny—far too small to hire a permanent clergyman. They thus looked to the church's growing number of licensees for preaching and other pastoral services.[4]

Philip would have been perfectly content staying near Betsy and the friends who inhabited his native soil, but he did not want to work as a substitute preacher any longer. The lack of long-term opportunities at home led him to request an "honourable and legal Dismission" from the Philadelphia Presbytery so that he might place himself under the care of another presbytery that needed his services. The Philadelphia Synod granted his wish in April 1775. As shots rang out in the Massachusetts towns of Lexington and Concord and Cohansians mustered for war, Philip began preparations for a trip to the backcountry. The synod appointed him (and his friend Andrew Hunter Jr.) to two preaching tours—one among the trans-Susquehanna congregations of the Donegal Presbytery and the other among the Shenandoah River Valley Presbyterians of the Hanover Presbytery. If time permitted, Philip and Andrew were free to travel into the North Carolina backcountry (Orange Presbytery) to visit the small but growing Presbyterian population that had recently settled there. Each tour was scheduled to last three months.[5]

On his first trip Philip would travel into parts of the northern Shenandoah Valley and the Pennsylvania backcountry. Many of the towns he would visit were less than a decade old. Some of them were communities of scattered farmers with few of the amenities needed to live what Philip would have called a civilized life. He reflected on what awaited him in the backcountry with an air of the enlightened gentleman he had become. On receiving his assignment, he wrote that he "must Away to the Westward, over Mountains & sylvan Wilds; Among I know not what kind of People—Possibly it may be my Lot to go among Men barbarous, clownish, & ungospelized as the Indians who have lately been compell'd, by Violence, to leave those Lands!" The backcountry was an ideal place for Philip to strengthen his identity as a man of improvement. The region and its settlements were primitive, lacking churches, schools, and other institutions of "civilized" culture. If Philip had any doubts about how far his way of improvement had taken him over the course of the previous decade, his visits to parts of the Pennsylvania and Virginia frontier would put them to rest. However, Philip also saw great potential in some of these places. It would be only a matter of time, he believed, before the civilizing power of Enlightenment progress—with its accompanying economic and cultural blessings—would reach these areas. As we will see in Chapter 8, such progress was intricately wedded to the success of the American Revolution.[6]

On May 9 Philip bid farewell to his family, Betsy, and his Greenwich friends and headed west with Andrew. After leaving New Jersey and before crossing the Susquehanna River, Philip and Andrew spent a few days with Presbyterian congregations along the Pennsylvania-Maryland border. In Georgetown, Maryland, they stopped to hear a sermon by Joseph Montgomery, a fellow Princeton graduate (1755) and one of the many Nassau Hall alumni who would provide Philip with useful conversation during his preaching tours. The "Princeton Circle," as the historian Mark Noll has called the alumni, trustees, and instructors affiliated with the College of New Jersey, extended deep into the early American backcountry.[7] Later that afternoon Philip preached a specially appointed fast-day sermon, a form of public oration that was becoming increasingly more common among colonial Presbyterians as relations with England grew tense. With little time to prepare something new, he recycled a sermon on the Book of Lamentations that he had preached earlier in the year at a similar fast day in Egg Harbor, New Jersey. The following Sunday he preached again at Georgetown to a congregation half the size of the one present for his fast-day sermon. Apparently the Presbyterians of Georgetown were more interested in hearing a message on how to respond to the current political climate than they were in hearing a traditional exposition of a biblical passage. Even those who did show up for Philip's second sermon, he lamented, "had not that deep Attention."[8]

After stops at several towns along what would later become the Mason-Dixon Line, Philip and Andrew crossed the Susquehanna River (probably at Nelson's Ferry) on May 16 and headed into the Pennsylvania backcountry. Philip had never seen such a "mountainous" landscape before and commented on the rocks that formed "huge Islands" in the middle of the river. After a 37-mile ride across this rugged ground, they arrived at York-Town, a "considerable village" that served as the economic center of York County. After a brief stay, Philip and Andrew began their travels along the Philadelphia Wagon Road, a 435-mile highway extending into the southernmost settlements of the Shenandoah River Valley. The Wagon Road was a busy thoroughfare by eighteenth-century backcountry standards. In its earlier manifestation as an Indian trail, it served as the primary route into the valley for those German and Scots-Irish migrants from Pennsylvania who first settled this region in the 1730s. By the time of the American Revolution, it had become a well-traveled two-way road. Migrants still followed it on their way to North Carolina or Kentucky, and residents of the Shenandoah Valley utilized it as the primary route to get their grain to market.[9] On May 17 and 18 Philip and Andrew traveled 45 miles along the Wagon

Road, making short stops among the hospitable "Dutch [German] Lutheran" communities of Berwick, Pennsylvania, and Hunterstown and Hagerstown, Maryland. They crossed the Potomac River at Williams Ferry and headed into Virginia. Philip's trip had hardly begun, but he was already enthused about his "ramblings into other Provinces." He observed that he and Andrew "were in the Province of Pennsylvania this Morning; we have passed through the Colony of Mary-land [today]; And are now in Virginia—!"[10] Fueled by these cosmopolitan wanderings, the itinerants crossed the Potomac and entered Berkeley County, Virginia, the home of Andrew Hunter Jr. Andrew had left the family homestead on the Red House Farm outside of Martinsburg following the death of his father and had moved to Greenwich to start his schooling under the direction of his uncle Andrew, Philip's patron and the minister of the Greenwich Presbyterian church.

Over the course of the next month Philip and Andrew occasionally went their separate ways in order to meet the needs of the Presbyterian communities along the Wagon Road more effectively. Philip passed through Winchester ("Frederick-Town") and then rode thirty-seven miles to Stephensburg (contemporary Stephens City). He would spend the next several weeks there, staying with Joseph Holmes, a store owner and leader of the local militia, which was preparing for war with England. Though Philip was bothered by some unnamed "Inaccuracies" in Holmes's "domestic Life," he could not have asked for a better host on this leg of his journey. Holmes had a library full of "useful & amusing Books" that included "The Spectators, Popes Works, Shakespear's Works, Gay's Works, & many single valuable Books." Philip pored through Holmes's copies of *Macbeth* and *The Taming of the Shrew* ("poor Kate," he noted; "she was tamed indeed!"), Pope's "Essay on the Characters of Women," and Gay's "tragical" *Dione*. When he was not preparing or preaching sermons, "Reading & Scribling" were his "chief Amusements."[11]

In the rural area of Opequon, located about three miles outside of Stephensburg, Philip found himself mixed up in a local religious controversy.[12] The longtime clergyman at Opequon was John Hoge, who for most of the history of white settlement in this region was the equivalent of a Presbyterian pope. He was a 1749 graduate of the College of New Jersey and had been the settled minister at Opequon for over twenty years. Hoge's grandfather William Hoge was one of the earliest settlers to this region and had donated the land for the church where his grandson presided. Reverend Hoge at one point was responsible for all of the Presbyterian congregations in the Shenandoah Valley.[13] When Philip arrived at Opequon, the elders invited him to preach two sermons to the congregation. Hoge was out of town. Philip preached "with some Warmth & satisfaction" and noted that the "People [were] very attentive." He received several invitations for dinner following his morning sermon and the following day wrote: "It is hinted to me that my Performance yesterday is approved."[14] The next time Philip preached at Opequon, Reverend Hoge was in the audience. Following the sermon Joseph Holmes introduced his house guest to Hoge (Philip called Hoge a "lusty and well made Man"), who wasted no time in querying Philip concerning his "future Purpose" and "design of leaving home." Hoge invited him to his house for dinner and further conversation. Philip could not understand why, if Hoge was present for the Sunday morning service, he had not preached. He urged Hoge to deliver a sermon in the afternoon service, but the veteran minister "wholly declined it." Philip now felt awkwardly out of place. He could "not avoid supposing that the People wished rather to have the Labour of their old Minister, than to hear me an unexperienced Novice!" Despite these concerns, Philip preached again that evening to another large crowd, which included "Several Store-Keepers, & People of Note."[15]

At some point during his stay Philip was informed why he, and not Hoge, was preaching to the Opequon congregation. Apparently Hoge's authority among the Presbyterians of the Shenandoah Valley was starting to erode. Over the course of the previous three years the people of Opequon had grown "highly enraged" at Hoge's "Conduct" and had made every effort to prevent him from preaching. When Hoge did preach, the people "never attend on his Sermons." We do not know for sure why Hoge had been censored by his congregation, but Philip wrote, "He is desirous of being reinstated & is jealous of my having an Intention to supplant him."[16] Hoge saw Philip as a threat, and for good reason. Following his June 11 sermons Philip was entertained by members of the Opequon session and invited, by more than one elder, to stay permanently as the congregation's settled minister. On one occasion Lewis Stephens (the town proprietor) and his wife "both attacked me, & urged me, by many Arguments to agree & stay in this Society." Philip was tempted by the offers. In his short stay he had grown to "respect and love the People" of Opequon. He claimed that he would "gladly" settle with them if it were not for the controversy surrounding Hoge. Privately, as he admired the natural beauty of the Shenandoah Valley, he could not help but daydream about the possibility of living in this place with Betsy, but he also did not want to "injure Mr. Hoge." Philip knew that the controversial minister had a large family and would have "no way of supporting them" if he were removed from his post. Philip thus decided, perhaps wisely, to turn down the Opequon congregation's job offer. The synod had appointed him to carry out an itinerant tour, and he was intent upon completing it.[17]

Philip would return to the Shenandoah Valley later in the year, but now, as the summer approached, his appointed tour took a northeasterly turn back into Pennsylvania. He arrived in Upper West Conococheague (Mercersburg) on June 20 for the meeting of the Donegal Presbytery to receive more details concerning what awaited him on the remainder of his trip. Philip's itinerary (Andrew Hunter Jr. would not join him in the Pennsylvania backcountry) would take him across the Juniata River en route to Northumberland-Town and Sunbury, relatively new towns laid out at the convergence of the western and eastern branches of the Susquehanna River. He would then follow the Susquehanna's west fork past the settlements that would later become Williamsport and Lock Haven before turning southward once again. By the end of the summer he planned on coming full circle, passing through the Kishacoquillas Valley and present-day Mifflin and Huntingdon Counties on his way back to the Philadelphia Wagon Road, and he would do it all in three months.[18]

After the meeting of the presbytery, Philip mounted his horse Jack and rode for roughly 120 miles, making numerous "Circumvolutions and Regradations" along the way, through the valleys (Path and Tuscarora) formed by the ridges of the Allegheny Mountains. He was reminded of the region's remoteness (160 miles from Philadelphia, he estimated) by the dark, narrow, and stony pathways over which he passed. Philip forded the Juniata River at present-day Mifflintown and made his way through the woods to the forks of the Susquehanna, his first extended stop.[19] On June 27 he crossed the Susquehanna River's main branch and arrived in Sunbury, the site of the former Indian trading village of Shamokin. He then plied back over the river to Northumberland-Town, where he would spend most of his time during the next month. Northumberland-Town was a shipping village of about forty houses serving the growing number of grain farmers beginning to populate the area of the upper Susquehanna Valley. Philip was surprised by the amount of economic activity in the town, writing, "this infant Village seems busy & noisy as a Philadelphia Ferry-House." He spent the next several days visiting the Presbyterian faithful, dining and supping with the town's most prominent residents, meditating and praying along the banks of the Susquehanna, and indulging in "humour & Friendship" (on at least one occasion until 3:00 A.M.) with his new acquaintances.[20]

Philip preached at Northumberland-Town on July 2 and promised to deliver a fast-day sermon later in the month. He then traveled eighteen miles along a recently laid-out road following the course of the west branch of the Susquehanna. This was "fertile, level, goodly Country," he wrote, thick with wheat, rye, and oat fields. It was reaping season in the upper Susquehanna Valley settlements at Buffalo Valley and Warrior Run, and Philip marveled at the bountiful harvests that the region's farmers were able to collect. The writer J. Hector St. John de Crèvecoeur,

Figure 9. Travels of Philip Vickers Fithian (Pennsylvania backcountry), May to September 1775.

who had traveled in this region the previous year, was similarly moved by the abundance: "I never saw a greater display of plenty in my life than these people possessed; they had every kind of grain that they chose to sow, excellent cattle, great number of swine in the woods, venison and fish for catching." Much of Philip's pastoral visiting took place in the fields among the reapers, whom he described as "merry & civil." The sight of harvesters taking in their grain, the ubiquitous presence of irritating mosquitoes (which "bepurpled" his face), and the opportunities afforded by the Susquehanna for recreation and reflection made him nostalgic for his beloved Cohansey. Philip could often be found during the evenings playing the fife along the river's banks and thinking about home.[21]

Because the settlements along the Susquehanna River were so young, the Presbyterian communities of the region lacked ministers, meeting-houses, and any real sense of religious order. John Fleming, Philip's host at the settlement along Bald Eagle Creek, informed him that he was the "first orderly Preacher" who had come to this region. Philip was surprised by this news and wrote, "Truly I am in the Woods." Success in the backcountry required ministers to adapt to the primitive conditions. It demanded skills that were not part of John Witherspoon's Enlightenment-based curriculum at Princeton. For example, Philip began preparing for his Northumberland-Town fast-day sermon in the barn of William Gray, his host in Buffalo Valley, and completed it in Gray's small joiner's shop amid the sounds of saws, planes, and chisels. The backcountry preaching conditions were not much better. Philip delivered sermons "among the Trees," on the banks of the river, in barns, and from the beds of wagons. His congregations were often seated on the ground and "peeping" at him "through the Bushes." Philip reminded the people of the region to "attend with Carefulness & Reverence" to "God's Sabbaths," particularly during seasons when visiting ministers were scarce.[22]

Philip returned to Northumberland-Town on July 17 and three days later preached on the occasion of the "Solemn Continental Fast." Since the town did not have a meetinghouse (Philip had been shown the site along the Susquehanna River where the people hoped to erect one), the fast-day service was held at the yet-to-be-completed home of "Mr. Chatham," a local layperson. The inhabitants of the town and the surrounding countryside packed their way into the unpartitioned chamber of Chatham's house. Some stood in the cellar, and others listened to the sermon from outside the partially framed walls. The people of Northumberland-Town were eager to hear the young preacher's sentiments on the strained relationship between England and her colonies, and Philip wrote that he had never preached before so "nice an Audience." Though we do not know the content of his sermon that day, the occasion to preach on the sacred cause of liberty to a group of like-minded patriots overwhelmed him. He claimed to speak "in great Fear & dread," noting that "my Lip's quivered; my Flesh shrunk; my Hair rose up; my Knees trembled" and "I was wholly confused, til' I had almost closed the Sermon."[23]

Following his fast-day sermon Philip left Northumberland-Town. He was saddened by the proposition of departing since he had found in this brand-new frontier town the kind of social networks that he had enjoyed among his friends in Cohansey. On the evening before his departure he dined with some local Presbyterians and chatted about "Books & Litterary

Improvements." Philip was in the "Company of Gentlemen where there is no Reserve," and when they spoke, "Every Sentence was Sentiment." Indeed, he was "most highly entertained." As these new friends talked along the banks of the Susquehanna, the "heavy Thoughts of War were for a While suspended." The town's Presbyterians, hopeful for regular preaching, made him an offer to stay and settle with them, but Philip knew it was time to move on. "Cruel Destination," he wrote sorrowfully, "Tommorrow morning I must be broken off & ramble up the River." He worried about the possibility of future encounters with "quarrelsome Yankees, insidious Indians, & at best lonely Wilds." As he thought about the prospect of mingling with these people, Philip once again had to remind himself that he was traveling "in the Cause of my God."[24]

Philip retraced some of his steps north and west along the Susquehanna River past Bald Eagle Creek (present-day Flemington). He then headed southwest through the woods to Bald Eagle's Nest (present-day Milesburg, about one hundred miles west of Northumberland-Town) and followed the Penn's Valley road south (along the path of present-day Route 322) to Penn's Valley (present-day Old Fort), Spring Mills, and eventually to the Kishacoquillas Valley towns of Reedsville and Belleville. Heading west again, he crossed the Juniata River just south of Huntingdon and preached at Fort Shirley (present-day Shirleysburg) and Fort Louden before stopping briefly at Berkeley Springs, Virginia. This was the most physically demanding part of the trip. It required following the Penn's Valley road through several ridges of the Allegheny Mountains, a journey that demanded both "patience and perseverance." Philip's horse Jack did not fare well through this region. Despite his faithfulness, Jack had traveled "too hard" through the frontier. After arriving in the Kishacoquillas Valley, Philip traded his "able, steady, useful Friend" for a "smaller, neat-carriaged, black Horse of four Years Old," which he named "Bullrock."[25] This last leg of the trip lasted close to two months, and Philip traversed some of the most remote and undeveloped settlements that he would encounter in all of his travels in Pennsylvania. A year earlier Crèvecoeur had noted surprise at the "boldness, the indifference with which these new settlers scatter themselves here and there in the bosom of such an extensive country without even a previous path to direct their steps and without being in any number sufficient either to protect or assist one another."[26] Consequently, this was also the part of Philip's journey in which he expressed the most complaints about the primitive conditions.

After he left Northumberland-Town, Philip began to mention more frequently his encounters with Indians. By the time of his arrival, white settlement had pushed most of the upper Susquehanna Valley's diverse Native American population to the west. Indians, however, could still be found trading venison and skins in white communities. Their presence was enough to get Philip's attention. As he reached Lycoming Creek near present-day Williamsport, Pennsylvania, Philip noted that he was now entering Indian country. He saw his first two Indians at Bald Eagle Creek and remarked in his journal that he could not "bring myself to a Pleasant Feeling when I look upon or even think of, these heathenish Savages." As he rode through the woods to Bald Eagle's Nest (Milesburg) he was "terrified very much" by what he described as the "Whoop, Whoop" of two Indians nearby. Philip was certain that a hoard of Indians, "who were lying in Ambush," would leap from the woods "to shoot us when we disturbed their property." Later he described these yells as "hollowing" and "frantic Screams, not less fearful than inebriated Demons, howling til' we were out of Hearing." His host in these parts of the woods, Andrew Boggs, invited Indians into his home to trade. On one particular morning three of them showed up for morning prayers, sitting motionless on the floor as Philip conducted the exercises. Philip's most harrowing experience with Indians, however, occurred one July evening when he was awakened from sleep by "Six large Indians" who had arrived at Boggs's house with knife and "Tom-Hawk" in hand. The Indians did not harm him, but they certainly gave him a scare. After this experience Philip could only conclude, "For all this Settlement I would not live here . . . not for five hundred [pounds] a Year—nothing would persuade me!"[27]

Indians remained a concern throughout Philip's trip, but the conditions he experienced among the white settlements in this part of the Pennsylvania backcountry received the most attention in his diary. If Philip was ever an "insufferable prig," as the early twentieth-century editors of his journal described him, it was during this stage of his preaching tour. He felt out of place among these settlements and made his thoughts about the residents' uncivilized ways of life abundantly clear on the pages of his journal. His refined sensibilities were most evident in his remarks about the unclean houses in which he was forced to stay. Andrew Boggs's cabin, for example, "look[ed] and smell[ed] like a Shambles" as a result of his practice of trading venison and other animal meat with the Indians, who frequently stopped by unannounced. Philip commented on the "raw Flesh & Blood in every Part—Mangled, wasted Flesh on every Shelf—Hounds licking up the Blood from the Floor." He had a habit of judging (privately, of course) the people he encountered based on their attention to cleanliness.[28]

Unclean dwelling places, according to Philip, were the natural extension of the uncivilized behavior of the region's settlers. As in many early American frontier regions, the overuse of alcohol was a problem. In the Kishacoquillas Valley the people consumed a "Great Quantity & Variety of strong Liquors, which grow poisonous by untimely & immodest Application." Philip added that the liquors did "stop up & darken the Understanding, they effect that Langour & burdensome Dullness which makes Life & all her Duties appear to many tiresome beyond Measure." In Huntingdon he observed that small frontier towns "go before every other Place in most Sorts of Vice; but especially in Drinking." He entered this town in disguise—covering his clerical cloth so that he would not have to deal with intoxicated town dwellers mocking the arrival of a traveling holy man. Philip's observations of frontier life extended beyond condemnations of drunkenness. He was also appalled, for example, at the "Custom in these back Woods, almost universally with Women, to go barefooted" and the habit of Men to wear "Mockisons, or Indians Shoes." In addition, the women of Reedsville practiced the "Vulgar Custom" of fortune-telling through the reading of tea leaves (they prophesied that Philip had been "for a considerable Time fond of a middle-sized, fair-Faced, grave young Woman"). Philip complained too that few of the houses had desks, forcing him on occasion to write on a log in the woods with his paper pressed against his knee.[29]

Philip complained most often about his sleeping arrangements. The beds in Chilisquaqua were filled with "Fleas biting" and "Bugs crawling!" and other "leaping insects." In the heat of summer he found himself "on a hard board, surrounded by a snoring Family!" On another occasion, as he slept under an open window at the home of James Potter in Penn's Valley, a large dog jumped into his room and "bedded himself, dripping with Water & Mud" among his "clean, new washed Clothes!" Because the houses he stayed in were primitive by Cohansey standards, Philip was often forced to share a bed chamber with multiple members of the host family. "One thing here I do not like," he wrote from Chilisquaqua, "[is that] in almost all these rural Cots I am under the Necessity of sleeping in the same Room with all the Family." He continued, "It seems indelicate, at least new, to strip, surrounding by different Ages & Sexes, & rise in the Morning, in the Blaze of Day, with the Eyes of, at least, one blinking Irish Female, searching our Subjects for Remark." Later, from Reedsville, he again complained: "this going to Bed & rising in the same Room, & in full view of the whole Family—This, to be sure, puts me often to Blush." On one occasion in Bald Eagle's Nest he was forced to stay in bed late into the morning because he was embarrassed to get up while the daughters of his host, John Fleming, were working in the room. Philip was learning that bodily privacy—an important part of refined living—had not yet found its way to the eighteenth-century Pennsylvania backcountry.[30]

Philip saw little chance of improvement in these more remote regions. Without large waterways such as the Susquehanna, these settlements, he believed, were culturally barren. They were unable to access the transportation infrastructure that carried civilization into the back-country. Philip did encounter a few inhabitants with books (James Potter, his host at Penn's Valley, had a library that included the writings of Pope, Blackstone, and James Hervey), but overall this region was "remote from Navigation which I dearly love—It is out of the Way of news; [and] we have no Tea." The flow of water, at least in Philip's mind, provided opportunities for sociability. It brought conversation partners—a necessary ingredient for self-improvement—to the frontier from new and faraway places. Even when experienced in isolation, a flowing river provided the right kind of natural environment to cultivate sympathy for one's fellow creation. "A Man of Thought & Taste," Philip reflected, "in his most sour unphilosophical Hours, will not be able to stand on the shady Banks of a fine River without Refinement; his Heart must be softened & moulded into a similar Complexion with these Charms of Nature."[31]

The social relationships between the people of this region, from Philip's point of view, were unrefined. The inhabitants who lived in this "unneighborhooded Valley" lacked the "sympathetic, invisible Cord, which . . . ties minds together." Invoking the novelist Laurence Sterne, as he had done as a tutor on Robert Carter's plantation, Philip longed for "secret efficacious Stamina, which like the Effluvia of the Loadstone, attract & bring Souls together." He found the backcountry settlers' inability to sustain this kind of moral community to be "repulsive," and he hoped to leave as soon as possible. As we will see, he was also wrestling with his own feelings of nostalgia for the social world of Cohansey and the circles of benevolent friends that his homeland had offered him. Philip could always find people to talk with, but the conversation, unless it was conducted with a gentleman traveler from the East or a member of the "Princeton Circle," was rarely "useful." The frontier was a "Simple Society." The people Philip met and conversed with were not "indecent or wicked"; they were simply incapable of engaging in any form of enlightened discourse. Philip described them as the kind of people "in which you may talk a whole half Day, & never hear a distinct Opinion, unless you are kind enough, for a Rarity, to introduce one yourself." Making his point more clearly, he added, "I do therefore prefer an Occasional, & periodical Death, rather than the Bondage of Dullness or Nonsense." Philip made every effort to avoid such social torture. On more than one occasion he would "feign myself indisposed & unable to attend to the Entertainment of Company," asserting that "in all similar Cases it is justifiable." Philip may have been an "insufferable prig" in his descriptions of this part of backcountry Pennsylvania, but he was reflecting the enlightened culture in which he had been trained and to which he was now accustomed.[32]

While Philip was staying at Fort Shirley, he managed to get access to a Philadelphia newspaper and learned that the Reverend Andrew Hunter, his spiritual mentor and friend, had died. The news put him into a deep state of sorrow, and he mourned the death of his pastor privately on the pages of his diary: "Oh! DEATH! DEATH! DEATH! O DEATH!—Thou has at last struck down & removed my *Patron*, my *Teacher*, & my *Father*—!" Hunter died on July 20, more than a month before Philip learned about it in the *Pennsylvania Packet*. He composed an obituary on the pages of his diary, describing Hunter as "My late dear much-honoured *Father* & *Mother's* most intimate Companion" and his "best of Friends, to whose Benevolence I owe my *Education*, & Improvement." He then prayed that he would someday see Hunter in "Abraham's Bosom, drinking at the Fountain of eternal Life!"[33] In the meantime he would honor his teacher by continuing to perform the work for which Hunter had prepared him. Philip was overcome with grief, but at some point after the mourning ended he must have certainly thought about the pulpit that now sat empty at his home church in Greenwich.

By the end of September 1775 Philip was back in Cohansey. He may have "left home" when he headed off to the backcountry, but he still could not control his affections for this beloved place. With a steady flow of job offers coming his way and the exciting possibility of fulfilling his calling in a region that needed the religious order his presence could provide, it may be surprising that Philip's bouts with homesickness persisted. Yet, as long as the faint hope of returning permanently to Cohansey continued to exist, he would feel a homeward tug. During his backcountry trip he was desperate to hear news about life in Cohansey and described chance meetings with those who were familiar with his homeland. In Falling Water Meetinghouse, about ten miles outside of Martinsburg, Virginia, he met a resident who had visited Deerfield and had conversed with Enoch Green and some of Philip's other Cohansey friends. "It is pleasant, it is desirable, to hear of home," Philip noted after this encounter. Later, when he met a "distressed Countryman" from Deerfield in the fields of Cowpasture, Virginia, he wrote, "I felt warm toward him—I should see with transport the very Sand of Cohansie."[34]

Philip walked the banks of the upper Susquehanna River in the summer of 1775, and his mind wandered down its mighty currents into the Chesapeake Bay, along the Elk River in Maryland and Delaware, across the Delaware Bay, and up the Cohansey River to Greenwich. "Much of my Heart teizes me about Home," he wrote, and "It hangs steadily there which Way soever I turn, so that my whole Train of thinking leans that Way also." As he moved southward into the remote Kishacoquillas

Valley, his longings became more intense: "I feel sick—sick at my Heart! If this is what they call *Homesick* I pity the poor *Irish*." As an educated gentleman and a Christian minister, Philip was aware of the irrationality of these feelings, writing: "Foolish, fluttering, mistaken Thing! . . . Here I am so far as I can see, in the very Spot allotted to me to labour in, according to the Course of my Education; let me then be wholly content."[35] His thoughts about Cohansey seemed to be getting in the way of his vocation. He turned down job offer after job offer in the backcountry and wondered whether he was effectively carrying on the work he had been called to do. In Virginia, Philip worried that his "ardent Expectation" of seeing home was distracting him from "honestly striving to assist the Souls of our Fellow Creatures."[36]

It would be impossible, of course, to talk about Philip's longings for home without mentioning his love for Elizabeth Beatty. Philip could never quell his passions for Cohansey as long as Betsy remained there. Whatever reservations Betsy may have once had about pursuing a relationship with Philip had all but disappeared. As he prepared to head west, he paused for a heartfelt and emotional good-bye with the woman he loved: "She wep't, & her powerful Tears quite drowned me in melancholy Rapture—! She was silent, I was literally dumb—She held me by the Hand, & I sat reclined, in a mournful Posture, by her Side—But at last I must leave her." He compared leaving Cohansey to leaving "Paradise" and all of its "heavenly Joys."[37] Philip continued his sentimental longings for Betsy at nearly every point of his backcountry tour. They occasionally exchanged letters, but it was difficult in the frontier to maintain regular communication. A whippoorwill's song reminded him of a similar sound they had heard together in Cohansey at the time of Philip's departure. (It also prompted him to reflect on "Mr. Locke's Doctrine of Association of Ideas.") He carved their names on a beech tree on a small island in the Susquehanna River, praying that as the trees grew, so would the "*Love & Friendship*" between them. He imagined the Susquehanna carrying him home to Betsy's arms: "my Wishes fly across the Country, & centre in the Peace of my fair Eliza. Your Company, my dear Laura, with Health & Rest & Plenty, on the Margin of this transparent Water, would rival, to me, the happiest Elysium that was ever exprest by the Language, or entertained in the Fancy, of the softest or most inventive Poet."[38]

The couple had clearly spent time discussing marriage before he left for the backcountry because Philip often reflected, in a more practical and specific way than he ever had before, about his future with Betsy. He also began to ponder the moral bands needed to sustain a marriage. He had heard some depressing stories of backcountry marriages that had fallen apart, and he wondered if his and Betsy's relationship could survive the storms of life. He asked,

Will any of the Qualities which have so deeply smitten me retain the Power of pleasing, when She will have lost her Beauty, & be furrowed by Age? When I picture her, in Fancy, & place her before me at the Age of sixty, conflicting with the Infirmities of Age, added to those which always belong to her feeble Sex, would my Heart have such warm Emotions towards her as I feel now? Shall I love *Eliza* with the same Ardour, if indulgent Heaven has allotted her to me & will preserve us together til' that Time, when I view her sitting, in the Corner, over a slow-burning Fire, in a low Chair, bended downwards with Years, resting her hoary, withered Head, upon the hollow of her shaking Hand & with the other Hand, poorly supporting a Pipe in her Toothless Mouth—When her Voice is weak & inarticulate; when her enfeebled Limbs will scarcely bear her up; When her flimsy Eyelids overhang half her deadened Eyes; When the Roots of all her Nails, & the Hollows under her Eyes, are turned to a livid Blue—! Should I walk then, with the same Satisfaction, enfolded Arm in Arm, as I do now? Should I clasp my Arms, with the same Transport, round that Death-like, Rib-encircled Waist? Should I view with such Astonishment her flabby, wrinkled Bosom? Should I kiss, with such unceasing Pleasure, those quivering Lips, when they are sunk down, like a mouldered Grave, upon her wasted Gums! Short indeed is the Empire of Beauty! What then, I ask, is the Security for my Happiness with *Eliza*?[39]

Philip's description of Betsy in old age was unflattering, if not overly graphic in nature, but he was also quick to answer these questions on the pages of his diary. As much as Philip was attracted to Betsy's youthful appearance, he knew that a marriage remained "strong and durable" when it was rooted in "Kindness & Fidelity," the kind of virtues and "Constancy of Temper" that he had long admired in her.[40]

Philip and Betsy's relationship had had its share of difficult moments, but it now appeared to be coming to fruition in marriage. Yet, Philip was also aware that his romantic passion for Betsy would need to compete with political jealousy—that "laudable passion" informing the patriotism of the American colonies. Political jealousy might put a damper on their wedding plans. "Surely," Philip wrote from Pennsylvania, "I may not enter into any such Connexion [as marriage], however willing—however desirous I am—til' the Fate of America be known & settled." If Philip and Betsy were temporarily to put off their future together, it would be because the commitment of marriage might make it more difficult for Philip to come to the aid of his country: "Probably in the Conflict I may be called to the Field, & such a Connexion, in its Nature, would make me less capable, & less willing, to answer so reasonable a Call. I will not, therefore, marry, till our American Glory be fixed on our permanent Foundation, or taken entirely from us!"[41] For once Philip was willing to curb his passions for Betsy in order to pursue an equally if not *more* "laudable" passion—a call to the sacred and enlightened cause of liberty.

Or so it seemed. Whatever convictions Philip had about postponing his marriage until the American Revolution was over seemed to vanish once he arrived home from Pennsylvania. His diary is silent during this period, but we do know that he and Betsy were married on October 25, 1775, at the Deerfield Presbyterian church. His former teacher Enoch Green conducted the service. For all of his musings about Betsy in letters and diaries, it is ironic that we know nothing about the months leading up to or immediately following this momentous event in Philip's life. One would expect that Philip's siblings, Uncle Samuel, and a host of friends were present for the celebration, but Betsy's family members, with the exception of her sister Mary (who was married to Enoch Green), were absent.[42] Whatever kind of honeymoon the newlyweds enjoyed was short-lived. Philip needed to finish his tour of the backcountry. He would spend the next three months in Virginia while Betsy remained with her sister and Enoch Green in Deerfield.

By mid-November, Philip was back on the road. Andrew Hunter Jr., who also got married during their Cohansey hiatus, was with him. This leg of his journey required stops at some of the same congregations and towns that he and Andrew had visited on their earlier tour of the region. This time, however, they would continue farther south along the Philadelphia Wagon Road into the upper Shenandoah Valley. Philip left home with yet another dramatic good-bye that was only intensified by his marriage to Betsy: "Farewell Cohansie: —Farewell my near & agreeable Friends,—Farewell my kind & benevolent Relations—Farewell also my dear dear Betsey, O farewell—! He asked his new wife to pause for prayer each evening at eight o'clock so that they could "mutually implore our Almighty Creator, that we may both be preserved & in rapturous Pleasure meet again."[43]

Philip and Andrew merged onto the Wagon Road outside of York-Town, crossed the Potomac River, and by November 18 were visiting again with Andrew's family outside of Martinsburg. The Hunters congratulated Philip on his marriage to Betsy, and the conversation during their two-day stay undoubtedly revolved around the death of the Reverend Andrew Hunter the previous summer and Andrew Jr.'s recent marriage to Ann Riddell, whom he affectionately called "Nancy."[44] On November 20 Philip left Andrew with his family and headed for Stephensburg, where he was reunited with Joseph Holmes, his host during his earlier visit ("Here I seem at Home," Philip wrote, "In the Captain's office I have a Room & Books for my Amusement and Improvement.") This was a difficult trip due to the unusually harsh

Shenandoah Valley weather. After arriving in Stephensburg, Philip claimed that he was "much unwell. Feverish at Night. Pains in my Bones. Weakness and Faintness in my Breasts, All I believed, the Effect of our Cold Ride." In addition to his physical ailments he continued to battle homesickness: "How impatient of Home am I at this Distance, in so inclement a Season . . . —Home, Home, Home, O' dear Home; & best of Women to me, my lovely Betsy, from you I am also absent." Yet, Philip pressed on "in Hopes a more decent Feeling will possess me." He prayed that time spent in good conversation would "harden" him to "this painful Absence & Weakness."[45]

After preaching at Opequon (he did not mention John Hoge this time) and Cedar Creek, he traveled eighty miles along the Wagon Road to Staunton, the southern valley's largest town. Philip was now leaving the German-dominated northern part of the valley and entering one of the most concentrated pockets of Scots-Irish population in America. "All here are Irish—all are Presbyterians," he observed.[46] As he rode through the rain and sleet, he again wrestled with God over his calling, writing that he had wished he was going the "Other Way," back toward New Jersey. Indeed, these were "Bad Times for poor itinerant Preachers." When he arrived at Staunton, he found a room, drank a glass of brandy, ate a "moderate Supper," and went straight to bed.[47]

The weather was not the only dangerous part of Philip's tour of the Shenandoah Valley. After arriving at Stephensburg he heard news that the earl of Dunmore, the royal governor of Virginia, had declared martial law in the colony and had offered freedom to slaves who would leave their masters and join the British army. According to Philip, the Presbyterian patriots of the Shenandoah Valley were "deeply alarmed" by Dunmore's proclamation. Patrick Henry, the leader of Virginia's opposition to the Crown, sent orders from Williamsburg to all local militia commanding them, as Philip put it, "to fill up their Companies forthwith." Philip was advised not to continue his travels any farther into the backcountry since, with the slaves roaming free, "public safety is greatly interrupted." Assuming Betsy had heard the news of Dunmore's proclamation, Philip wrote home to calm his new bride and let her know he was safe. "If I was now at home," he told her, "I should surely think it my Duty to continue there til Spring."[48] Yet, despite the potential peril, Philip once again entrusted his future to God and moved forward with his assignment.

During his visits in Virginia, Philip had the opportunity to meet and converse with several ministerial graduates of the College of New Jersey. Nine Presbyterian licensees, all Princeton alumni and former classmates of Philip, were preaching in the Shenandoah Valley. "Nine raw inexperienced Candidates," he wrote, "not one of whom are ordained—Almost as many Shepherds as Sheep you will say."[49] In Staunton he heard that

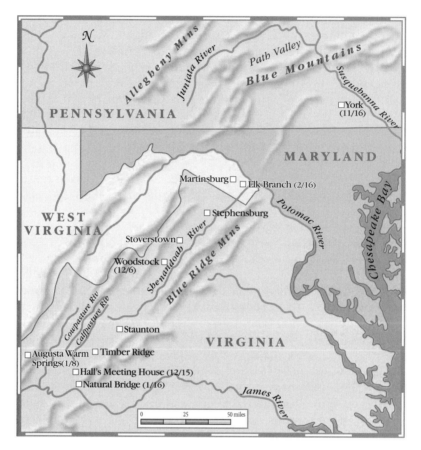

Figure 10. Travels of Philip Vickers Fithian (Shenandoah Valley), November 1775 to February 1776.

John McMillan, a fellow member of the class of 1772, was ministering in the area. Always on the lookout for enlightened conversation, Philip concluded that he "must see him." With little hesitation he mounted his horse and drove eight miles to visit McMillan and then spent several days with him sharing memories from Nassau Hall and commiserating about the demands of frontier preaching. At Timber Ridge, Philip stayed at the home of John Brown, a member of the class of 1749, who ran a small academy in the area and presided over the Timber Ridge and New Providence churches. Philip remarked that Brown's wife "was at no Loss in talking of any trifling Incident which has taken place at Princeton since my first Acquaintance at College." Brown's assistant was William Graham, who was a year behind Philip at Nassau Hall. When

Graham heard that Philip was in the valley he summoned him to a meeting, and the young Presbyterians had a "comfortable Interview" together. Indeed, if he had to spend extended time in these remote parts of the Shenandoah Valley, Philip would not be at a loss for conversation partners. The "Princeton Circle" had a wide circumference.[50]

Philip was a studious observer of Presbyterian life in the Shenandoah Valley. The Presbyterians of the region were overwhelmingly New Side in their religious orientation, and Philip was often pleased with their "well-tempered" zeal. Yet, as a minister who had drunk deeply from the British Enlightenment, he also commented on how "Some of the Pretenders to our divine religion have no Morality" and worried about the inroads being made among Presbyterians by the enthusiastic Methodist preachers and their "Doctrine of universal Restitution."[51] In addition to their evangelical sensibilities, the region's Presbyterians upheld a rigid adherence to Calvinist beliefs. Scots-Irish Presbyterians were known for their strong commitments to Westminster orthodoxy. "Election, Election, Election! O this Election & Reprobation!" wrote Philip from Stephensburg, Virginia. "I am much troubled with these Doctrines—Poor unmeaning Persons, perplexed with a fictitious airy Fury, & never in Expectation of full Satisfaction, till the Die is cast—."[52] Philip, of course, was also a Calvinist, but his theological convictions, as we have seen, were seasoned by an Enlightenment belief in the power of human reason that softened his understanding of traditional Reformed doctrines such as divine election and human depravity.

Philip also learned that Virginia backcountry Presbyterians frowned on preachers who read their sermons. He thus made sure to put additional time into his preparations so as not to rely too heavily on his notes from the pulpit. At Cedar Creek, Philip remarked that a minister who can "Preach without Papers" and "seem earnest & serious" will be "listened to with Patience & Wonder." This style of preaching, which was popular among eighteenth-century evangelicals, also had its share of social perks. According to Philip, ministers who were not wed to a text in their delivery would be greeted after the service with handshakes of appreciation and invitations to dinner. However, even the most learned or elegantly written sermon—one that possessed the soundness of John Witherspoon or the ease of Samuel Davies—would not please Shenandoah Presbyterians if it was read instead of preached: "Backs will be up at once, their Attention all gone, their Noses will grow red as their Wigs,—And, let me whisper this, you may bet your Dinner where you Breakfasted."[53]

The Scots-Irish Presbyterians of the Shenandoah Valley were intellectually curious and eager to talk about religious and theological matters with their visiting ministers. Unlike some of the inhabitants of the undeveloped parts of Pennsylvania that Philip had traversed, the people of the Shenandoah Valley were "civilized and religious." In Staunton, Philip's host, James Trumble, was so eager to dialogue with his guest on matters of religion, politics, and Indian affairs that the young preacher complained that Trumble's regular visits were a deterrent to study: "The Prospect of a little Study lies here before me this Week. I have a Room, and the Promise of my Time. But like every former Hope, It is all in vain. Good-natured Mr. *Trumble . . .* comes smiling in with a Pot of Cyder, & then we both sit chatting over it til' it is gone, & with it our full Hour." Similarly, in the settlements at Cowpasture, Philip's host John Dickinson bombarded Philip with "Questions in Divinity, Morality, Oeconomy, Politicks, & c." Philip whined that he could "find no Time for Study not the scanty Loan of an Hour to myself." He added, "If I do not converse, I am reserved, clumsy, dull, every way unfavourable to good Society." Since he needed to memorize all of his sermons so that he could preach them without reading from his text, these distractions were particularly annoying.[54]

Philip spent the first half of December 1775 preaching in and around Staunton among the Presbyterians who made up the congregations of Timber Ridge, Hall Meeting House, and North River. He then crossed North Mountain, the easternmost ridge of the Allegheny range, and entered the scarcely populated Presbyterian settlements at Calfpasture and Cowpasture in one of the more remote portions of the Shenandoah Valley. Philip was immediately taken by the agricultural abundance of the people living along these plains: "The Country at once surprizes me— Meadow Ground of the best Quality!" Philip was quick to note that the people of the region did not have "Coffee, Chocolate, nor many other of what is allow'd to be needful in polite life," but they did have "Bread, Meat of many Kinds, Milk, Butter, & Cheese, & all in great Plenty, & of the best Quality."[55] While he was in Calfpasture, Philip's travels were plagued again by the Shenandoah Valley winter of 1775–76.[56] On December 23 he wrote, "Perhaps I never felt a more cold Day." As Christmas approached, the ground was covered with snow and the rivers were filled with floating chunks of ice, making them difficult to ford. This was indeed, as Philip put it, "Nature in rough, hardy Majesty!" On Christmas Eve, Philip preached to a few brave souls who fought the frigid conditions to attend his sermon. Since the weather was too treacherous for him to travel to the Calfpasture meetinghouse, he held the service in the house of a member of the congregation. He spent the rest of the evening with the family of his host, singing hymns "at the good Peoples Desire." The following week, in Lower Cowpasture, Philip preached in a "small, open, damp, log House" but was able to continue only for a few minutes because it was so cold. As the new year dawned, local Presbyterians could not get enough of Philip's sermons. He obliged them by preaching wherever and whenever he could get an audience.[57]

By early January, Philip, now reunited with Andrew, began to consider just how much farther he would continue into the backcountry. Shortly after it passed through the town of Fincastle, the Philadelphia Wagon Road split off in three directions. Philip and Andrew could go west into the Trans-Allegheny region along the Greenbrier River, southwest toward the backcountry settlements in Kentucky (on roads carved out of the wilderness by Daniel Boone), or south into the Carolinas.[58] They had authority from the Philadelphia Synod to visit any of these regions, and all three places had considerable Presbyterian populations. However, the itinerants were growing tired of fighting the weather, and both of them were eager to return home to their new brides. Philip had initially planned to travel into the Greenbrier Valley but was forced to turn back after reaching Augusta Warm-Springs due to icy horse paths and "thick, damp, sleety Air." A trip to the Presbyterians in this outpost would have to wait until spring. On his return to Staunton he encountered a "most violent Rain" that forced him to navigate Bullrock through treacherous mountain trails. "Of all Places which I have ever seen for Horse & Baggage," he wrote, "this is the worst." He described the trip as "purgatory." Philip and Andrew also concluded that the weather was too severe to continue their travels southward and thus opted to forgo a visit to the Presbyterians in North Carolina or Kentucky. They agreed to make every effort to visit these outposts the following summer, but for now they would begin their long journey home in the hopes of making it to Cohansey sometime by mid-March. "I am now contented," Philip wrote with a sense of relief at the prospect of his itinerant tour coming to an end, "I will return & gladly, to my dear, dear Betsey."[59]

Before beginning their return trip, Philip and Andrew took some time for recreation and sight-seeing. The two ministers and a local guide visited the Natural Bridge, a popular eighteenth-century tourist site that happened to lie on land owned by Thomas Jefferson. Philip marveled at the "stupendious Grandieur" of this mass of limestone that had been eroded by the continual flow of Cedar Creek to form a natural overpass. He estimated it to be 100 feet long and 85 wide and suspended 360 feet above the ground. In a more playful moment, the ministers positioned themselves on the edge of Cedar Creek and threw stones at the underside of the bridge's arch. Philip recorded a bit of lore, passed on by their guide, that only three men—one of whom was George Washington (who had surveyed the area surrounding the bridge)—had ever hit the bottom of the arch with a stone. To do so, he wrote, "is a Prooff of Manhood." After failing to hit the arch by throwing, Philip and Andrew removed their garters and used them to sling stones at the arch. Andrew managed to hit his target once, but Philip concluded, after several tries, "I think my fullest Ability by Habit & Desire could never do it." They eventually climbed to the top of the bridge, but neither preacher had the nerve to stand on the formation and admire the view. Their guides informed them that Charles Beatty, Betsy's father, had at one time visited the bridge and "stood boldly on a Rock on the outmost Margin & looked over!" Philip was impressed.[60]

Philip and Andrew spent the rest of January and the first half of February 1776 revisiting the congregations around Staunton. The riding continued to be difficult in the snow and ice, but such hardships were eased considerably by the pleasing conversation with the Brown family at Timber Ridge and the rest of the "Princeton Circle" who served the churches in the area. Philip relished the "social Friendship" that these ministers and their families provided him. He enjoyed the Virginia hospitality: "Should I continue here a Month, I should surely fatten, upon plenty of Cyder & perpetual Good Humour. I think my face already begins to widen & my pointed chin to double." He spent time with William Graham and participated in a special religious service called to "pray for the Revival of vital Religion" and for God's "Interposition & Mercy to save us from the Judgments which are falling upon us." Philip remained pleased with the piety of the Presbyterians in the southern Shenandoah Valley: "Laudable Design! I would to God in the Warmth of my Heart, that such a Spirit was universal!" He continued to think about this region of spiritual and economic abundance as a place where he and Betsy might possibly settle one day: "I am in a perplexing Dilemma, whether I ought not to determine also that it shall be, remote & wild as it is, the Habitation of me & my lovely Betsey." He had already received an invitation from the church at Calfpasture to be that congregation's permanent minister.[61]

With the help of the occasional glass of Madeira and some good conversation, Philip managed to make his way through the wind and snow toward home. He arrived sometime in late February or early March, a bit earlier than he and Andrew had projected. We know little about what he did during the next three or four months. He certainly spent some much-needed and longed-for time with Betsy. They made a home together in Greenwich, probably in the same farmhouse in which he was raised. As they started their life together they no doubt pondered where they would spend the rest of it. Philip had job offers from Presbyterian congregations in Opequon, Northumberland-Town, West Kishacoquillas Valley, and Cowpasture. The opportunities to leave home had never been more available, but for now the Fithians were going to stay put in Cohansey. On his return the Philadelphia Presbytery requested that he preach "as often as he can" at the Greenwich church. The church session was searching for a suitable candidate to replace the recently deceased Andrew Hunter, and Philip was available to supply the pulpit while they deliberated. It all seemed so providential.[62] In May 1776 Philip asked the Philadelphia Presbytery to take him back. "Mr. Philip Vickers Fithian," the minutes note, "who took Dismission from this Presbytery at our Meeting last Spring in Order to put himself under the Care of some other Presbytery, being present informs the Presbytery, that he has not found it expedient to put himself under the stated Care of another Presbytery, but desires to return to us as formerly." With Betsy by his side and an open pulpit at Greenwich, it was certainly not "expedient" for him to leave home now. The presbytery "cheerfully" granted Philip's request, and the elders from the Greenwich church who were present at the Philadelphia meeting immediately asked that he be allowed to supply their pulpit on a regular and continual basis until November. The presbytery granted this request as well.[63]

Once again Philip was home. He would plan to spend the next six months preaching every Sunday as the visiting minister at his home church with the hopes of being ordained there as the successor to Andrew Hunter. There was a very real possibility that this would indeed be the case. It was common for Presbyterian congregations to hire permanently the young licensees appointed to supply their pulpits during periods of vacancy. Philip was a known commodity in Greenwich, he had recently been awarded a master's degree from Princeton, and his backcountry experience had seasoned him to the demands of the Presbyterian ministry. His chances of "fix[ing] down" on his "native dear Sod" had just grown exponentially. One year earlier he had been resigned to leave Cohansey for good, and now his long way of improvement seemed at last to be leading him home.

This, at least, was how things were supposed to proceed. However, the Presbyterian God worked in mysterious and unpredictable ways. Only a few weeks into his preaching stint at Greenwich, duty called once again.

Chapter 8

Duty

On the morning of November 13, 1776, Philip was in Salem, New Jersey, waiting to depart on his trip to the Shenandoah Valley. It was cold, and part of him was dreading the fact that he was leaving Betsy and Cohansey to embark on this second leg of his mission to the backcountry. He was scheduled to meet Andrew Hunter Jr. in Salem at noon. From there the two Presbyterian itinerants would head south through the "hard" and "frosty" northwesterly winds that were whipping along the Delaware River. As he waited for Andrew to arrive, Philip struck up a conversation with Samuel Neglee, an officer in the Continental army who had come to Salem to recruit soldiers. Neglee was also having second thoughts about his work. He had been in this Quaker stronghold (he called Salem a "dull Town") for four days and had recruited only five men. As Philip and Neglee chatted, their spirits were raised by one another's company. Neglee could not help but observe that he and Philip, though engaged in different work, were pursuing similar callings. "I have left my Relations, Friends, & broke from inglorious Ease to serve my country," he told Philip proudly. "And you also, Parson," he continued, "have, a few hours ago, left all, even your dear, dear Betsey, tho' so very lately connected with her, & are now going on the Service of your God." Neglee concluded, "we are both in an honourable Cause, let us then defend it with our Property & blood, if the Call is so loud." Eventually both men went their separate ways. Andrew Hunter arrived, and the young preachers left on their trip.[1]

By November 1775, as Philip's encounter with Neglee suggests, it was becoming more difficult to separate the mission of the Presbyterian Church from the cause of American liberty. Philip's way of improvement and his call to serve God reached a convergence in this revolutionary moment. The universal ideals for which the Revolution was being waged—liberty, freedom, natural rights—were enlightened ones. They transcended any particular place or nation and were thus worthy of defense by all people, especially those in the cosmopolitan republic of letters. However, modernity was rushing forward in America faster than any other place on the globe. This made the colonies and their

Revolution exceptional. As Thomas Paine had put it so eloquently in *Common Sense*, "The cause of America is in a great measure the cause of all mankind."[2]

Philip and his friends in the Princeton Circle believed that there was a providential dimension to all of this. While they seldom talked about the colonies in terms of their "chosen" status, as the seventeenth-century Puritans had done, they did believe that the ideals nudging this Revolution onward were ordained by God. The Presbyterian Deity favored liberty over political slavery. Providence was on the side of human progress, and God called true believers to resist the evil encroachments of tyrannical government intent on slowing the inevitable advancement of freedom. Presbyterian patriots had no difficulty embracing the American Revolution's progressive vision and also remaining true to a providential view of human events.[3] Driven by this powerful synergy between the enlightened call of liberty and the will of God for the nations, Philip would leave home—one more time—to perform his sacred duty to his country.

In the months following the skirmishes at Lexington and Concord, Philip's diary became a running chronicle of how liberty was penetrating the backcountry regions of Pennsylvania and Virginia. Wherever he traveled he paid careful attention to the ways in which local frontier communities were experiencing the Revolution. In fact, the diary often goes into more detail about the revolutionary spirit of particular towns than about the spiritual or religious conditions of these places. In Georgetown, Maryland, the inhabitants were "warmed with a martial spirit," and the women of the town lined the streets to observe the mustering and "wish well to our common & sacred Cause." In York-Town, Pennsylvania, the German and Scots-Irish settlers were "enthusiastic in the American cause." In Stephensburg, Virginia, "Mars, the great God of Battle, is now honoured," and "all" the townspeople were in a "Hunting-Shirt Uniform & Bucks Tale in their hats." In Staunton the drums were "beating for recruits," a sound that Philip described as "Music in my Ears." Similar scenes of local mustering, complete with drums and fifes, could be found in Northumberland-Town, Sunbury, New Castle, and all along the Philadelphia Wagon Road as it pierced the heart of the Shenandoah Valley.[4] News related to the imperial crisis filled the pages of Philip's diary. Whenever he arrived at a new backcountry town it was his habit to find a Philadelphia newspaper in order to bring himself up to speed on events back east.

Philip had been recording his thoughts in journals for close to a decade by the time he departed Cohansey for the backcountry. The diary he kept between May 1775 and September 1776, however, was drafted, more than any of his previous efforts, with posterity in mind. Philip's scrawlings were composed for multiple audiences. As a Presbyterian clergyman, he wrote to describe religious life on the frontier so that he might accurately report back to the Philadelphia Synod. He certainly wrote to provide a record of his experiences for Betsy and their future children. However, Philip also wrote because he realized that he was living through an important moment in history. He wanted to represent as accurately as possible for his readers, whoever they might be, the story of American liberty and his place within it.

As early American historians are aware, Philip is one of the eighteenth century's most insightful diarists. Much of the praise he has received for his astute observations of colonial life has been lavished on the journal he wrote in 1773 and 1774 as a tutor at Robert Carter's plantation on Virginia's Northern Neck. The twentieth-century publication of his Northern Neck journal made Philip's plantation musings accessible to post–World War II historians and their students and lifted the name Philip Vickers Fithian from historical obscurity.[5] Yet, if Philip were alive today, he would have been surprised to find that his Carter diary has received so much attention, especially since it was the 1775–76 journal (and not the plantation diary) that he tailored most specifically for future readers. Philip spent considerable time during his backcountry preaching tour doing the historian's work of writing, rewriting, and "altering and abridging" his "Manuscripts" in order to portray correctly the course of the Revolution in the places he visited. He makes several references to his "Readers" or, more specifically, to those "who shall read these Papers a couple of hundred Years hence."[6]

Like all diaries, the journal Philip kept between 1775 and 1776 is largely personal in nature and focuses on the experiences of one man. Yet, to the degree in which it can be considered a public work, it is loosely modeled after the historical writers of the eighteenth-century Enlightenment. David Hume, William Robertson, and Lord Kames, to name a few of these historians, wrote to chronicle the advancement of societies through various stages of civilization. Human societies had evolved (or were evolving) from a condition of incivility or barbarity (associated with hunter-gatherers and pastoral societies) to a more modern state characterized by agriculture and, eventually, commerce. While these "stages of civilization" were often discussed in terms of economic development, they could also be applied to the political and moral lives of a particular culture. These optimistic authors wrote based on the premise that the present—in all its dimensions—was more enlightened and civilized than the past. History could thus be defined as the unrelenting march of human progress. Such a way of understanding the course of human events would become especially useful to those American writers—such as David Ramsay and Mercy Otis Warren—who would record the first histories of the American Revolution. By the first half of the nineteenth century, American historians—often described as "Whig"—had begun to tell the story of their country in terms of the gradual decay of European ways under the slow and steady assault of political liberty and democracy.[7]

As Philip described the coming of the American Revolution, he wrote from the center of this tradition of enlightenment historiography. The ideas presented in his diary and the Whig interpretation of American history stem from the same Enlightenment roots. Philip's commitment to this progressive view of the Revolution was only enhanced by the venue in which he wrote. As we saw in the previous chapter, he believed he was visiting a region at a lower stage of civilization than the more cosmopolitan early American cities on the eastern seaboard or, for that matter, his Cohansey home. Yet, he also saw great potential in the backcountry. He prompted his future readers to understand the American Revolution as a catalyst for improvement in these communities. For example, during his first itinerant tour of the Shenandoah Valley in the summer of 1775, Philip rode through Martinsburg, the newly settled seat of Berkeley County, Virginia. The town was only two years old at the time of Philip's visit but would grow over the next decade into a vibrant regional trading center for the northern valley. He counted about thirty houses, a stone prison, and a courthouse (under construction) "of no considerable size and Eligance." Philip believed that Martinsburg would benefit economically "if American Liberty be established." The Revolution was more than just a political break from a tyrannical British Crown; it was also the means by which Enlightenment progress would go forward in America: "this, with many other infant Villages, in a Series of Years, will be populous & wealthy Towns, grand in Appearance, & busy with Commerce."[8] A commercial society was one functioning at the highest stage of civilization attainable in the modern age. Economic liberty—the freedom to pursue wealth through free markets—went hand in hand with political liberty. A break from the shackles of tyranny would bring growth to America. Capitalism would replace mercantilism, trade restrictions would be lifted, and prosperity would inevitably follow.[9] Throughout his trip Philip expressed his affinity for what his former Princeton classmate Hugh H. Brackenridge called (in a commencement oration at which Philip was present) "The Rising Glory of America." In Northumberland-Town, Philip wrote, "in short, this Town, without Doubt in a few Years, will be grand & busy." In the Shenandoah Valley, Philip praised the Scots-Irish churches and singing schools, reflecting on how "beautiful" it is "to behold the Progress of Civilization." The promise of the Revolution, according to Philip, resided in these small communities and backcountry towns. The possibilities for America, whether moral, religious, economic, or cultural, were endless: "O America! Unwieldy Mass of Earth, pleasant & unhealthful, tho' various in thy Climes—Fertile of every useful Support of Life—On thy Bosom, exuberant of Nourishment, have been raised a wise & gigantic People—They are now flourishing in Learning & Arts, & chiefly at present, urged on by a misjudging Ministry, are preparing with a Confidence of Success, to rival the whole World in Milatary Honour—O America! with Reverence I look forward, & view thee in distinguished Majesty—It is not rash to assert, without the Aid of Prophecy, that thy Commerce, & Wealth, & Power, are Yet to rule the Globe!"[10]

The Enlightenment vision of history differed considerably from earlier histories of America—such as William Bradford's *Of Plymouth Plantation* (circa 1650) or Cotton Mather's *Magnali Christi Americana* (1702)—that were written to explain God's providential ordering of the past. These older works were designed to bring glory to the Creator for bestowing his blessings on America. They were not meant to tell the story of human progress. Philip, however, seemed to have no problem reconciling these differing approaches. The American Revolution was just as much an event ordained by the Author of history as it was another stage in the cultural development of Western civilization. Witherspoon's lectures on history taught Philip that "History presents us with a plan of providence, of the power and mercy of God."[11] A Calvinist view of God's providence over human history was not incompatible with Enlightenment historical narratives. The Scottish historians of the era, as Karen O'Brien has argued, believed that "Christianity is literally progress itself." The spread of Protestantism was an essential prerequisite for the transition from barbarity to civility. The advancement of the gospel, in other words, would both please God and contribute to a civil society. As we have seen from Philip's moral thought, eighteenth-century enlightened Presbyterians believed that Christianity—even evangelical Protestantism in certain cases—could be a useful stimulus for the improvement of society. If God was a historian, he would certainly be a Whig.[12]

Yet, for Presbyterians, God wanted liberty to progress within an ethical framework informed by his law as revealed in both Holy Scripture and the human conscience. Consequently, Philip's account of the Revolution's spread through the backcountry was tempered by these moral sensibilities. The progressive march of freedom always needed to be balanced with a healthy dose of virtue, and Philip was quick to comment whenever the patriotic behavior of backcountry inhabitants failed in this regard. For example, he had received news from home that some Pittsgrove, New Jersey, slaves, infused with revolutionary zeal, had murdered their owner and fled the scene of the crime. Other slaves, he added, were "running off daily." Servants, apparently taking advantage of the breakdown of authority in the colonies, were stealing horses and "many other things." If these were only a small sampling of the types of "Civil Discord" occurring throughout the colonies, "Good Lord! What then is her real Self!" Philip wrote with a sense of alarm. In parts of the Shenandoah Valley the mustering of troops degenerated into a venue for drinking, horse racing, and "carousing." Philip did not question the patriotism of these Scots-Irish militiamen; they were eager to receive news of events in Boston or, if necessary, come to the aid of their fellow New England countrymen. However, Philip could not fathom how they were able to carry the mantle of patriotism when they conducted themselves in such a "preposterous" manner. He concluded that they were "serving the Father of Deception under the Colour of Patriotism." He continued to rant, "Forbid it Decency & Valour that sacred Patriotism should be so cursedly prostituted, to subserve such Diabolical Purposes!"[13] Philip could not separate the moral character of the American Revolution from its political dimensions. He was probably just as disappointed by the way these raucous patriotic celebrations corrupted Presbyterian moral beliefs as he was by the way immoral behavior degraded patriotism.

As he observed and recorded the movement of the Revolution through the backcountry, Philip was hardly a detached observer. If God was on the side of the American Revolution, then Philip wanted to make it clear to his future readers that he was too. For the first time he started consciously to make reference to his path of self-improvement, which had begun when he was an eighteen-year-old Cohansey farm boy and had advanced—through Deerfield, Princeton, and Nomini-Hall—to the Presbyterian ministry and ultimately to his participation in the American Revolution. In November 1775 he noted that he was beginning his seventh volume—presumably a reference to the number of diaries he had filled since he first commenced writing over a decade earlier. He also started to organize his diary into chapters. Philip made sure to explain how his chapters told the story of his improvement: "Chapters, like the distinct Periods of my Time, are still increasing; every one carries me farther from the Place of beginning." The next several chapters of his life would be written within the larger context of the Revolution's progress and reach their culmination at the end of "volume seven" with his service in the Continental army.[14] Philip was now, in a very real sense, writing autobiography.

Although Philip made a new effort to construct himself for his audiences, he continued to express his deepest thoughts and convictions about the American Revolution in his diary. During his months in the backcountry he went through nothing less than a conversion to the cause of American liberty. In order to understand this transformative event, it is helpful to compare it to his evangelical conversion experience in the winter of 1765. As we saw in Chapter 2, most Presbyterian conversions were experienced by people who were familiar with the tenets of the gospel. Philip was an ideal candidate for conversion because he had been baptized as an infant and had attended church his entire life. Through his catechism and early grammar school training under the direction of Rev. Andrew Hunter he was familiar with Presbyterian beliefs and teachings. His spiritual conversion was thus more about embracing, on his own terms, the faith of his parents and community and less about responding to the teachings of the gospel. The authenticity of his conversion was confirmed by his decision to dedicate his life to the service of God.

In much the same way that Philip had been schooled in the theological confessions of Presbyterianism, he had also been educated to believe that the American Revolution was a sacred cause. He could explain that "political jealousy" was a "laudable passion" before an audience of distinguished guests at Princeton's commencement exercises in 1772. He could articulate the ways in which Whig political thought was compatible with Presbyterian ethics. He had a firm intellectual grasp on his church's approach to the imperial crisis with England. However, like his spiritual conversion as an eighteen-year-old, he now had to move beyond a mere rational understanding of the Revolution's justness and come to grips with whether or not he was willing to dedicate, or perhaps even sacrifice, his life to this cause. The Pennsylvania and Virginia backcountry would provide the bucolic setting for such a transformation to take place.

There has been a long-standing tradition in Christianity that the gospel is advanced most effectively through the testimony of people who practice their faith genuinely in everyday life. In other words, when it comes to winning converts, actions often speak louder than words. A similar form of public witness influenced Philip's personal conversion to the American Revolution. The patriotic spirit he saw firsthand on the frontier served as a powerful testimony of what a life truly dedicated to the rising glory of America might look like. The zeal with which backcountry residents were willing to take up arms for the cause of liberty was an inspiration to him. Capt. Joseph Holmes, his host in Stephensburg, Virginia, was willing "to leave his Family, his Store, & on the first Demand, march to the Relief of any Part of America." The call to serve one's country required sacrifice—perhaps even leaving one's home and family. Philip no doubt wondered if he could pull himself away from Cohansey and Betsy long enough to do the same. He watched with awe as the young men from Northumberland-Town headed east to join the Continental army. Philip's twenty-three-year-old brother Josiah had signed on for a year of service and would soon be with the army in Canada. Philip wrote proudly of Josiah's decision to enlist: "Brave Youth! his Bosom is warmed with genuine patriotic Fire!—Our Captain honours his Fortitude; he calls it noble—A young Man in Ease & Independence at Home, to enter with a Private's laborious Duty & Scanty Pay—To do this discovers Virtue." With such devotion surrounding him, how could Philip not do his part for the cause?[15]

During the course of his pastoral duties in Pennsylvania, Philip pondered the state of America with the same kind of intensity with which he had reflected on the state of his soul ten years earlier. On July 1, 1775, he spent the better part of the evening on the banks of the Susquehanna River thinking about the Revolution and his potential contribution to it: "I wandered pensive, slow, & alone, ruminating, with my Arms folded on my Breast, & my Eyes sometimes on the smooth, gently-moving Water, & sometimes on the Ground before me, upon the melancholy State of our dear Country! O if Tears driven out by Grief & real Sorrow could bring any Help, I would with much Pleasure & Desire have passed the Night and wept with the Genius of this Water, til our Tears had increased the Flood—! If Grief & Sympathy will not do, I stand ready, & am willing to hazard *Life* & *Credit*, & *Property*, in general, and needful Contest for what is our *All.*"[16] Philip, in his own dramatic way, was coming to terms with what the American Revolution might require of him. Duty to country might cost him his life. It was one thing to offer intellectual assent to the principles of Christianity or the cosmopolitan ideals of the Revolution and quite another to consider the real possibility of martyrdom for those beliefs. This distinction was at the heart of his conversion to "sacred patriotism."

Several weeks following his Susquehanna River musings, Philip was a bit more definitive about his duty to his country: "I have professedly enlisted in his Cause; & taken up Arms to oppose his Enemies." From his assignment in the East Kishacoquillas Valley he prayed that God would grant him "Wisdom & Ability" as he performed such future service. In late August, while picking plums in the woods around Fort Shirley, Pennsylvania, he sat down on a "great Rock, on the side of the Mountain" and spent several hours (in what he called a "visionary Trance") contemplating "our present most melancholy State." He imagined himself as a "private Soldier" encamped with the American militia near Boston and engaged in a skirmish with "cruel General Howe." He claimed to be "in the highest Transport of Satisfaction in a strong Persuasion of the Justice of the Cause, & Certainty of Success." As his daydream continued, he envisioned being struck by a bullet. When he broke from his daze, he concluded that even in the "Terror of Dying I seemed satisfied."[17]

With his clear willingness to surrender his life if necessary, Philip's conversion to the American Revolution was nearly complete. However, as was the case with any true conversion experience, his commitment to liberty would require action. As he completed his backcountry tour and settled into a comfortable life of supply preaching in Greenwich, he would be called to put his faith in America to the test. Shortly after Philip began his assignment at the Greenwich Presbyterian church, the Provincial Congress of New Jersey voted in favor of independence. Philip's mentor John Witherspoon would represent the colony in the Second Continental Congress in Philadelphia, while other members of the Provincial Congress—many of them Presbyterians—would begin to write a new state constitution. William Franklin, the last royal governor of New Jersey, was removed from office in June.[18] In Cohansey the patriotic spirit was also growing more intense. In January 1776, with the Continental army engaged in a siege of Quebec, the Continental Congress called on the New Jersey Provincial Congress to raise a battalion of infantry. New Jersey had contributed two battalions to the Continental army the previous October, but few of these soldiers had come from southwestern New Jersey. This third battalion of infantry, however, would draw extensively from Cumberland County and its environs.[19]

Joseph Bloomfield, Philip's former classmate at Green's academy and the Bridge-Town lawyer who defended the Greenwich tea burners, was chosen by the Cumberland County Committee as a captain of one of this battalion's companies. On February 9, 1776, Bloomfield began to "beat up" recruits. His work would not be difficult, especially among the Presbyterian patriots of Cumberland County. By the end of the month 106 men had enlisted and his company was considered "full." Bloomfield described his soldiers as "young Men whose Parents are Men of good Property, Family, & Circumstances & who could not be induced to enter the Service from Interest, but from Motives purely to Service their Country." He selected Josiah Seeley as his first lieutenant and Ebenezer Elmer as his ensign. Both men were friends of Philip and fellow tea burners. After a sermon by Enoch Green at Deerfield, the company left Cohansey on March 27. They marched to Salem County, where they tarred and feathered a particularly troublesome Tory, and were present with the third New Jersey battalion (under the command of Col. Elias Dayton) by mid-April. They would soon be fighting the British in upstate New York.[20]

By June the New Jersey Provincial Congress was fielding another request for troops. With the greater part of the Continental army moving to Manhattan after the successful siege of Boston, the Continental Congress requested 13,800 militiamen to support the army as it prepared for a British invasion of New York City. New Jersey would be responsible for providing 3,300 of these troops. On June 14, 1776, the New Jersey Provincial Congress responded to this call by raising five battalions of militia under the command of Col. Nathaniel Heard. Heard had gained fame for his leadership of the militia unit that had arrested William

Franklin earlier in the month. Each battalion in "Heard's Brigade" would include eight companies of 78 men. The soldiers would agree to serve until December 1.[21] Every one of Heard's regiments would be assigned a chaplain in accordance with the current policy set forth by the Continental Congress. The congress required the officers of each battalion in the Continental army to "procure Chaplains accordingly." They would be paid "thirty-three dollars and one-third per month" and were to be "persons of good character and exemplary lives, to see that all inferior officers and soldiers pay them suitable respect and attend carefully upon religious exercises." The congress affirmed that "the blessing and protection of Heaven are at all times necessary but especially in times of public distress and danger." Chaplains would help every member of the army "to live and act as becomes a Christian soldier defending the dearest rights and liberties of this country."[22]

It is unclear exactly how Philip became a chaplain. We also have no record as to how members of the Greenwich Presbyterian church responded to losing their regular supply minister, although it would be hard to imagine that the laity of this revolutionary-charged congregation would have objected to their pastor's enlistment. By the end of June, Philip had left his post at the church and joined Silas Newcomb's battalion, one of the five regiments in Heard's Brigade. Newcomb was fifty-three years old and had served New Jersey with honor as an officer in the French and Indian War. He had been an active member of the Cumberland County Committee but had fallen out of favor with this body earlier in 1775 when he refused to stop consuming British tea. He had since repented of this serious revolutionary sin and was chosen to lead eight companies of soldiers from Burlington, Cumberland, Gloucester, and Salem Counties. Newcomb was a member of the Fairfield Presbyterian church, a local judge, and a former Cumberland County sheriff. He probably knew Philip quite well. Philip and Newcomb's son were probably fellow conspirators in the Greenwich tea burning. The colonel had the authority to recruit his own chaplain, so he most likely chose Philip personally for this important position.[23]

Since chaplains were appointed at the battalion level during the first two years of the war (in 1778 they would be appointed at the brigade level), Philip would spend the next six months with many young men from his homeland. Some may have attended the Greenwich Presbyterian church. The major in Newcomb's battalion was Ebenezer Howell, another tea burner and one of the young men responsible for the *Plain Dealer*. The regiment's surgeon was one of Philip's best friends, Thomas Ewing. Philip, as we have seen, grew up with Thomas and his brother James (who would later also serve as an officer in the army). They had burned tea together, exchanged letters of friendship, and conversed with one another as part of the Bridge-Town Admonishing Society. Thomas Ewing's assistant, the battalion's "surgeon's mate," was James Patterson, another close friend. Patterson was a schoolmaster from Wilmington who had recently married Amy Hunter Ewing, the sister of Thomas and James Ewing. His bride was named after Andrew Hunter, the now-deceased Greenwich minister. Quartermaster Abijiah Holmes was also an acquaintance of Philip, and the two company captains from Cumberland County, William Kelsey and James Ogden, were both from long-standing Cohansey families.[24]

At the time of Philip's enlistment, American regiments had been present in New York City for over four months. George Washington, the commander of the army, anticipated that the British would attack the city following William Howe's Saint Patrick's Day retreat from Boston. He thus sent troops under the command of Lord William Stirling to prepare fortifications on Manhattan and along the Jersey shore at Paulus Hook (Jersey City), Amboy, and Elizabeth. After the British evacuation of Boston was complete, Washington moved his army south to New York. By April the city was under martial law and English trading ships were prevented from passing through the Upper Bay and the East River. Washington arrived on April 13 with approximately ten thousand troops. He organized them into four divisions under the command of Generals William Heath, Nathanael Greene, Joseph Spencer, and William Stirling. Greene's division was sent to Long Island, and the other three, at least for the moment, remained in New York to build more fortifications. During the course of the next two months, Washington worked closely with the Continental Congress in Philadelphia to raise more troops.[25]

Meanwhile the British navy ended its short hiatus in Halifax, Nova Scotia, and began trickling into New York's Lower Bay. Most of the fleet had docked on Staten Island during the first week of July. William Howe, the British commander in chief, arrived on June 24, and his brother, Adm. Richard Howe, would come a few weeks later. At the time of the Howe brothers' arrival, the British had 427 ships and thirty-four thousand men at Staten Island. Curious and anxious New Yorkers climbed to the roofs of their houses to peer across the Upper Bay in the hopes of getting a glimpse of this imposing naval force. Washington quickly moved more troops across the mouth of the East River to Long Island, where he expected at least part of the British invasion to take place. As both sides prepared for battle, the New York Provincial Assembly approved the Declaration of Independence. On the evening of July 9 Washington received a copy of the Declaration and read it to his troops. The army responded with great exuberance. Many of them marched down Broadway and removed the statue of George III on horseback that had prominently kept watch over the city since 1770. The following day, after receiving a harsh rebuke from Washington for their unruly and overheated behavior the previous evening, the Continental army continued its work on fortifications. Unsure of the enemy's next move, Washington prepared for the worst—a dual attack on both New York City and Long Island.[26]

On July 2 Philip was in Cohansey writing his will. In the event of his death, his father's plantation would be passed to his brothers and sister. His entire estate—both real and personal—was willed to Betsy. This included his horse Bullrock, his watch, his five volumes of Witherspoon's works, and his eight-volume set of the *Spectator*. If Betsy had a son or daughter by him after he died, the estate would be divided between his wife and child.[27] We do not know exactly where Philip was when the Second Continental Congress declared independence from England. If he was still in Cohansey, he would have certainly been present at the county seat in Bridge-Town on July 7 when the patriots of Cumberland County, accompanied by the local militia, paraded to the courthouse to hear the first public reading of the Declaration of Independence and the New Jersey Constitution. Those in attendance heard Jonathan Elmer, the chairman of the Cumberland County Committee, announce that a "new era in politics had commenced." Philip would have been pleased with Elmer's speech. The distinguished Cohansey physician and politician warned his audience not to allow the Revolution to degenerate into "faction and party spirit." Elmer added with a certain historical flair that "Anarchy" and "confusion" would open the door to tyranny and the very real chance that "a Julius Cesar, or an Oliver Cromwell, will spring up among ourselves." He asked his hearers to "keep a strict and jealous eye, over our own internal police and constitution" in order to avoid "the fate of Greece, Rome, Carthage, and Great Britain." Elmer urged the people of Cohansey to get involved in the ensuing war for independence. "Every member of this state, who enjoys the benefits of its civil government," he announced, "is absolutely bound, by the immutable law of self-preservation, the laws of God and of society, to assist in protecting and defending" liberty. He added that "it is impossible for any one, possessed of the spirit of a man, who is a friend to the united states, and whose conscience does not furnish him with an excuse, to stand by, as idle spectator, while his country is struggling and bleeding in her own necessary defence."[28]

Those who refused to support the cause of liberty, Elmer argued, "should be shunned as enemies or despised as cowards." In an obvious reference to Cohansey Quakers, he addressed the problem of those whose "conscience" provided them an excuse not to fight. Elmer respected the Quakers' testimony of peace and affirmed that any person's "conscience ought to be free from compulsion," but at a moment such as this, Quaker pacifism only stood in the way of the Revolution's forward movement. Elmer was firm in his conviction that Quakers, at least for a time, should be prevented from participating in government. Not only would involvement in the affairs of the Revolution force them to violate their collective conscience, but such participation would also be a detriment to the safety of Cohansey inhabitants, and all New Jersey citizens, in a time of war. "It is plain," he noted, "that to entrust the affairs of our government, at this juncture, to such people, is as dangerous, as to entrust the management of a ship, in a violent storm, to an infant or an idiot." The Revolution needed patriots—those willing to shed their blood to defeat the "despicable minions of tyranny and oppression" and the "haughty and imperious Task masters."[29]

If Philip was in Cohansey on July 7, he did not stay long. Two days later he was with Newcomb's regiment in Philadelphia making final preparations for joining the Continental army. As a staging area for militia companies from the Delaware Valley preparing for service in New York, the City of Brotherly Love was abuzz with military activity. Philip wrote home to Betsy describing the scene: "Several Companies go out of Town this day for New Jersey, in which are many of our Friends . . . I cannot form to you the Picture which this Day shows: Suffice it to say, all are in Arms."[30] On July 11 Philip passed through Newark, New Jersey. He was traveling with Abijiah Holmes, Newcomb's quartermaster and another member of the Cumberland County Committee. The two men were headed by stage to Paulus Hook, where they planned to ferry across the North (Hudson) River to New York. Their travel plans, however, were temporarily put on hold by the first shots of the campaign. At precisely the time of their arrival at the North River on July 12, the British began a preliminary naval assault on the American fortifications. Admiral Howe sent two warships, the HMS *Phoenix* and the HMS *Rose*, up the North River to prevent the Americans from drawing supplies from regiments stationed in Albany. Philip heard the cannon fire as he rode closer to Paulus Hook. "The Country was in great Consternation & Tumult" as cannonballs ripped through houses in New York to the west and the Paulus Hook ferry house to the east. It was Philip's first exposure to the guns of war.[31]

As New Yorkers fled the city in the aftermath of this British naval demonstration, Philip finally got a chance to cross the North River and join his battalion. He showed his commission papers to Nathaniel Heard and for the next week remained in Manhattan while the rest of the companies assigned to Newcomb's regiment made their way to the city.[32]

Philip bunked with Abijiah Holmes and William Kelsey in one of New York's many vacated houses (it was a "good House—without furniture"). He wrote, both in his diary and in a letter to Betsy, about his sleeping arrangements: "We sleep on the Floor in a Blanket; Lodging, you will say hard enough, I think so too." Yet, despite the hardships, he told Betsy that "all is good." He reminded himself that "It is American Liberty we are trying to support, & there are many thousands in this Town, as well as me, who are resolved to suffer more before we give it up."[33] Philip devoted the next several days to familiarizing himself with New York. Most of the eighteenth-century population of the city was clustered in a square mile at the southern tip of Manhattan Island. This area was now filled with American soldiers. The rest of the Continental army was concentrated along the East and North Rivers, on the Jersey shore from Paulus Hook to South Amboy, and on Long Island and Governors Island, a small island near the mouth of the East River. "But dreadful indeed is the Aspect of this City," Philip wrote. It was "full of Soldiers—the streets barricaded—the Shores & neighbouring Parts, lined with Fortifications—Women, Children, & the Aged fled." There were, by his estimation, 130 British ships across the bay at Staten Island. Their presence inspired him with a sense of what the defense of liberty and, more specifically, the defense of the city of New York might demand of the thousands of soldiers filling the streets: "On every Hand perplexity! The Fears of Death should be laid aside by every Person who enters on the Service, for the Course of our Duty will require the Hazards of it almost daily." Philip spent the remainder of July 13 visiting the site where troops had four days earlier removed the statue of George III.[34]

As he was a chaplain, Philip's primary responsibility was to conduct required daily prayer meetings—at 5:30 A.M. and 6:00 P.M.—with the companies of Newcomb's battalion. Following evening prayers he visited sick and wounded soldiers confined to makeshift military hospitals. On Sunday mornings the troops attended one of several New York City churches. Philip took advantage of his morning off by visiting some of the Protestant congregations still holding services during the army's occupation of the city. He heard sermons from some of revolutionary America's most well-known dissenting clergymen, including John Rogers at the First Presbyterian Church, John Henry Livingston at the "North Dutch Church," John Mason of the Cedar Street (Seceder) Church, and John Gano of the First Baptist Church. He even occasionally preached in these churches. As a gentleman in the camp, Philip was not expected to help with the building of fortifications or participate in combat (although he did occasionally take exercise with the troops during their marches). His days were free for study, socializing, or observing his regiment at work. He told Betsy that his duty, for the most part, "is easy."[35]

Though Philip's daily schedule was less physically demanding than that of an ordinary private, his job of helping troops to "live and act" as Christian soldiers was no "easy" task. Most of the men in Newcomb's battalion were Christians affiliated with southern New Jersey churches. However, the daily demands of war often distracted them from tending to their souls to the degree that would please their chaplain. On July 24, for example, morning prayers were canceled because, according to Philip, "We had Business of greater importance!" As the fighting with the British on Long Island drew near, Philip wrote that "the Sabbath is scarcely known in the Army. Profaned is all religious Exercises. Dreadful is the thought that Man who expect an Engagement every Day with a obstinate, wise, & powerful Enemy should dare be so ungodly. But the God of this World has blinded the Mind." Philip worried that the lack of religion among the troops might have a direct bearing on the army's success in New York: "It were happy if we could see some Signs of the Enlargement of Religion; if Christ was honoured more; if his venerable Name was profaned less, we might expect a more effectual Blessing on our Arms; but alas, swearing abounds, all Classes swear, most disregard holy Duties, & will not be thoughtful for their precious Spirits."[36]

Philip's "easy" schedule left him plenty of time to socialize. The networks of friends and acquaintances that brought him happiness and contributed to his self-improvement all seemed to intersect on the southern tip of Manhattan Island. The young men of the "Princeton Circle" could be found serving the Continental army as officers, chaplains, and physicians. Philip ate regularly with Andrew Hunter Jr. (who was also serving as a chaplain in Heard's brigade), Israel Evans (his friend from college), and his brothers-in-law, Reading, John, and Erkuries ("Arky") Beatty. He walked the potential fields of battle with colonels, captains, and lieutenants from Heard's Brigade and listened to their plans for battle. If Philip got homesick, he could surround himself with friends from Cohansey. New York City and Long Island were filled with Cohansians on the eve of the engagement. In addition to Andrew Hunter Jr., Robert Patterson, and the Ewing brothers, William Hollingshead, the pastor of the Fairfield Presbyterian church, was also in New York doing chaplain duty. Philip conducted daily prayers before a host of familiar faces from Newcomb's regiment, and those Cohansey men who were not serving often came to visit, delivering letters from Betsy and providing him with news from home.[37]

By mid-July, Adm. Richard Howe, who in addition to his role as commander of the Royal Navy served as a delegate of the British peace commission, was trying to convince the American revolutionaries to rescind the Declaration of Independence and avoid the possibility of an engagement with the powerful British fleet. George Washington and the Continental Congress, however, would have none of it. The Americans refused to consider every offer of peace that Howe proposed. Philip had heard about the rejection of the British peace offers and, with a sense that an armed conflict was now inevitable, wrote, "The Fleet appears formidable; but our Army is couragious." As the Continental Army continued to fortify its defenses and wait for the British to make the first move, Philip wrote home to Betsy. With all efforts to avoid battle apparently exhausted, he contemplated the possibility that he might never see his wife again on this side of eternity: "I have told you that nothing but direful War should detain me long from you. And surely unnumbered Curses await that Wretch who has occasioned the Division of such near Alliances. But we shall meet again—in the World to come, if not in this. Be not then unduely troubled; If I fall in Battle, or otherwise; This I ask, let my Memory be dear to you, think of me as a Person, who never viewed you without Emotion; & was never in your Company a Moment but with the highest Pleasure!" The day after he penned this letter Philip was dispatched, with part of Silas Newcomb's battalion, to Long Island, where the Continental army was preparing a line of defense along the hills of Brooklyn Heights.[38]

The good news about being transferred to Long Island was that Philip no longer had to sleep on the floor. While the soldiers in Newcomb's regiment slumbered in tents and barns, Philip found food and lodging behind the American fortifications at the house of a local Dutch widow. For the next month or so, as he enjoyed the comforts of a bed and regular meals, Philip commented on the poor health conditions faced by ordinary soldiers in the Continental army. The construction of the Brooklyn Heights breastworks required troops to live in close proximity to one another, making them all the more susceptible to a host of camp diseases. Without proper sanitation, the Continental army inadvertently polluted the men's water supply. Philip wrote on July 19 that "the vile water here sickens us all. I am very sick; troubled with continual lax." Philip was nursed back to health by his Dutch landlady, but for soldiers without nursemaids, dysentery, an extreme and disgusting form of diarrhea, was particularly troublesome. Philip made regular pastoral visits to the army hospitals, where dozens of troops were suffering from this sickness. The drought inflicting New York City in late July only enhanced the dehydration that usually accompanied dysentery. In addition to the putrid water, Philip attributed the army's health problems to the change in diet—brought on by the scarcity of fresh vegetables—that most soldiers experienced after joining the army. He thought twice before visiting soldiers suffering from "contagious" and "horrible" disorders, but he viewed this work as part of his pastoral and patriotic calling: "I am

Figure 11. Fithian and the battle for New York, summer 1776.

willing to hazard & suffer equally with my Countrymen since I have a firm Conviction that I am in my Duty."[39]

As July passed into August, Philip and the Continental Army could do little more than wait for the British to mount their invasion. As Washington and his generals tried to guess (due to a lack of solid intelligence) where the Howe brothers would strike, Philip spent his days wandering with friends along the American lines on Long Island and Manhattan. He continued to watch with awe as the British fleet on the other side of the bay prepared for an attack. On July 31 he returned to Manhattan and moved into a house on Broadway (with Andrew Hunter Jr.), where he claimed to "have a perfect view of the Ferry & good Prospect of the River." Philip also thought about his new wife back home in Cohansey, writing, "How do you pass these burning july Suns and dewy Evenings.

O tell me!"[40] His passionate love for Betsy once again filled his letters
to her:

My Desire of seeing you is already grown so strong that I am not without many
uneasy Hours every Day, which have no other Foundation than bare Absence
from the Woman that I have fixed my Heart to love & protect. You will have no
Occasion to think it Flattery or Enthusiasm when I assure you that I bear a separation from you now, with more Anxiety, & real Distress than ever I have done before. . . . If we meet again, surely we shall be tenfold Happy. If not here—if not
My charming Betsy, I bespeak your Friendship on the other side of Death! . . .
Your Interest, my dear Creature, lies on my Soul next to my bleeding Country—
Next to my dear Jesus do I place, in my Regard our suffering Land; & next to our
suffering Land, do I place my unfeigned Esteem, the Girl that lies in my Bosom &
deserves my Love—Oh! nothing but the necessity of defending & establishing sacred Freedom should detain me long from your loving Arms![41]

In addition to these bursts of romantic desire, Philip's letters to Betsy
were means of exchanging news and passing along instruction in household affairs. Philip was eager to hear about the health of his Uncle
Samuel and the condition of his horse Bullrock, and he kept Betsy up to
date on the activities of her brothers in New York. In one letter Betsy informed Philip that Andrew Hunter Jr.'s wife Nancy had given birth to a
son (Philip referred to him as an "infant General"). He reminded her to
visit Nancy and "Mrs. Hunter," the widow of Rev. Andrew Hunter, as
often as possible. He also asked her to visit Maskell Ewing (the father of
James and Thomas) on Ye Greate Street to make sure he returned
Philip's copy of "Mr. Chesterfield's Letters." Betsy was to retrieve the volumes and "put them up safe." She was also instructed to have a bed ticking woven for their house in Greenwich and to settle some of her
husband's outstanding debts. Philip requested that Betsy, at her earliest
convenience, send him his overcoat, a new shirt, a sheet and pillow, and
his Psalm Book—a clear sign that he believed that the war would not
stop anytime soon and that he would probably need to serve out his entire appointment. Sometime in late July, Betsy had moved from the
Fithian house in Greenwich and gone to Deerfield to live with Enoch
Green and her sister Mary. Green would soon be leaving to do chaplain
work as well, and perhaps Betsy wanted to keep her sister company while
their spouses were absent. Philip supported her decision, but since
Deerfield did not receive as many visitors and travelers as Greenwich or
Bridge-Town did, he worried that his correspondence with his wife
would be limited.[42]
    During the first and second weeks of August rumors circulated
throughout the camps about British naval movements, and Philip responded in his journal every time he heard the cannon fire of an enemy
ship. With little else to do but wait, Philip's thoughts continued to dwell

on Betsy. "I have often heard it said, & so have you," he wrote from New York, "that Hours go heavily along to absent Lovers. It is Sentiment . . . to say that I experience this every Day." As his passion for Betsy raged, Philip noted that such "real" and "constant" sentiment had failed to weaken the "vigor in the Cause I came here to support." On one level, Philip probably saw this as a good thing. He could not let his passions for Betsy interfere with his patriotism, that "laudable passion." However, on another level, Philip was concerned that his embrace of a manly revolutionary identity, fueled by his experience with the Continental army, was eroding away his softer side—the sentimental feelings that characterized a true gentleman and person of refinement. "I must have lost totally every soft Feeling of the Heart," he told Betsy, "& degenerated into a Condition coarser than Brutality." He added, "it is hard Necessity that detains me here."[43]

On August 7 Philip left his boardinghouse in New York and began eating meals with the troops. A British attack seemed imminent: "Tolling Bells!" Philip wrote, "Dolefully do they call for our Notice." Members of Newcomb's battalion were ordered to prepare their guns for battle, fill their canteens with water, and man their posts through the night. George Washington was still uncertain about what the Howe brothers would do. On August 9 he received word that the British had invaded Long Island, but he later found out that it was "only a Feint to amuse us." False alarm or not, Philip urged the troops to place their "whole Dependence on God's Assistance."[44] On August 13 Heard's entire brigade, chaplains included, was moved back to Long Island. As the transfer took place, Philip watched the ships from the Manhattan batteries: "they lie in a long, thick Cluster," he wrote, "we had a good Glass, but could not precisely tell their Numbers, we think there is near two hundred Sail, probably more!" Philip marched with the troops the following day and "gave them a short Address on the Expectation of an Attack." He then took up lodging at the house of Mrs. Borum, the Dutch widow with whom he had boarded during his earlier stay on Long Island.[45]

On August 15, the day that eight thousand German ("Hessian") soldiers arrived on Staten Island to bolster the British ground troops, the American division commander Nathanael Greene, who had been appointed major general the previous week, fell ill with typhoid fever. George Washington replaced him with John Sullivan, who had recently returned from combat in Canada. Greene's sickness was a huge loss to the Continental army. He had been the architect of the American defense lines on Long Island and knew the terrain better than any other general. It rained most of the day, but the American officers still felt that a British attack was coming at any moment. The men in Newcomb's battalion were called to their posts at 3:00 A.M. to wait "under Arms." Many of them did not have blankets or coats to protect them from the hard rainfall. Philip spent the day sick in bed and was once again nursed back to health by his landlady. As he lay ill, he worried about his own safety. What if the enemy attacked Long Island while he was confined to his room? How would he be able to retreat back to New York City? It did not take long, however, before he realized that he was letting his pessimism get the best of him. His worries, he came to believe, were unwarranted. His faith in the American army and the God who sustained it would not let him or his country down: "Curses must follow the Executors of such ill Designs. Heaven will not pass them by unpunished. This healing Thought distends my Heart; tho sick I am yet strong." By the end of his journal entry for August 15 Philip's confidence had grown by leaps and bounds. "I fear not *George's Tory Fleet & Army*," he wrote with a sense of courage and honor; "Let them ride yonder before our Town, & Fortifications, in their highest Grandieur, we dread them not. . . . May the God of Peace fill them all with Confusion because they came from their Homes to rob us our *Peace* & *Freedom*. Do it, good Lord. Amen. Amen."[46]

The following day Philip left Mrs. Borum's house and began boarding, with Andrew Hunter Jr., closer to the shore of the East River. His new landlady, "Mrs Coburn," was the wife and mother of a "genteel, sober, and patriotic family."[47] Philip's new room was "free of noise," was "well-furnished," and had a "good bed." From his window he could see the British fleet in the bay. "Some say our Situation is dangerous," he wrote, but Philip preferred to be in a position on the waterfront where he could monitor closely the movements of the enemy navy. He was feeling better—in terms of both his health and America's chances.[48] On August 18 the *Phoenix* and the *Rose* finally made their way back down the North River. At 6:45 A.M. from his new room Philip heard the "Crack, Crack, Crack!" of the New York City batteries firing at the British vessels. Fifteen minutes later he watched as the American cannons on Governors Island and Red Hook continued the bombardment. "For about four Minutes the firing was indeed tremendous," Philip wrote with wonder. The ships sailed past the American batteries "in the midst of a perpetual Blaze," and Philip saw cannonballs splashing in the water between Governors Island and his waterfront boardinghouse. Later in the day the Howe brothers began to move fifteen thousand men on transport boats toward Long Island.[49]

When the British forces under the command of Gen. Charles Cornwallis landed on Long Island during the early morning hours of August 21, the American breastworks at Brooklyn Heights ran three miles in length. Cornwallis's troops quickly brushed aside American riflemen stationed along the coast at Gravesend Bay and by the end of the day were positioned within a few miles of the American fortifications.

George Washington, thinking that the British were still planning a simultaneous attack on Manhattan, shifted only six regiments to Long Island to help strengthen the American line. He had grossly underestimated the size of the army, assuming that the Howe brothers did not have any more than eight thousand men on the island when in reality they had almost twice that many troops. With the British on Long Island, the Continental army was on the alert. Philip described the troop movement: "Crack: Crack!: An Alarm from Red-Hook. Crack! Crack! Crack! The Alarm repeated from Cobble Hill. Orders are given for drums to beat to *Arms*. The Enemy have been landing for some time down at the Narrows, & it is said, have now ashore several thousand." In the midst of a thunderstorm that Philip described as "so violent as I have not seen since about this time in August 1773" and that Andrew Hunter claimed killed several American soldiers, Newcomb's battalion was sent to guard Fort Box, on the far west flank of the American defenses on Brooklyn Heights. Philip grabbed his gun, canteen, knapsack, and blanket and entered the fort with his regiment. Other battalions from Heard's Brigade were sent to stop the advance of British ground forces. Philip would later write to Betsy, "For one single Hour . . . my heart fluttered—All was new! To see the Ravages of War presented visibly in view." His battalion spent the afternoon fortifying Fort Box. "The Men work with Vigor," Philip observed, "a Sense of Necessity, & the Security of Life, are strong Springs to Industry." By evening the British advance had been halted and the enemy settled for the night at Flatbush, about four miles from the American lines. Philip thought correctly that it was the hilly terrain around Brooklyn and Gowanus Heights that held them back. Members of Newcomb's battalion were permitted to rest until 2:00 A.M. before returning again to their posts. "No officer or Soldier," Philip wrote, "is to take off his Clothes; & all are to lye on their Arms."[50]

On August 23 George Washington arrived on Long Island and replaced Andrew Sullivan with Israel Putnam. Hessians and American forces skirmished near Flatbush, and Richard Howe's ships bombarded the American troops from the bay. Silas Newcomb's New Jersey militia was sent to spend the night in the woods near Red Hook, close to where the Royal Navy was directing its cannon fire. The following morning the British under Cornwallis had still not advanced from their position at Flatbush, and Philip took the opportunity to take a walk to the front lines where his regiment was stationed. He found some of the men "sitting under shady trees and conversing about the Occurences of the Day: who were killed, or wounded, or taken Prisoners, & which Army, on the Whole gained Ground or lost." Others were "preparing their Victuals, & eating" or "securely sleeping." Those who were on duty were "standing among whistling Bullets" and "taking trees for Security & shooting when they can." The skirmishing was constant, but Philip prayed that the British would "lose their Strength & Courage & return to their Ships with Shame." Unfortunately, God did not answer this prayer—at least in the way Philip had hoped.[51]

On Sunday, August 25, Philip began his daily diary entry with a lament: "Another holy Sabbath presents to our View. No social Worship to be performed this Day." The American troops did not pause to worship because the enemy now had close to twenty thousand men on Long Island. Most of the approximately eleven thousand American soldiers on the island were behind the fortifications at Brooklyn Heights, although Israel Putnam, with the approval of George Washington, had placed three thousand troops on the high ground at Gowanus Heights, a few miles south of the American line. Philip described the scene as Continental army soldiers headed out to Gowanus Heights. "Carts & Horses driving every Way among the Army," he wrote, "Men marching out & coming in to & from the front Camp—Small Arms & Field Pieces continually firing; all in Tumult." Not willing to let the Sabbath go by without some kind of acknowledgment of the God he believed to be protecting the American army, Philip conducted prayers with his regiment in the afternoon, shortly before they returned to the woods to guard against the coming British invasion.[52]

By evening on August 26 the Americans had formed a two-mile line along Gowanus Creek to serve as a buffer between the British army and the Brooklyn Heights fortifications. Lord Stirling commanded the forces on the right flank, and Andrew Sullivan was in charge of two hundred men on the left flank protecting the Jamaica Road entrance to Gowanus Heights. Sensing that the American left flank was weak, British general Henry Clinton proposed a surprise attack on Gowanus Heights via the lightly defended Jamaica Road. He would march through the night with four thousand troops and join the rest of the British and Hessian infantry in the morning for a full-scale assault on the Continental army. Philip, completely ignorant of what was happening to the southeast, ended the day by noting that there was "no very important movement of the Enemy To Day." He did, however, feel that sooner or later something significant was bound to happen. The possibility of death filled his thoughts. That evening he wrote to Betsy, once again reflecting on his own mortality: "if Providence should divide me from you, think it not a very great Breach upon your Felicity—turn your Attention more to him who gave & took away—& say 'Philander loved me & was kind; but as all things here are uncertain, when Providence took him I freely gave him up.'"[53]

The Battle of Long Island began early on the morning of August 27, 1776. Clinton's plan worked. By daylight his expeditionary troops had united with six thousand additional men under the command of William Howe to overrun the American left flank at Gowanus Heights successfully. They were now positioned between Gowanus Heights and Brooklyn Heights, making it difficult for American troops on Gowanus Heights to retreat. The Americans had been driven off the hill before noon. "O doleful! doleful! doleful!—Blood! Carnage! Fire!" Philip wrote that evening. "Our people drove this Morning within their Lines ... Many Battalions of excellent Men, went out into the Woods on the right & left Wing of the Enemy;—Alas! numbers went never to return!—The Enemy surrounded them." The British had approached the American line on Brooklyn Heights at least twice, but Howe decided to turn back, perhaps remembering the disaster that had occurred when he attacked the heart of the American defenses at Bunker Hill the previous year. Instead, he chose to dig trenches in preparation for a slow but steady advance. With superior numbers, it would be only a matter of time before he could overpower the American forces on Brooklyn Heights. Historians debate how many Americans were killed on this day, but the best estimates suggest that Washington's army lost about three hundred men to death and another one thousand to capture. On the evening of August 27 the Continental army was tending to soldiers' wounds and contemplating its next move. The British were just over one mile away, building earthworks in preparation for a siege. It was, as Philip described it, "a most dismal Scene."[54]

Over the course of the next two days the British worked relentlessly in the pouring rain on their trenches, inching ever closer to the American fortifications on Brooklyn Heights. Washington continued to supply the lines until about ninety-five hundred men were on the island, but he was still heavily outnumbered. As the British soldiers dug, they were protected by riflemen and artillery. During the course of the battle on August 27, Generals Sullivan and Stirling were both captured by the British, and behind the American lines, according to Philip, there reigned a sense of chaos that could not be controlled simply by the arrival of more troops. American soldiers were "running promiscuously" to deter the British siege, but their weapons were soaked by the "violent Rain." As the enemy moved closer to Brooklyn Heights, Philip noted that the American position was "overflowed with water" and that some of the troops had been on guard for more than twenty-four hours. "Sickness," he concluded, "must follow." The only good news was that heavy winds prevented the British navy from controlling the East River.[55]

On August 29, with the British entrenched in the earth only yards away from the American fortifications and a terrible rainstorm brewing, Philip was surprised to hear that Heard's Brigade was ordered to "move over to New-York, & from thence up the North River to some Place of greater

Security." At 7:00 P.M. members of the brigade began to abandon their posts and "parade . . . with all the Baggage" to ferries that would take them across the East River back to Manhattan. Philip and Andrew Hunter Jr. decided that "no Rest can be had if we pass over so late" and thus decided to return to their boardinghouse. They planned to leave Long Island early the next morning. At midnight their landlady woke them to inform them that the entire American army was leaving Long Island. She was joining the evacuation party and wanted to take with her the bed on which Philip was sleeping. Philip gave up his bed, but for whatever reason, he thought that the woman was spinning an "idle Tale" about the mass evacuation. He and Andrew thus chose to lay their blankets on the floor and continue sleeping. The next morning the two chaplains realized that their landlady had been correct. They frantically rushed to shore and managed to sail across the river on one of the last boats available. Philip added that the vessels which left the island after them "were fired at, & in one of them five were badly wounded."[56]

What Philip had experienced was the Continental army's famous retreat from Long Island. Washington, after the previous day's defeat, removed the entire army from the island under the cover of darkness. Between 7:00 P.M. and the following morning he evacuated nearly ten thousand Continental troops. Washington was aided by a dense fog that lingered over the East River long enough to shield the American ferries from the sight of the British navy. The following day, as the weather became more "settled & fair," Philip wrote about the events he had just lived through: "Many Opinions there are about the Retreat from Long-island—some say it was too secret; some that it was a Mark of Fear; some that we are sold." Philip preferred to call it a "brave & useful Manoeuvre," affirming that the army left the island "with Profit and Hounour, for they could have surrounded us." Though he was unsure about the ability of the Continental army to hold New York City for much longer, he did not give up hope, telling Betsy that the losses the army suffered were "reparable" and that he expected "it will by the common Assistance of Providence, be made up to us with Advantage before the Campaign is finished."[57]

After his return to New York, Philip continued to perform his regular routine of conducting morning prayers, dining with officers, and visiting friends from Cohansey. British ships were lurking south of the city, while others were cruising up the East River to explore the possibility of mounting an attack from the northern part of Manhattan Island. Washington sent troops to Kings Bridge, on the Harlem River, to guard against this distinct possibility. On September 3 Newcomb's battalion was ordered to march north along the river to Mount Washington. The men planned to spend the next several weeks in northeastern Manhattan working on the construction of what would become Fort Washington. "Adieu New-York," Philip wrote, "perhaps forever!"[58] After settling into the fortification at Mount Washington, Philip wrote to Betsy to catch her up on the traumatic events of the previous few days. He continued to wonder if he would ever see his wife again. He blamed George III for forcing him to consider this possibility: "Cruel George, why, without Reason, are so many Mothers robbed of their beloved Children—So many Lovers forever divided?—Why, since all must lie on thy guilty Head! But Tyrany & Ambition have no control." He wrote each letter to Betsy as if it were his last: "Not a single Rival have you had in my Breast since the Hour you consented to be mine—I have Reason to believe the same of you. I trust our Hearts are undivided. Let us then go hand in hand, in spite of any Interruptions from this gay seducing World, onwards to the peaceful Gates of Paradise: However thorny & rocky we find the Way; at the End is the flowery Garden of God—The Tree of Life—the New Jerusalem—that great beautiful, everlasting City!"[59]

Philip continued to assert that in serving his country he was also serving his God. If he would need to give his life for the cause of liberty, he was now more than ready. He was willing to "lie here on the crimsoned Field and bleed out my life" in order to save his beloved Betsy from the evil grasp of tyranny. Indeed, he wrote, "This has been my Desire & Endeavour, especially of late. The Days are Evil; Future contingencies are most uncertain—I have given up myself to him who lent me to the World; if I have done my fellow Creatures any Service at all, the Profit is theirs, & be the Glory God's—But the all-important Design of my Life has been to prepare for Eternity; this thought too I have diligently & soberly traced; And the Issue is; that resting on the Promises in the Word of God, with a firm & only Reliance on the Merits of the gracious Saviour of Sinners, I resign my Soul & my Body to my Maker, trusting in his forgiving Mercy."[60] Yet, even as Philip thought seriously about death, he also had hope in the possibility that he would one day return to Cohansey. He advised Betsy on matters of everyday life as if such a return were certain. Philip was pleased to hear, for example, that Betsy was spinning him a new coat. He wondered if their new bed ticking had been completed and asked again how Bullrock was faring. He conducted Cohansey visits vicariously through Betsy, urging her to spend time with friends and family throughout the region. His term of service was to be finished in December, and he concluded one of his letters by reminding Betsy, "The Months are marching along, & if my Life is spared, if we are Victors, I shall soon be with you. . . . Only a few Days divide us, if we are to meet again—And if we are so much blessed, I pray it may not be soon to part."[61]

After arriving at Mount Washington, Philip described his new surroundings with a sense of optimism that, as we will see, would turn out to be tragically ironic: "Glad was I to be on land—the Land here looks promising of Health, very hilly, woody, & romantic; Our men we hope will be more healthy." Philip was no longer in the comfortable boarding-house where he had stayed on Long Island. He slept, like the soldiers, in tents. As the late summer nights grew colder he looked forward with dread to autumn: "All our clothes we put over us now, & then the Weather will be five times colder—We trust only our growing more hardy." Everyday life at Mount Washington centered on digging fortifications and trying to guess the enemy's next move from the sound of British cannons being fired from the East River and Long Island. On September 9 Philip was taken with a bad case of ague and fever. His brother-in-law and physician John Beatty came to his aid and took Philip to spend the night with him in Morrisiana (present-day Bronx). When Philip returned to Mount Washington the following day the sounds of bombing and cannonading had grown louder—"More fierce than heretofore."[62]

Philip also noted that more and more American troops were arriving at Mount Washington. This was a result of George Washington's decision to abandon New York City. With British ships surrounding Manhattan, Washington and his generals felt that they could no longer hold the city. Most of the Continental army was transferred to the northeastern portion of the island, with the bulk of the troops positioned at Harlem Heights, approximately two miles south of Mount Washington. Once again members of Newcomb's battalion were ordered to fill their canteens and prepare their weapons for the possibility of an imminent attack. The British cannon fire continued to rumble during this second week of September, and each day Philip described it as "brisker" or "heavier" than the day before. In the process he had grown accustomed to the flying cannonballs and whirring bullets. He and Andrew Hunter Jr. took daily walks south to Harlem to examine the American fortifications and view the British positions on the East River. By the evening of September 13 the American retreat from New York City was nearly complete, and the British were preparing to make their invasion of Manhattan. The American troops at Mount Washington were "very dull-spirited" about Washington's decision to give up the city to the British, but they were also eager to fight. Philip described their habit of writing the phrase "Let us fly no more" on the sides of their tents and houses.[63]

The anxious soldiers in Philip's battalion would get their wish. After a hard day of work constructing Fort Washington, the troops were awakened to their posts at 2 A.M. on the morning of Sunday, September 15. Later that day the British sent three ships, cannons roaring, up the North River, but by noon the Americans had learned that this was only a diversion. The real activity was occurring roughly five miles to the southeast on the lower East River. Philip recorded hearing a cannonade that "grew to be the heaviest I ever heard" coming from that direction. The British had finally begun their invasion of Manhattan. What Philip heard was the sound of five enemy ships bombarding the island from Kips Bay. His battalion was called "to march downwards" to meet the enemy. By the afternoon the British had landed four thousand troops on Manhattan, and Philip's Princeton classmate Aaron Burr, a major in the Continental army, rushed to send a message urging the remaining American troops in New York City to retreat. Newcomb's battalion had traveled as far south as Harlem Heights, where they were ordered to join Washington's line of defense now extending from the Harlem River on the east to the North River on the west. By the end of the day Washington had his troops in place ready to defend Harlem Heights and prevent the British from moving farther up the island to Kings Bridge. If the Howe brothers could control the bridge, they could use their navy to completely surround the American army on Manhattan Island and trap it. "Our Lads I hope will stand," wrote Philip, "for the Honour of their State; for the Safety of the Land, & for their Own Reputation, I hope they will stand."[64]

On September 15 the British gained control of New York City and the Continental army was hunkered down at Harlem Heights. As any good Presbyterian patriot would have done, Philip tried to make sense of the day in theological terms. He wrote a brief jeremiad, in a style reminiscent of the seventeenth-century Puritans, which combined Whig political thought and Christian doctrine with a healthy dose of Calvinist providentialism: "But New York we have lost this Day . . . Just Heaven thy Judgments are equal—We are a sinful Nation, O Lord. But is it written in thy Book concerning us that we must always fly before our Enemies?—Must this great, & formerly happy Country, submit at Length to despotic Domination?—Must Oceans of our Blood yet stain our own Land? Must not the widowed Lovers, & the fatherless Orphans for a long Time to come cease to increase!—We pray, good Lord for thy interposing Mercy; O spare us, & spare our Land."[65] His battalion would spend the night lying in trenches on Harlem Heights with their "Arms secure." Early the following morning Philip ate breakfast with James Ewing and Robert Patterson and then examined the American line on the Heights. He noted that the previous evening the troops had grown "dispirited" from all of the retreating, but after a night of sleep they seemed to be "much improved" and in "good spirit." At 11:00 A.M. the British attempt to penetrate the American defenses had begun. By midafternoon the soldiers had even more reason for optimism after repulsing the British offensive and holding their line. Philip wrote, "The Appearance of Success fills them with Life & Spirit."[66]

Following the engagement at Harlem Heights, Philip's battalion was sent back to Mount Washington. They set up camp in a new position

Figure 12. Chalk sketch of Philip Vickers Fithian drawn near Fort Washington, New York, by an unknown artist. Courtesy, Department of Rare Books and Special Collections, Princeton University Libraries, Princeton, N.J.

roughly a quarter of a mile north of the fort, closer to Kings Bridge. "All is quiet," Philip wrote on September 17. "Our Army stand boldly against them, & are hourly rooted still deeper in the Earth." Back in camp the soldiers all slept "sweetly," and Philip spent the next several days visiting with his Cohansey friends, taking walks to Kings Bridge, and picking peaches and peppers along the way. Silas Newcomb kept his battalion sharp by parading them around the fort, and Philip finally got back to a regular schedule of prayer services. He was particularly pleased to see Timothy Elmer, a close Cohansey friend (and the brother of Jonathan and Ebenezer Elmer), who was serving as the captain of a militia unit from Cumberland County that had been guarding fortifications in Perth Amboy, New Jersey. On September 21 Philip had breakfast with Elmer and Reading Beatty. "Most agreeably do we pass the Time while our Friends are round us," he wrote in his diary. Philip had a chalk portrait of himself made—apparently sketched by a local artist in the camp. The portrait is our only glimpse into his physical appearance. As the Continental army on Harlem Heights continued to repulse British advances and a mysterious fire began to rage throughout New York City, Philip noted that two of his Cohansey associates, James Ewing and James Patterson, had grown ill. Dysentery was beginning to emerge again in the battalion, though Philip credited the rise in sickness among the troops to the "damp & hard lying in Tents without Boards on the Ground." On Sunday, September 22, Newcomb's battalion was ordered to continue digging fortifications, and there was little time for rest or prayers. "Our Lads grow tired," Philip wrote, "& begin to count the Days of their Service which yet remain."[67]

Philip also had some free time to write to Betsy. He reminded her that "Amidst all of the Distress & Ruin of this dreadful War I am yet alive & yours." As usual, he wrote with great anticipation of seeing her again, this time noting the exact day—December 10—when he would come home. This letter included a catalog of all the letters he had written to her since he had arrived in New York—a sort of summation of their correspondence similar to the one he had compiled during their courtship. Philip had written fifteen letters to Betsy between July and September and had received three in return. He ended this epistle with a prayer: "Peace, & God's Blessing be with my Betsey, my dear Wife, forever may you be happy."[68] It was the last letter he would ever write.

Chapter 9

Conclusion

We will never know how Philip would have harmonized his citizenship in the republic of letters with his love of home or his religious faith in the years following the American Revolution. His way of improvement came to an abrupt end on October 8, 1776. Philip died of complications related to dysentery while encamped with Silas Newcomb's battalion outside Fort Washington, New York. His last journal entry, written on September 22, noted that many soldiers in the battalion were "disordered at present." Six days later Philip also got sick. He spent the next week lying on the hard floor of an army tent, exposed to the elements. He was burning with fever, and his skin was covered with boils. Andrew Hunter Jr. had the "very disagreeable Task" of informing Betsy of her husband's condition. He asked her to come to New York as soon as possible.[1]

By October 4 Philip's friends had found him a feather bed, but his prospects of survival looked grim. William Hollingshead confided in his diary that his friend had been "reduced to the lowest state one would imagine possible for human nature to support under." Hollingshead and Andrew Hunter cared for Philip in his final days, seeing to his comfort and helping him to prepare for his "departure into the World of Spirits." Betsy never did arrive. She probably did not receive Hunter's letter in time. Only a few hours before Philip's death, Thomas Ewing sent another letter to Betsy advising her not to come to New York as it was too late. Ewing wrote that her presence "can be no satisfaction either to him or you now." Later that morning Hunter recorded in his journal, "about 10 O'Clock Mr. Fithian closed his Eyes upon the Things of Time and is gone to try a Spiritual World." Philip was buried the following day. His funeral was attended by the officers and soldiers of Newcomb's battalion and was conducted with "as much Decency as the nature of the Case would allow."[2]

Of course, life went on without Philip Fithian. In November the British overran the Continental army at Fort Washington, forcing George Washington's troops to retreat to New Jersey. The army would live to fight another day and eventually would secure the American freedom for which Philip had hoped and prayed.[3] Enoch Green, Philip's teacher at Deerfield, was with a regiment of Pennsylvania soldiers near Kings Bridge at the time of Philip's fatal illness (he was back in Deerfield on a brief leave on the day Philip died). He would fall victim to camp fever as well. Green died on December 2 at the age of forty-two, leaving Mary, Betsy's sister, to care for their three young children. In an early draft of Green's will, written in September 1775, he assigned the responsibility for his children's education to Philip. Mary would obviously need to make other arrangements.[4]

Meanwhile, Andrew Hunter Jr. continued his service with the Continental army. Following the disbandment of Heard's Brigade he was ordained to the Presbyterian ministry and named chaplain of the Third New Jersey Brigade. He ministered to New Jersey troops throughout the remainder of the war and was present with Washington's army at the battles of Monmouth and Yorktown. Following the war he would preside over several academies (including one he founded in Bridge-Town), continue to supply Presbyterian pulpits, teach at the College of New Jersey, and serve as chaplain of the United States Navy.[5]

Back in Cohansey, Philip's Uncle Samuel succumbed to illness in 1777. According to local tradition, he suffered an attack of paralysis while sitting on the bench of the Cumberland County Court of Common Pleas. Philip's disabled brother, Enoch, would die roughly around the same time. Josiah, who had fought with the Continental army in upstate New York, died shortly after his year of service came to an end. The tragedy of an early death, however, did not befall all of the Fithians. Philip's sister, Rebecca, was married in 1778, and his younger brothers all lived into old age. Amos would eventually reside on his father's homestead. On the religious front, the Greenwich Presbyterian church was without a settled minister until 1781. With Philip gone and many Presbyterian ministers off serving the Continental army as chaplains, the church could not find a suitable replacement to fill the pulpit. Had Philip returned from New York, he would have undoubtedly occupied this post permanently. His way of improvement would have truly led him home. Also in 1781 Presbyterians returning from war began to join Cohansey's churches, triggering a massive religious revival (by local standards) in the region. Philip would have been pleased at this local awakening's calm and sensible character.[6]

What became of Betsy? Shortly after her husband's death she moved to Princeton, residing with the wife of her brother Dr. John Beatty, who was serving the Continental army in New York. After mourning the loss of Philip, Betsy married again. She did not, however, need to change her name. On the evening of February 2, 1780, at her brother's house in Princeton, John Witherspoon presided over the wedding ceremony of Betsy and Joel Fithian, Philip's cousin. Joel was the son of Samuel

Fithian, and he and Philip had grown up together. He was an elder in the Greenwich Presbyterian church, one of the young men who had burned tea in December 1774, a member of the Cumberland County Committee, and a New Jersey legislator after the Revolution. He was also the coexecutor of Philip's will. At the time of his marriage to Betsy, Joel was widowed and had a young son. His first wife, Rachel Holmes, had died in 1779. Immediately following the wedding, Betsy returned with Joel to the familiar surroundings of Cohansey. Her brother Reading Beatty surmised that Betsy's "partiality for that Country" and the fact that Joel was a "good Fat farmer" convinced her to remarry. Their courtship probably lacked the passion of Betsy's relationship with Philip, but Joel certainly offered his new bride stability and security. Joel and Betsy would have nine children together. They named their third son Philip.[7]

What can we learn from the life of Philip Vickers Fithian? He reminds us that Enlightenment cosmopolitanism always existed in compromise with local attachments. Ironically, Philip died away from his beloved Cohansey. It is doubtful, however, that he would have been disappointed with the place where he passed from this life, for he died in service to the cause of liberty. He had truly imbibed John Witherspoon's advice about the public duty required of the man of letters in defense of Enlightenment values such as political independence and freedom. In this sense, he died not only on behalf of his country but also on behalf of the universal and cosmopolitan ideals—ideals that transcended individual nations—that he believed were essential to the betterment of all humankind. Yet, even as he remained geographically removed from what he had once longingly called his "place of nativity," Philip died as a chaplain to a battalion of soldiers from Cohansey. Though Betsy could not be at his side, William Hollingshead, Andrew Hunter Jr., Thomas Ewing, and a host of close friends and advisers were present. As during much of his short life, Philip died performing the responsibilities of a member of the republic of letters *and* a citizen of a particular place. If true republicans were also true world citizens, then Philip's cosmopolitan spirit was nurtured within the context of Cohansey's local brand of Presbyterianism, complete with the social networks of friends, relatives, and loves that came with it.

Philip's story teaches us that the abstract, urban, and elite-centered republic of letters that has so captivated early American historians over the past two decades had a real impact on individual human experience. He struggled with the implications that citizenship in this imagined community might have for his commitments to family, friends, and home. He declined every offer—and there were several—to move elsewhere. When he had the opportunity to go home, he took it every time. Throughout his short life, Philip asked not only how he might improve himself but also what might be permanently lost in the process. He rarely acted without considering carefully the answers to both of those queries. Philip's life reveals the need for the local as the anchor of a modern and revolutionary self in the eighteenth century.

Many middling, relatively unprivileged, and educated early Americans living in places teetering between the medieval and the modern understood local attachments—not world citizenship—as the necessary starting point in the construction of a modern self. Rather than rejecting commitments to the particularities of place, good patriots and republicans such as Philip strove to participate in the eighteenth-century equivalent of intellectual and cultural globalization in the context of their own locales. Philip's networks of friends, letter-writing circles, admonishing societies, pastoral commitments, reading groups, and revolutionary activities were all means of being cosmopolitan in a given place. Philip's life challenges us to be ever more mindful that the ideals of the transatlantic republic of letters could have a profound influence on the remote precincts of British America and the social worlds of the people who inhabited them.

Philip's biography also reveals how much Christianity adapted to the Enlightenment in eighteenth-century America and, conversely, how much the Enlightenment found its primary place of influence within the world of early American Christianity. Such mutual accommodation, as might be expected, diluted both the Enlightenment and Christianity. In its purest form, the Enlightenment presented a fierce attack on orthodox Christianity in the Western world. Thomas Jefferson believed that the Enlightenment was a secular movement that would eventually annihilate organized Christianity. The contemporary historian Henry May has described enlightened people as those who believe that "we understand nature and man best through the use of our natural faculties" (rather than through an encounter with God or Divine revelation). One of his colleagues, Peter Gay, wrote about the Enlightenment as the "Rise of Modern Paganism."[8] However, such explanations fall short of explaining the Enlightenment in America. The religious beliefs of the American people, even if they did not always translate into church membership, were just too strong on the ground to allow the Enlightenment to dominate cultural life. Thomas Paine, for example, was a great hero in the colonies when he advocated the universal values of liberty and freedom—values that he shared with many American Christians. However, when he directed his secular Enlightenment toward religious belief, he was burned in effigy. Americans have always preferred the Paine of *Common Sense* to the Paine of *The Age of Reason.*

Philip Vickers Fithian could never embrace *all* of the Enlightenment and still call himself a "Christian." His commitment to a modern life defined by the forward rush of progress could go only so far before it ran smack up against the religious boundaries of his worldview. The world was not moving toward a secular utopia defined by human freedom. It was instead moving, in God's time, toward the return of Jesus Christ and the ultimate initiation of a heavenly kingdom. Philip knew that Enlightenment progress could not cheat death—life's ultimate limit. The train of progress would eventually reach the station, and, as in the case of Philip's parents and Philip himself, it just might arrive ahead of schedule. For all his love of Cohansey and the friends and relations who gave it meaning, heaven was his real "home"—the place where his restless soul would be at peace for eternity in the presence of his Savior. Philip's purpose in life was to bring glory to his Creator and prepare himself for such a home-going. His pursuit of self-improvement was tempered by these beliefs. Philip sought the Enlightenment with every ounce of his being and yet wholeheartedly rejected its most fundamental teachings about where human history was heading. This was the great paradox of an eighteenth-century enlightened life.

Similarly, ambition—the inner drive and passion that motivated him to move beyond the agrarian life of limits that his father offered him—was understood by Philip in the context of the Christian doctrine of vocation. Enlightened ambition and the spiritual discipline of obeying a call from God were not incompatible to him. A properly fashioned life of self-betterment did not necessarily have to result in a rejection of Christianity, either in the way that Thomas Jefferson had argued when he predicted the end of organized religion or in the way that Benjamin Franklin exemplified in his move from Puritan Boston to Enlightenment Philadelphia. Philip's call to an educated and enlightened life and his call to serve God were often one and the same.

If the Enlightenment in America found itself limited by Christian belief, Christianity also made some substantial accommodations to the Enlightenment. Such accommodations have been well rehearsed by religious and intellectual historians, but they are worth noting here in the context of Philip's story.[9] For example, by making his peace with modern ways of thinking, Philip—even as a Presbyterian minister—seemed always to be more focused on *this* world than the next. His Cohansey home had been a haven of otherworldly evangelicalism in the early 1740s. However, by the time of his birth, and especially by the time of his conversion, Presbyterians had become equally concerned with how their ordered approach to Christianity, void of passion and enthusiasm and saturated with enlightened gentility, might contribute to the improvement of society. It is worth noting that nowhere in Philip's writings, including those from the years after he was licensed as a Presbyterian minister, does he describe an attempt to convert another person to the Christian gospel in the fashion made popular a generation before by evangelicals such as George Whitefield and Gilbert Tennent. This, of course, does not mean that Philip was uninterested in winning souls but that he was more interested, at least in terms of what he chose to record for posterity, in the role that Christianity played in bringing moral order and civility to the dark places of British America. For him, all transcendent or unexplainable encounters with the Divine needed to be carefully monitored, controlled, or rationalized.[10]

Philip's Enlightenment embrace was especially relevant in the area of morality. He rejected, following his mentor John Witherspoon, the idea that ethical behavior in this world could stem *only* from an encounter with God. While the Bible and personal piety were still important sources of virtue, they now stood on equal footing with the conscience and its cultivation through education, reading, and sociability. Indeed, if Philip were going to improve himself by making peace with the spirit of the age, he would need to come to grips with a way of understanding his moral life that did not rely entirely on what Jonathan Edwards called "benevolence to Being in general." Morality became separated from the process of Christian sanctification. Fitting with the universal flavor of the Enlightenment, a virtuous life was now something that *all* people could strive to obtain. Philip's moral compass was governed by a hodgepodge of ideas stemming from the Bible, classical literature, popular novels, and coffeehouse magazines such as the *Spectator*. The highest aim of religion was to know God *and* to live a happy and ethical life here on earth.[11]

Philip's accommodation to modernity also meant that his faith would be bound with the political concerns of the Enlightenment. This translated into a warm support of the American Revolution. Philip was firmly convinced, at least for the moment, that God was on the side of freedom and liberty. He and his fellow enlightened Presbyterians were confident in their ability to decipher the will of a sovereign God in relation to the American founding. The Calvinist belief that human sin clouded one's capacity to discern God's providence was exchanged for a modern certainty that the Revolution was divinely inspired. There was little room for mystery.[12] God's actions in the political realm were clearly knowable by his creation. Consequently, Christianity became wedded to the advancement of the United States of America. As the historian Mark A. Noll has argued, the nineteenth-century emergence of an American civil religion, the fusing of God and country, and the notion that America was exceptional because it had been chosen by the Divine were perhaps the greatest legacies of this convergence of Christianity and the Enlightenment.[13]

When these compromises between world citizenship and local attachments, and between Christianity and the modern age, are considered in depth, people like Philip become our best windows into the way the Enlightenment in America was lived. Philip moved freely through Princeton, Virginia, and Pennsylvania, but he also remained committed to the type of moral improvement his Cohansey home could offer him, even to the point of suffering from serious bouts of homesickness. He envisioned the American Revolution as the culmination of Enlightenment progress, but he curbed his optimism with a strong dose of Calvinist providentialism. He did his best to control his passions but was seldom successful. In addition, his ambition and desire for self-improvement were balanced by his sense of Christian calling.

Not much has changed since Philip's death. Americans still pursue self-betterment through higher education and career advancement in record numbers. They travel around the world and boast about their cosmopolitanism. They are often willing to fight and die for modern ideas such as liberty and freedom. Yet, they also long for the passion, love, and faith that bring meaning, in a transcendent way, to their lives. They search for roots as part of attempts to connect to particular pasts or places. They cherish unlimited progress—both for themselves and for society—even as they prepare themselves for death. Many bind their nationalism to a sovereign God. These tensions seem always to have defined the American experience. Perhaps, as Philip shows us, the way of improvement really does lead home.

Appendix
A Note on the Fithian Diaries

Most of the diaries, letters, and other writings that make up the Fithian papers collection at Princeton's Firestone Library were transcribed from the originals into small notebooks by Enoch Fithian, Philip's disabled brother. Since Enoch died shortly after his older brother, he certainly must have begun transcribing before Philip's death. It is also apparent that Enoch did not finish the job since Philip's diary of life with the Continental Army is written in a different hand and is slightly smaller than the other notebooks. This may be the only part of the extant papers actually written by Philip. John R. Williams, the first scholar to publish a collection of Fithian papers, has speculated that whatever errors in grammar, punctuation, or capitalization there are in these writings can be traced to Enoch's habits of transcription. (I have chosen to cite from Enoch's transcriptions.) Since no twentieth-century historian has ever seen the original manuscripts, it is impossible to know if Williams is correct in his assessment. The papers were donated to Princeton in 1908 by a member of the Fithian family and have been bound into the ten volumes I have referenced in the notes of this book.[1]

Notes

Introduction

1. Journal of Philip Vickers Fithian, July 16–19, 1773, in Philip Vickers Fithian Journals and Commonplace Books, 1766–76, General Manuscripts, CO1099, no. 349, vol. 7, Princeton University Libraries, Princeton, N.J. (Fithian Papers hereafter).

2. See, for example, Ned Landsman, *From Colonials to Provincials: American Thought and Culture, 1680–1760* (Ithaca, N.Y.: Cornell University Press, 2000); Norman S. Fiering, "The Transatlantic Republic of Letters: A Note on the Circulation of Learned Periodicals to Early Eighteenth-Century America," *William and Mary Quarterly* 33 (October 1976): 642–60; Michael Warner, *Letters of the Republic: Publication and the Public Sphere in Eighteenth-Century America* (Cambridge, Mass.: Harvard University Press, 1990); Richard D. Brown, *Knowledge Is Power: The Diffusion of Information in Early America* (New York: Oxford University Press, 1989).

3. Fiering, "Transatlantic Republic of Letters"; Lorraine Daston, "The Ideal and Reality of the Republic of Letters in the Enlightenment," *Science in Context* 4 (winter 1991): 367; Landsman, *From Colonials to Provincials*, 31–56.

4. Hunter Dickinson Farish's edited version of the diary was first published by Colonial Williamsburg in 1943, with subsequent editions in 1945 and 1957. A paperback edition was issued by the University Press of Virginia in 1968. See *Journal & Letters of Philip Vickers Fithian 1773–1774: A Plantation Tutor of the Old Dominion,* ed. Hunter Dickinson Farish (Williamsburg, Va.: Colonial Williamsburg, Inc., 1943; repr., Charlottesville: University Press of Virginia, 1968).

5. On Colonial Williamsburg, see http://www.colonialwilliamsburg.com/history/teaching/enewsletter/volume2/march04/primsource.cfm. Timothy M. Russell, a historical reenactor based in Williamsburg, interprets Fithian for general audiences. See http://tmruss.people.wm.edu/CW.html. On *Liberty,* see http://www.pbs.org/ktca/liberty/. Fithian was played by the noted character actor Anthony Heald.

6. Vincent S. McCluskey, "The Life and Times of Philip Vickers Fithian" (Ph.D. diss., New York University, 1991); *Philip Vickers Fithian: Journal and Letters, 1767–1774,* ed. John R. Williams (Princeton, N.J.: Princeton University Press, 1900; repr., Freeport, N.Y.: Books for Libraries Press, 1969); *Philip Vickers Fithian: Journal, 1775–1776, Written on the Virginia-Pennsylvania Frontier and in the Army around New York,* ed. Robert Greenhalgh Albion and Leonidas Dodson

(Princeton, N.J.: Princeton University Press, 1934). Another collection of published Fithian material was edited by the local Cumberland County, New Jersey, historian Alan F. Palmer; see *The Beloved Cohansie of Philip Vickers Fithian* (Greenwich, N.J.: Cumberland County Historical Society, n.d.). Palmer published only those materials related directly to Fithian's life in the Cohansey River townships of Cumberland County. As a result, his volume contains large gaps in Fithian's life. Palmer's editorial remarks throughout the text are sometimes helpful, but his selective coverage and typographical errors made this collection very difficult to work with.

7. Some of this material has been published in Palmer, ed., *The Beloved Cohansie of Philip Vickers Fithian.*

8. For an attempt to teach Fithian to undergraduates, see my "Teaching the JAH" feature on the Web site of the *Journal of American History,* www.indiana.edu/%7ejah/teaching/2003_09/index/shtml

9. Gordon Wood, *The Radicalism of the American Revolution* (New York: Knopf, 1992), 221. On eighteenth-century cosmopolitanism, see Thomas J. Schlereth, *The Cosmopolitan Ideal in Enlightenment Thought: Its Form and Function in the Ideas of Franklin, Hume, and Voltaire, 1604–1790* (Notre Dame, Ind.: University of Notre Dame Press, 1977); Ian Dyck, "Local Attachments, National Identities, and World Citizenship in the Thought of Thomas Paine," *History Workshop Journal* 35 (autumn 1993): 117–35; and Alan D. McKillop, "Local Attachments and Cosmopolitanism—The Eighteenth Century Pattern," in *From Sensibility to Romanticism: Essays Presented to Frederick A. Pottie,* ed. Frederick W. Hilles and Harold Bloom (Oxford: Oxford University Press, 1965). For recent theoretical works on this ideal, see Pheng Cheah and Bruce Robbins, eds., *Cosmopolitics: Thinking and Feeling beyond the Nation* (Minneapolis: University of Minnesota Press, 1998); Martha C. Nussbaum et al., *For the Love of Country: Debating the Limits of Patriotism* (Boston: Beacon Press, 1996); and Kwame Anthony Appiah, *Cosmopolitanism: Ethics in a World of Strangers* (New York: W. W. Norton, 2006).

10. Henry May, *The Enlightenment in America* (New York: Oxford University Press, 1976), xi–xiv; Ned C. Landsman, *From Colonials to Provincials: American Thought and Culture, 1680–1760* (Ithaca, N.Y.: Cornell University Press, 1997), 60. For a recent treatment of Enlightenment cosmopolitanism in Europe that stresses its incompatibility with Christianity, see Margaret C. Jacob, *Strangers Nowhere in the World: The Rise of Cosmopolitanism in Early Modern Europe* (Philadelphia: University of Pennsylvania Press, 2006), especially Jacob's even more recent essay on the History News Network, "Thoughts on the Impossibility of Being Both Deeply Religious and Cosmopolitan (http://hnn.us/articles/29011.html).

11. Max Hilbert Boehm, "Cosmopolitanism," quoted in Schlereth, *Cosmopolitan Ideal in Enlightenment Thought,* xiii.

Chapter 1

1. Journal of Philip Vickers Fithian, March 21, 1766; March 16, 1767; March 21, 1766; May 7, 1767, in Philip Vickers Fithian Journals and Commonplace Books, 1766–76, General Manuscripts, CO1099, no. 349, vol. 1, Princeton University Libraries, Princeton, N.J. (hereafter Fithian Papers).

2. Al Zambone, e-mail to author, March 21, 2006. This paragraph borrows heavily, in both content and prose, from Zambone's description of the Cohansey River.

3. Wallace Stegner, *Where the Bluebird Sings to the Lemonade Springs: Living and Writing in the West* (New York: Random House, 1992), 205.

4. Karl Marx, *Eighteenth Brumaire of Louis Bonaparte* (1849), in *Karl Marx and Frederick Engels: Selected Works* (New York, International Publishers, 1968), 97, cited in Allan Kulikoff, *From British Peasants to Colonial American Farmers* (Chapel Hill: University of North Carolina Press, 2000), 5.

5. Yi-Fu Tuan, *Space and Place: The Perspective of Experience* (Minneapolis: University of Minnesota Press, 1977), 6, 102, 159, 179, 183–84; Kent C. Ryden, *Mapping the Invisible Landscape: Folklore, Writing, and the Sense of Place* (Iowa City: University of Iowa Press, 1993), 38. Edmund Morgan has made a similar argument for the fourth and fifth generations of Virginia freemen; see his *American Slavery, American Freedom: The Ordeal of Colonial Virginia* (New York: W. W. Norton, 1975), 368.

6. Ryden, *Mapping the Invisible Landscape*, 39–40, 64. Ryden has noted, "To live in a place is to see and know what the people who lived there before you did with it; to hear talk about a place is to understand what else happened there that has been deemed worth remembering" (64).

7. Fithian Journal, December 17, 29, 1766, Fithian Papers, vol. 1.

8. On the links between genealogy and the sense of place, see Barbara Allen, "The Genealogical Landscape and the Southern Sense of Place," in *Sense of Place: American Regional Cultures,* ed. Barbara Allen and Thomas J. Schlereth (Lexington: University Press of Kentucky, 1990), 152–63. Allen writes: "In these genealogical conversations, people frequently refer not only to an individual's kinship ties but also to his or her 'homeland,' suggesting that where people live or have lived is just as significant in establishing personal identity as who their relatives are" (ibid., 158).

9. Bernard Bailyn, *The Peopling of British North America: An Introduction* (New York: Vintage Books, 1988), 17–26; Alison Games, *Migration and the Origins of the English Atlantic World* (Cambridge, Mass.: Harvard University Press, 1999), 164–65; Allan Kulikoff, "Internal Migration," in *Encyclopedia of the North American Colonies,* ed. Jacob Ernest Cooke (New York: Scribner, 1993), 2:329–44.

10. Joseph and Hannah were wed on July 31, 1740. See Enoch Fithian, "Fithian Family History" (1834), transcribed on rootsweb.com/pub/usgenweb/pa/Philadelphia/history/family/.

11. "The Agreement Between ye Purchasers of Fairefield," September 1, 1697, Thomas Bridge Letter File, MG 23, New Jersey Historical Society, Newark; Thomas J. Farnham, *Fairfield: The Biography of a Community* (West Kennebunk, Maine: Phoenix Publishing for the Fairfield Historical Society, 1988), 17; Aaron Leaming and Jacob Spicer, *The Grants, Concessions, and Original Constitutions of the Province of New Jersey* (Philadelphia: W. Bradford, 1758), 556–57. The purchasers were John Bateman, Samuel Bellnap (Belknap), John Bennett, Thomas Bennett, John Chatfield, Joshua Curtis, Robert Dallglesh, John Fairchild, Zachariah Ferris, Samuel Foster, John Griffin, Joseph Grimes, Michael Hanna, Nicholas Johnson, Thomas Jones, Thomas Kernes, Edward Lummis, John Mills, Jonathan Morehouse, John Ogden, John Roberts, Joseph Sayre, Joseph Seeley, Eleazar Smith, John Smith, Joseph Smith, Daniel Westcott, and Joseph Wheeler. I will use "Fairfield" and "New England Town" interchangeably to describe this settlement.

12. On Fenwick's colony, see John E. Pomfret, *The Province of West Jersey* (Princeton, N.J.: Princeton University Press, 1956); "Fenwick's Proposal for Planting His Colony of New Caesarea or New Jersey," *Pennsylvania Magazine of History and Biography* 6 (1882): 86–90; Joseph Sickler, *The History of Salem County,*

New Jersey (Salem, N.J.: Sunbeam Publishing, 1937); Robert G. Johnson, *An Historical Account of the First Settlement of Salem in West Jersey* (Philadelphia: Orrin Rogers, 1839; repr., Salem, N.J.: Salem County Historical Society, 1991).

13. This theme is ubiquitous in the literature of early New England. For general assessments, see Lois Kimball Matthews, *The Expansion of New England: The Spread of New England Settlement and Institutions to the Mississippi, 1620–1865* (Boston: Houghton-Mifflin, 1909); Kulikoff, "Internal Migration," 337; Peter C. Mancall, "Landholding," in *Encyclopedia of the North American Colonies*, ed. Cooke, 656–57; Games, *Migration*, 171–72.

14. Farnham, *Fairfield*, 17, 29, 30–31; Jackson Turner Main, *Society and Economy in Colonial Connecticut* (Princeton, N.J.: Princeton University Press, 1985), 64. On land distribution practices in seventeenth-century New England towns, see John Frederick Martin, *Profits in the Wilderness: Entrepreneurs and the Founding of New England Towns in the Seventeenth Century* (Chapel Hill: University of North Carolina Press, 1991), 149–61; Virginia DeJohn Anderson, *New England's Generation: The Great Migration and the Formation of Society and Culture in the Seventeenth Century* (New York: Cambridge University Press, 1991), 31–32, 89–99.

15. Farnham, *Fairfield*, 17, 29, 31, 33; Elizabeth Schenk, *The History of Fairfield* (New York: By the author, 1889), 140; Bruce C. Daniels, *The Connecticut Town: Growth and Development, 1635–1790* (Middletown, Conn.: Wesleyan University Press, 1979), 121.

16. Farnham, *Fairfield*, 33–34, 37, 51; Schenk, *History of Fairfield*, 255.

17. Schenk, *History of Fairfield*, 68; Fairfield Town Minutes, May 23, 1687, Fairfield Historical Society, Fairfield, Conn.; Fairfield Town Grants, vol. A, p. 207, Fairfield Town Hall, Fairfield, Conn.; Fairfield Town Grants of Land, pp. 221, 469, Fairfield Town Hall, Fairfield, Conn.; Rod MacKenzie to the author, e-mail correspondence, August 30, 2005. I am thankful to Rod MacKenzie of the Fairfield (Conn.) Historical Society for his assistance in this research.

18. They were the families of Samuel Barnes, Nathaniel Bishop, John Bishop, Thomas Diament, John Fithian, Samuel Fithian, Charles Howell, Hezekiah Love, Nathan Lawrence, James Mason, John Miller, William Mulford, Nicholas Osborn, Thomas Parvin, Howell Powell, David Sayre, Ephraim Sayre, Edmund Shaw, John Shaw, and Benjamin Stratton.

19. Purcell B. Robertson, "Profiles of the Early Settlers of the Town of East Hampton, Long Island," vol. 2 (unpublished manuscript, Long Island Collection, East Hampton Library, East Hampton, N.Y., 1979), 1. On the migration from Lynn to East Hampton, see Faren R. Siminoff, *Crossing the Sound: The Rise of Atlantic American Communities in Seventeenth-Century Eastern Long Island* (New York: New York University Press, 2004), 87–109.

20. T. H. Breen, *Imagining the Past: East Hampton Histories* (Reading, Mass.: Addison Wesley Publishing Co. Inc., 1989), 90–91, 113–14, 138.

21. Ibid., 148–49, 166–67, 198–99; Matthews, *Expansion of New England*, 52; Brendan McConville, *Those Daring Disturbers of the Public Peace: Agrarian Unrest and the Struggle for Political Legitimacy in New Jersey, 1701–1776* (Ithaca, N.Y.: Cornell University Press, 1999), 13; Jeffrey Dorwart, *Cape May County, New Jersey: The Making of an American Resort Community* (New Brunswick, N.J.: Rutgers University Press, 1992), 14, 21.

22. Robertson, "Profiles of the Early Settlers," 1–2; Dean Failey, "A Tradition of Craftsmen: The Dominy Craftsman of East Hampton" (lecture delivered to the East Hampton Library, 350th Anniversary of the Town of East Hampton, October 1998, http://www.easthamptonlibrary.org/lic/350thlectures.html).

23. Robertson, "Profiles of the Early Settlers," 2; Henry P. Hedges, *History of East Hampton, NY* (Sag Harbor, N.Y.: J. H. Hunt, 1849), appendix (list of officeholders—Fithian, overseer in 1667), consulted on-line at http://longislandgenealogy.com/histehampton.html, n.p.

24. Robertson, "Profiles of the Early Settlers," 3–4; Thomas Cushing and Charles E. Sheppard, *History of the Counties of Gloucester, Salem, and Cumberland, New Jersey* (Philadelphia: Everts & Peck, 1883), 512, 568, 664, 685; Will and Inventory of Samuel Fithian, March 1703, Salem Record of Wills, Book 3 (1698–1703), 150–51, 170–72, New Jersey State Archives, Trenton; Will and Inventory of Josiah Fithian Esq., March 31, 1741, Salem County Wills, New Jersey State Archives, Trenton.

25. Kulikoff, *From British Peasants to Colonial American Farmers,* 114–15.

26. John Fenwick Will and Inventory, in Frank H. Stewart, *Major John Fenwick* (Salem, N.J.: Salem County Historical Society, 1964), 39–44 ("town bank"). Greenwich was also referred to as "Cohanzick on the Caesarea River" and "Antioch."

27. Cushing and Sheppard, *History of the Counties of Gloucester, Salem, and Cumberland,* 680; Joseph Sickler, *Tea Burning Town* (New York: Ubelard Press, 1950); Lewis D. Cook, *Families of South Jersey, Philadelphia & Bucks County,* Family Files, Cumberland County Historical Society, Lummis Library, Greenwich, N.J.; Leaming and Spicer, *Grants, Concessions, and Original Constitutions,* 542–43; Roger T. Trindell, "The Ports of Greenwich and Salem in the Eighteenth Century," *New Jersey History* 86 (1968): 199–214.

28. Cushing and Sheppard, *History of the Counties of Gloucester, Salem, and Cumberland,* 512, 507; Will Abstract of Thomas Harris, October 24, 1749, in *Documents Relating to the Colonial History of the State of New Jersey,* ed. A.Van Doren Honeyman, 1st ser., vol. 30: Calendar of Wills, Administrations, Etc. . . . , vol. 2: 1730–50 (Somerville, N.J.: Unionist-Gazette Association, 1918), 222; Frank D. Andrews, *Residents of Greenwich, New Jersey Who Paid Taxes in the Year 1843* (Vineland, N.J.: By the author, 1916), 9.

29. "Subscribers to the Construction of the Greenwich Presbyterian Church, 1735," in Enoch Fithian, *History of the Presbyterian Church, Greenwich* (Bridgetown, N.J.: Office of the Chronicle, 1871), 8.

30. See Peter O. Wacker and Paul G. E. Clemens, *Land Use in Early New Jersey: A Historical Geography* (Newark: New Jersey Historical Society, 1995).

31. My survey includes all of the first generation of Cohansey settlers who left wills (including those who did not arrive from East Hampton or Fairfield, Connecticut). I examined New Jersey will abstracts from *New Jersey Archives* 30, 1730–50 (Somerville, N.J.: Unionist-Gazette Association, 1918); Salem Deeds, Liber B, in Salem Deeds, vols. 1–7 (1664–1703), in *Documents Relating to the Colonial History of the State of New Jersey,* vol. 21: *Calendar of Records in the Office of the Secretary of State, 1664–1703,* ed. William Nelson (Paterson, N.J.: Press Printing and Publishing Co., 1899), 565–642. Kenneth Lockridge makes a similar point for Suffolk County, Massachusetts, from 1750 to 1759; see Lockridge, "Land, Populations and the Evolution of New England Society," *Past and Present* 39 (1968): 70n24.

32. Mildred Campbell, *The English Yeoman under Elizabeth and the Early Stuarts* (New Haven, Conn.: Yale University Press, 1942; repr., New York: Barnes and Noble, 1959), 4, 10, 25–34; Keith Wrightson, *English Society, 1580–1680* (New Brunswick, N.J.: Rutgers University Press, 1982), 20–21, 31–37, 134–36; Peter Laslett, *The World We Have Lost* (New York: Scribners and Sons, 1965), 43–44; Margaret Spufford, *Contrasting Communities: English Villages in the Sixteenth and*

Seventeenth Centuries (London: Cambridge University Press, 1974), 38–39; Mark Overton, *Agricultural Revolution in England: The Transformation of the Agrarian Economy, 1500–1850* (Cambridge: Cambridge University Press, 1996), 40–41.

33. Allan Kulikoff, *Agrarian Origins of American Capitalism* (Charlottesville: University Press of Virginia, 1992), 34–36; Main, *Society and Economy in Colonial Connecticut,* 30; Roger Thompson, *Mobility and Migration: East Anglian Founders of New England, 1629–1640* (Amherst: University of Massachusetts Press, 1994), 101, 253n38; Ronald Jager, *The Fate of Family Farming: Variations on an American Idea* (Hanover, N.H.: University of New England Press, 2004), xv–xvii.

34. See n. 31.

35. Charles E. Eisinger, "The Freehold Concept in Eighteenth-Century American Letters," *William and Mary Quarterly,* 3rd ser., 4 (1947): 42–59; Campbell, *English Yeoman,* 54–65; Kulikoff, *From British Peasants to Colonial American Farmers,* 27; Thompson, *Mobility and Migration,* 232 ("style"); Anderson, *New England's Generation,* 125; Jessica Kross, *The Evolution of an American Town: Newtown, NY, 1642–1775* (Philadelphia: Temple University Press, 1983), 215.

36. Kulikoff, *Agrarian Origins,* 41, 64; McConville, *Daring Disturbers of the Public Peace,* 46–47, 168–69.

37. William B. Scott, *In Pursuit of Happiness: American Conceptions of Property from the Seventeenth to the Twentieth Century* (Bloomington: Indiana University Press, 1977), 10, 16; Jager, *Fate of Family Farming,* xv–xvii.

38. Governor Hunter to the Lords Commissioners for Trade and Plantations at London, cited in Cushing and Sheppard, *History of the Counties of Gloucester, Salem, and Cumberland,* 520.

39. *New Jersey Archives* (1918), 4:214–15.

40. Will and Inventory of Philip Vickary, April 8, 1703, Salem County Wills, New Jersey State Archives, Trenton; Will and Inventory of Philip Vickers, February 17, 1758, Cumberland County Wills, New Jersey State Archives, Trenton.

41. Kulikoff, *Agrarian Origins,* 66; Wrightson, *English Society,* 21, 136; Campbell, *English Yeoman,* 33–35.

42. John J. McCusker and Russell R. Menard, *The Economy of British America, 1607–1789* (Chapel Hill: University of North Carolina Press, 1985), 189–205.

43. Mancall, "Landholding," 661; David E. Dauer, "Colonial Philadelphia's Intraregional Transportation System: An Overview" (Working Papers of the Regional Economic History Research Center, Baltimore, Md., 1978), 2; Kulikoff, *From British Peasants to Colonial American Farmers,* 210–11.

44. For census data, see "An Account of the Dwelling Houses and Inhabitants of . . . the said Provinces of New Jersey . . . from the 1st of July, 1771 to the 1st of July, 1772," in *Documents Relating to the Colonial, Revolutionary, and Post Revolutionary History of the State of New Jersey* (Newark: New Jersey Historical Society, 1886), 10:452–53. For the phrase "Spartan Common-Wealth," see Philip Fithian to John Peck, August 12, 1774, in *Journal and Letters of Philip Vickers Fithian: A Plantation Tutor of the Old Dominion,* ed. Hunter Dickinson Farish (Williamsburg, Va.: Colonial Williamsburg, Inc., 1943; repr. Charlottesville: University Press of Virginia, 1968), 160. Farm sizes were calculated from the 1773–74 tax lists for Deerfield, Fairfield, Greenwich, and Hopewell. See Kenn Stryker-Rodda, ed., "New Jersey Tax Ratables, 1773–1774," *Genealogical Magazine of New Jersey* 38 (1963): 57–60, 62–64, 129–35. None of the region's inhabitants owned more than five hundred acres of improved land.

45. Rodda, "New Jersey Tax Ratables," 134 (Samuel Fithian's farm). F. Alan Palmer has suggested that the Fithian farm was situated between Molly Wheaton

Run and Sheppard's Mill Creek; see Palmer, ed., *The Beloved Cohansie of Philip Vickers Fithian* (Greenwich, N.J.: Cumberland County Historical Society, n.d.), 32.

46. Will and Inventory of Josiah Fithian Esq., March 31, 1741, Salem County Wills, New Jersey State Archives, Trenton; Will and Inventory of Samuel Fithian, January 21, 1776, Cumberland County Wills, New Jersey State Archives, Trenton; Inventory of Joseph Fithian, March 7, 1772, Cumberland County Wills, New Jersey State Archives, Trenton; Rodda, "New Jersey Tax Ratables," 134.

47. Philip Fithian to Joseph Fithian, August 10, 1767, Fithian Papers, vol. 2 ("limited necessary"). On the education of mid-Atlantic farm children, see Kulikoff, *From British Peasants to Colonial American Farmers*, 247.

48. Fithian Journal, July 28, 1775, in *Philip Vickers Fithian: Journal, 1775–1776, Written on the Virginia-Pennsylvania Frontier and in the Army around New York*, ed. Robert Greenhalgh Albion and Leonidas Dodson (Princeton, N.J.: Princeton University Press, 1934), 75–76.

49. Most of my understanding of agricultural life in Cohansey comes from Wacker and Clemens, *Land Use in Early New Jersey*, especially 231–63.

50. For an overview of Fithian's activities, see his "Workbook," December 17, 1766, through March 6, 1767, Fithian Papers, vol. 1. On wheat and rye culture in the early American Northeast, see Stevenson Whitcomb Fletcher, *Pennsylvania Agriculture and Country Life, 1640–1840* (Harrisburg: Pennsylvania Historical Commission, 1950), 99–100; Wacker and Clemens, *Land Use in Early New Jersey*, 144–46, 210, 237; Darwin P. Kelsey, "Early New England Farm Crops: Small Grains," Old Sturbridge Village Online Resource Library, 1980, http//www.osv.org/learning/DocumentViewer.php?DocID=779.

51. For references to dressing flax, see Fithian Journal, December 17, 1766, through March 6, 1767, Fithian Papers, vol. 1. On the production of flax, see Adrienne Hood, *The Weaver's Craft: Cloth, Commerce, and Industry in Early Pennsylvania* (Philadelphia: University of Pennsylvania Press, 2003), 40–66; Fletcher, *Pennsylvania Agriculture*, 160–62; Ellen J. Gehret and Alan G. Keyser, "Flax Processing in Pennsylvania: From Seed to Fiber," *Pennsylvania Folklife* 22 (1972): 10–34; Darwin P. Kelsey, "Early New England Farm Crops: Flax," Old Sturbridge Village Online Resource Library, 1980, http//www.osv.org/learning/DocumentViewer.php?DocID=729.

52. For a glimpse of Fithian's work patterns during the spring, see Fithian workbook, March, 9, 1767, to June 13, 1767, Fithian Papers, vol. 1. See also Fithian Journal, May 16, 1766 ("noble green"); ibid., April 13, 1767 ("extremely weary"); ibid., June 13, 1767 ("much fatigued"); ibid., March 30, 1767 ("bottoming some chairs"). On the usefulness of dung, see Wacker and Clemens, *Land Use in Early New Jersey*, 14.

53. Fithian Journal, August 10, 1766, Fithian Papers, vol. 1.

54. For economic liberalism of the early Delaware Valley, see James Lemon, *The Best Poor Man's Country: A Geographical Study of Early Southeastern Pennsylvania* (New York: W. W. Norton & Company Inc., 1972); Barry Levy, *Quakers and the American Family: British Settlement in the Delaware Valley* (New York: Oxford University Press, 1988).

55. Fithian Work Journal, June 28, 1766, to July 19, 1766, and June 24 to July 14, 1766, Fithian Papers, vol. 1. On at least one occasion Philip was paid for his work on neighboring farms. See ibid., June 28, 1766. For a brief discussion of the eighteenth-century harvest season, see Richard L. Bushman, *The Refinement of America: People, Places, Cities* (New York: Vintage Books, 1992), 22–23.

56. Kimberly R. Sebold, *From Marsh to Farm: The Landscape Transformation of Coastal New Jersey* (Washington, D.C.: National Park Service, 1992), 1, 5, 21–23, 30, 41; Gabrielle M. Lanier, *The Delaware Valley in the Early Republic: Architecture, Landscape, and Regional Identity* (Baltimore: Johns Hopkins University Press, 2005), 119–28; Matthew G. Hatvany, "The Origins of the Acadian A*boiteau*: An Environmental-Historical Geography of the Northeast," *Historical Geography* 30 (2002): 121–37.

57. Sebold, *From Marsh to Farm*, 2, 21–23; Fithian Work Journal, July 26, 31, 1766, Fithian Papers, vol. 1; ibid., August 1, 13, 1766; ibid., September 11, 1766.

58. Peter Kalm, *Peter Kalm's Travels in North America* (1770), English translation in 2 vols. (New York: Dover Publications, 1937), vol. 2, October 1, 1748, p. 78.

59. Ibid., November 30, 1748, p. 192.

60. Fithian Work Journal, August 29, 1766, to September 11, 1766, Fithian Papers, vol. 1; Fithian Journal, August 11, 1775, in *Philip Vickers Fithian: Journal, 1775–1776*, ed. Albion and Dodson, 98.

61. Fithian Journal, April 24, 1766; August 23, 1766; September 22, 27, 1766; October 7, 1766; December 22, 1766, Fithian Papers, vol. 1; *The Autobiography of Thomas Harris of New England Town in Cohansey, West New Jersey* (Greenwich, N.J.: Cumberland County Historical Society, 1989), 13.

62. Fithian Journal, August 9, 1775, Fithian Papers, vol. 6.

63. Fithian Work Journal, September 17, 1766, to October 21, 1766, Fithian Papers, vol. 1; Palmer, *Beloved Cohansie of Philip Vickers Fithian*, 42–43 ("700 gallons"); Fithian Work Journal, September 26, 1766 ("water Cyder"), Fithian Papers, vol. 1; Fletcher, *Pennsylvania Agriculture*, 209–10, 212, 411; David Freeman Hawke, *Everyday Life in Early America* (New York: Harper & Row, 1988), 79–80.

64. Fithian Journal, June 28, 1766, Fithian Papers, vol. 1. The *Oxford English Dictionary* credits Philip with the first use of the term "Nor'Easter."

65. Fithian Journal, April 29, 1766; June 28, 1766; July 7, 1766, Fithian Papers, vol. 1.

66. Ibid., July 6, 9, 1766.

67. Ibid., July 10, 8, 1766.

68. Philip Fithian, "Declamation on the Dreadful Appearance of a Drouth, pronounced at Deerfield," August 13, 1769, Fithian Papers, vol. 2.

69. Cushing and Sheppard, *History of the Counties of Gloucester, Salem, and Cumberland*, 682; Enoch Fithian, "Fithian Family History" (1834).

Chapter 2

1. Journal of Philip Vickers Fithian, March 30, 1766, Philip Vickers Fithian Journal and Commonplace Books, 1766–76, General Manuscripts, CO1099, no. 349, vol. 1, Princeton University Libraries, Princeton, N.J. (hereafter Fithian Papers).

2. Ibid., March 31, 1766.

3. For a good introduction to Puritans, see David D. Hall, *Puritans in the New World: A Critical Anthology* (Princeton, N.J.: Princeton University Press, 2004).

4. The classic treatment remains Edmund Morgan, *Visible Saints: The History of a Puritan Idea* (Ithaca, N.Y.: Cornell University Press, 1965).

5. Leonard J. Trinterud, *The Forming of an American Tradition: A Re-examination of Colonial Presbyterianism* (Philadelphia: Westminster Press, 1948), 15–19, 28–29; Bryan F. LeBeau, *Jonathan Dickinson and the Formative Years of American Presbyterianism* (Lexington: University Press of Kentucky, 1997), 15, 25. For a full

treatment of the move toward Presbyterianism in seventeenth-century New England, see James F. Cooper Jr., *Tenacious as Their Liberties: The Congregationalists in Colonial Massachusetts* (New York: Oxford University Press, 1999), 68–87.

6. The East Hampton and Fairfield, Connecticut, churches were both independent in church governance. See Lyman Beecher, *A Sermon Containing a General History of the Town of East Hampton* (Sag Harbor, N.Y.: Spooner, 1806), 19; Wilbur Stone Deming, *The First Church of Fairfield* (Bridgeport, Conn.: Cutting & Woods Inc., 1963), 2–5; Frank Samuel Child, *An Old New England Church: Established Religion in Connecticut* (Fairfield, Conn.: Fairfield Historical Society, 1910), 37–47; LeBeau, *Jonathan Dickinson*, 15; Trinterud, *Forming of an American Tradition*, 16, 18. Fairfield, Connecticut, settlers to Cohansey, like the rest of the churches in Connecticut, were moving closer to a Presbyterian form of church polity through the formation of county consociations of ministers that were invested with limited authority over the colony's congregations.

7. Minutes of the Philadelphia Presbytery, May 19, 1708, in *Minutes of the Presbyterian Church in America, 1706–1788*, ed. Guy Klett (Philadelphia: Presbyterian Historical Society, 1976), 4; Trinterud, *Forming of an American Tradition*, 24, 33.

8. I have arrived at this estimate by comparing the 1773 tax ratables lists (the earliest ratables lists available for these communities) for Fairfield, Deerfield, Greenwich, and Hopewell with all extant Presbyterian church records for the congregations that resided in these townships. See Session Minutes, Fairfield Presbyterian Church, 1759–1812, Presbyterian Historical Society, Philadelphia; Alan F. Palmer, *The Deerfield Presbyterian Church, Records of the Session, 1737–1827* (Deerfield, N.J.: Published by the author, 1988); Greenwich Presbyterian Church Session Minutes, 1747–89, manuscript located in Greenwich Presbyterian Church, Greenwich, N.J.; New Jersey Tax Ratables, 1768–1846, New Jersey Archives, Trenton.

The Philadelphia Presbytery did not begin recording the numbers of communicants per church until the turn of the nineteenth century, but the numbers from these early reportings are telling and provide us with some sense of just how much the Cohansey region was a Presbyterian stronghold in the eighteenth century. With the exception of Philadelphia, the Cohansey congregations at Fairfield (1697), Greenwich (1707), Deerfield (1737), Pittsgrove (1741), and Bridgeton (1792) had the largest numbers of communicants in the entire presbytery. For example, in 1809 the Fairfield church reported 124 communicants and the Bridgeton and Greenwich churches reported a combined 169 communicants. The only non-Philadelphia Presbyterian churches with numbers even close to those of Cohansey churches were the Great Valley and Charleston (Pa.) congregation at 69 communicants, Neshaminy (Pa.) at 68 communicants, and Newton and Bensalem (Pa.) at 68 communicants. The Cape May (N.J.) congregation reported 62 communicants. Philadelphia's Third Presbyterian Church reported 303 communicants, and Philadelphia's First Presbyterian Church reported 156. It should also be noted that the Cohansey-area parishes of Pittsgrove and Deerfield did not report to the presbytery in 1809, but in 1807 the Deerfield church reported 58 "in full communion" while the Pittsgrove church reported 95 communicants. These statistics, of course, do not reflect the realities of the second half of the *eighteenth* century, but they do suggest that outside the city of Philadelphia there were more Presbyterians worshiping in Cohansey than anywhere else in the Delaware Valley. See Minutes of the Philadelphia Presbytery, 1706–1959, Presbyterian Historical Society, Philadelphia. Such an estimate, however, must remain *very* conservative since it accounts only for individuals listed in official church records. Not all churchgoers were members or pew holders in a given congregation. On any given Sunday morning Cohansey Presbyterians would have had considerably more people in their pews than names on their communicant rolls. See Patricia Bonomi and Peter Eisenstadt, "Church Attendance in the Eighteenth-Century British-American Colonies," *William and Mary Quarterly* 39 (1982): 245–86.

9. Martin Lodge, "The Crisis of the Churches in the Middle Colonies, 1720–1750," *Pennsylvania Magazine of History and Biography* 95 (1971): 195–210; Patricia U. Bonomi, *Under the Cope of Heaven: Religion, Society, and Politics in Colonial America* (New York: Oxford University Press, 1986), 74–79. The shortage of ministers in the first half of the eighteenth century in colonial America is a major theme that runs through Bonomi, *Under the Cope of Heaven;* and Trinterud, *Forming of an American Tradition.*

10. Isaac Foster, "Historical Report of Pittsgrove Church, 1794," Presbyterian Historical Society, Philadelphia.

11. A sense of what Jon Butler has called "denominational order" arrived rather late to this part of the Delaware Valley. See Jon Butler, *Power, Authority, and the Origins of American Denominational Order: The English Churches in the Delaware Valley, 1680–1730* (Philadelphia: American Philosophical Society, 1978).

12. *Minutes of the Presbyterian Church,* ed. Klett, 1–191. A close examination of the available ministerial roll calls at Philadelphia Presbytery and Synod meetings between 1706 and 1743 reveal that Cohansey clergymen rarely attended these gatherings unless they were held—as they sometimes were when ordinations and installations took place—in nearby communities. When Rev. Daniel Lawrence was called by the Presbyterians at Cape May, located approximately forty miles south of Cohansey, he had to wait nearly a year before being installed "in as much as none of the Members of the Presby. can conveniently take a Journey to Cape May this Summer." See Minutes of the Abington Presbytery, May 16, 1753, typescript copy, Presbyterian Historical Society, Philadelphia.

13. "Brief History of the Formation and establishment of the Presbyterian church at Greenwich in the county of Cumberland in New Jersey" (n.d., probably late eighteenth century), manuscript in the possession of the Presbyterian Historical Society, Philadelphia.

14. See, for example, the cases of Samuel Exall, James Moorehead, and Henry Hook: "A Letter to the people of Cohanzy," September 1711, Letter-Book of Philadelphia Presbytery, in *Minutes of the Presbyterian Church,* ed. Klett, 77–78; Minutes of the Philadelphia Synod, September 1720, ibid., 43; Minutes of the Philadelphia Synod, September 1722, ibid., 55–57.

15. While the Awakening wreaked havoc on this rural Presbyterian community—dividing it between New Side and Old Side factions—it has also been a point of contention for historians of colonial religious life. Some historians of the Awakening described it as an event that connected culturally the previously disparate colonies of British North America. In this scenario, revivals united colonists of different Protestant persuasions around a shared and imagined evangelical experience. The colonywide preaching of George Whitefield and other itinerants in the early 1740s created a regenerate community of saints; fashioned a common understanding of how to resist clerical, and later British, authority; or brought a renewed intensity to congregations languishing in a state of spiritual decline. See Timothy Hall, *Contested Boundaries: Itinerancy and the Reshaping of the Colonial Religious World* (Durham, N.C.: Duke University Press, 1994); Harry S. Stout, *The Divine Dramatist: George Whitefield and the Rise of Modern Evangelicalism* (Grand Rapids, Mich.: Eerdmans Publishing Co., 1991); Frank Lambert, *Pedlar*

in Divinity: George Whitefield and the Transatlantic Revivals (Princeton, N.J.: Princeton University Press, 1994); Frank Lambert, *Inventing the 'Great Awakening'* (Princeton, N.J.: Princeton University Press, 1999).

Others, however, emphasize the divisiveness of the Awakening. These historians focus much of their attention on the way the revival divided churches into Old Light/Old Side and New Light/New Side factions and disrupted the religious life of local communities. See, for example, Jon Butler, *Awash in a Sea of Faith: Christianizing the American People* (Cambridge, Mass.: Harvard University Press, 1990); Gregory Nobles, *Divisions throughout the Whole: Politics and Society in Hampshire County, Massachusetts, 1740–1775* (New York: Cambridge University Press, 1983), 36–58; Brendan J. McConville, *Those Daring Disturbers of the Public Peace: Agrarian Unrest and the Struggle for Political Legitimacy in New Jersey, 1701–1776* (Ithaca, N.Y.: Cornell University Press, 1999), 83–89. My tack here follows the latter approach. The Great Awakening only enhanced the already existing struggles that Cohansey Presbyterians were facing in their attempts to plant strong churches in the southern New Jersey countryside. For an approach that stresses both the unifying and divisive nature of the Awakening in its local context, see Ned Landsman, "Revivalism and Nativism in the Middle Colonies: The Great Awakening and the Scots Community in East New Jersey," *American Quarterly* 34 (1982): 149–63.

16. See John Thomson, *The Government of the Church of Christ* (Philadelphia: A. Bradford, 1741), 26.

17. These differences are summarized nicely in LeBeau, *Jonathan Dickinson*, 129.

18. Thomson, *Government of the Church of Christ*, 48, 8.

19. Tennent, cited in ibid., 7; Gilbert Tennent, *Remarks upon a Protestation* (Philadelphia: B. Franklin, 1741), 20.

20. Minutes of the Philadelphia Synod, May 1737, in *Minutes of the Presbyterian Church*, ed. Klett, 150; Minutes of the Philadelphia Synod, May 1738, ibid., 153. On the disruptive nature of evangelical itinerancy in the eighteenth century, see Hall, *Contested Boundaries*.

21. [Francis Alison], *An Examination and Refutation of Mr. Gilbert Tennent's Remarks* (Philadelphia: B. Franklin, 1742), 13–14, 21, 52; *The Querists, Part III* (Philadelphia: B. Franklin, 1741), 12.

22. Minutes of the Philadelphia Synod, May 29, 1738, in *Minutes of the Presbyterian Church*, ed. Klett, 157; Minutes of the Philadelphia Synod, May 26, 1739, ibid., 162.

23. The best account of these events remains Trinterud, *Forming of an American Tradition*.

24. Ibid., 88–89; Milton J. Coalter, *Gilbert Tennent, Son of Thunder* (New York: Greenwood Press, 1986), 71–72.

25. "Brief History of the Formation and establishment of the Presbyterian church at Greenwich."

26. "The History of the Presbyterian Church at Deerfield in the State of New Jersey" (1797), manuscript in the possession of the Presbyterian Historical Society, Philadelphia.

27. George Whitefield, *Journals* (Edinburgh: Banner of Truth Trust, 1960), 496; "Number of People in New Jersey, Taken in 1737–38," *New Jersey Archive* (1880–1928) 6: 242–44.

28. Minutes, New Brunswick Presbytery, 1738–56, Presbyterian Historical Society, Philadelphia.

29. Minutes of the Philadelphia Presbytery, 1733–46, typescript copy, July 1736, Presbyterian Historical Society, Philadelphia. On the power of the laity to

remove ministers who were not in conformity with revival evangelicalism, see Marilyn J. Westerkamp, *The Triumph of the Laity: Scots-Irish Piety and the Great Awakening, 1625–1760* (New York: Oxford University Press, 1988).

30. Minutes of the Philadelphia Presbytery, 1733–46, transcript copy, May 1739, June 1739, Presbyterian Historical Society, Philadelphia; Richard Webster, *A History of the Presbyterian Church in America from Its Origins until the Year 1760* (Philadelphia: Joseph Wilson, 1858), 505.

31. Lucius Q. C. Elmer, *History of the Early Settlements and Progress of Cumberland County* (Bridgeton, N.J.: George F. Nixon, 1869), 92–93; Will of Nathan Lawrence, November 23, 1744, in *Documents Relating to the Colonial History of the State of New Jersey*, ed. A. Van Doren Honeyman, 1st ser., vol. 30, Calendar of Wills, Administrations, Etc., vol. 2, 1730–50 (Somerville, N.J.: Unionist-Gazette Association, 1918), 305.

32. Elmer, *History of Cumberland County*, 92–93.

33. "History of the Fairfield Church," 1794, manuscript in possession of the Presbyterian Historical Society, Philadelphia; Elmer, *History of Cumberland County*, 97–98.

34. Minutes of the Philadelphia Synod, May 1754, in *Minutes of the Presbyterian Church*, ed. Klett, 240.

35. Robert Jenney to Bishop of London, June 29, 1743, cited in *Historical Collections . . . American Colonial Church*, vol. 2, *Pennsylvania* ed. W. S. Perry (Hartford, Conn.: Church Press, 1871), 234–35.

36. Steven Bullock, *Revolutionary Brotherhood: Freemasonry and the Transformation of the American Social Order, 1730–1810* (Chapel Hill: University of North Carolina Press, 1996), 57–59; Robert A. Ferguson, *The American Enlightenment, 1750–1820* (Cambridge, Mass.: Harvard University Press, 1997), 52–60.

37. Bullock, *Revolutionary Brotherhood*, 57–58; Deitmar Rothermund, *The Layman's Progress: Religious and Political Experience in Colonial Pennsylvania, 1740–1770* (Philadelphia: University of Pennsylvania Press, 1961), 35–56; Jack Marietta, *The Reformation of American Quakerism, 1748–1783* (Philadelphia: University of Pennsylvania Press, 1984).

38. Minutes of the Synod of New York and Philadelphia, May 1758, in *Minutes of the Presbyterian Church*, ed. Klett, 340–42; *The Plan of Union between the Synods of New York and Philadelphia* (Philadelphia: W. Dunlap, 1758).

39. [Francis Alison], *An Examination and Refutation of Mr. Gilbert Tennent's Remarks*, 9; Minutes of the Synod of Philadelphia, May 30, 1743, in *Minutes of the Presbyterian Church*, ed. Klett, 183–85; LeBeau, *Jonathan Dickinson*, 136–37, 144–45.

40. LeBeau, *Jonathan Dickinson*, 85–103; Jonathan Dickinson, *The Danger of Schisms and Contentions* (New York: Peter Zenger, 1739), 9–22; Henry May, *The Enlightenment in America* (New York: Oxford University Press, 1976), 54–55; Nina Reid Maroney, *Philadelphia's Enlightenment, 1740–1800: Kingdom of Christ, Empire of Reason* (Westport, Conn.: Greenwood Press, 2001), 77–94.

41. Webster, *History of the Presbyterian Church*, 189–91.

42. Ned C. Landsman, *From Colonials to Provincials: American Thought and Culture, 1680–1760* (Ithaca, N.Y.: Cornell University Press, 1997), 125. See Gilbert Tennent, *The Danger of Spiritual Pride Represented* (Philadelphia: William Bradford, 1745); Gilbert Tennent, *Brotherly Love Recommended* (Philadelphia: B. Franklin, 1748); Gilbert Tennent, *Irenicium Ecclesiasticum, or a Humble Impartial Essay Upon the Peace of Jerusalem* (Philadelphia: W. Bradford, 1749); Gilbert Tennent, *Blessedness of Peace–Makers Represented* (Philadelphia: W. William Bradford, 1765); Trinterud, *Forming of an American Tradition*, 120.

43. Norman Fiering, *Jonathan Edwards's Moral Thought in Its British Context* (Chapel Hill: University of North Carolina Press, 1981), 48. Fiering has described "moral theology" as "supernatural ethics" or the study of how "happiness might be attained through the practice of virtue but included in its scope the next world as well as this one." On the idea that religion began to become increasingly more concerned with "behavior in everyday life," see James Turner, *Without God, Without Creed: The Origins of Unbelief in America* (Baltimore: Johns Hopkins University Press, 1985), 32.

44. See Mark Valeri, *Law and Providence in Joseph Bellamy's New England: The Origins of the New Divinity in Revolutionary America* (New York: Oxford University Press, 1994).

45. Samuel Davies, *Religion and Publick Spirit: A Valedictory Address to the Senior Class, Delivered in Nassau Hall, September 21, 1760* (New York: James Parker and Company, 1761), 4, 5, 7, 9.

46. All verses quoted from the King James Version of the Bible. Each of these verses appeared in Tennent's *Irenicum Ecclesiasticum*, 7, 10, 73.

47. Tennent, *Irenicum Ecclesiasticum*, 10.

48. Daniel Walker Howe, *The Making of the American Self: Jonathan Edwards to Abraham Lincoln* (Cambridge, Mass.: Harvard University Press, 1997), 5–10, 21–22; May, *Enlightenment in America*, 55; Landsman, *From Colonials to Provincials*, 68–69.

49. Enoch Green, *Slothfulness Reproved and the Example of the Saints Proposed for Imitation* . . . (Philadelphia: D. Hall and W. Sellers, 1772), 6.

50. Tennent, *Irenicum Ecclesiasticum*, 85, 92, 98, 100.

51. May, *Enlightenment in America*, 42.

52. Gilbert Tennent, *A Sermon Preached in Greenwich, September 4, 1746 at the Ordination of Mr. Andrew Hunter* (Philadelphia: William Bradford, 1746).

53. Elmer, *History of Cumberland County*, 97–99.

54. Webster, *History of the Presbyterian Church*, 670.

55. "History of the Fairfield Church," 1794, Presbyterian Historical Society, Philadelphia.

56. Ibid.

57. S. R. Anderson, *Historical Account of the Presbyterian Church at Fairfield, Cumberland County, New Jersey* (Fairfield, N.J.: Fairfield Presbyterian Church, 1876), Presbyterian Historical Society, Philadelphia, n.p.

58. "History of the Fairfield Church," 1794.

59. Session Minutes, Fairfield Presbyterian Church, Presbyterian Historical Society, Philadelphia.

60. Quoted in Anderson, *Historical Account of the Presbyterian Church at Fairfield*, n.p.

61. "The Roll of Communicants," Fairfield Presbyterian Church Parish Register, 1759–1970, Presbyterian Historical Society, Philadelphia. In the five years prior to the revival, Fairfield averaged fewer than two admissions annually, and in the years immediately following the revival, from 1767 to 1773, the church on average received less than one new admission per year.

62. "Brief History of the Formation and establishment of the Presbyterian church at Greenwich"; Foster, "Historical Report of the Pittsgrove Church, 1794."

63. Enoch Green, *Slothfulness Reproved, and the Example of the Saints proposed for Imitation: A Sermon Occasioned by the Death of the Reverend William Ramsey* . . . (Philadelphia: D. Hall and W. Sellers, 1772), 26.

64. Fithian Journal, February 23, 1766, Fithian Papers, vol. 1; Michael Craw-ford, *Seasons of Grace: Colonial New England's Revival Tradition in Its British Context* (New York: Oxford University Press, 1991), 180.

65. Green, *Slothfulness Reproved*, 28.

66. Landsman, *From Colonials to Provincials*, 125–28.

67. Jonathan Elmer, *Funeral Eulogium: Sacred Memory of the late Reverend William Ramsey*... (Philadelphia: D. Hall and W. Sellers, 1772), 7, 8.

68. Journal of Ebenezer Elmer, cited in Elmer, *History of Cumberland County*, 99.

69. Fithian Journal, January 20, 1766, Fithian Papers, vol. 1.

70. Ibid., January 26, 1766; February 9, 1766.

71. Ibid., January 22, 23, 25, 1766.

72. Ibid., January 22, 23, 26, 1766.

73. Ibid., February 9, 1766; January 29, 1766; February 8, 1766.

74. Ibid., February 16, 9, 1766.

75. Ibid., March 5, 1766.

76. Ibid., April 20, 27, 1766.

77. Philip Vickers Fithian, Spiritual Reflection, April 7, 1766, Fithian Papers, vol. 1.

78. Fithian Journal, May 10, 11, 1766, Fithian Papers, vol. 1. On Presbyterian communion seasons, see Leigh Eric Schmidt, *Holy Fairs: Scottish Communions and American Revivals in the Early Modern Period* (Princeton, N.J.: Princeton University Press, 1989).

79. *The Journals of Henry Melchior Muhlenberg*, trans. Theodore G. Tappert and John W. Dobberstein, 3 vols. (Philadelphia: Muhlenberg Press, 1945), 2:181.

80. Fithian Journal, June 26, 1775, in *Philip Vickers Fithian: Journal, 1775–1776, Written on the Virginia-Pennsylvania Frontier and in the Army around New York,* ed. Robert Greenhalgh Albion and Leonidas Dodson (Princeton, N.J.: Princeton University Press, 1934), 38.

81. I am borrowing here from Michael Walzer's notion of a "dense moral cul-ture" in *Interpretation and Social Criticism* (Cambridge, Mass.: Harvard University Press, 1987), 16.

Chapter 3

1. Philip Fithian to Joseph Fithian, August 10, 1767, Philip Vickers Fithian Journals and Commonplace Books, 1766–76, General Manuscripts, CO1099, no. 349, vol. 2, Princeton University Libraries, Princeton, N.J. (hereafter Fithian Papers); Journal of Philip Vickers Fithian, March 27, 1767; July 29, 1766; May 13, 1767; July 30, 1766, Fithian Papers, vol. 1; Fithian Work Journal, March 27, 1767; July 29, 1766; May 13, 1767; July 30, 1766, Fithian Papers, vol. 1.

2. Philip Fithian to Joseph Fithian, September 28, 1769, Fithian Papers, vol. 2; Joseph F. Kett, *The Pursuit of Knowledge under Difficulties: From Self-Improvement to Adult Education in America, 1750–1990* (Stanford, Calif.: Stanford University Press, 1994), 30.

3. Philip Fithian to Joseph Fithian, August 10, 1767, Fithian Papers, vol. 2.

4. Philip Fithian to Joseph Fithian, September 28, 1769, Fithian Papers, vol. 2.

5. Philip Fithian to Joseph Fithian, August 10, 1767, Fithian Papers, vol. 2.

6. Philip Fithian to Joseph Fithian, September 28, 1769, Fithian Papers, vol. 2.

7. Ibid. On the "stages of civilization" theory, see Ronald L. Meek, *Social Science and the Ignoble Savage* (New York: Cambridge University Press, 1976).

8. Philip Fithian to Joseph Fithian, September 28, 1769, Fithian Papers, vol. 2.

9. Jason M. Opal, "Beyond the Farm: Ambition and the Transformation of Rural New England, 1770s–1820s" (Ph.D. diss., Brandeis University, 2004), 16–17.

10. Jack Scott, ed., *An Annotated Edition of Lectures on Moral Philosophy by John Witherspoon* (Newark: University of Delaware Press, 1982), 71.

11. Andrew Hunter to Philip Vickers Fithian, June 26, 1773, in *Journal and Letters of Philip Vickers Fithian*, ed. Hunter Dickinson Farish (Williamsburg, Va.: Colonial Williamsburg, Inc., 1943; repr. Charlottesville: University Press of Virginia, 1968), 3.

12. Frederick Tolles, *MeetingHouse and CountingHouse: The Quaker Merchants of Colonial Philadelphia* (Chapel Hill: University of North Carolina Press, 1948); Barry Levy, *Quakers and the American Family: British Settlement in the Delaware Valley* (New York: Oxford University Press, 1988).

13. Philip Vickers Fithian, "A Piece on Ambition: Composed for an Exercise in the respectable Whig Society at Nassau-Hall Written May 20, Anno 1771," Fithian Papers, vol. 2.

14. Fithian Journal, April 4, 1774, in *Journal and Letters of Philip Vickers Fithian*, ed. Farish, 91; Philip Vickers Fithian, "On Education & Example, their Influence on our Actions, being an Exercise prepared for the Whigg Society at Nassau Hall, Performed, June 1, 1771," Fithian Papers, vol. 2.

15. Fithian Journal, August 6–17, 1767, Fithian Papers, vol. 1; ibid., July 2, 1773, Fithian Papers, vol. 7.

16. Douglas Sloan, *The Scottish Enlightenment and the American College Ideal* (New York: Columbia University Press, 1971), 38–39, 281–84; Elizabeth Nybakken, "In the Irish Tradition: Pre-Revolutionary Academies in America," *History of Education Quarterly* 37 (summer 1997): 173–74; Nina Reid-Maroney, *Philadelphia's Enlightenment, 1740–1800* (Westport, Conn.: Greenwood Press, 2001), 77–94. Neither Sloan, Nybakken, nor Reid-Maroney includes Green's school in a list of Presbyterian academies.

17. Sloan, *Scottish Enlightenment and the American College Ideal*, 38–41, 65.

18. Ned Landsman, *From Colonial to Provincials: American Thought and Culture, 1680–1760* (Ithaca, N.Y.: Cornell University Press, 1997), 130; Francis L. Broderick, "Pulpit, Physics and Politics: The Curriculum of the College of New Jersey, 1746–1794," *William and Mary Quarterly*, 3rd ser., 6 (1949): 42–68.

19. Nybakken, "In the Irish Tradition," 178; Richard A. Harrison, *Princetonians, 1769–1775: A Biographical Dictionary* (Princeton, N.J.: Princeton University Press, 1980), xxi.

20. For biographical sketches of all of these students, see John Fea, "Rural Religion: Protestant Community and the Improvement of the South Jersey Countryside, 1676–1800" (Ph.D. diss., State University of New York at Stony Brook, 1999), 452–57.

21. Susan Purviance, "Intersubjectivity and Sociable Relations in the Philosophy of Francis Hutcheson," *Eighteenth Century Life* 15 (1991): 26; Lawrence Blum, "Friendship as a Moral Phenomenon," in *Friendship: A Philosophical Reader,* ed. Neera Kapur Badhwar (Ithaca, N.Y.: Cornell University Press, 1993), 192–210.

22. Thomas Ewing to Philip Vickers Fithian, March 13, 1766; February 7, 1766, Fithian Papers, vol. 1.

23. Philip Vickers Fithian, "An Epistle to Miss Amy Fithian on the Excellencies of Friendship, Written at Greenwich, December 8, 1769," Fithian Papers, vol. 2.

24. Augustine, *Confessions,* book 4, cited in Gilbert Meilander, *Friendship: A Study in Theological Ethics* (Notre Dame, Ind.: University of Notre Dame Press, 1981), 18.

25. Fithian, "Epistle to Miss Amy Fithian."

26. Ned C. Landsman, "Esther Edwards Burr and *The Nature of True Virtue*: Books and Conversation, Piety and Virtue in the Presbyterian Enlightenment," paper presented to the Columbia Seminar in Early American History, Columbia University, 1995 (in John Fea's possession, cited with permission).

27. On the impact of the republic of letters in America, see Norman Fiering, *Jonathan Edwards's Moral Thought and Its British Context* (Chapel Hill: University of North Carolina Press, 1981), 14–23; Landsman, *From Colonials to Provincials*, 31–56; Michael Warner, *Letters of the Republic* (Cambridge, Mass.: Harvard University Press, 1990).

28. The circle of correspondents took classical names such as Amasio, Theron, Hortentio, and Diores. Philip took the name Irenio. See Amasio to Philip Vickers Fithian, March 3, 1767, Fithian Papers, vol. 1; Philip Fithian to Sally Dare, June 8, 1767, ibid., vol. 3. On scribal communities, see Harold Love, *Scribal Publication in Seventeenth Century England* (New York: Oxford, 1993), esp. 179–82.

29. Philip Vickers Fithian, "An Epistle to Rowena, written at Deerfield, July 7, 1769," Fithian Papers, vol. 2; James Ewing to Irenio, July 27, 1767, ibid., vol. 3.

30. Richard Bushman, *The Refinement of America: Persons, Houses, Cities* (New York: Vintage Books, 1992), 90–92; Konstantin Dierks, "Letter Writing, Gender, and Class in America, 1750–1800" (Ph.D. diss., Brown University, 1999).

31. John Witherspoon, "Address to the Senior Class," 1775, quoted in Sloan, *Scottish Enlightenment and the American College Ideal*, 144. On Witherspoon's Princeton, see Mark A. Noll, *Princeton and the Republic, 1767–1822. The Search for a Christian Enlightenment in the Era of Samuel Stanhope Smith* (Princeton, N.J.: Princeton University Press, 1989), 16–58; and Howard Miller, *The Revolutionary College: American Presbyterian Education, 1707–1837* (New York: New York University Press, 1976), 101.

32. Kett, *Pursuit of Knowledge*, 14, 15.

33. Miller, *Revolutionary* College, 89. On the New Moral Philosophy, see Norman Fiering, *Jonathan Edwards's Moral Thought and Its British Context* (Chapel Hill: University of North Carolina Press, 1981).

34. Miller, *Revolutionary College*, 88–89; Sloan, *Scottish Enlightenment and the American College Ideal*, 123–24, 136; Scott, *Annotated Edition of Lectures on Moral Philosophy by John Witherspoon*, 83–85. On Edwards's understanding of virtue, see Fiering, *Jonathan Edwards's Moral Thought;* and George M. Marsden, *Jonathan Edwards: A Life* (New Haven, Conn.: Yale University Press, 2003), 464–71. See also James Turner, *Without God, Without Creed: The Origins of Unbelief in America* (Baltimore: Johns Hopkins University Press, 1985), 33.

35. Scott, *Annotated Edition of Lectures on Moral Philosophy by John Witherspoon*, 109–12, 113n4.

36. Ibid., 110. Witherspoon, in his *Address to the Natives of Scotland Residing in America* (1776), does avow a certain degree of national feeling.

37. Broderick, "Pulpit, Physics and Politics," 61; Ralph Ketcham, "James Madison at Princeton," *Princeton University Library Chronicle* 28 (1966): 27.

38. Philip Fithian to Joseph Fithian, November 30, 1770, Fithian Papers, vol. 2.

39. Ketcham, "James Madison at Princeton," 27, 30.

40. Philip Fithian to Joseph Fithian, November 30, 1770, Fithian Papers, vol. 2; Hannah Fithian to Philip Vickers Fithian, January 10, 1771, ibid.; John Maclean, *History of the College of New Jersey* (Philadelphia: J. B. Lippincott, 1877), 302.

41. Philip Fithian to Joseph Fithian, November 30, 1770, Fithian Papers, vol. 2; Ketcham, "James Madison at Princeton," 31.

42. Philip Fithian to Joseph Fithian, November 30, 1770, Fithian Papers, vol. 2.

43. Ibid.; John M. Murrin, "Christianity, Enlightenment, and Revolution: Hard Choices at the College of New Jersey after Independence," *Princeton University Library Chronicle* 50 (1988): 228.

44. Philip Vickers Fithian, "On Habit: An Exercise in the Whig Society at Nassau Hall," October 2, 1771, Fithian Papers, vol. 2.

45. Maclean, *History of the College of New Jersey*, 362; William S. Dix, "The Princeton University Library in the Eighteenth Century," *Princeton University Library Chronicle* 40 (1978): 1–102.

46. Broderick, "Pulpit, Physics and Politics," 60.

47. Harrison, *Princetonians, 1769–1775*, xxvi; Philip Vickers Fithian, "An Oration, the First in the Junior Winter," November 1771. Princeton, N.J.

48. Philip Vickers Fithian, "The Advantages of Union in Members of Societies Being an Exercise when Assistant to the Moderator in the Whig Society," June 20, 1771, Fithian Papers, vol. 2; Harrison, *Princetonians, 1769–1775*, xii; Vincent S. McCluskey, "The Life and Times of Philip Vickers Fithian" (Ph.D. diss., New York University, 1991), 66, 89, 94. Brackenridge, who came from poor western Pennsylvania farmers, may have distinguished himself with this group due to his superior literary talents.

49. Fithian Journal, June 29, 1774, in *Journal and Letters of Philip Vickers Fithian*, ed. Farish, 127.

50. Fithian Journal, September 19, 1774, in *Journal and Letters of Philip Vickers Fithian*, ed. Farish, 192–93.

51. McCluskey, "Life and Times of Philip Vickers Fithian," 55–58; Philip Fithian to Hannah Fithian, January 12, 1772, Fithian Papers, vol. 2.

52. Kett, *Pursuit of Knowledge*, 12; Philip Fithian to Hannah Fithian, January 12, 1772, Fithian Papers, vol. 2; Fithian Journal, September 19, 1774, in *Journal and Letters of Philip Vickers Fithian*, ed. Farish, 192–93; Harrison, *Princetonians, 1769–1775*, xxii–xxiii.

53. Harrison, *Princetonians, 1769–1775*, xxiv–xxv, xxxi; Philip Vickers Fithian, "Oration," November 1771; Philip Fithian to Joseph Fithian, January 13, 1772, Fithian Papers, vol. 2.

54. Philip Fithian to Hannah Fithian, January 12, 1772, Fithian Papers, vol. 2.

55. Rev'd Andrew Hunter to Philip Fithian, February 10, 1772, Fithian Papers, vol. 3.

56. Philip Vickers Fithian to Polly Bullock, May 10, 1772; Philip Vickers Fithian to Sally Bullock, May 10, 1772, Fithian Papers, vol. 2.

57. Fithian Journal, August 30, 1774, in *Journal and Letters of Philip Vickers Fithian*, ed. Farish, 181; Hannah Fithian to Philip Vickers Fithian, January 10, 1771, Fithian Papers, vol. 2; Hannah Fithian to Philip Vickers Fithian, March 4, 1771, ibid.; Philip Vickers Fithian to Hannah Fithian, January 12, 1772, ibid.

58. Philip Vickers Fithian to "Betsy," June 7, 1767, Fithian Papers, vol. 3; Philip Vickers Fithian to Polly Bullock, January 11, 1773, ibid., vol. 2; Philip Vickers Fithian to Sally Pennington, July 12, 1772, ibid.; Philip Vickers Fithian to "Madam," September 1769, ibid.

59. Fithian Journal, September 1, 1773, Fithian Papers, vol. 7.

60. Philip Vickers Fithian to Elizabeth Beatty, July 15, 1770, Fithian Papers, vol. 7.

61. Ellen K. Rothman, *Hands and Hearts: A History of Courtship in America* (Cambridge, Mass.: Harvard University Press, 1987), 9.

62. Philip Vickers Fithian to Elizabeth Beatty, February 15, 1772, Fithian Papers, vol. 7; Philip Vickers Fithian to Elizabeth Beatty, June 20, 1772, ibid.; Nicole Eustace, "'The Cornerstone of a Copious Work': Love and Power in Eighteenth-Century Courtship," *Journal of Social History* 34 (2001): 542n23.

63. Philip Vickers Fithian to Elizabeth Beatty, June 20, 18, 1772, Fithian Papers, vol. 7.

64. Philip Vickers Fithian to Elizabeth Beatty, September 22, 1772, Fithian Papers, vol. 7.

65. Philip Vickers Fithian to Elizabeth Beatty, October 2, 1772, Fithian Papers, vol. 7.

Chapter 4

1. William Nelson, ed., *Extracts from American Newspapers Relating to New Jersey*, vol. 9, 1772–73 (Paterson, N.J., 1916), 271ff.; Vincent S. McCluskey, "The Life and Times of Philip Vickers Fithian" (Ph.D. diss., New York University, 1991), 87–98.

2. Susan Purviance, "Intersubjectivity and Sociable Relations in the Philosophy of Francis Hutcheson," *Eighteenth Century Life* 15 (February 1991): 35.

3. Charles Clinton Beatty to Elizabeth Beatty, September 25, 1773, Letters of Charles Clinton Beatty, Beatty Family Collections, General Manuscripts, C1010, Princeton University Libraries, Princeton, N.J.

4. Samuel Leake to Philip Vickers Fithian, September 23, 1769, Philip Vickers Fithian Journal and Commonplace Books, 1766–76, General Manuscripts, CO1099, no. 349, vol. 3, Princeton University Libraries, Princeton, N.J. (hereafter Fithian Papers).

5. Philip Vickers Fithian to Benjamin Armitage Jr., March 11, 1773, Fithian Papers, vol. 2.

6. Philip Vickers Fithian to Oliver Reese, February 19, 1773, Fithian Papers, vol. 2; Philip Vickers Fithian to Betsy Armitage, March 12, 1773, ibid.; Philip Vickers Fithian to Polly Bullock and Laura Armitage, April 24, 1773, ibid.; Amanda to Philip Vickers Fithian, November 11, 1772, ibid.; Philip Vickers Fithian to Amanda, November 13, 1772, ibid.

7. Donna Landry, *The Invention of the Countryside: Hunting, Walking and Ecology in English Literature, 1671–1831* (New York: Palgrave-Macmillan, 2001), 1–2; Christopher Lasch, *The True and Only Heaven: Progress and Its Critics* (New York: W. W. Norton, 1991), 84.

8. Philip Vickers Fithian to Polly Bullock and Laura Armitage, April 24, 1773, Fithian Papers, vol. 2.

9. Fithian Journal, July 7, 8, 9, 10, 12, 14, 1773, Fithian Papers, vol. 7.

10. On Doddridge, see Daniel Walker Howe, *The Unitarian Conscience: Harvard Moral Philosophy, 1805–1861* (Middletown, Conn.: Wesleyan University Press, 1988), 152; Mark A. Noll, *The Rise of Evangelicalism: The Age of Edwards, Whitefield and the Wesleys* (Downers Grove, Ill.: InterVarsity Press, 2003), 42; Lawrence Cremin, *American Education: The Colonial Experience, 1607–1783* (New York: Harper & Row, 1970), 281–85; Douglas Sloan, *The Scottish Enlightenment and the American College Ideal* (New York: Teachers College Press, 1971), 66–67.

11. Benedict Pictet, *Christian Theology*, trans. Frederick Reyroux (Philadelphia: Presbyterian Board of Publication, 1845); Fithian Journal, July 2, 1773, Fithian Papers, vol. 7.

12. Thomas Ridgeley, *Body of Divinity: Wherein the Doctrines of the Christian Religion Are Explained and Defended*, 2 vols. (New York: Robert Carter & Brothers, 1855); Fithian Journal, January 2, 1774, in *Journal and Letters of Philip Vickers Fithian*, ed. Hunter Dickinson Farish (Williamsburg, Va.: Colonial Williamsburg, Inc., 1943; repr. Charlottesville: University Press of Virginia, 1968), 46.

13. Carl J. Richard, *The Founders and the Classics: Greece, Rome, and the American Enlightenment* (Cambridge, Mass.: Harvard University Press, 1994), 10, 12, 20, 37–38. Witherspoon believed that the ethical thought of the ancients was worthy of study but that it was "pagan" in nature and "scarcely compatible" with the "quality of life taught by Jesus." See Jack Scott, ed., *An Annotated Edition of Lectures on Moral Philosophy by John Witherspoon* (Newark: University of Delaware Press, 1982), 119n2.

14. Fithian Journal, July 1, 1773, in *Journal and Letters of Philip Vickers Fithian*, ed. Farish, 4.

15. Will and Inventory of Philip Vickers Fithian, December 13, 1776, Cumberland County Wills no. 169, New Jersey Archives, Trenton; Ned Landsman, *From Colonials to Provincials* (Ithaca, N.Y.: Cornell University Press, 1997), 38–42; Erin Mackie, "Introduction," in *The Commerce of Everyday Life: Selections from* The Tatler *and* The Spectator (Boston: St. Martin's, 1998), 10–12; G. J. Barker-Benfield, *The Culture of Sensibility: Sex and Society in Eighteenth-Century Britain* (Chicago: University of Chicago Press, 1992), 62–67.

16. Landsman, *From Colonials to Provincials*, 55–56.

17. *Spectator* no. 69, May 19, 1711, in Spectator On-Line Project, Rutgers University, http://tabula.rutgers.edu/spectator/text/may1711/no69.html.

18. Fithian Journal, July 28, 1775, in *Philip Vickers Fithian: Journal, 1775–1776, Written on the Virginia-Pennsylvania Frontier and in the Army around New York*, ed. Robert Greenhalgh Albion and Leonidas Dodson (Princeton, N.J.: Princeton University Press, 1934), 75–76.

19. Philip Vickers Fithian to Elizabeth Beatty, December 2, 1772, Fithian Papers, vol. 7.

20. As Nicole Eustace has written concerning the nature of eighteenth-century courtship, "the period of courtship reversed the usual hierarchy of gender, making men subordinate to the whims of women and allowing women the final say, perhaps the only time in their lives they would have it." See Nicole Eustace, "'The Cornerstone of a Copious Work': Love and Power in Eighteenth-Century Courtship," *Journal of Social History* 34 (2001): 527.

21. Philip Vickers Fithian to Elizabeth Beatty, December 15, 1772, Fithian Papers, vol. 7.

22. Philip discusses the definition of gallantry in Philip Vickers Fithian to Elizabeth Beatty, November 28, 1774, Fithian Papers, vol. 7.

23. Philip Vickers Fithian to Elizabeth Beatty, December 29, 1772, Fithian Papers, vol. 7.

24. Oliver Reese to Philip Vickers Fithian, December 26, 1772, in *Philip Vickers Fithian Journal and Letters, 1767–1774*, ed. John Rogers Williams (Princeton, N.J.: Princeton University Press, 1960; repr., Freeport, N.Y.: Books for Libraries Press, 1969), 28.

25. Philip Vickers Fithian to Elizabeth Beatty, May 12, 1774, Fithian Papers, vol. 7.

26. Purviance, "Intersubjectivity and Sociable Relations in the Philosophy of Francis Hutcheson," 26. On Witherspoon, see Thomas Miller, *The Selected Writings of John Witherspoon* (Carbondale: Southern Illinois University Press, 1990),

36; and Scott, *Annotated Edition of Lectures on Moral Philosophy by John Witherspoon*, 78, 83–87, 118–19.

27. Fithian Journal, August 27, 1773; July 20, 1773; September 1, 16, 17, 1773, Fithian Papers, vol. 7.

28. Ibid., July 28, 29, 30, 1773, Fithian Papers, vol. 7.

29. The following discussion is indebted to Ned Landsman, "Esther Edwards Burr and *The Nature of True Virtue*: Books and Conversation, Piety and Virtue in the Presbyterian Enlightenment," paper presented to the Columbia Seminar in Early American History, Columbia University, 1995 (in John Fea's possession, cited with permission). See Francis Brooke, *The History of Lady Julia Mandeville* (1763; New York: D. Appleton and Company, 1920); and Lorraine McMullen, *An Odd Attempt at a Woman: The Literary Life of Frances Brooke* (Vancouver: University of British Columbia Press, 1983).

30. Fithian Journal, July 21, 1773, Fithian Papers, vol. 7.

31. Landsman, "Esther Edwards Burr." On interpretive communities of novel readership, see Cathy Davidson, *The Revolution and the Word: The Rise of the Novel in America* (New York: Oxford University Press, 1986), 9, 45, 49.

32. Philip Vickers Fithian, "An Exercise in the Admonishing Club," March 16, 1773, Fithian Papers, vol. 2.

33. On the rise of these clubs, see David T. Shields, *Civil Tongues and Polite Letters in British America* (Chapel Hill: University of North Carolina Press, 1997).

34. Fithian, "Exercise in the Admonishing Club."

35. Fithian Journal, July 30, 1773, in *Journal and Letters of Philip Vickers Fithian*, ed. Farish, 6.

36. On Robert Carter, see Andrew Levy, *The First Emancipator: The Forgotten Story of Robert Carter, the Founding Father Who Freed His Slaves* (New York: Random House, 2005).

37. Hunter Dickinson Farish, "Introduction," in *Journal and Letters of Philip Vickers Fithian*, ed. Farish, xxv–xvii; Louis Morton, *Robert Carter of Nomini Hall* (Charlottesville: University Press of Virginia, 1941); Elizabeth Brown Pryor, "An Anamolous Person: The Northern Tutor in Plantation Society, 1773–1860," *Journal of Southern History* 47 (August 1981): 363–92; Fithian Journal, February 12, 1774; April 6, 1774, in *Journal and Letters of Philip Vickers Fithian*, ed. Farish, 64–65, 93–94.

38. Fithian Journal, January 2, 1774, in *Journal and Letters of Philip Vickers Fithian*, ed. Farish, 46.

39. Ibid.; Fithian Journal, October 12, 1774, in *Journal and Letters of Philip Vickers Fithian*, ed. Farish, 203–4; "Virginia Journal, 1762–1763," Enoch Green Papers, 1762–63, Rutgers University Library Special Collections, Rutgers University, New Brunswick, N.J.

40. Philip Vickers Fithian to Elizabeth Beatty, August 17, 1773, in *Journal and Letters of Philip Vickers Fithian*, ed. Farish, 9; Fithian Journal, August 9, 1774; August 17, 1773, ibid., 6–7; Fithian Journal, August 10, 12, 13, 1773, Fithian Papers, vol. 7.

41. Philip Fithian to John Witherspoon, August 30, 1773, in *Journal and Letters of Philip Vickers Fithian*, ed. Farish, 9–10; Fithian Journal, September 19, 1773, ibid., 14.

42. Fithian Journal, January 2, 1774, in *Journal and Letters of Philip Vickers Fithian*, ed. Farish, 46.

43. Fithian Journal, October 12–13, 1773, in *Journal and Letters of Philip Vickers Fithian*, ed. Farish, 16, 17.

44. Fithian Journal, October 14–20, 1773, in *Journal and Letters of Philip Vickers Fithian*, ed. Farish, 17–18.

45. Philip Vickers Fithian to Elizabeth Beatty, March 2, 1773, Fithian Papers, vol. 7.

46. Ibid.

47. Philip Vickers Fithian to Elizabeth Beatty, March 20, 1773, Fithian Papers, vol. 7.

48. Elizabeth Beatty to "Sir," n.d., in Frank D. Andrews, ed., "Letters to Elizabeth Beatty Fithian of Cumberland County, N.J. from 1772 to 1802," *Vineland Historical Magazine* 15 (July 1930): 265.

49. Fithian Journal, August 14, 15, 16, 1773, Fithian Papers, vol. 7.

50. Philip Vickers Fithian to Elizabeth Beatty, August 17, 1773, in *Journal and Letters of Philip Vickers Fithian*, ed. Farish, 8.

51. Philip Vickers Fithian to Elizabeth Beatty, August 31, 1773, in *Journal and Letters of Philip Vickers Fithian*, ed. Farish, 10–11; Philip Vickers Fithian to Elizabeth Beatty, October 1, 1773, Fithian Papers, vol. 7.

52. Philip Vickers Fithian to Elizabeth Beatty, October 1, 1773, Fithian Papers, vol. 7; Philip Vickers Fithian to Elizabeth Beatty, December 21, 1773, in *Journal and Letters of Philip Vickers Fithian*, ed. Farish, 35–36.

53. John Fea, "The Way of Improvement Leads Home: Philip Vickers Fithian's Rural Enlightenment," *Journal of American History* 90 (2003): 462–90.

Chapter 5

1. Fithian Journal, October 20–28, 1773; November 1, 12, 1773, in *Journal and Letters of Philip Vickers Fithian*, ed. Hunter Dickinson Farish (Williamsburg, Va.: Colonial Williamsburg, Inc., 1943; repr. Charlottesville: University Press of Virginia, 1968), 18–19, 20, 22; Philip Vickers Fithian to Enoch Green, November 2, 1773, ibid., 21.

2. Richard Beale Davis, *Literature and Society in Early Virginia, 1608–1840* (Baton Rouge: Louisiana State University Press, 1973); Richard D. Brown, *Knowledge Is Power: The Diffusion of Information in Early America, 1700–1865* (New York: Oxford University Press, 1989), 46–47.

3. Rhys Isaac, *Landon Carter's Uneasy Kingdom: Revolution and Rebellion on a Virginia Plantation* (New York: Oxford University Press, 2004), 99–100; Kathleen M. Brown, *Good Wives, Nasty Wenches, and Anxious Patriarchs: Gender, Race, and Power in Colonial Virginia* (Chapel Hill: University of North Carolina Press, 1996), 248–52, 263.

4. Philip Fithian to Enoch Green, December 1, 1773; March 1774; September 10, 1774; March 3, 1774, in *Journal and Letters of Philip Vickers Fithian*, ed. Farish, 26, 83, 108, 69.

5. Philip Fithian to John Peck, August 12, 1774, in *Journal and Letters of Philip Vickers Fithian*, ed. Farish, 159–61. Fithian, however, lowered (to five thousand pounds) the value his own education had in Virginia because the northern tutors were not familiar with some Virginia plantation social graces.

6. Ibid.

7. On the social structure of Virginia and the status of the planter class, see Rhys Isaac, *The Transformation of Virginia: 1740–1790* (Chapel Hill: University of North Carolina Press, 1982). For "anxious patriarch," see Brown, *Good Wives*, 323, 365. For "threatened by a revolutionary spirit," see Isaac, *Landon Carter's*

Uneasy Kingdom. On Carter, see Andrew Levy, *The First Emancipator: The Forgotten Story of Robert Carter, the Founding Father Who Freed His Slaves* (New York: Random House, 2005), 33–93.

8. Hunter Dickinson Farish, "Introduction," in *Journal and Letters of Philip Vickers Fithian,* ed. Farish, xvi–xvii; Brown, *Knowledge Is Power,* 50–52; Brown, *Good Wives,* 265.

9. Philip Fithian to John Peck, August 12, 1774, in *Journal and Letters of Philip Vickers Fithian,* ed. Farish, 162.

10. Brown, *Good Wives,* 269–73; Isaac, *Landon Carter's Uneasy Kingdom,* 235–37.

11. Fithian's references to dinner-table conversations are scattered. See, for example, Fithian Journal, December 23, 1773; March 5, 1774; July 17, 1774; August 11, 1774, in *Journal and Letters of Philip Vickers Fithian,* ed. Farish, 37, 71, 145, 158.

12. Brown, *Good Wives,* 272–73.

13. Fithian Journal, December 17, 1773, in *Journal and Letters of Philip Vickers Fithian,* ed. Farish, 33.

14. Ibid.; Isaac, *Transformation of Virginia,* 81.

15. Fithian Journal, December 12, 1773; February 6, 1774, in *Journal and Letters of Philip Vickers Fithian,* ed. Farish, 29, 63; Philip Fithian to John Peck, August 12, 1774, ibid., 167; Fithian Journal, April 17, 1773, ibid., 100.

16. Edward L. Bond, *Damned Souls in a Tobacco Colony: Religion in Seventeenth-Century Virginia* (Macon, Ga.: Mercer University Press, 2000), 252–66.

17. Fithian Journal, December 12, 13, 1773, in *Journal and Letters of Philip Vickers Fithian,* ed. Farish, 29; Philip Fithian to John Peck, August 12, 1774, ibid., 167.

18. March 6, 1774, in *Journal and Letters of Philip Vickers Fithian,* ed. Farish, 73–74.

19. December 23, 1773; March 24, 1774, in *Journal and Letters of Philip Vickers Fithian,* ed. Farish, 38–39, 84–85.

20. Isaac, *Transformation of Virginia,* 143–205.

21. Philip Fithian to John Peck, August 12, 1774; December 5, 12, 1773; March 6, 1774; April 1, 1774, in *Journal and Letters of Philip Vickers Fithian,* ed. Farish, 167–68, 28, 29, 73–74, 88.

22. Bond, *Damned Souls in Tobacco Colony,* 266; John K. Nelson, *A Blessed Company: Parishes, Parsons, and Parishioners in Anglican Virginia, 1690–1776* (Chapel Hill: University of North Carolina Press, 2001), 207.

23. Ned Landsman, *From Colonials to Provincials* (Ithaca, N.Y.: Cornell University Press, 1997), 63–66, 78; Nelson, *Blessed Company,* 206; Jack Scott, ed., *An Annotated Edition of Lectures on Moral Philosophy by John Witherspoon* (Newark: University of Delaware Press, 1982), 35–37; Mark A. Noll, *America's God: From Jonathan Edwards to Abraham Lincoln* (New York: Oxford University Press, 2002), 97.

24. Isaac, *Transformation of Virginia,* 192–93; Fithian Journal, March 6, 1774, in *Journal and Letters of Philip Vickers Fithian,* ed. Farish, 72–73.

25. Richard Beeman, *The Evolution of the Southern Backcountry: A Case Study of Lunenberg County, Virginia, 1746–1832* (Philadelphia: University of Pennsylvania Press, 1984), 57, 58, 104.

26. Fithian Journal, July 17, 31, 1774, in *Journal and Letters of Philip Vickers Fithian,* ed. Farish, 145, 151–52.

27. Fithian Journal, March 6, 1774, in *Journal and Letters of Philip Vickers Fithian,* ed. Farish, 73. Rhys Isaac has suggested that Presbyterians acquired only a "measure of respectability in the eyes of the [Anglican] gentry." See Isaac, *Transformation of Virginia,* 154.

28. Fithian Journal, January 30, 1774, in *Journal and Letters of Philip Vickers Fithian*, ed. Farish, 61.

29. Daniel Walker Howe, *Making the American Self: Jonathan Edwards to Abraham Lincoln* (Cambridge, Mass.: Harvard University Press, 1997), 1–20; Brown, *Good Wives*, 324–27. For an introduction to the history of emotions in America, see Peter N. Stearns and Jan Lewis, eds., *Emotional History of the United States* (New York: New York University Press, 1998).

30. Philip Vickers Fithian, untitled sermon, in Philip Vickers Fithian Journals and Commonplace Books, 1766–76, General Manuscripts, CO1099, no. 349, vol. 9, Princeton University Libraries, Princeton, N.J. (hereafter Fithian Papers); Fithian Journal, April 7, 1766; January 27, 1767; May 2, 1766, Fithian Papers, vol. 1; Fithian Journal, January 2, 1774, in *Journal and Letters of Philip Vickers Fithian*, ed. Farish, 46; Philip Fithian to Joseph Fithian, September 28, 1769, Fithian Papers, vol. 2; Howard Miller, *The Revolutionary College: American Presbyterians and Higher Education, 1707–1837* (New York: New York University Press, 1976), 88–89.

31. Alan D. McKillop, "Local Attachment and Cosmopolitanism—The Eighteenth Century Pattern," in *From Sensibility to Romanticism: Essays Presented to Frederick A. Pottle*, ed. Frederick W. Hilles and Harold Bloom (Oxford: Oxford University Press, 1965), 191–204.

32. Fithian Journal, July 4, 1774, in *Journal and Letters of Philip Vickers Fithian*, ed. Farish, 131.

33. Fithian Journal, October 16, 12, 1773; December 26, 1773; January 16, 1774, in *Journal and Letters of Philip Vickers Fithian*, ed. Farish, 17, 16, 41, 55–56.

34. Fithian Journal, June 5, 1774 in *Journal and Letters of Philip Vickers Fithian*, ed. Farish, 114–15.

35. Fithian Journal, August 18, 1774, in *Journal and Letters of Philip Vickers Fithian*, ed. Farish, 171.

36. Svetlana Boym, *The Future of Nostalgia* (New York: Basic Books, 2002), 3–12; William Cullen, *A Synopsis of Methodical Nosology* (Philadelphia: Parry Hall, 1793), 153–54.

37. Boym, *Future of Nostalgia*, 8–11; Christopher Lasch, *The True and Only Heaven: Progress and Its Critics* (New York: W. W. Norton, 1991), 82–119.

38. Fithian Journal, May 25, 1774, in *Journal and Letters of Philip Vickers Fithian*, ed. Farish, 108.

39. Fithian Journal, October 18, 1774, in *Journal and Letters of Philip Vickers Fithian*, ed. Farish, 207; Philip Vickers Fithian to Elizabeth Beatty, December 21, 1773, ibid., 35–36; Fithian Journal, March 22, 1774; December 15, 1773, ibid., 84, 32.

40. Fithian Journal, July 8, 1774, in *Journal and Letters of Philip Vickers Fithian*, ed. Farish, 134.

41. Fithian Journal, July 4, 1774, in *Journal and Letters of Philip Vickers Fithian*, ed. Farish, 129. On Sterne, see Arthur Cash, *Laurence Sterne: The Later Years* (London: Methuen & Co., Ltd., 1986); Elizabeth Kraft, *Laurence Sterne Revisited* (New York: Twayne, 1996); and John Mullan, *Sentiment and Sociability: The Language of Feeling in the Eighteenth Century* (Oxford: Clarendon Press, 1988), 147–200.

42. Laurence Sterne, *Letters from Yorick to Eliza* (Philadelphia: John Dunlap, 1773). Philip Vickers Fithian to Elizabeth Beatty, August 31, 1773, in *Journal and Letters of Philip Vickers Fithian*, ed. Farish, 10. I have consulted the 1792 version of the *Letters:* Sterne, *Letters from Yorick to Eliza* (Burlington, N.J.: Isaac Neale, 1792).

43. See, for example, Philip Vickers Fithian to Elizabeth Beatty, September 10, 1773; December 21, 1773, in *Journal and Letters of Philip Vickers Fithian*, ed. Farish,

12–13, 35–36; Philip Vickers Fithian to Elizabeth Beatty, May 14, 1774; January 26, 1775, in Fithian Papers, vol. 7.

44. Sterne, *Letters from Yorick to Eliza* (1792), 57; Philip Vickers Fithian to Elizabeth Beatty, October 1, 1773, Fithian Papers, vol. 7.

45. Sterne, *Letters from Yorick to Eliza* (1792), 40; Philip Vickers Fithian to Elizabeth Beatty, May 12, 1774, Fithian Papers, vol. 7.

46. Sterne, *Letters from Yorick to Eliza* (1792), 35–36; Philip Vickers Fithian to Elizabeth Beatty, May 14, 1774, Fithian Papers, vol. 7. Fithian replaced Sterne's final phrase, "saw, read, or heard of," with the phrase "yet behold."

47. G. J. Barker-Benfield, *The Culture of Sensibility: Sex and Society in Eighteenth-Century Britain* (Chicago: University of Chicago Press, 1992). In the American context, see Andrew Burstein, *The Inner Jefferson: Portrait of a Grieving Optimist* (Charlottesville: University Press of Virginia, 1995), 3–28.

48. For an overview of this literature, see Barker-Benfield, *Culture of Sensibility*; Mullan, *Sentiment and Sociability*; R. F. Brissenden, *Virtue in Distress: Studies in the Novel of Sentiment from Richardson to Steele* (New York: Barnes & Noble, 1974); and Janet Todd, *Sensibility: An Introduction* (New York: Methuen & Co., 1986).

49. Mullan, *Sentiment and Sociability*, 13, 25, 192.

50. Ibid., 26–27, 56, 198–200; Barker-Benfield, *Culture of Sensibility*, 62–68, 105–19, 151 ("softened stoicism"); Andrew Burstein, *Sentimental Democracy: The Evolution of America's Romantic Self-Image* (New York: Hill and Wang, 1999, 11 ("moderated sensibility"); Martha Thomave Blauvelt, "The Work of the Heart: Emotion in the 1805–35 Diary of Sarah Connell Ayer," *Journal of Social History* 35 (2002). 579 ("tears not sobs").

51. On novel reading among eighteenth-century Reformed evangelicals, see Landsman, *From Colonials to Provincials*, 46–52, 133–34; *The Works of Laurence Sterne* (Philadelphia: James Humphreys, 1774), 3–14. William Smith, the provost of the College of Philadelphia, and Benjamin Rush, professor of chemistry, also subscribed.

52. Scott, *Annotated Edition of Lectures on Moral Philosophy by John Witherspoon*, 71.

53. Ibid., 133.

54. "Reflections on Marriage," *Pennsylvania Magazine* (September 1775): 409, 410, 411; (March 1776): 110.

55. Ibid. (March 1776): 110; (September 1775): 410, 412.

56. Fithian Journal, October 12, 1774, in *Journal and Letters of Philip Vickers Fithian*, ed. Farish, 203–4.

57. I am borrowing this metaphor, with slight variation, from Alfred Lubrano, *Limbo: Blue Collar Roots, White Collar Dreams* (Hoboken, N.J.: John Wiley & Sons, 2004).

Chapter 6

1. Fithian Journal, October 31, 1774; November 1–3, 1774, in *Philip Vickers Fithian: Journal, 1775–1776, Written on the Virginia-Pennsylvania Frontier and in the Army around New York*, ed. Robert Greenhalgh Albion and Leonidas Dodson (Princeton, N.J.: Princeton University Press, 1934), 245–46; Minutes of Philadelphia Presbytery, May 1774, August 1774, November 1774, Presbyterian Historical Society, Philadelphia.

2. Fithian Journal, December 6, 1774, in *Philip Vickers Fithian: Journal, 1775–1776*, ed. Albion and Dodson, 246–47.

3. Fithian Journal, June 3, 1766, Philip Vickers Fithian Journals and Common-place Books, 1766–76, General Manuscripts, CO1099, no. 349, vol. 1 (hereafter Fithian Papers).

4. Fithian Journal, January 24, 1774, in *Journal and Letters of Philip Vickers Fithian*, ed. Hunter Dickinson Farish (Williamsburg, Va.: Colonial Williamsburg, Inc., 1943; repr. Charlottesville: University Press of Virginia, 1968), 59; Philip Fithian to Samuel Fithian, June 8, 1774, ibid., 117; Fithian Journal, June 21, 1774; July 26, 1775, ibid., 122–23, 149.

5. J. G. A. Pocock, *The Machiavellian Moment: Florentine Political Thought and the Atlantic Republican Tradition* (Princeton, N.J.: Princeton University Press, 1975); Gordon S. Wood, *The Creation of the American Republic, 1776–1787* (Chapel Hill: University of North Carolina Press, 1967).

6. Jack Scott, ed., *An Annotated Edition of Lectures on Moral Philosophy by John Witherspoon* (Newark: University of Delaware Press, 1982), 141, 145.

7. Susan M. Purviance, "Intersubjectivity and Sociable Relations in the Philosophy of Francis Hutcheson," *Eighteenth-Century Life* 15 (February, May 1991): 24; Jack P. Greene, "The Concept of Virtue in Late Colonial British America," in *Imperatives, Behaviors, and Identities: Essays in Early American Cultural History*, ed. Jack P. Greene (Charlottesville: University Press of Virginia, 1992), 210–34, esp. 234; Mark A. Noll, *America's God: From Jonathan Edwards to Abraham Lincoln* (New York: Oxford University Press, 2002), 53–113.

8. On the convergence of the vocabularies of evangelicalism, republicanism, and the New Moral Philosophy, see Mark A. Noll, "The American Revolution and Protestant Evangelicalism," *Journal of Interdisciplinary History* 23 (winter 1993): 615–38; James T. Kloppenberg, "The Virtues of Liberalism: Christianity, Republicanism, and Ethics in Early American Political Discourse," *Journal of American History* 74 (June 1987): 9–33; Ruth Bloch, "The Gendered Meanings of Virtue in Revolutionary America," *Signs* 13 (autumn 1987): 37–57; and John M. Murrin, "Religion and Politics in America from the First Settlements to the Civil War," in *Religion and American Politics: From the Colonial Period to the 1980s*, ed. Mark A. Noll (New York: Oxford University Press, 1990), 19–43.

9. Fithian Journal, December 18, 1774; December 25, 1775, in *Philip Vickers Fithian: Journal, 1775–1776*, ed. Albion and Dodson, 247, 248.

10. Ibid., January 1, 8, 22, 1775, pp. 248, 249.

11. Ibid., March 14, 1775, p. 256.

12. Ibid., March 10, 1775, pp. 253–54 ("eight hours"); Peter O. Wacker, *Land and People: A Cultural Geography of Preindustrial New Jersey* (New Brunswick, N.J.: Rutgers University Press, 1975), 10–13, 90–91.

13. Carl M. Anderson, "Pastor Wrangel's Trip to the Shore," *New Jersey History* 87 (1969): 20–25; Fithian Journal, January 30, 1775, in *Philip Vickers Fithian: Journal, 1775–1776*, ed. Albion and Dodson, 249.

14. Fithian Journal, February 5, 12, 1775; March 12–13, 15, 1775; February 13, 26, 8, 25, 1775, in *Philip Vickers Fithian: Journal, 1775–1776*, ed. Albion and Dodson, 251, 252, 254–55, 257–58; Philip Vickers Fithian to Enoch Green, February 17, 1775, Fithian Papers, vol. 6.

15. Fithian Journal, October 18, 1774, in *Journal and Letters of Philip Vickers Fithian*, ed. Farish, 207.

16. Philip Vickers Fithian to Elizabeth Beatty, March 11, 1775, Fithian Papers, vol. 7.

17. Ibid.; Philip Vickers Fithian to Elizabeth Beatty, November 30, 1774, in *Journal and Letters of Philip Vickers Fithian*, ed. Farish, 210–11.

18. Philip Vickers Fithian to Elizabeth Beatty, November 30, 1774, in *Journal and Letters of Philip Vickers Fithian*, ed. Farish, 210–11.

19. Philip Vickers Fithian to Elizabeth Beatty, November 29, 1774, Fithian Papers, vol. 7.

20. Philip Vickers Fithian to Elizabeth Beatty, January 16, 1775, Fithian Papers, vol. 7.

21. Ibid.

22. Ibid.

23. Philip Vickers Fithian to Elizabeth Beatty, January 26, 1775, Fithian Papers, vol. 7; Fithian Journal, January 30, 1775, in *Philip Vickers Fithian: Journal, 1775–1776*, ed. Albion and Dodson, 249.

24. Philip Vickers Fithian to Elizabeth Beatty, February 2, 1775, Fithian Papers, vol. 7.

25. Anonymous to Philip Vickers Fithian, February 27, 1775, Fithian Papers, vol. 7.

26. Anonymous to Philip Vickers Fithian, March 1, 1775, Fithian Papers, vol. 7.

27. Anonymous to Philip Vickers Fithian, March 3, 1775, Fithian Papers, vol. 7.

28. Philip Vickers Fithian to Elizabeth Beatty, March 5, 1775, Fithian Papers, vol. 7.

29. Ibid.

30. Scott, *Annotated Edition of Lectures on Moral Philosophy by John Witherspoon*, 141–42, 145.

31. John Witherspoon, *The Dominion of Providence over the Passions of Men* (Philadelphia: R. Aitken, 1770), in *Political Sermons of the American Founding Era, 1730–1805*, ed. Ellis Sandoz (Indianapolis: Liberty Fund, 1990), 550, 549.

32. Witherspoon, *Dominion of Providence over the Passions of Men*, 535, 538, 539, 543, 544, 545–46. For an analysis of this sermon, see Richard B. Sher, "Witherspoon's *Dominion of Providence* and the Scottish Jeremiad Tradition," in *Scotland and America in the Age of the Enlightenment*, ed. Richard B. Sher and Jeffrey R. Smitten (Princeton, N.J.: Princeton University Press, 1990), 46–64.

33. Witherspoon, *Dominion of Providence over the Passions of Men*, 549, 551, 552.

34. Ibid., 553–54.

35. The classic statement on republican critiques of luxury remains Wood, *Creation of the American Republic*, 108–16.

36. Witherspoon, *Dominion of Providence over the Passions of Men*, 556.

37. "A Pastoral Letter & c., May 1775," in *Minutes of the Presbyterian Church in America, 1706–1788*, ed. Guy S. Klett (Philadelphia: Presbyterian Historical Society, 1976), 543–46, esp. 545 and 543.

38. Ibid.; Ann Fairfax Withington, *Toward a More Perfect Union: Virtue and the Formation of American Republics* (New York: Oxford University Press, 1991), 15–16.

39. Enoch Green Sermon to Bloomfield's Company, March 22, 1776, quoted in R. Craig Koedel, "Stories of Remembrance," in Enoch Green File, Box 9, Princeton University Archives, Mudd Manuscript Library, Princeton, N.J.

40. Philip Vickers Fithian, "An Exercise at the Public Commencement at Princeton College," September 10, 1772, Fithian Papers, vol. 2; John Trenchard and Thomas Gordon, *Cato's Letters* (1755; 2 vols., Cambridge, Mass.: Da Capo Press, 1971), 1:260–61; James H. Huston, "The Origins of the 'Paranoid Style' in American Politics: Public Jealousy from the Age of Walpole to the Age of Jackson," in *Saints and Revolutionaries: Essays in Early American History*, ed. David D. Hall, John Murrin, and Thad W. Tate (New York: W. W. Norton, 1984), 334–72.

41. Fithian Journal, December 18, 1775, in *Philip Vickers Fithian: Journal, 1775–1776,* ed. Albion and Dodson, 247.

42. T. H. Breen, *The Marketplace of Revolution: How Consumer Politics Shaped American Independence* (New York: Oxford University Press, 2004), 300. Much of the following paragraph relies heavily on Breen, especially 294–331.

43. Charles Clinton Beatty to "Laura" Beatty, April 6, 1775, Beatty Family Collections, General Manuscripts, Princeton University Libraries, Princeton, N.J.; Breen, *Marketplace of Revolution,* 304.

44. Breen, *Marketplace of Revolution,* 302, 325–26.

45. Ibid., 306.

46. Philip Vickers Fithian to Elizabeth Beatty, January 16, 1775, Fithian Papers, vol. 7.

47. Reading Beatty to Enoch Green, December 10, 1775, Enoch Green File, Box 9, Princeton University Archives, Mudd Manuscript Library, Princeton, N.J.

48. Witherspoon, *Dominion of Providence over the Passions of Men,* 557.

49. Ibid.

50. Fithian Journal, December 18, 22, 1775, in *Philip Vickers Fithian: Journal, 1775–1776,* ed. Albion and Dodson, 247; Thomas Cushing and Charles E. Sheppard, *History of the Counties of Gloucester, Salem, and Cumberland New Jersey* (Philadelphia: Everts & Peck, 1883), 536; Larry Gerlach, *Prologue to Independence: New Jersey in the Coming of the American Revolution* (New Brunswick, N.J.: Rutgers University Press, 1076), 232, 458n16; *New Jersey Archives* 10 (1917): 530–31; Richard A. Harrison, *Princetonians, 1769–1775: A Biographical Dictionary* (Princeton, N.J.: Princeton University Press, 1980), 395.

51. Fithian Journal, December 23, 1775, in *Philip Vickers Fithian: Journal, 1775–1776,* ed. Albion and Dodson, 248.

52. Gerlach, *Prologue to Independence,* 200, 445n118, 445n123. The traditional list of tea burners included Ebenezer Elmer, Timothy Elmer, James Ewing, Thomas Ewing, Joel Fithian, Philip Vickers Fithian, Alexander Moore Jr., Ephraim Newcomb, Silas Newcomb, Clarence Parvin, Stephen Pierson, Lewis Howell, Richard Howell, James B. Hunt, John Hunt, Andrew Hunter Jr., Joel Miller, Henry Seeley, Josiah Seeley, Abraham Sheppard, Silas Whitakar, David Pierson, and Henry Stacks. Abraham Sheppard was the only non-Presbyterian in the group; he was a Quaker. For brief biographical sketches of the participants, see John Fea, "Rural Religion: Protestant Community and the Moral Improvement of the South Jersey Countryside, 1676–1800" (Ph.D. diss., State University of New York at Stony Brook, 1999), 452–57.

53. Fithian Journal, December 23, 1774, in *Philip Vickers Fithian: Journal, 1775–1776,* ed. Albion and Dodson, 248.

54. Cushing and Sheppard, *History of the Counties of Gloucester, Salem, and Cumberland,* 536.

55. Gerlach, *Prologue to Independence,* 198–202.

56. Robert Gibbon Johnson, *An Historical Account of the First Settlement of Salem in West Jersey* (Philadelphia: Orrin Rogers, 1839), 124; Cushing and Sheppard, *History of the Counties of Gloucester, Salem, and Cumberland,* 537; Fithian Journal, October 22, 1774, in *Journal and Letters of Philip Vickers Fithian,* ed. Farish, 209.

57. Breen, *Marketplace of Revolution,* 302–9.

58. "Journal of Ephraim Bateman," March 12, 1801, *Vineland Historical Magazine* 14 (April 1929): 127.

59. Committee for the County of Cumberland to the Honourable Delegates of the Thirteen United Colonies in General Congress Assembled, September 30,

1775, in *American Archives,* 4th ser., ed. Peter Force, 9 vols. (Washington, D.C.: By the author and M. St. Clair, 1837–53), 3:849–50.

60. "Muster Roll of the Minutemen of Pittsgrove," September 20, 1775, Revolutionary War File, Salem County Historical Society, Salem, N.J.; "Records of the Presbyterian Congregation in Pittsgrove," Presbyterian Historical Society, Philadelphia; Pittsgrove Presbyterian Church, "Subscription Lists, Receipts, and Correspondence, 1766–1792," Presbyterian Historical Society, Philadelphia.

61. Minutes of the Cumberland County Committee, March 6, 1775; May 11, 1775, in *American Archives,* ed. Force, 2:34–35.

62. "Journal of Ebenezer Elmer," July 21, 22, 1775, in Cushing and Sheppard, *History of the Counties of Gloucester, Salem, and Cumberland,* 539.

63. Gerlach, *Prologue to Independence,* 275; "Journal of Ebenezer Elmer," July 21, 22, 26, 1775, in Cushing and Sheppard, *History of the Counties of Gloucester, Salem, and Cumberland,* 539.

64. Fithian Journal, November 13, 1775, in *Philip Vickers Fithian: Journal, 1775–1776,* ed. Albion and Dodson, 131.

65. "Journal of Ebenezer Elmer," in Cushing and Sheppard, *History of the Counties of Gloucester, Salem, and Cumberland,* 538–39.

66. Enoch Green, "Upon His Appointment as Chaplain of the New Jersey Militia," manuscript sermon, 1776, Firestone Library, Dept. of Rare Books and Special Collections, Princeton University, Princeton, N.J.; Enoch Green, manuscript sermon, Titus 2:14, Presbyterian Historical Society, Philadelphia. For the blending of theological and political concepts in revolutionary-era sermon literature, see Harry S. Stout, *The New England Soul: Preaching and Religious Culture in Colonial New England* (New York: Oxford University Press, 1986); and Nathan O. Hatch, *The Sacred Cause of Liberty: Republican Thought and the Millennium in Revolutionary New England* (New Haven, Conn.: Yale University Press, 1977).

67. "To the Public," *Plain Dealer,* Introduction, December 21, 1775, Rutgers University Library Special Collections, New Brunswick, N.J. The entire manuscript was reprinted in *The Plain Dealer,* ed. William Nelson (privately printed, 1894).

68. Ibid. We know the identity of at least one of the authors. Ebenezer Elmer noted in his 1776 journal that he "wrote a piece for the plain Dealer." See Journal of Ebenezer Elmer, "Die Venins 19th mo," Box 1, Folder 4, Ebenezer Elmer Papers, New Jersey Historical Society, Newark. The anonymity of the authors and the revolutionary impulse of many of the entries placed the *Plain Dealer* squarely within the "public sphere"—a site, as described by Jurgen Habermas, where large portions of the citizenry could express their opinions on political matters and criticize established and ruling authorities. See Jurgen Habermas, *The Structural Transformation of the Public Sphere: An Inquiry into a Category of Bourgeois Society,* trans. Thomas Burger (Cambridge, Mass.: MIT Press, 1991).

69. Philip Vickers Fithian to Elizabeth Beatty, March 5, 1775, Fithian Papers, vol. 7; Fithian Journal, November 13, 1775, in *Philip Vickers Fithian: Journal, 1775–1776,* ed. Albion and Dodson, 133. During the height of the revolutionary activity in the wake of the Greenwich tea party, Philip told Laura that he would be going that evening to Bridge-Town, where he was eager to hear "Mr. Leeks [Leake's] Declamation from which I find there are high Expectations with several of the Members."

70. The secretaries encouraged "several persons whose genius & inclination for many years past have led them to Study and contemplation" to submit essays to the newsletter. See "To the Public," *Plain Dealer* 1, December 25, 1775.

71. *Plain Dealer* 1, December 25, 1775.

72. Ibid.

73. *Plain Dealer* 2, January 1776.

74. "To Capt. Bloomfield's Company of Continental Forces Delivered the Evening Before They March'd," *Plain Dealer*, March 26, 1776.

75. *Plain Dealer* 7, February 5, 1776.

76. Richard Godbeer, *Sexual Revolution in Early America* (Baltimore: Johns Hopkins University Press, 2002), 46–55; Laurel Thatcher Ulrich, *Good Wives: Image and Reality in the Lives of Women in Northern New England, 1650–1750* (New York: Vintage Books, 1980), 122–23; Daniel Scott Smith and Michael S. Hindus, "Premarital Pregnancy in America, 1640–1971: An Overview and Interpretation," *Journal of Interdisciplinary History* 5 (spring 1975): 537–70; Ellen Rothman, *Hands and Hearts: A History of Courtship in America* (Cambridge, Mass.: Harvard University Press, 1984), 46–49. See also Henry Stiles, *Bundling: Its Origins, Progress, and Decline in America* (1871; New York: Book Collectors Association Inc., 1934).

77. *Plain Dealer* 4, January 15, 1776.

78. Ibid.

79. On the links between immoral social and cultural practices and colonial resistance to British "slavery," see Withington, *Toward a More Perfect Union.*

Chapter 7

1. Fithian Journal, May 9, 1775, in *Philip Vickers Fithian: Journal, 1775–1776, Written on the Virginia-Pennsylvania Frontier and in the Army around New York,* ed. Robert Greenhalgh Albion and Leonidas Dodson (Princeton, N.J.: Princeton University Press, 1934), 1. Fithian personalized this passage from Ovid's *Metamorphoses* by changing the subject from third-person singular (*gaudebat*) to the first-person singular (*gaudebam*). I am thankful to Joseph Huffman for his help in deciphering Philip's Latin.

2. Genesis 17:7–8; Luke 18:29.

3. Fithian Journal, January 25, 1776; May 9, 1775, in *Philip Vickers Fithian: Journal, 1775–1776,* ed. Albion and Dodson, 174, 1.

4. For a recent examination of the migration of Ulster Scots to America and their settlement of the Virginia and Pennsylvania backcountry, see Patrick Griffin, *The People with No Name: Ireland's Ulster Scots, America's Scots-Irish, and the Creation of British Atlantic World, 1689–1764* (Princeton, N.J.: Princeton University Press, 2001), 157–73.

5. Fithian Journal, May 9, 1775, in *Philip Vickers Fithian: Journal, 1775–1776,* ed. Albion and Dodson, 1; Minutes of the Philadelphia Presbytery, April 4, 1775, Presbyterian Historical Society, Philadelphia; Minutes of the Philadelphia Synod, May 23, 1775, in *Minutes of the Presbyterian Church in America, 1706–1788,* ed. Guy S. Klett (Philadelphia: Presbyterian Historical Society, 1976), 548.

6. Fithian Journal, May 9, 1775, in *Philip Vickers Fithian: Journal, 1775–1776,* ed. Albion and Dodson, 1. On the backcountry in eighteenth-century America, see Eric Hinderaker and Peter C. Mancall, *At the Edge of Empire: The Backcountry in British North America* (Baltimore: Johns Hopkins University Press, 2003), esp. 153, 171–72.

7. Mark A. Noll, *Princeton and the Republic, 1768–1822* (Princeton, N.J.: Princeton University Press, 1989), 3.

8. Fithian Journal, May 9–15, 1775, in *Philip Vickers Fithian: Journal, 1775–1776,* ed. Albion and Dodson, 2–7, esp. 6.

9. Ibid., May 16–17, 1775, pp. 7–8; Robert Mitchell, *Commercialism and Commerce: Perspectives on the Early Shenandoah Valley* (Charlottesville: University Press of Virginia, 1977), 149.

10. Fithian Journal, May 17–19, 1775, in *Philip Vickers Fithian: Journal, 1775–1776*, ed. Albion and Dodson, 8–10.

11. Ibid., May 23, 25, 1775; June 7, 10, 14, 1775, pp. 14, 15, 25, 26, 29.

12. Warren R. Hofstra, "Land, Ethnicity, and Community at the Opequon Settlement, Virginia, 1730–1800," in *Ulster and North America: Transatlantic Perspectives on the Scotch-Irish*, ed. H. Tyler Blethen and Curtis W. Wood (Tuscaloosa: University of Alabama Press, 1997), 167–71. On the Presbyterian churches of the Shenandoah Valley, see Freeman H. Hart, *The Valley of Virginia in the American Revolution, 1763–1789* (Chapel Hill: University of North Carolina Press, 1942), 34–35.

13. Dorsey D. Ellis, *Look unto the Rock: A History of the Presbyterian Church, U.S. in West Virginia, 1719–1974* (Parsons, W.Va.: McClain Publishing Company, 1982), 10.

14. Fithian Journal, May 28–29, 1775, in *Philip Vickers Fithian: Journal 1775–1776*, ed. Albion and Dodson, 17.

15. Ibid., June 11, 1775, p. 26. The tension between Hoge and the Opequon congregation may have had something to do with Hoge's long-standing disputes over his salary. See Richard Webster, *A History of the Presbyterian Church in America* (Philadelphia: Joseph M. Wilson, 1857), 663.

16. Fithian Journal, June 11, 1775, in *Philip Vickers Fithian: Journal, 1775–1776*, ed. Albion and Dodson, 26.

17. Fithian Journal, June 12, 14, 11, 1775, in *Philip Vickers Fithian: Journal, 1775–1776*, ed. Albion and Dodson, 29, 30, 27.

18. Ibid., June 20–22, 1775, pp. 32–35.

19. Ibid., June 22–26, 1775, pp. 34–38.

20. Ibid., June 27–July 5, 1775, pp. 38–49, esp. 39, 45, 49; J. Hector St. John de Crèvecoeur, *Letters from an American Farmer*, ed. Albert E. Stone (New York: Penguin Books, 1981), 372.

21. Fithian Journal, June 27, 1775, to July 26, 1775; July 26, 1775, in *Philip Vickers Fithian: Journal, 1775–1776*, ed. Albion and Dodson, 38–72; Crevecoeur, *Letters from an American Farmer*, 371. On the upper Susquehanna River Valley during the time of Philip's visit, see Peter C. Mancall, *Valley of Opportunity: Economic Culture along the Upper Susquehanna, 1700–1800* (Ithaca, N.Y.: Cornell University Press, 1991), esp. 36–37, 95–96, 113–14, 126–29.

22. Fithian Journal, July 28, 7, 9, 10, 11, 16, 30, 1775 in *Philip Vickers Fithian: Journal, 1775–1776*, ed. Albion and Dodson, 77, 51, 52, 53, 54, 59, 80–81.

23. Ibid., July 20, 1775, p. 64.

24. Ibid., July 20, 21, 1775, pp. 65–66. The reference to "Yankees" referred to the land dispute between Connecticut and Pennsylvania over this territory. Settlers from the Connecticut-based Susquehanna Land Company had been in this region since the late 1760s.

25. Fithian Journal, August 8, 22, 1775, in *Philip Vickers Fithian: Journal, 1775–1776*, ed. Albion and Dodson, 92, 115.

26. Crèvecoeur, *Letters from an American Farmer*, 372.

27. Fithian Journal, July 17, 25, 26, 1775; August 1, 1775; July 31, 1775; August 2, 1775, in *Philip Vickers Fithian: Journal, 1775–1776*, ed. Albion and Dodson, 61, 70, 71, 82, 84, 83, 86. On the Indian population in the upper Susquehanna Valley, see Mancall, *Valley of Opportunity*, 72–78. Philip was crossing the boundary

of the "New Purchase" territory established by the Treaty of Fort Stanwix in 1768.

28. *Philip Vickers Fithian: Journal, 1775–1776, ed. Albion and Dodson* , "Introduction," xvi; July 31, 27, 1775, 82, 72.

29. Fithian Journal, August 10, 21, 23, 14, 7, 1775, in *Philip Vickers Fithian: Journal, 1775–1776,* ed. Albion and Dodson, 95, 110, 117, 101–2, 90.

30. Ibid., July 22, 25, 1775; August 6, 1775; July 24, 1775; August 10, 1775; July 27, 1775, pp. 67, 69, 89, 68, 95, 72. On bodily privacy as a sign of refinement, see C. Dallett Hemphill, *Bowing to Necessities: A History of Manners in America, 1620–1860* (New York: Oxford University Press, 1999), 143–44.

31. Fithian Journal, August 3, 4, 1775, in *Philip Vickers Fithian: Journal, 1775–1776,* ed. Albion and Dodson, 86, 87.

32. Ibid., August 4, 3, 1775; July 28, 1775, pp. 87, 88, 86, 76.

33. Ibid., August 25, 1775, pp. 118–19.

34. Ibid., May 21, 1775; January 3, 1776; August 28, 1775; November 20, 1775, pp. 12, 13, 159, 122, 134.

35. Ibid., July 9, 1775; August 11, 1775, pp. 53, 97–98.

36. Ibid., August 9, 26, 1775; December 17, 1775, pp. 93, 120, 143.

37. Ibid., May 9, 1775, p. 3.

38. Ibid., May 15, 1775; June 29, 1775; July 18, 28, 12, 1775, pp. 6, 7, 40, 61, 77, 58.

39. Ibid., July 29, 1775, pp. 78–79.

40. Ibid., p. 79.

41. Ibid., July 17, 1775; August 11, 1775, pp. 60–61, 98.

42. Vincent S. McCluskey, "The Life and Times of Philip Vickers Fithian" (Ph.D. diss., New York University, 1991), 272.

43. Philip Vickers Fithian to Elizabeth Fithian, November 9, 1775, in *Philip Vickers Fithian: Letters to His Wife,* ed. Frank D. Andrews (Vineland, N.J.: Smith Printing House, 1932), 14.

44. Fithian Journal, November 18, 20, 1775, in *Philip Vickers Fithian: Journal, 1775–1776,* ed. Albion and Dodson, 133, 134.

45. Ibid., November 20, 1775, p. 134.

46. Ibid., December 10, 1775, p. 139; Mitchell, *Commercialism and Frontier,* 34, 151; Hart, *Valley of Virginia in the American Revolution,* 35.

47. Fithian Journal, December 7–10, 1775, in *Philip Vickers Fithian: Journal, 1775–1776,* ed. Albion and Dodson, 138–39.

48. Ibid., November 28, 1775, p. 135; Philip Vickers Fithian to Elizabeth Beatty, December 2, 1775, in *Philip Vickers Fithian: Letters to His Wife,* ed. Andrews, 15–16.

49. They were, in addition to Philip, John McKnight (1773), Andrew Hunter (1772), William Linn (1772), James McConnell (1773), Samuel McCorkle (1772), Robert Archibald (1772), and William Graham (1773). See *Philip Vickers Fithian: Journal, 1775–1776,* ed. Albion and Dodson, December 10, 1775, p. 139. See also Richard Harrison, *The Princetonians: A Biographical Dictionary, 1769–1775* (Princeton, N.J.: Princeton University Press, 1980).

50. Philip Vickers Fithian: Journal, 1775–1776, ed. Albion and Dodson, December 10, 8, 12, 23, 1775, pp. 139, 138, 141, 148–49.

51. Fithian Journal, January 28, 1776; May 26, 1775, in *Philip Vickers Fithian: Journal, 1775–1776,* ed. Albion and Dodson, 176, 16.

52. Ibid., June 7, 1775, p. 25.

53. Ibid., June 4, 1775, p. 22.

54. Ibid., January 23, 1776; December 30, 1775, pp. 172, 155.

55. Ibid., December 20, 1775, p. 145; Mitchell, *Commercialism and Frontier*, 39, 135.

56. Mitchell, *Commercialism and Frontier*, 21n11.

57. Fithian Journal, December 23, 31, 1775, in *Philip Vickers Fithian: Journal, 1775–1776*, ed. Albion and Dodson, 147, 150.

58. Hart, *Valley of Virginia in the American Revolution*, 21.

59. Fithian Journal, January 8, 9, 15, 1776, in *Philip Vickers Fithian: Journal, 1775–1776*, ed. Albion and Dodson, 161, 163–64, 166.

60. Ibid., January 16, 1776, pp. 167–69; Pamela H. Simpson, *So Beautiful an Arch: Images of the Natural Bridge, 1787–1890* (Lexington, Va.: Washington & Lee University, 1982), 3–4.

61. Fithian Journal, January 18, 24, 1776; December 23, 1775, in *Philip Vickers Fithian: Journal, 1775–1776*, ed. Albion and Dodson, 169–70, 173, 148.

62. Arthur D. Pierce, *Smugglers Woods: Jaunts and Journeys in Colonial and Revolutionary New Jersey* (New Brunswick, N.J.: Rutgers University Press, 1960), 163–64.

63. Minutes of the Philadelphia Presbytery, May 1776, Presbyterian Historical Society, Philadelphia.

Chapter 8

1. Fithian Journal, November 13, 1775, in *Philip Vickers Fithian: Journal, 1775–1776, Written on the Virginia-Pennsylvania Frontier and in the Army around New York*, ed. Robert Greenhalgh Albion and Leonidas Dodson (Princeton, N.J.: Princeton University Press, 1934), 130–31.

2. Thomas Paine, *Common Sense* (New York: Penguin, 1986), 63.

3. See Chapter 6. See also Karen O'Brien, *Narratives of the Enlightenment: Cosmopolitan History from Voltaire to Gibbon* (repr., New York: Cambridge University Press, 1997), 123–25.

4. Fithian Journal, May 11, 17, 1775; June 6, 17, 14, 1775, in *Philip Vickers Fithian: Journal, 1775–1776*, ed. Albion and Dodson, 4, 8, 24, 31, 29. See also ibid., June 14, 17, 28, 1775; July 4, 1775; November 13, 1775, pp. 29, 31, 40, 49, 132.

5. *Journal and Letters of Philip Vickers Fithian: A Plantation Tutor of the Old Dominion, 1773–1774*, ed. Hunter Dickinson Farish (Williamsburg, Va.: Colonial Williamsburg Inc., 1943; repr. Charlottesville: University Press of Virginia, 1968).

6. Fithian Journal, August 24, 1775; December 24, 1775; August 23, 1775, in *Philip Vickers Fithian: Journal, 1775–1776*, ed. Albion and Dodson, 117, 149, 117.

7. O'Brien, *Narratives of the Enlightenment*, 93–166, 204–33; Ned C. Landsman, *From Colonials to Provincials: American Thought and Culture, 1680–1760* (New York: Twayne, 1997), 55–56; Herbert Butterfield, *The Whig Interpretation of History* (London: G. Bell and Sons, 1959). See also Peter C. Messer, *Stories of Independence: Identity, Ideology, and History in Eighteenth-Century America* (DeKalb: Northern Illinois University Press, 2005). In the early nineteenth century the Whig interpretation was particularly associated with the works of the historian George Bancroft. See George Bancroft, *The History of the United States from the Discovery of the Continent*, 10 vols. (Boston: Little, Brown and Company, 1834–75). For a discussion of Bancroft that downplays the tension between his historicism and his providentialism, see Jonathan Tucker Boyd, "Holy Hieroglyph: Providence and

Historical Consciousness in George Bancroft's Historiography" (Ph.D. diss., Johns Hopkins University, 1999).

8. Fithian Journal, May 19, 1775, in *Philip Vickers Fithian: Journal, 1775–1776*, ed. Albion and Dodson, 11; Robert Mitchell, "The Settlement of the Shenandoah Valley, 1790–1860: Pattern, Process, and Structure," in *After the Backcountry: Rural Life in the Great Valley of Virginia, 1800–1900*, ed. Kenneth E. Koons and Warren R. Hofstra (Knoxville: University of Tennessee Press, 2000), 37–38.

9. This position was advocated by revolutionaries from Thomas Paine to John Witherspoon. See Paine, *Common Sense*; Ned C. Landsman, "Witherspoon and the Problem of Provincial Identity in Scottish Evangelical Culture," in *Scotland and America in the Age of the Enlightenment*, ed. Richard B. Sher and Jeffrey R. Smitten (Princeton, N.J.: Princeton University Press, 1990), 40–42.

10. Fithian Journal, July 1, 1775; January 19, 1776; June 1, 1775, in *Philip Vickers Fithian: Journal, 1775–1776*, ed. Albion and Dodson, 45, 175, 20.

11. Philip Fithian, Notes on Lectures on History, Nassau Hall, December 10, 1771–January 9, 1772, in Philip Vickers Fithian Journals and Commonplace Books, 1766–76, General Manuscripts, CO1099, no. 349, vol. 3, Princeton University Libraries, Princeton, N.J.

12. O'Brien, *Narratives of the Enlightenment*, 123–25; James Turner, *Without God, Without Creed: The Origins of Unbelief in America* (Baltimore: Johns Hopkins University Press, 1995), 17, 40–42, 70.

13. Fithian Journal, June 17, 1775; January 1, 1776, in *Philip Vickers Fithian: Journal, 1775–1776*, ed. Albion and Dodson, 131, 132, 158.

14. Ibid., November 13, 1775; January 8, 1776, pp. 130, 163.

15. Ibid., June 3, 28, 1775; November 13, 1775, pp. 21, 40, 131.

16. Ibid., July 1, 1775, pp. 44–45. This episode is also recounted in Charles Royster, *A Revolutionary People at War: The Continental Army and American Character, 1775–1783* (Chapel Hill: University of North Carolina Press, 1979), 89–90.

17. Fithian Journal, August 9, 23, 1775, in *Philip Vickers Fithian: Journal, 1775–1776*, ed. Albion and Dodson, 93, 117.

18. Larry Gerlach, *Prologue to Independence: New Jersey in the Coming of the American Revolution* (New Brunswick, N.J.: Rutgers University Press, 1976), 327–58.

19. Mark E. Lender and James Kirby Martin, eds., *Citizen Soldier: The Revolutionary War Journal of Joseph Bloomfield* (Newark: New Jersey Historical Society, 1982), 6–7.

20. Ibid., 35–38; Thomas Cushing and Charles Sheppard, *History of the Counties of Gloucester, Salem, and Cumberland, New Jersey* (Philadelphia: Everts & Peck, 1883), 36–37. Seeley would eventually be replaced as first lieutenant by Constant Peck.

21. William S. Stryker, *Official Register of the Officers and Men of New Jersey in the Revolutionary War* (Trenton, N.J.: William T. Nicholson & Co., 1872), 334; Robert K. Wright, *The Continental Army* (Washington, D.C.: Center for Military History, United States Army, 1983), 76–78, 82.

22. Military Dispatch from Norfolk, Virginia, July 9, 1776, in *American Archives*, ser. 5, vol. 1, ed. Peter Force, p. 225 "Newcomb's Regiment on Foot," Sept. 19, 1776, microfilm no. 246, Revolutionary War Rolls, 1775–83, Roll 64, New Jersey Jacket numbers 62 through 91–92 (Washington, D.C.: National Archives and Records Administration, 1957).

23. Roll of Communicants, Fairfield Presbyterian Church, Presbyterian Historical Society, Philadelphia; Kenn Stryker-Rodda, "New Jersey Tax Ratables,

1773–1774," *Genealogical Magazine of New Jersey* 38 (1963): 64. On Revolutionary War chaplains, see Royster, *Revolutionary People at War*, 161–74.

24. Stryker, *Official Register*, 335–36, 397, 403; Cushing and Sheppard, *History of the Counties of Gloucester, Salem, and Cumberland*, 616. Kelsey was the son of Robert Kelsey, minister of the Cohansey Baptist church.

25. David Hackett Fischer, *Washington's Crossing* (New York: Oxford University Press, 2004), 11, 82–83; Barnet Schechter, *The Battle for New York: The City at the Heart of the American Revolution* (New York: Walker Publishing Company, 2002), 85, 88, 90–91.

26. Schechter, *Battle for New York*, 97, 99, 4, 102–3; Fischer, *Washington's Crossing*, 31–32, 29.

27. Will of Philip Vickers Fithian, July 2, 1776, no. 609, Cumberland County Wills, New Jersey Archives, Trenton (microfilm reel 315).

28. *Pennsylvania Journal*, August 28, 1776.

29. Ibid.

30. Philip Vickers Fithian to Elizabeth Fithian, July 10, 1776, in *Philip Vickers Fithian Letters to His Wife Elizabeth Beatty Fithian*, ed. Frank D. Andrews (Vineland, N.J.: Smith Printing House, 1932), 17–18.

31. Fithian Journal, July 12, 1776, in *Philip Vickers Fithian: Journal, 1775–1776*, ed. Albion and Dodson, 185–86; Schechter, *Battle for New York*, 104–6; Fischer, *Washington's Crossing*, 83.

32. Fithian Journal, July 12, 1776, in *Philip Vickers Fithian: Journal, 1775–1776*, ed. Albion and Dodson, 186–88.

33. Ibid., July 13, 1776, p. 187; Philip Fithian to Elizabeth Fithian, July 10, 1776, in *Philip Vickers Fithian Letters*, ed. Andrews, 19; Schechter, *Battle for New York*, 90.

34. Fithian Journal, July 13, 1776, in *Philip Vickers Fithian: Journal, 1775–1776*, ed. Albion and Dodson, 187; Philip Fithian to Elizabeth Fithian, July 19, 1776, in *Philip Vickers Fithian Letters*, ed. Andrews, 18.

35. Philip Fithian to Elizabeth Fithian, August 12, 1776, in *Philip Vickers Fithian Letters*, ed. Andrews, 27–28.

36. Fithian Journal, July 24, 1776; August 11, 1776, in *Philip Vickers Fithian: Journal, 1775–1776*, ed. Albion and Dodson, 194, 205–6. See also ibid., August 25, 1776, p. 218. On swearing in the camps, see Royster, *Revolutionary People at War*, 76–77.

37. Fithian Journal, July 15, 18, 19, 20, 24, 25, 26, 28, 29, 1776; August 5, 6, 8, 21, 24, 1776; September 1, 12, 18, 20, 21, 1776, in *Philip Vickers Fithian: Journal, 1775–1776*, ed. Albion and Dodson, 189, 190, 191, 194–97, 199, 204–6, 214, 217, 223, 229, 237, 239–41. On Princetonians in the American Revolution, see Richard A. Harrison, *Princetonians, 1769–1775: A Biographical Dictionary* (Princeton, N.J.: Princeton University Press, 1980), xxxi.

38. Fithian Journal, July 16, 20, 1776, in *Philip Vickers Fithian: Journal, 1775–1776*, ed. Albion and Dodson, 189, 191; Philip Fithian to Elizabeth Fithian, July 19, 1776, in *Philip Vickers Fithian Letters*, ed. Andrews, 18–20.

39. Fithian Journal, July 19, 22, 23, 26 1776, in *Philip Vickers Fithian: Journal, 1775–1776*, ed. Albion and Dodson, 190, 192–93, 196–97; Fischer, *Washington's Crossing*, 87–89.

40. Fithian Journal, August 1, 1776, in *Philip Vickers Fithian: Journal, 1775–1776*, ed. Albion and Dodson, 202; Andrew Hunter Diary, July 31, 1776, General Manuscripts, CO199, Series H, Box 537, Princeton University Library, Princeton, N.J. (hereafter Hunter Diary); Philip Fithian to Betsy Fithian, July 29, 1776, in *Philip Vickers Fithian Letters*, ed. Andrews, 21–23.

41. Philip Fithian to Betsy Fithian, August 6, 1776, in *Philip Vickers Fithian Letters*, ed. Andrews, 25–27.

42. Fithian Journal, July 29, 1776; August 3, 6, 1776, in *Philip Vickers Fithian: Journal, 1775–1776*, ed. Albion and Dodson, 99, 204, 205.

43. Philip Fithian to Elizabeth Fithian, August 12, 1776, in *Philip Vickers Fithian Letters*, ed. Andrews, 27.

44. Fithian Journal, August 7, 9, 10, 1776, in *Philip Vickers Fithian: Journal, 1775–1776*, ed. Albion and Dodson, 206, 207.

45. Ibid., August 13, 14, 1776, p. 209; Hunter Diary, August 13, 1776. According to Barnet Schechter, *Battle for New York*, 114, the British fleet had reached full strength on August 13. It included twenty-four thousand soldiers, four hundred transport ships and smaller land craft, thirty warships, and ten thousand sailors.

46. Fithian Journal, August 15, 1776, in *Philip Vickers Fithian: Journal, 1775–1776* ed. Albion and Dodson, 209–10; Fischer, *Washington's Crossing*, 189; Schechter, *Battle for New York*, 121.

47. Andrew Hunter Jr. notes that the landlady was "Mrs. Seaburn." See Hunter Diary, August 16, 1776.

48. Fithian Journal, August 16, 1776, in *Philip Vickers Fithian: Journal, 1775–1776*, ed. Albion and Dodson, 210.

49. Ibid., August 17, 1776, pp. 211–12; Philip Fithian to Elizabeth Fithian, August 18, 1776, in *Philip Vickers Fithian Letters*, ed. Andrews, 28–29; Schechter, *Battle for New York*, 115–16, 123.

50. Fithian Journal, August 20–22, 1776, in *Philip Vickers Fithian: Journal, 1775–1776*, ed. Albion and Dodson, 213–16; Philip Fithian to Elizabeth Fithian, August 26, 1776, in *Philip Vickers Fithian Letters*, ed. Andrews, 33–36; Hunter Diary, August 21, 1776; Schechter, *Battle for New York*, 121, 126–29; Fischer, *Washington's Crossing*, 89–92.

51. Fithian Journal, August 23–24, 1776, in *Philip Vickers Fithian: Journal, 1775–1776*, ed. Albion and Dodson, 216–17; Fischer, *Washington's Crossing*, 90–94.

52. Fithian Journal, August 25, 1776, in *Philip Vickers Fithian: Journal, 1775–1776*, ed. Albion and Dodson, 218; Fischer, *Washington's Crossing*, 93; Schechter, *Battle for New York*, 130–32. Hunter described it as a "Lamentable Day" (Hunter Diary, August 27, 1776).

53. Fithian Journal, August 26, 1776, in *Philip Vickers Fithian: Journal, 1775–1776*, ed. Albion and Dodson, 218; Philip Fithian to Elizabeth Fithian, August 26, 1776, in *Philip Vickers Fithian Letters*, ed. Andrews, 33–36; Schechter, *Battle for New York*, 132–38.

54. Fithian Journal, August 27, 1776, in *Philip Vickers Fithian: Journal, 1775–1776*, ed. Albion and Dodson, 218–19; Fischer, *Washington's Crossing*, 95–99; Schechter, *Battle for New York*, 139–54.

55. Fithian Journal, August 28, 29, 1776, in *Philip Vickers Fithian: Journal, 1775–1776*, ed. Albion and Dodson, 220; Fischer, *Washington's Crossing*, 99–100; Schechter, *Battle for New York*, 156–58.

56. Fithian Journal, August 29, 30, 1776, in *Philip Vickers Fithian: Journal, 1775–1776*, ed. Albion and Dodson, 220–21.

57. Fischer, *Washington's Crossing*, 99–100; Schechter, *Battle for New York*, 158–63; Fithian Journal, August 30, 31, 1776, in *Philip Vickers Fithian: Journal, 1775–1776*, ed. Albion and Dodson, 221–22; Philip Fithian to Elizabeth Fithian, September 1, 1776, in *Philip Vickers Fithian Letters*, ed. Andrews, 37–39. Philip did not discuss the fortunate change in weather at Long Island in providential

terms—an interpretation of the events of August 27, 1776, that was common among later providential historians and some of the religious soldiers.

58. Fithian Journal, September 1–3, 1776, in *Philip Vickers Fithian: Journal, 1775–1776*, ed. Albion and Dodson, 223–24; Schechter, *Battle for New York*, 171.

59. Philip Fithian to Elizabeth Fithian, September 1, 3, 1776, in *Philip Vickers Fithian Letters*, ed. Andrews, 38, 41.

60. Ibid., 37–42.

61. Ibid.

62. Fithian Diary, September 4–9, 1776, in *Philip Vickers Fithian: Journal, 1775–1776*, ed. Albion and Dodson, 225–28.

63. Schechter, *Battle for New York*, 171–77; Fischer, *Washington's Crossing*, 101–2; Fithian Journal, September 10–13, 1776, in *Philip Vickers Fithian: Journal, 1775–1776*, ed. Albion and Dodson, 228–31.

64. Fithian Journal, September 15, 1776, in *Philip Vickers Fithian: Journal, 1775–1776*, ed. Albion and Dodson, 232–34.

65. Ibid., 234.

66. Ibid., September 16, 1776, pp. 235–36; Schechter, *Battle for New York*, 197–201.

67. Fithian Journal, September 17–22, 1776, in *Philip Vickers Fithian: Journal, 1775–1776*, ed. Albion and Dobson, 236–41. The sketch remains somewhat of a mystery since Philip does not mention it in his journal. According to tradition, the portrait was returned to Betsy with the rest of Philip's papers following his death and remained in the possession of the Fithian family until it was sold to private collectors. A photo of the sketch can be found in Fithian's Princeton University alumni file with the inscription "Charcoal on paper, done by an unknown artist when Fithian was in camp, ca Oct. 1776, not long before his death." See Philip Vickers Fithian File, Princeton University Archives, Alumni Files, Box 24, Mudd Manuscript Library, Princeton University, Princeton, N.J.

68. Philip Fithian to Elizabeth Fithian, September 19, 1776, in *Philip Vickers Fithian Letters*, ed. Andrews, 46–47.

Chapter 9

1. Fithian Journal, September 22, 1776, in *Philip Vickers Fithian: Journal, 1775–1776*, ed. Robert Greenhalgh Albion and Leonidas Dodson (Princeton, N.J.: Princeton University Press, 1934), 241; Andrew Hunter to Betsy Fithian, September 28, 1776, in *Philip Vickers Fithian's Letters to His Wife*, ed. Frank D. Andrews (Vineland, N.J.: Smith Printing House, 1932), 47; "Newcomb's Regiment on Foot," Sept. 19, 1776, Microfilm No. 246, Revolutionary War Rolls, 1775–83, Roll 64, New Jersey Jacket nos. 62 through 91–92 (Washington, D.C.: National Archives and Records Administration, 1957).

2. Journal of William Hollingshead, October 4–6, 1776, cited in *Philip Vickers Fithian: Journal, 1775–1776*, ed. Albion and Dodson, 242; Journal of Andrew Hunter, October 7–9, 1776, cited in ibid.; Thomas Ewing to Elizabeth Fithian, October 8, 1776, in *Philip Vickers Fithian's Letters to His Wife*, ed. Andrews, 48.

3. Barnet Schechter, *The Battle for New York: The City at the Heart of the American Revolution* (New York: Penguin, 2002), 231–57.

4. Reading Beatty to Elizabeth Fithian, October 3, 1776, in "Letters to Elizabeth Beatty Fithian of Cumberland County, New Jersey," ed. Frank D. Andrews, *Vineland Historical Magazine* 15 (1930): 287.

5. Richard A. Harrison, *Princetonians, 1769–1775: A Biographical Dictionary* (Princeton, N.J.: Princeton University Press, 1980), 225–29.

6. Enoch Fithian, "Fithian Family History," 1834, transcribed on rootsweb .com/pub/usgenweb/pa/Philadelphia/history/family/; "Indenture between Joel Fithian and Elizabeth Fithian on one hand, and Amos Fithian on the other," November 21, 1788, Fithian Family Deeds, Princeton University Library, Collection CO199, Princeton, N.J.; John Fea, "'The Chosen People of God': Presbyterians and Jeffersonian Republicanism in the New Jersey Countryside," *American Nineteenth Century History* 2 (2001): 10–13.

7. "Letters to Elizabeth Beatty Fithian of Cumberland County, New Jersey," ed. Andrews, 289; ibid., *Vineland Historical Magazine* 16 (January 1931): 23; Enoch Fithian, "Fithian Family History."

8. Henry May, *The Enlightenment in America* (New York: Oxford University Press, 1976), xiv; Peter Gay, *The Enlightenment: An Interpretation: The Rise of Modern Paganism* (New York: Vintage, 1966).

9. See, for example, May, *Enlightenment in America*; Mark A. Noll, *America's God: From Jonathan Edwards to Abraham Lincoln* (New York: Oxford University Press, 2002); James Turner, *Without God, Without Creed* (Baltimore: Johns Hopkins University Press, 1985); Ned Landsman, *From Colonials to Provincials: American Thought and Culture, 1680–1760* (New York: Twayne, 1997).

10. Much of my thinking about Fithian in this paragraph borrows from Turner, *Without God, Without Creed*, 7–72.

11. Turner, *Without God, Without Creed*, 86.

12. Ibid., 37.

13. This is the thesis of Noll, *America's God.*

Appendix

1. Philip Vickers Fithian Journals and Commonplace Books, 1766–76, General Manuscripts (Bound), CO1099, no. 349, vol. 6, Princeton University Library, Princeton, N.J.; *Philip Vickers Fithian: Journal and Letters, 1767–1774*, ed. John R. Williams, (Princeton: Princeton University Press, 1900; reprint, Freeport, N.Y.: Books for Libraries Press, 1969), xv.

Index

Acknowledgments

Many people have helped me bring this book to completion. Not only did Ned Landsman critique several chapters of the manuscript, but most of my thinking about the relationship between religion and the Enlightenment has been influenced by his work. I could not have asked for a better mentor on this project, and to him I owe my greatest intellectual debt.

I am also the beneficiary of a generous program of faculty development, led by Rhonda Jacobsen, at Messiah College. The Messiah work-reallocation program, two scholarship grants, and a 2005–7 Scholar Chair allowed me time away from teaching in order to finish this book. My colleagues in Messiah's history department—Joseph Huffman, Jim LaGrand, Bernardo Michael, David Pettegrew, Cathay Snyder, Anne Marie Stoner-Eby, and Norm Wilson—have provided a wonderful community in which to work and have offered much encouragement along the way. Cali Pitchel, my student research assistant, performed part of the indispensable role of checking quotations and digging through the Fithian diaries for references to various themes. Dee Porterfield and her staff of student workers in the Murray Library interlibrary loan department tracked down many obscure sources.

The early stages of this project were supported by a grant from the New Jersey Historical Commission and a fellowship from the McNeil Center for Early American Studies at the University of Pennsylvania. I am especially thankful to the center's director, Richard Dunn, for inviting me to join an extraordinary community of early American scholars while at the same time exhorting me to spend part of the week tending to the needs of my young family back on Long Island. The latter stages of this project were funded by grants from the American Philosophical Society and the Spencer Foundation.

In the research stages, I was aided by the dedicated staffs of Princeton's Firestone and Mudd Libraries (which granted permission to quote from the Fithian manuscripts), the Presbyterian Historical Society (especially conversations with Ken Ross), the New Jersey Historical Society, the New Jersey State Archives, the Cumberland County (N.J.) Historical Society, the Fairfield County (Conn.) Historical Society, and the East Hampton (N.Y.) Library.

This project has been improved by the formal conference comments, general encouragement, words of inspiration, and informal remarks of several people, including Dee Andrews, Richard D. Brown, Richard Bushman, Jayber Crow, Jay Green, Allen Guelzo, Kevin Gumieny, Marsha Hamilton, Rhys Isaac, David Jaffee, Eric Miller, Mark Noll, Elizabeth Nybakken, Donna Rilling, Mark Schwehn, and Nancy Tomes. Al Zambone, who like Philip Vickers Fithian is a native Cohansian who spent some time in Virginia, read the entire manuscript and offered very helpful comments. Dallett Hemphill and an anonymous reader offered excellent suggestions for improvement as readers for the University of Pennsylvania Press, but I want particularly to thank Dallett for some well-timed thoughts during the late stages of the revision process. It was also a pleasure to work with Gerry Kreig in the design of the book's maps.

I would not have been able to write this book without the constant support of local historians. Rod MacKenzie at the Fairfield County (Conn.) Historical Society uncovered some genealogical information at a critical stage of the writing process. Paul Schopp and Jim Turk answered my many e-mails filled with questions about early south Jersey history. Jonathan Wood of the Cumberland County Historical Society first introduced me to Philip Vickers Fithian's homeland. I enjoyed discussing Fithian with Jonathan during our driving tours of Cohansey and lunches in Dutch Neck Village.

I first wrote about Philip Vickers Fithian in a 2003 essay published in the *Journal of American History*, and I am grateful to the Organization of American Historians for permission to quote freely from that essay. I have also learned much from e-mail exchanges with dozens of educators who have used Fithian's story to teach about Revolutionary America through the article's "Teaching the JAH" companion Web site, a resource that provides pedagogical tools for using the essay in undergraduate and high school classrooms. Informal conversations with some of my own students have sharpened my thinking and ultimately made this a better book. I especially want to thank Justin Bollinger, Matt Bucher, Matt Caliguire, Megan Giordano, Joe Hackman, Josh Roth, Cali Pitchel, and Nathan Tillman—young women and men who, like Fithian, grapple regularly with the tensions between cosmopolitan ambitions, local attachments, and the call of God in their lives.

I am honored that Dan Richter saw fit to include this book in the University of Pennsylvania Press's Early American Studies series. Dan's careful reading of an earlier and quite different draft of this work led me to return to my basement study and rethink exactly what I wanted to write about. Bob Lockhart at the University of Pennsylvania Press has carefully guided this book to publication. He saw the potential in this project from the start and has patiently answered, always with good cheer, my endless questions along the way.

I am blessed that my "way of improvement" always "leads home." I cannot sit down at our family computer these days without Caroline wondering if I have "made a book" yet. I am thrilled that Allyson graciously put down her copy of *Nancy Drew* and allowed me to read to her the sections of this book dealing with Philip's courtship with Elizabeth Beatty. Her intense interest in these passages helped me to realize that parts of this book may appeal to more people than just the usual academic audience. Joy has read parts of this book in manuscript form, nudged me to get to work as deadlines approached, listened to me talk endlessly about Philip Vickers Fithian, and took on the bulk of the household duties while I was away on research trips. More important, her love has spurred me on—both in this project and in life.